THE GREATEST SHOWS ON EARTH

THE GREATEST SHOWS ON EARTH

World Theatre from Peter Brook
to the Sydney Olympics

John Freeman

First published in 2011 by Libri Publishing

Copyright © John Freeman

Authors retain copyright of individual case studies

ISBN: 978 1 907471 54 4

All rights reserved. No part of this publication may be reproduced, stored in any retrieval system or transmitted in any form or by any means, electronic, mechanical, photocopying, recording or otherwise, without the prior written permission of the copyright holder for which application should be addressed in the first instance to the publishers. No liability shall be attached to the author, the copyright holder or the publishers for loss or damage of any nature suffered as a result of reliance on the reproduction of any of the contents of this publication or any errors or omissions in its contents.

A CIP catalogue record for this book is available from The British Library

Photograph of John Freeman by Leigh Brennan

Photograph on front cover by (c) Maarten Vanden Abeele, Brussels, 2004.
In the photograph : Actress Viviane De Muynck in the theatre production *Isabella's Room* from director Jan Lauwers & Needcompany.

Cover design and typesetting by Carnegie Book Production

Printed in the UK by Halstan Printing

Contents

Chapter 1	John Freeman **The Best Seat in the House**	1
Chapter 2	Colin Chambers **Shakespeare for My Time**	17
Chapter 3	Edward Lewis **'I've been Nicked!':** *The Life and Adventures of Nicholas Nickleby* **by Charles Dickens, Adapted for the Stage by David Edgar**	35
Chapter 4	Jean-Marc Larrue **Robert Lepage and Théâtre Repère:** *Trilogie des Dragons*	53
Chapter 5	Anthony Mawson & Ursula Raffalt ***Styx***	69
Chapter 6	Kevin J. Wetmore Jr. **Third World Bunfight's** *Ipi Zombi?*	87
Chapter 7	Peter Snow **Performing Nation: The Opening Ceremony of the Sydney 2000 Olympic Games**	105
Chapter 8	Allan Owens ***Pilgrim*: Taichi-kikaku**	125
Chapter 9	Guilherme Mendonça ***O ACHAMENTO DO BRASIL*, Foco Musical**	145
Chapter 10	David Jortner **Faustian Fears:** *Dr. Atomic*, **National Anxiety and J. Robert Oppenheimer**	163

Chapter 11 Kathy Foley
*Odalan Bali: An Offering of Music
and Dance* by Gamelan Çudamani   181

Chapter 12 Constantin Chiriac
**Silviu Purcărete's *Faust*:
an Encyclopedia of the Emotional**   201

Chapter 13 John Freeman
Life is a Cigarette: *Isabella's Room***, Jan Lauwers
and Needcompany**   219

Chapter 14 Anne Pellois
*Impromptu XL***: Tg STAN:
Theatre as a Memory Machine**   235

Chapter 15 David Mason
The Oberammergau Passionsspiele   255

Contributors' Biographies   277

Index   282

Leave unchanged the hands that I have kissed.

CHAPTER ONE

The Best Seat in the House

JOHN FREEMAN

Theatre is not about the flowering fantasy of the artist, it's about the imagination of the audience.
Heiner Goebbels: 'Polyphony or Essential Solitude', February 2010

As the title suggests, this book is about great theatre, about all that is made visible or audible on stage, about *mise en scène* as an imaginative organisational concept. And, with barely a mention of semiotics, it is a book about a system of signs working together to produce meaning and resonance. In being a book about fourteen performances, described by fifteen contributors, this is also a book that wrestles with the challenge of describing on the page that which exists in time and space and, most significantly, within specific contexts. Published scripts tell us plenty, but even more is left out. Where text is considered in various chapters it is approached primarily in the sense of *performance text*, as the result of choices made by performers, directors, designers, writers and spectators... choices that are made concrete in the work's presentation and reception. In this way the book nails its colours cleanly to the mast of performance as an event occuring over time rather than to literary criticism aligned to the object of text as it appears in print. Where Tom McAlindon is suspicious of writing which 'valorises performance rather than substance' (McAlindon, 2004, p.20) this book's prime concern is with the very substance of performance. This is not to discredit the value of the written script (where such exists) so much as to engage with the idea that dramatic text is as likely to be used in the service of performance as *vice versa*.

Because each chapter will focus on a particular production seen on one or more occasion and at one or more venues, the role of the spectator is made central. This is not as obvious an element of writing about theatre as it may at first appear. Library shelves are heavy with the weight of books written about productions never seen at first hand by the authors and, whilst this form of more distanced and usually historical scholarship is undoubtedly valuable, it is not what *The Greatest Shows on Earth* is about. For many, the greatest shows on earth are the shows they (we) never saw: those performances that the history books tell us were wonderful – Helene Weigel's 1949 portrayal of the title role in Brecht's *Mother Courage*; Marlon Brando's sweat-stained swagger onto the 1947 Broadway stage in Tennessee Williams' *A Streetcar Named Desire*; Trevor Nunn's pared-down *Macbeth* of 1976 with the electrifying Ian McKellen and Judi Dench; David Hare and Howard Brenton's mid-'80s *Pravda*, replete with Anthony Hopkins' bravura Lambert Le Roux. Even without having seen these productions live, I find myself dropping easily into the language of borrowed praise, so that the productions function as a barometer to other works' standing, tempering the rapture of immediacy with the measure of critical weight and canonical significance. All of this is true and inevitable, as well as having been hard-earned by the relevant personnel: but it is not what is driving this book. Where *The Greatest Shows on Earth* drifts (as it surely shall) into hyperbole, then those moments of extravagance and exaggeration are at least harnessed to feelings gained at no further remove than the distance between the seating rake and the stage.

The etymology of 'theatre' is *theatron*, a place where spectators go to watch. *Theatron* incorporates both spectacle and contemplation and in this way comprises the location and theory of looking. It is in this meeting of performance as spectacle and spectatorship as a contemplative act that this book functions… not as an idea of what theatre might be, as some form of cultural medicine, moral good or aestheticised intellectual imperative, but as something made real and made witness in the moment. In this sense and within the context of this book, 'theatre' is a term that is approached inclusively, so that the conventions of theatre, all of those traditions and experimentations, all of theatre's histories and all of its endless potential for change, serve as reference points for a series of chapter-length discussions and departures.

If prostitution is widely held to be the world's oldest profession, closely followed by soldiering, then theatre's long history gives it a noble third place. The first recorded theatrical event is of the myth of Osiris and Isis in 2500 BC in Egypt; and through its subsequent flourishing in Ancient

Greece between 550 and 220 BC, our notions of Western theatre have their origins in these faint traces of documentation. Performance scholars such as Ernest T. Kirby (1975), Richard Schechner (1988) and Victor Turner (1985) have suggested earlier understandings of theatre, beginning with the ur-drama of shamanist ritual, where participants took on and portrayed identities other than their own. This is a view that Eli Rozik sees as fallacious on the grounds that it 'overlooks the internal viewpoint of the culture within which the shaman performs... the shaman is definitely not enacting the character of a spirit, but constitutes a means for its revelation in the human world.' (Rozik, 2003, p.120) Rozik's rebuttal is as emphatic as Schechner et al.'s is suggestive, not least in his determination that to include ritualistic behaviour as part of the history of theatre reflects little more than a postmodern malaise morphing itself into nostalgia. Despite the anthropological appeal of the argument, Rozik is adamant that 'the medium of theatre could not have originated in ritual'. (Ibid., p.139)

It is only on paper and within university seminars that theatre's real or imagined past is ever cause for discussion. In the theatre, everything is in the moment and our own moment can be taken in more ways than one. The recent rise in UK theatre attendance is cause for optimism, as is the fact that at any one time in the last ten years there have been many thousands of undergraduates studying Drama, Theatre or Performance at British universities, alongside an ever-increasing number studying the subjects at GCSE, A Level and BTEC. This growth pattern has so extravagantly over-reached its critical and natural mass that it attracted the Damoclean sword of a government that no longer regards performance study as the provision of a public good largely financed by public funds. It is also true that those same students have made up a vast slice of herded-in audiences, at the same time as they have put a lot of ticks in the box marked 'Audience Development'. Nevertheless, the cries of 'Theatre in Crisis' that were heard throughout the latter part of the 20th century have all but died away. So much so that Matt Wolf's *London Evening Standard* article, 'Why This is a Great Age of Theatre', appeared neither tongue in cheek nor vainglorious. (Wolf, 2009)

Great age it may be, but the concept of what makes a particular performance great is endlessly contestable and the productions that are left out of this book's chapters will inevitably leave gaps that some readers (and even at times this editor) will surely bemoan. Decisions as to which works to include are unavoidable, despite the certain knowledge that every decision is also a loss. Ultimately, perhaps, the book's value lies as much in its absences as its inclusions, inasmuch as any book that presumes to list the greatest shows on earth is bound to ruffle some feathers. Shakespeare gets an appreciatively learned nod from Colin Chambers, and a number of his plays are listed in the index, but there's no Schiller; there's no Beckett, no Brecht, no Albee or Ayckbourn, no Miller, no Wilde, nor Williams, nor Wooster Group; no Tadeusz Kantor, no Sarah Kane, no Caryl Churchill, no Harold Pinter, no David Mamet: a list of significant others that is itself contentious in the names of the great and the good it excludes. There is no circus, come to that, which seems a remarkable omission given this book's recycling of the 1952 film's title. Shorter chapters would have allowed for more performances to be discussed, but the list of the left out would always be greater than the included. So what we get is an extremely partial view.

The limits of recall have much to do with choice, as does geography, as does my own editorial access to contributors... informed and decided as it is by my own not-always-consciously-knowing decisions about who to approach and why. Apropos of which it is worth saying that the productions described in these pages were chosen by the contributors. No search was made, for example, for somebody to write about Robert Lepage's *The Dragons' Trilogy*; rather an approach was made to Jean-Marc Larrue based on respect for his ability to write persuasively about his chosen experiences and about the work that affected him most profoundly at the time he saw it. In this way what international, formal and thematic diversity exists in the stretch from Peter Snow's response to the Sydney 2000 Olympics Opening Ceremony to Kevin J. Wetmore's *Ipi Zombi?* and Kathy Foley's *Odalan Bali* stems from the diversity of the contributors' interests as much as from any driving editorial desire to encompass such a range of work. In this sense, my approach has been considerably more curatorial than editorial. The standard generosity of spirit that acknowledges all errors as belonging to the editor and all qualities being credited to contributors is added to here by the confession of a shameless desire to build this book on the knowledge of others.

The biographies that come towards the end of this book reveal the international flavour of the contributors no less than the origins of the work they discuss; and this resistance to the usual suspects of Anglo North American theatre in books published in England is further evidenced in the index, where an international eclecticism is not so much a by product of the book as its *raison d'être*. As the biographies further assert, and as the chapters confirm, many of this book's contributors are employed, at least partly, in academia. Others, such as Guilherme Mendonça and Constantin Chiriac, are significantly not influenced by primarily academic careers; whilst others still – Peter Snow and Kevin J. Wetmore Jr. being perfect cases in point – have succesfully combined university employment with ongoing practical and professional outcomes. Whilst this does not mean that contributors will be writing uniquely informed pieces on their chosen works (in fact, many contributors have opted to write on work that falls beyond their established and/or published areas of expertise), it does mean that productions will be discussed from positions of some authority within the wider fields of performance practice and scholarship and that the chapters will be oftentimes academic in intent if not always in tone. Academic is as academic does: the chapter provided by Anthony Mawson and Ursula Raffalt, for instance, offers a meditation on the craft of performance making that complements the critical spectator-driven focus that informs the bulk of the book; David Jortner's chapter, whilst focusing on a specific performance, sheds as much light on a US sense of Homeland Insecurity as it does on theatre *per se*; David Mason's analysis of the passion play at Oberammergau tells more about the relationship between religion and performance than the production itself. And so it is and so it goes: the performances covered in this book are very different, and so are the ways in whch they are addressed, and so are each contributor's intentions, agendas and interests.

Central to the conceit of this embrace of difference is the belief that academic writing has to be recognised by more than its abundance of sixty-dollar terms and the erudition-by-demonstration of endless references; by more than the 'nihilism and cynicism that exists and has become accepted as the correct tone', a tone which the celebrated polymath Mike Figgis warns against. (In ten Cate, 1996, p.8) What gives strength to academic writing is its need always to be predicated upon argument, upon an overriding thesis that the writing strives to explore and explain... on those Big Ideas that secure publication and tenure, and on writing that builds on the kind of constructive bias facilitated in and through a book such as this. Accordingly, subjectivity and its sinister twin, prejudice, will often be foregrounded profoundly in academic writing. Whilst the majority of this book's contributors are also experienced theatre reviewers, the book's drift is away from standard responses suggesting that 'the audience felt this' and towards provocative essays based around 'I felt this'. Accordingly a number of the chapters function as attempts to see if something (a thesis) fits, rather than as seemingly objective appraisals of performance quality.

That said, a key intention of *The Greatest Shows on Earth* is to dissolve some of the more invidious distinctions between theory and practice, critic and academic, essay and review, so that what binds the chapters together into more than a collection of thoughts is an attempt to do some justice to the ephemerality of performance through the permanence of words on the page. The flipside of ephemerality is memory, and our memories are always also inventions, re-tellings of the past that tell as much about what we would like to have seen and how we would like ourselves to be seen in the subsequent tellings as what we actually saw. As Luis Bunuel saw it, 'Our imagination, and our dreams, are forever invading our memories; and since we are apt to believe in the reality of our fantasies, we end up transforming our lies into truth'. (In Zinder, 1980 p.40) If Bunuel is right, then very little objectivity remains, and few claims for such are sought in this book's pages, despite the cultural standing of a great deal of the work under discussion. This is more than mere word play. Subjectivity acknowledges meaning as an act of personal interpretation rather than collective understanding; seeing responses as being generally rooted in a state of mind, whilst objectivity is beyond interpretation, existing instead as something shared to the point of common acceptance. As George Ivanovitch Gurdjieff sees it, in objective art there is nothing indefinite. (In Ouspensky, 1949, pp.295–7) Gurdjieff's statement makes assumptions that take it beyond this first chapter's embrace, which is not to say that all of the book's contributors share my levels of skepticism: a skepcis that does not quite yet amount to a charlatan's total faith in relativism, so much as a championing, in this book if not always elsewhere, of the individual's right to hold his or her views on performance in spite of a dearth of supporting critical commentary. That the individuals holding these views have an obligation to make their case in the light of resistant opinion is axiomatic. Susan Bennett suggests that the act of theatre-going tells us much about what society affords its citizens; (Bennett, 1997, p.vii) and in a similar vein, the responses of theatre goers might tell us something about what it is that successful productions afford spectators.

As is always the case when writing about performance, the transient nature of the moment does battle with both memory and the permanence of print. That which we write may not have happened in precisely the way we remember it, but the way we remember is all we have to give: half-memories and half-hopes of what we think we experienced and what we wish the productions to have been. All of this seems true, and yet responses based significantly on emotional and sometimes idiosyncratic connectedness are seen as problematic in performance despite the fact that every audience member is unique, with different beliefs, value systems, experiences, hopes and expectations. Even knowing this, we slip effortlessly into often-historical discussions of an audience as something collective, as a single being responding to performance with commonality. This has done much to channel students at all levels into the recycling of ideas without evidence, so that we describe Brecht's original productions as having distanced his audiences without ever feeling any pressing need to search for the testimony of individual spectators in support. When John Cage famously responded to the question of what was the best seat in the house by stating that every seat was the best, he was saying more than the obvious fact that the perspective created by spectators' positions in auditoria was at once deliberately distinct and equally valuable; he was reminding us that the perceptual frames we carry inside our heads are stronger determinants in the way we see than the seat we see from. Roland Barthes' ideas of readerly work, which seeks out a common response, and his notions of writerly product, which invites spectators to create their own meanings, add the language of deconstruction to Cage's primarily practice-based and practice-informed suggestions.

Contemporary performance has been quick to pick up on this, with shows that make conscious appeals to our individualistic responses acting as the distillation of theatre's inevitable truism: that regardless of written text, *mise en scene* and climactic denouement, each member of an audience will always read work in their own sweet way. Where *The Daily Telegraph* theatre critic Charles Spencer argues that one of the great things about theatre is that it is an activity that brings people together, so that we enter an auditorium as a group of individuals and emerge as a community, (Spencer, 2009) offering a reminder through theatre that no man is ever quite an island, then the experience of spectatorship shows us too that in our seated togetherness we could not be more resolutely alone… or, as Tim Etchells sees it, 'Watching the best theatre and performance we are together and alone'. (In Brine and Keidan, 2007, p.26)

That a performance happens in a particular venue and at a particular time amounts to an objective reality based on a shared understanding of time and place. A spectator's belief that this performance was great is a subjective response. Objectivity and subjectivity are logical seeming definitions until they cross over. When an entire audience finds the same performance great then a series of singular subjective realities begins to assume the characteristics of a shared objective reality. The performance is now regarded as objectively great, and the term 'great' becomes fact. The possibility then that individual spectators who thought the work dreadful would find themselves in a minority would not make their opinions wrong so much as singularly subjective in the face of shared objective belief. Those readers who have found themselves in this position, outside the circle of appreciation and seemingly alone with the criticisms that nobody wants to hear will understand this feeling of estrangement only too well.

In place of objective worldviews, the chapters of this book form an embrace and acknowledgement of subjectivity. Whether the work in question was lauded by critics or garlanded with prizes, what remains central is the way the work made this book's contributors feel as well as think, the way the chapters' events created a considered framework for a range of emotional experiences. What emerges through the chapters is a profound sense of contact and communication between a responsive spectator and a finely crafted performance. As Wetmore points out, what Brett Bailey's *Ipi Zombi?* might or might not mean on the page is less important here than the way the work plays on the stage. Similarly, the notion of great theatre is as much here about what is created in the minds of the watcher–writers as that which is created in performance: whilst much of the work under discussion would be classed as objectively 'great', greatness elsewhere is suggested as much by the thinking subject as by the objects of thought. In this the works' qualities are filtered quite overtly through the characteristics of personal evaluation: characteristics that stress the attitudes and opinions of the writer. In this sense too feelings become as important as findings… indeed, the feelings invoked by the work *are* the findings. If feelings can be defined as that which arises spontaneously rather than through conscious effort, then the emotions of joy, love and rapture become as significant to our understanding of successful performance as the more logical and deductive processes that see each work as a crime scene, each onstage moment as a clue to be intellectually solved and each essay as a flawed attempt to prove ourselves sharper than the artists who made the work.

Writing about work from Brook's *Lear* of 1962 to the present means also writing about the ways in which technology has impacted on the making and receiving of live performance. Despite the telling impact of digital innovations and interventions, it remains the case that we go to the theatre in order to have a (usually communal) visceral connection with (usually live) performers. However, this very notion of liveness has been thrown into relief by approaches to interactivity and doubling that are some distance away from the voice manipulation of Laurie Anderson's 1970s work and the swathe of Forced Entertainment inspired television monitors that flanked the newly experimental stages of the mid-to-late 1980s. Concerns that technology should aid an artwork rather than defining it have given way, at least in part, to an audience embrace that is symptomatic of our own increasingly tech-reliant lives. On one level this has resulted in initiatives such as the National Theatre's NT Live presentation of the Jean Racine/ Ted Hughes' *Phèdre*, directed by Nicholas Hytner, which was broadcast live via satellite in 2009 to 280 international screen venues and which reached a widespread audience of over 50,000. Critical response to the event was positive, with the consensus being that seeing the work on screen was 'by no means a second best option to live performance but an innovative alternative.' (National Theatre, 2010) On a very different level, the performance artist Stelarc, who sees the organic body as obsolete in a world of technological development, made *Pingbody* (1995) in which his own electrode covered body was jerked into action via a 60-volt muscle interaction system operated by interested individuals on touch-screen computers around the world. Whichever end of this scale our personal tastes and interests lead us to, the fusing of digital technology and live performance has become a given of our time, to the extent that the *Guardian* theatre critic Lyn Gardner sees the growth of pervasive media as something that offers theatre makers and audiences 'unprecedented new challenges and opportunities' and which will soon be as ubiquitous as Facebook or mobile phones. (Gardner, 2010) The shorthand term 'Cyberperformance' can be taken to include work presented entirely online or to an actual audience watching and/or interacting with performers appearing digitally and it is a term that sits comfortably within the ouevre of Robert Lepage and Peter Sellars – as witnessed by Jean-Marc Larrue and David Jortner.

Larrue writes about the occasion in 1987 when Robert Lepage and Théâtre Repère staged *The Dragons' Trilogy* in a disused hangar in the Old Port of Montreal. The piece was a magnificent poetic epic that drew on interdisciplinarity, deconstructed time and space, exoticism, multilingualism, identity and heritage issues, romantic relationships, intercultural and interracial relations, and violence. Despite its revolutionary character, the show became an instant classic that appealed to international audiences by virtue of its portrayal of the major concerns of the moment. Twenty years on, the moment was *Faust*. In London the remarkable company Punchdrunk turned an abandoned warehouse into a vision of hell, and in the same year Silviu Purcărete's production opened in Romania on its way to massive European success, whilst at the time of writing the Icelandic company Vesturport are at London's Young Vic Theatre with their Nick Cave-scored stab at Marlowe's classic tale. The celebrated Romanian actor and director Constantin Chiriac explores Purcărete's *Faust* as an 'encyclopedia of the emotional'; as a performance that proposes an androgenic Mephisto who ultimately finds himself humanised by suffering. From a production perspective, Chiriac's chapter describes too some of the managerial aspects, which made possible the participation of this massively complex *Faust* as a main event at the Edinburgh International Theatre Festival. Chiriac's chapter is laced through with pride in his city, his country and his countrymen, as well as with a sense of wonder at all that theatre can achieve. Purcărete described *Faust* as one of the 'few stories of humanity that cannot be avoided, in any age, at any time, in any century.' (Barnett, 2009) David Jortner's chapter makes this timelessness explicit in his exploration of John Adams and Peter Sellars' collaboration on the *Faust* motif in their 2005 work *Dr Atomic*. *Dr. Atomic* recasts Faust in the form of J. Robert Oppenheimer, the 'father' of the atomic bomb, and Adams and Sellars mirror the Faust story in the events leading to the first detonation of the bomb in New Mexico. As it was in 1594 so is it now, and just as *Doctor Faustus*' wayward scientist spoke to Elizabethan audiences at a time of national crisis and confusion of nationality, so the re-imagination of Oppenheimer as Faust constructs the scientist as a synecdoche for post-9/11 and post-Iraq fears about national identity, ethics and responsibility.

Not all performance that changes lives is epic in form. For Anthony Mawson, his first ten-minute experience of *Styx* opened, as he describes it, a door into another world which was new but also strangely familiar… remarkable because it was the sort of performance that could only come from a deeply committed outsider, unconcerned with, even innocent of, the 'rules' of theatre making. Mawson's chapter, written with Ursula Raffalt, seeks to cut through the boundaries of spectatorship and performance, intimacy and art, aesthetic credo and method. Colin Chambers' analysis of Peter Brook's 1962 *King Lear* locates the production in the extraordinary trajectory of Brook from deeply committed insider and *enfant terrible* via

West End showman to Grotowski proponent and eventually the great helmsman guru of intercultural performance. In doing so, Chambers does more than locate Brook's *Lear* within a body of practice that has redefined Shakespeare interpretation since the Second World War; in placing the production in the context of the newly formed Royal Shakespeare Company he foregrounds the RSC's emergent identity as harbinger of theatrical innovation. Contextualisation is at the heart of Edward Lewis' chapter on the RSC production of Charles Dickens' *Nicholas Nickleby*. For Lewis this work was absolutely of its time, wedded to the political climate of both its construction and his acts of repeated spectating. Lewis depicts the production as representing the best of British subsidised theatre, not only in its audience appeal and artistic integrity but also in the working practices that shaped its creation: practices that were popular without being populist, innovative without being impenetrable, political without being pedantic and didactic without being dictatorial. Implicit in Lewis' analysis is the production's importance to the mainstream British theatre that, even today, is still capable of drawing in significant audiences.

In her chapter on the durational work *Impromptu XL* by the actors' company Tg STAN, Anne Pellois considers reiteration and repetition, the reproducable and the ephemeral in a way that questions the actor's existence on stage. In Pellois' view, the particularities of Tg STAN create a new type of relation between the stage and the audience, making the public feel 'at home' in the theatre, rather than as a guest… or worse, as some form of voyeur.

The idea of celebration is central to the Oberammergau Passion play, a work which has been presented in Garmisch-Partenkirchen just south of Munich every ten years since 1634, as well as on key anniversaries. In David Mason's analysis, the Passionsspiele constructs a world that may well never have been, a performative world which comes into existence within the theatre in which it plays, inviting willing and often devoted audience members to function as co-creators. Mason sees the work as a play that presents not history, but meta-history: a narrative where truth does not depend on accuracy, but enfolds constancy and change, the sacred and the secular, the people of the past and of the present in its always immediate significance. In this way, the Oberammergau production not only reiterates the cycle play tradition of medieval Europe but resembles devotional theatre around the world. The Passionsspiele is possessed of a near 400-year history, whereas the chapter I am offering on Needcompany's *Isabella's*

Room had enjoyed a comparatively brief five-year run before I first saw the work in Sarajevo in late 2009. Its inclusion here does not necessarily mean that this work is the best production I have ever seen, although it is one on a very short list. I do not feel that focusing on this work leads to an argument (even with myself) that it is better than the stellar Brook/Carriere *Mahabharata*, Kantor's *Today is My Birthday*, The Wooster Group's *L.S.D.*, Bill T. Jones' *Still Here*, Wilson's *Dr Faustus Lights the Lights*, Nederland Subtheatre's *Theatrum Anatomicum*, DV8's *Dead Dreams of Monochrome Men*, the exquisite small-scale beauty of the Curious production, *The Moment I Saw You I Knew I Could Love You* or, had I seen it early enough for consideration here, the beguiling inventiveness of Teatro Sunil's *Donka: A Letter to Chekhov*.... What I am saying is that *Isabella's Room* is the piece that made me fall in love with theatre again after a lengthy absence and that it is possessed of all of those features that, from my own perspective, make live performance the heart-stopping experience we always wish – and so rarely find – it to be.

Guilherme Mendonça adopts a similar standpoint in his analysis of Foco Musical's *O ACHAMENTO DO BRASIL*. For Mendonça, the quality of the work in question is technically deficient, dramatically simplistic and of an overall standard that is far from the highest; and yet the performance creates an electrifying and life-changing experience. The ways in which this seeming contradiction are realised through social, political, educational and community imperatives drive Mendonça's study and create an open dialogue with Kathy Foley's interpretation of I Dewa Putu Berata and I Nyoman Cerita's *Odalan Bali*. Foley sees this work as a modern spectacle which attempts to revitalise Balinese performance through a linking of tradition and innovation, the local and the global and intercultural training with international presentation, multi-cultural East–West performance and performer training in the 1990s.

Kevin J. Wetmore's recalling of *Ipi Zombi?* as a remarkable experience involving a bonfire, drumming, the Devil, ghost boys emerging from a cupboard, and a lip-syncing, dancing transvestite fuses scholarly research and personal reflection into an extraordinarily immersive response to this work in particular and also to the field of African theatre. Peter Snow discusses the opening ceremonies of the Sydney 2000 Olympic Games as a millennial demonstration of the new world's relationship with the old, personified by an elderly Aboriginal man and a young white girl with a stripe of sun cream on her nose. If this ceremony was a performative embodiment of one version of nationhood, Snow's chapter situates the ceremony within the wider contexts of other events at the Games and of other social and cultural events in turn-of-the-century multicultural Australia. Allan Owens' chapter on Taichi-Kikaku's *Pilgrim* at the Nihon Kogakuin Digital Open Space, Kamata, Tokyo, focuses on the way the group runs counter-culturally in Japan and yet draws overtly on tradition. Owens acknowledges Taichi-Kikaku's roots in ancient Japanese sensibility and primordiality and the influence of Noh plays, haiku and Tanka poetry forms alongside a post-industrial concern with alternatives to materialism and a distinctive focus on the spiritual as it relates to contemporary urban life. Few practitioner–scholars enjoy as wide an international profile as Owens and it is no surprise to note the way he explores the importance of travel for a company that in 21 years has visited 50 capital cities in 21 countries.

From Shakespeare at the RSC to versions of *Faust* and an Olympic opening ceremony, the idea of great shows is wrapped always here around theatre, if not always around work that takes place within theatres. In his seminal publication, Peter Brook wrote that one could take any empty space and call it a bare stage, and that a man walking across this space whilst being watched was all that was needed for an act of theatre to take place. (Brook, 1968) During a post-show debate at London's Barbican Theatre on 9 February 2010, Brook went further in suggesting that a physical theatre does not exist at all. That it is no more than a box, a cave, or cavern... a vehicle, where what is inside it is what matters. Perhaps it is safest within the pages of *The Greatest Shows on Earth* to approach theatre as an invitation based on conventions that spectators might not easily understand but which are nevertheless willingly accepted: not so much an empty space as an act of shared faith. That theatre can exist without this sharing is the stuff of Drama Studies 101, where notions of theatre as no more than that which engages our senses are woven into essay questions and batted back and forth in discussion groups. We well know that a lecturer (actor) standing behind a lectern (set), speaking semi-prepared words (text) to seated students (spectators) is possessed of all the salient elements of theatre... just as we know in our hearts and our minds that a lecture is patently *not* theatre, for when theatre becomes a definition based solely on theoretical whimsy then terminology destroys practice and intellectualism serves a death knell on art.

The professional status of contributors notwithstanding, deciding on what theatre is great is an activity with no need for academic study's rhetoric of confirmation bias dressed up in erudition. What matters most, in fact the only thing that matters, is how any given production makes us respond. This is not quite tantamount to the old postmodern embrace of all things being equal (as long as our things are more equal than yours): we know that Brecht's work is likely to retain more historical significance than Ben Elton's, and that in *that* type of high-culture framework *Mother Courage* will always outstrip *We Will Rock You*... but that matters little to the spectator whose eyelids grow heavy with all of that alienation and wide with wonder at the chutzpah of a show that makes us sing along. We can probably say that great theatre allows spectators to discover new possibilities through its own fearless curiosity; that it allows always for the possibility of change; that its concern is with transportation to a place of difficulty, doubt and disorientation; that it is at once real and unreal, extraordinary and familiar, and that its pursuit is the restlessness of truth rather than the very different value of box office receipts.

In concluding this chapter, an invitation is made for us to celebrate theatre that simply works... albeit not theatre that always works simply. For if theatre serves as a reflection and representation of life, it serves too to transform the ways in which we engage with a world both of and beyond our own. This is what makes theatre as valuable to us as it is, and this is what binds the seemingly disparate chapters to come; because there are certain performances, theatre events, which unsettle us. There might be some intricacy that we cannot quite follow, some strange aspect that sits outside of our customary understanding of what theatre might be, and of what it might do. We might find ourselves mesmerised and also, perhaps, irritated, angered even; for greatness does not automatically equate with either immediacy or pleasure; conversely, we might find ourselves so utterly delighted by everything the performance achieves that we know, in the act of watching, that like Thomas Hardy's lifelong affection for a girl who smiled at him once as she rode fleetingly by on a horse, our lives will never be quite the same again. These are the works we think about afterwards, the works that haunt us because they provide some plus-factor... something that lasts, and something that outlives a work's applause.

Readers will note the absence of a bibliography at the close of the book. Works are referenced by each contributor in their chapters, whether as a concluding list or in notes; as such, there was no need to duplicate information. Readers will also note that rather than placing each chapter next to one that bathes it in reflective and possibly misleading light, the book's sequence is based solely on the dates productions were first seen by their chroniclers here: starting with Brook's *King Lear...*

Works Cited

Barnett, L. (2009) 'Faust's blood, sweat and hell-fire', *Guardian*, 18 August 2009, http://www.guardian.co.uk/culture/2009/aug/18/faust-edinburgh-festival (Accessed 27 August 2010)

Bennett, S. (1997) *Theatre Audiences: A theory of production and reception*, London & New York: Routledge

Brine, D. & L. Keidan (2007) *Programme Notes: Case Studies for Locating Experimental Theatre*, London: Live Art Development Agency

Brook, P. (1968) *The Empty Space*, Victoria: Penguin Books Australia Ltd.

Gardner, L. (2010) 'A new stage age: why theatres should embrace digital technology', *Guardian*, http://www.guardian.co.uk/stage/theatreblog/2010/mar/23/stage-theatre-digital-technology-ished (Accessed 24 March 2010)

Kirby, E. T. (1975) *Ur-Drama*, New York: New York University Press

McAlindon, T. (2004) *Shakespeare Minus 'Theory'*, Aldershot: Ashgate

National Theatre (2010) http://www.nationaltheatre.org.uk/59800/nt-live/feedback-from-audiences.html (Accessed 25 June 2010)

Ouspensky, P. D. (1949) *In Search of the Miraculous: Fragments of an Unknown Teaching*, New York: Harcourt, Brace

Rozik, E. (2003) 'The Ritual Origin of Theatre – A Scientific Theory or Theatrical Ideology?', *Journal of Religion and Theatre*, Vol. 2, No. 1, Fall 2003 (105–140), Houghton: University of Michigan

Schechner, R. (1988) *Essays on Performance Theory*, New York: Routledge.

Schechner, R. & V. Turner (1985) *Between Theater and Anthropology*, Pennsylvania: University of Pennsylvania Press

Spencer, C. (2009) 'Theatre and the credit crunch: drama is thriving in a crisis', *Telegraph*, 5 June 2009, http://www.telegraph.co.uk/culture/culturecritics/charlesspencer/5450480/html (Accessed June 11 2010)

ten Cate, R. (1996) *Man Looking for Words*, Amsterdam: Theater Insitut Nederland

Wolf, M. (2009) 'Why This is a Great Age of Theatre', *London Evening Standard*, 2 December 2009

Zinder, D. (1980) *The Surrealist Connection: Towards an Aesthetic of Surrealist Theatre*, Ann Arbor: UMI

CHAPTER TWO

Shakespeare for My Time

COLIN CHAMBERS

A wesome', 'towering', 'revolutionary': critics were competing for superlatives in November 1962 to describe the latest production in Stratford-upon-Avon of the still-young Royal Shakespeare Company.[1] I, however, was unaware of this acclaim when I took the bus from home to see *King Lear* on its transfer to the Aldwych Theatre, which had become the London end of the RSC operation only two years beforehand. I had never seen this play that I knew had been branded a masterpiece, and had a schoolboy expectation of watching from the upper circle the story of a pitiable old man who at a distance might pass for an Old Testament prophet or ancient pagan priest officiating at Stonehenge.

My main memories, which have been filtered through forty years of subsequent theatre-going and study: the stage seemed bare; there was a throne and, behind it, two huge off-white walls – one, at an angle and to the side, was adorned with an abstract shape that seemed Japanese or Chinese, and the other, also angled to the side, hung with a corroded rectangular metal sheet. There was no national anthem – a common ritual then at the start of a performance; the action began with the house lights remaining on as an actor (Tom Fleming playing Kent) appeared, dressed in worn leather jacket and trousers. A huddle of actors formed with a sense of purpose yet informally. Lear (Paul Scofield) entered not in a procession from upstage centre but quickly from the side. He wore a robe but not like Moses, and there were no flowing locks – he sported cropped grey hair under a plain crown and a close beard. He was dominant, bored and brusque, and rarely raised his voice. And when he did – to rage, I recall, in and at the storm or to mourn the death of Cordelia (Diana Rigg) – the effect was chilling. His daughters wore beehive hair-dos and dark eye-liner, bringing the court into the present while still inhabiting an imaginary past. The walls were moved to fashion new spaces, props were few, and the setting stayed simple, becoming even starker and more austere. Three giant rusty thunder sheets descended for the storm, which took place in bright light. In the second half, the human figures seemed even smaller in the void. There was little movement and the pace was measured, which made sudden eruptions of violence, like the overturning of the table at Goneril's castle, all the more disturbing. The speaking was clear, deliberate yet nimble and presented as if for your consideration.

Certain moments and images stand out: Scofield's laser eyes; his nasal, mesmeric voice; the way his body shape seemed to change as the play progressed; Lear and the Fool (Alec McCowen) – the one relationship I remember, especially the lines 'Oh, let me not be mad' and the tenderness of 'Art cold?'; the brutality of the blinding of Gloucester (Alan Webb), seen in full light to close the first half; the two old men, mad Lear and blind Gloucester, both humiliated and desecrated yet almost comic in their attempt to seek consolation in a savage world without shelter; the sightless Gloucester sitting cross legged on the empty stage staring as if accusingly at the audience while the din of battle sounded somewhere in the distance; and, at the end, Edgar (Brian Murray) dragging the body of his defeated brother upstage, both facing the audience, to the murmur of an indistinct yet foreboding noise. No reassurance. Bleak, harrowing, thought-provoking, exhilarating: I'd never guessed Shakespeare could be this raw, this enthralling.

Years later, I understood that this production had, indeed, become regarded as seminal, not just in its interpretation of the play and its staging of Shakespeare but also, by helping secure the identity of the RSC nationally and globally, in promoting the value of ensemble playing. It had also roused controversy for overthrowing the expected way of seeing the play and twisting its meaning to suit the misanthropy of its director, Peter Brook. Unsurprisingly, as a generation of scholars came to prominence that had not seen the production and its historical moment receded, the prominence of the production has altered. For some, it has been overshadowed by reference either to the film that it spawned or, more frequently, to the astonishing 1970 production of *A Midsummer Night's Dream*, which started its life in the same theatre and came from the same director and the same company.[2]

Both productions mark important stages in Brook's directorial journey as well as in the wider account of Shakespearean stage representation.

Brook's journey of curiosity and experiment has been well rehearsed, both by himself and by manifold commentators, as at root a journey of magpie accretion, trial and elimination. This pragmatic process of synthesis began in the club theatres of 1940s London and saw him in the following decade sample a range of genres from romantic comedy, opera and film to the musical and avant-garde modernist drama. Before the age of public subsidy of the arts, Brook with ruthless dedication had secured a position in the generally conservative English theatre scene as its 'enfant terrible', a label he was happy to carry long into his maturity. A brilliant craftsman, he moved easily between London's West End and Covent Garden, Stratford, Paris and Broadway, often with major stars at the centre of his shows yet very much his own man. He was aware of the transforming theatrical movements of the mid-1950s without being a part of them, offering instead his own individual stage alchemy, which was most apparent and consistently developed in his productions of Shakespeare. Brook began away from the national critics with an inventive *King John* at the Birmingham Rep in 1945 and followed this with a typically eye-catching debut at Stratford, the youngest director to work there.[3] His triumphant *Love's Labour's Lost* responded to the play's artificiality with his own invented and elegant style that self-consciously embraced anachronism. Then came distinctive productions of *Romeo and Juliet* (Stratford, 1947), *Measure for Measure* (Stratford, 1950), *The Winter's Tale* (Phoenix, 1951), *Titus Andronicus* (Stratford, 1955), *Hamlet* (Phoenix, 1955) and *The Tempest* (Stratford, 1957).

Echoes of reactions to the iconoclasm of *King Lear* can be found in critics' responses to *King John* and onwards: in that production Brook departed from the text, as he did thereafter, notably in *Romeo and Juliet* from which he cut the reconciliation of the warring houses. Many critics seemed to find this production uncomfortable and disliked it because it was not how they had envisaged the play. Responding that 'Shakespeare has become, for the ordinary playgoer... a bit of a bore', Brook said he had tried to break with the play as a 'pretty-pretty, sentimental love story'. The 'significant thing is that we have attempted a clean break with the accepted style of Shakespearean production, and the storm of controversy is some measure of our success'.[4]

Measure for Measure was noted for its uncompromising austerity as well as its unified vision, which Brook anchored by being the production's designer as well – a logical move for a director who believed in the primacy of the visual and in solving a production through the set. For *Titus Andronicus*, an incendiary retrieval of a play never before performed at Stratford because it was cast as the runt in the Bard's litter, Brook designed the costumes and set and composed the music in addition to directing. The success of this production with Laurence Olivier in the title role (it transferred to the West End and toured Europe) cemented Brook's reputation for rediscovering lesser Shakespeare plays by imposing his own view on them. Tackling *King Lear*, a play that many believed placed Shakespeare in the exalted company of Mozart, was therefore of great moment. It was also keenly anticipated because it would be Brook's first production for the RSC and would re-unite Brook and Scofield, who, during an absence from Stratford of fourteen years, had become one of Britain's major actors.[5]

Scofield had first worked with Brook in 1945 at the Birmingham Rep as John Tanner in *Man and Superman*, the Bastard in *King John* and Wangel in *The Lady from the Sea*. Scofield was 23 and Brook 20. Brook subsequently cast Scofield as Don Armado in *Love's Labour's Lost*, Mercutio in *Romeo and Juliet*, the twins in *Ring Round the Moon*, Pierre in *Venice Preserv'd*, and in three plays at London's Phoenix Theatre in 1955–6, including the title role in *Hamlet*. Scofield had come to the theatre public's attention mostly through his West End performances – at the time, before the advent of the RSC and the National Theatre, the main arena for high-profile stage actors. He had appeared in a variety of new work from thriller and comedy to drama, including an under-rated musical (*Expresso Bongo*), an award-winning performance in Graham Greene's *The Power and the Glory* and his most celebrated role as Thomas More in *A Man for All Seasons*, which he had performed in the West End and on Broadway and was later to reprise on film for which he won an Academy Award. His Shakespeare work, in addition to the roles he had performed with Brook, included appearances in Stratford in the 1946, 1947 and 1948 seasons, playing, among other parts, Aguecheek, Troilus, Pericles, Henry V and Hamlet. For a John Gielgud season in London, he had been Richard II, and in Stratford, Ontario Coriolanus. Unlike many star actors, Scofield was private and modest.[6]

Brook had long contemplated *King Lear* and knew he needed the right actor as the king before he embarked on it. He had chosen the play in 1953 when asked to direct on US television, an invitation that resulted in a studio-filmed, compressed version (73 minutes) starring Orson Welles. Brook felt 'it was unexciting Shakespeare' and that while Welles was good in close-up he lacked the stamina 'for the rhythm of a whole performance'.[7] Brook was confident in Scofield: 'The communication between us was now so deep that it required few words… we never discussed the theory or the meaning of what we were attempting, it was implied, unsaid.'[8]

In order to achieve the unity of vision he required, Brook had decided, once more, to design and compose. From *Measure for Measure*, *Titus Andronicus* and *The Tempest* (also frugal) to *King Lear*, he continued his struggle to find a singular set that would signify and encompass the totality of his view. He worked on the *Lear* set for around a year and came up with what he later described as a 'wonderful toy', 'very interesting and very complicated, with bridges that came up and down'.[9] Recalling the episode when he tore up his pre-prepared directorial plan for *Love's Labour's Lost* at the start of his career to rely instead on discovery in rehearsal, Brook says that just before rehearsals began for *Lear*, he destroyed the set when he realised it 'was absolutely useless'.[10] In its place he conjured a Spartan landscape, a harsh world of metal, leather and wood. The movable walls combined the indoors (security) and the outdoors (unforgiving), a contrast Brook saw as critical to the experience of Lear's world. He wanted to create a stage environment in which Shakespeare's combination of different styles and conventions could happily co-exist while placing the emphasis on what the actors were doing and saying. Brook also reduced – to what he assessed was the minimum – the music, sound, props and costumes (only the eight or nine main characters were given distinctive dress). This tightening the focus to achieve clarity and intensity, a process of stripping back and rejecting what was not useful or necessary, what claimed attention at the expense of something more important, continued during rehearsal (Brook was dissatisfied with the costumes and had new ones made in ten days) and was applied to rehearsal itself.[11]

As a powerful figure in his own right and as one of the triumvirate running the RSC (with Michel Saint-Denis and, at the apex, Peter Hall as Managing Director), Brook had won five weeks' rehearsal (not then common). Various accounts, from Brook, actors and chiefly his assistant Charles Marowitz, have provided a record of some of what occurred. At his first meeting with the actors, Brook assumed command by speaking in traditional and fearsome terms of the play as a mountain whose summit had never been reached, the ascent being strewn with the shattered bodies of stars such as Olivier and Charles Laughton. Brook intimated a challenge to preconceptions without offering an alternative. Instead, he summed up his rehearsal method by telling an Oriental fable: a neighbour's wife disappears and, when he is found sifting sand and asked why, he replies that she must be somewhere, so he has to look everywhere. In this process of looking everywhere, writes Marowitz, 'Every rehearsal session dictates its own rhythm and state of completion. If what is wrong today is wrong tomorrow, tomorrow will reveal it, and it is through this constant elimination of possibilities that Brook finally arrives at interpretation.'[12]

Brook believed a Shakespeare play was 'not only of a different quality', it was 'also different in kind'.[13] It did not matter who wrote the plays and what the biographical traces might be because 'it's something that actually resembles reality' with an 'unlimited number of interpretations, which is a characteristic of reality'. A Shakespeare play reaches us not 'as a series of messages' but 'as a series of impulses that can produce many understandings'. Brook believed Shakespeare had discovered 300 years before Picasso 'the cubism of the theatre', a 'realistic image of life'. The 'idea of the play is the play itself' and, therefore, a Shakespeare play is easier to understand if considered as an object, a many-faceted complex of form and meaning in which the line of narrative is only one amongst many aspects. With *Lear*, Brook did not approach the play as a linear narrative centred on one individual but as the story of a cluster of relationships. Many themes criss-cross the play's prismatic form, among them age and youth, the 'sclerosis opposing the flow of existence', and sight and blindness. When it comes to what Shakespeare means, Brook says, 'Wisely, Shakespeare refuses to answer.' In *Lear*, 'the whole field of experience is both question and answer… the meaning will be for the moment of performance.'

Much of the controversy aroused by the production stemmed from Brook's approach, which was akin to treating a Shakespeare text as a new play rather than following pre-ordained perspectives. Brook and the actors created innovative characterisations removed from the moralising, picture-frame world of 'goodies and baddies'. In the opening scenes, Brook found a denial of life in Lear's rusty ironclad power. The king was shrewd and wilful but trapped in his own world. Goneril (Irene Worth) and Regan (Patience Collier) were seen as sincere in their opening remarks, yet consequently even crueller in their later actions. Gloucester was presented as a condescending, self-important patriarch yet one who did not deserve his fate, Edmund (James Booth) was no longer a monster, the bully in loyal Kent came out, the fleet, angry Fool spoke truth unto power not nonsense, and with Poor Tom voiced the alarming lucidity of those perceived as mad.

Brook's radical approach also refashioned certain crucial moments, such as the petulant, wrecking aggression unleashed by Lear in Goneril's castle, which put the daughter in a sympathetic light, and the storm on the heath, which was based on the actors' actions. As Harley Granville Barker had done, Brook eschewed traditional special effects. Drawing on a Chinese opera tradition, in which a fight in the dark takes place in full light, Brook staged the scene in bright light. The vibrations of the menacing metal sheets grew as the storm worsened, and their sound and duration were cued in the prompt books to follow moments in the actors' performance.

As far as the cast was concerned, most members were performing in other RSC productions and were, as a result, already participants in the company's brief challenge to the complacency of British acting, searching for a style of expression rooted in the totality of the actor's craft. For Brook, faced with the prismatic cubism of the *Lear* text, the question was how 'to bring the actor... towards an understanding of this remarkable invention, this curious structure of free verse and prose'.[14] One tool was improvisation, which Marowitz was asked to organise for some of the cast, though not Scofield, but which met resistance. Mostly, as Tony Church, a founder member of the RSC who was playing Cornwall, recalls, 'the text was explored, and worried, and felt, and teased.' He thought that *King Lear* was 'the first RSC example of really "breaking down" a text and actually "feeling the way" into it.' Brook, he said, 'produces an extraordinary concentration. Every line was a minefield... one couldn't charge through it. One had to pick out the *exact* meaning of an image and the *exact* meaning of a thought.'[15] From the time of his early productions, Brook had developed a distinctive presentation of Shakespearean text. He would warn against the dropped inflection at the end of speeches, against generalisation individually and collectively, and against yielding to verse rhythm while arguing for the need to find the stress in order to find meaning, but then to find the rhythm of a character, which is as personal as handwriting without being eccentrically so. Balancing the formal and the naturalistic, Brook believed speaking text should alter the actor, who needs to enter the extravagance of an image yet not sound false. Brook sought to break the prevalent prejudice that new plays required real acting and Shakespeare a heightened form, whereas both involve a search for truth, a 'truth of emotion, truth of ideas, and truth of character – all quite separate and yet all interwoven'.[16]

The production had been announced in October 1961 and had sold a reported 30,000 tickets when Hall was forced to postpone it due to Scofield's exhaustion from performing for almost two years without a break in London, New York and Ontario. The delay serendipitously helped the

RSC. It gave Brook time to scrap his *Lear* set (and the new one cost less than planned) while Hall, instead of extending existing shows, captured the spirit of makeshift adventure that characterised the young RSC by rushing on a new production of the then-little-played *The Comedy of Errors* directed by Clifford Williams. On a simple raked platform, the clarity and attack of its ensemble cast, which included twelve of the *Lear* company, were greeted jubilantly and as marking the emergence of an RSC style.

This success lifted the spirits at Stratford and helped buoy the *Lear* cast, which was opening at the very end of the season. There were no previews. The *Lear* team had Sunday, Monday and Tuesday morning and afternoon in the theatre to get the show ready for a Tuesday evening opening. Running at around four hours, *King Lear* played only 13 performances in Stratford, but at the Aldwych heroically clocked up 74 performances, playing from January to April 1963 in rep with just another Brook production (Durrenmatt's *The Physicists*). *Lear*'s success was already ensured, and Scofield won the 1962 Evening Standard best actor award; but the production's international standing was secured by performances in France, where it won the 1963 Théâtre des Nations' Grand Prix, along with Theatre Workshop's *Oh, What A Lovely War!*, and by a revival in 1964 as part of the RSC celebrations for the four-hundredth anniversary of Shakespeare's birth. Three Aldwych performances were followed by a tour of Europe and the US along with *The Comedy of Errors*, ambassadors for a company inspired by magnificent continental ensembles such as the Moscow Art Theatre and Berliner Ensemble and now placed on a par with its distinguished forebears. Following the tour, Brook commented on the role of the different audiences in the different countries and compared favourably those in central and eastern Europe, which happened to be home to these ensembles as well as subject to totalitarian regimes, to those in the US (specifically, Philadelphia), who largely went to the theatre for conventional social reasons other than interest in the play.[17]

The reception and subsequent commentary was divided in opinion, with what was probably the majority elated (albeit some of them rather tentatively so) while others, which included many powerful voices, believed the play to have been deformed. To comprehend the response adequately would require more space than is available to detail the historical context of the production. Any useful account would need to include the backdrop of the cold war, a polarised, power-bloc world of extremes that induced a genuine sense of potential mutual destruction (*Lear* rehearsed during the Cuban missile crisis) and, at home, a stratified society that retained the death penalty, conscription and pre-production stage censorship, that banned abortion and homosexuality, and that still had more than a decade to go before implementing the Equal Pay Act. The 'swinging sixties' lay ahead and *Lear* was a sombre reminder that notions of progress should carry a health warning. Brook, who had filmed and edited the mephitic *Lord of the Flies* before rehearsing *Lear*, believed the last, troubling lines of the play were unique in Shakespeare because they do not presage an optimistic future.

Despite the mostly benign notices in national and regional media for *Lear*, there were notable dissenters, both in Britain and abroad. While some complained that Scofield's Lear was not a King (Olivier dubbed him Mr Lear) and the play was, therefore, no longer a tragedy, and a few scholars, viewing Shakespeare's characters as paradigms, cavilled at the human complexity the actors portrayed, the prime complaint was the apparent lack of emotional effect ('no heart' – the *Daily Sketch*[18]). Apparently, throughout the production history of *King Lear* 'the main test has been, surprisingly, whether the audience can be made to cry.'[19] Brook would have none of that. His use of bright light throughout, even in the blinding of Gloucester, executed viciously with a golden spur as the victim is roped to a chair, not only excluded the possibility of audience sympathy but also suggested audience complicity: the house lights gradually came on as Gloucester stumbled off, blanket over head, bumping into servants who went about their business rather than helping him. Through this complicity, the production invited the audience to make judgements, presented humans as responsible for their own actions rather than religious or other supernatural forces, and announced that the tragedy is ours not Lear's, nor any other individual's in the play.

The cardinal sin was Brook's alterations to the text to sustain what detractors called a nihilistic view, as if there were a definitive text and – more absurdly – a definitive (and therefore) unchanging interpretation.[20] Stratford had acquired and sometimes assumed a sense of guardianship if not ownership of Shakespearean text, a role reinforced by the RSC's attachment to textual scrutiny even if veracity did not mean unswerving loyalty. Yet long before *Lear* and the later commonplace of deconstructionist theory that pronounced the death of the author, Brook in his Stratford productions had abandoned Shakespearean text as an untouchable vessel of single truth waiting to be revealed through diligent rehearsal and against which benchmark all performance was to be evaluated. He had cut *Titus*, for instance, to avoid bathos, but this was acceptable because of the poor standing of the play, just as opposition to the massive editing of the history plays that produced the RSC's iconic *The Wars of the Roses* (1964) was similarly muted because the originals were considered lesser texts. But with *Lear*, what constitutes the 'original' is open to dispute. The texts and their interpretation have changed over time, beginning with the two earliest and different extant versions, the Quarto (1608) and the Folio (1623), the relationships of which to the play's author or to how the play was first performed remain unclear.[21] Nahum Tate in the seventeenth century thought the play needed a happy ending, Charles Lamb in the nineteenth century said it was impossible to act while William Thackeray found it boring and Leo Tolstoy believed it to be riddled with inconsistencies. The play's good reputation grew in the twentieth century, championed by those who thought it a masterpiece, such as Granville Barker and Brook, who never went as far as others, for instance his *Lear* assistant Charles Marowitz, in chopping up Shakespearean text to create something quite new. Such a fluid history, however, does not absolve interpreters of responsibility – but responsibility to what?

Brook defends both traditional respect for Shakespeare, as a genius who wrote sublime plays such as *King Lear*, and the right to alter his texts in the search for their meanings in a contemporary world. His production was not frivolous or wanton and falls firmly within the tradition of *Lear* interpretation, even while altering it. Compared to many *Lear* productions, Brook cut little, but what he did caused a rumpus. As he had done with *Romeo and Juliet*, Brook removed references in *Lear* to reconciliation, notably (but not only), in the blinding scene, the servants' lines showing pity for Gloucester, lines which do not appear in the Folio text. Even supporters found this unacceptable, but ignored by most commentators was the fact that Brook kept the only example of resistance by a servant, who wounds Cornwall before being killed.

Criticism of the alleged warping of the play touched on a debate on relevance, a debate which the RSC had entered at full tilt and which subsequently exercised the academy as well as media critics. In the aftermath of the Holocaust and the dropping of the A-bombs, the role of art and of commitment in art had become urgent topics. Within this debate the question was raised of how the classics and Shakespeare in particular could fit into any vision of vital theatre. Should a classic 'speak for itself' or speak through a distinctive directorial interpretation? Brook believed that because the traditions of Shakespearean production in his day were not those of Shakespeare's day but of the Victorian theatre, then 'If you just let a play speak, it may not make a sound. If what you want is for the play to be heard, then you must conjure its sound from it.'[22] Setting out to be simple, he thought, 'can be quite negative, an easy evasion of the exacting steps to the simple answer.' He supported the RSC's mission to create a new tradition, to question the whole process of interpretation, to revivify Shakespeare with contemporary means for contemporary spectators. Speech and style, he said, 'can only take their true place if the impulse to use words and images relates to experience of life.'[23] In practising this, he distinguished between the relevant and the topical, the contemporary and the present, insisting that meaning resided in the imaginative process not in replicating the familiar or the everyday.

Those accusing Brook of sacrificing *Lear* to the demands of relevance have overstated the influence on the production of the Polish critic Jan Kott, and of passages in his book *Shakespeare Our Contemporary* that connect *Lear* to Beckett, whose work was still relatively rarely produced in Britain. Brook's view was that he and Kott were thinking along similar lines and that, while it was only in the 1960s that Shakespeare was found in Beckett, Beckett already had been found in Shakespeare (for example, the *Lear* scene near Dover in which Edgar persuades Gloucester they are ascending a steep hill though remaining on the flat ground). Marowitz acknowledges the presence of Beckett in discussions with Brook about *Lear* – though Kott was not mentioned – and confirms that theory was not directly mentioned in the rehearsal room.

Emphasis on Kott and Beckett underplays other ideas that were important to Brook, such as those of Jean Genet (he had directed *The Balcony* in Paris in 1960), the radical notions of sanity and madness associated with the psychiatrist R.D. Laing, the French New Wave in novel and cinema, and Eastern Asian traditions of performance and philosophy. There was also the influence of Brecht, particularly on acting style rather than on political approach. Along with Beckett and the Theatre of the Absurd, Brook also saw Brecht in Shakespearean theatre, a theatre that goes beyond both: 'Our need in the post-Brecht theatre is to find a way forwards, back to Shakespeare.'[24]

Some critics seemed upset that a director had displayed any ideas at all – and Brook himself warns against being seduced by the bright idea if it does not survive rigorous testing in the laboratory of rehearsal and performance.[25] Brook was considered very un-English in his attraction to ideas, even though he was pragmatic in their application. Yet for me, one of the great pleasures of the production was this excitement and materiality of ideas, the insistence on the phenomenology of the experience of the performance. Brook's world embraced the compact, palpable power of the haiku and that of a modernist poem such as William Carlos Williams' *The Red Wheelbarrow*, in which one senses the real as opposed to realism, the conceptual existing in and through the thing itself. For Brook, Shakespeare's text is a reflection of reality, grasped imaginatively, yet the imagination lacks purchase while it stays in the mind, and it has to be made real. Brook describes how Scofield as Lear achieved this: 'He refused to be disturbed by my constant chiding that he was not portraying an old man. He remained himself, but by the force of inner conviction he projected to the audience the exact image that he had in mind.' In 'the meeting place between imitation and a transforming power called imagination', a 'seemingly abstract word "incarnation" suddenly took on a meaning.'[26]

In 1968, employing a minimalism of under-statement equivalent to that of his *Lear* production, Brook wrote: 'All I would claim regarding our *Lear* was that it presented an unusually complete text in bright white light with less elaboration than was customary at the time.'[27] This is a neat and, to my mind, accurate summation but what it understandably omits is the invigoration achieved by the production through its purposeful, focused vitality, and the density and depth of the experience which, while devoid of sentiment, was not devoid of emotion, and though forbidding, was not negatively passive.

Although for me the achievement of Scofield at the head of a terrific cast in an exemplary production is undoubtedly linked to the period in my life when I saw it and how it figured in my own embryonic interest in theatre, the production deserves attention because of its wider importance. It was not the novelty, though the innovations seemed fresh. Previous productions had, for instance, made Lear more a human being and less a royal symbol and had cut the text; Brook and other directors had already embraced anachronism, had presented characters against stereotype, seeing them from their own perspective, had offered multiple perspectives and had dispensed with decorative productions to focus on the actors (in the 1962 RSC season, this was evident in *Measure for Measure*, *Cymbeline* and *The Comedy of Errors*). Use of a bare stage in a major proscenium theatre, however, and deployment of architectural shapes reminiscent of Appia's and Craig's work were still unusual though not unknown. Unlike earlier isolated radical productions, however (for instance, of *Lear* by Komisjaresvky in 1936), Brook's synthesis for a particular company playing a particular theatre circuit at a particular moment did change the theatrical landscape of which it was a feature.

Whatever the production's flaws and inconsistencies, many witnesses attest to its unique effect in making Shakespeare live for its day. Here are just a few, drawn from across the years since the production occurred and across different constituencies: 'I know at least three playwrights', said David Hare, 'who will tell you they realised they wanted to make their lives in theatre when they saw Paul Scofield play King Lear. It was... the greatest classical performance of my lifetime: radical, humane and incredibly moving.' W.A. Darlington (*Daily Telegraph*) thought the production would go into theatrical history 'as the best performance of this tremendous play in modern times'. Roger Gellert (*New Statesman*) said Brook and Scofield 'have demonstrated shatteringly how it [*Lear*] can be acted for our generation'. Jack Kroll (*Newsweek*) called it a 'revolutionary production that can change the face of Shakespeare for our time'. Garry O'Connor in a biography of Scofield judged that 'no greater and more prestigious production of this masterpiece was to hold such sway for so long'; while in the academy, Jackie Bratton said it 'threw down the gauntlet of the late twentieth century to the classical tragic stage' and Alexander Leggatt thought that 'Shakespeare production, in England at least, was never the same again'.[28]

Brook's view of how to approach a Shakespeare play and, more broadly, of what constituted theatre, which he says changed radically for him through directing *Lear*, are major influences stemming from the production – both through his stage work and through the enormous influence of *The Empty Space*, which first appeared in 1968 based on a series of lectures in which he distilled what he had learned up to that point in his directing career.

The notion of the 'empty space' or the neutral platform, which in modern times can be traced through directors such as Poel, Copeau, and Granville Barker, is linked to Brook's minimalist setting in *Lear* and his attempts to overcome the limitations of the proscenium through use of the house lights to overlap with the action as well as full light throughout. This approach, which inscribes in the production's aesthetic acknowledgement of the audience as makers of meaning, looks forward to Christopher Morley's plain-box set for William Gaskill's 1966 production of *Macbeth* at the

Royal Court, which in turn fed into the permanent sets that became a feature of the RSC and Sally Jacobs' celebrated white-box set for Brook's RSC production of *A Midsummer Night's Dream*. This approach also led Brook and others towards smaller spaces, as if recognising the increasing difficulty of making commonly agreed meanings. The influence of *Lear* can be seen in the trend toward small-scale Shakespeare, which was propelled by the RSC's The Other Place in outstanding productions there, such as *Hamlet* (1975) by that venue's founder, Buzz Goodbody, with Ben Kingsley in the title role, and Trevor Nunn's production of *Macbeth* (1976) with Ian McKellen and Judi Dench.

King Lear affected the RSC in several other ways and, through the sway of the company, influenced the wider theatre world too. The production helped secure the company's hegemony in approaches to text, the dialectic between past and present, and mise en scène. The RSC had only just ditched the Memorial tag from the name of its Stratford theatre, thereby hoping to lose the mausoleum association; and yet the Swan, a pre-eminent symbol of Shakespearean veneration, still hung over the theatre's proscenium and the National Anthem still usually preceded performances there. Although Brook himself was not a company player, *Lear* helped promote the company as having decisively broken with the negative aspects of past bardolatry and establish itself as a large, publicly funded ensemble committed to the interaction of new plays and old. Appealing especially to a significant constituency which had enjoyed the post-war expansion of education and moves towards the democratisation of culture, the RSC's 'relevance' and modernity, however diffuse and contradictory, did connect with the developing political tenor of the time, and *Lear*, along with productions such as *The Wars of the Roses*, was at the heart of this relationship.

Lear led directly to Brook's next phase of work, stretching from the Theatre of Cruelty immediately afterward through to the International Centre for Theatre Research, which he founded in 1970 in order to create a theatre 'of doubting, of unease, of trouble, of alarm', focusing on the primacy of the actor, building a core ensemble and exploring the empty performance space often in non-conventional settings.[29] In this phase, Brook offered a critique of the RSC's methodology while still working with the company and enhancing its reputation; with the exception of an unremarkable *Antony and Cleopatra* in 1978, Brook did not work for the RSC again following his production of *A Midsummer Night's Dream* in 1970, which rivalled, if not surpassed, the clamour that greeted *Lear*.

As David Hare testifies, the inspiration of *Lear* went beyond the RSC and can be found in actors, directors, writers and other theatre professionals who came to shape British theatre in the subsequent decades. The impact of the production and what it represented can be found in later productions of the play on stage and film and, even if indirectly, in those who have mined *Lear* for their own fashionings, such as Edward Bond, Elaine Feinstein and Howard Barker. On a broader intellectual front, *Lear* contributed to the development of cultural materialism and new historicism and, in its validation of anachronism, multiplicity of viewpoints, recognition of the role of the audience and the importance of the aesthetic, contributed to the development of post-modernity and the post-dramatic, too.

When rediscovering or re-interpreting classics became a popular trend, novelty often became the norm, and directors ignored what Richard Eyre noticed about Brook: that his work is concerned with conferring authority on the performer rather than celebrating the director.[30] The Brook–Scofield *Lear*, as it was often called, may contain other things of value that have also been lost. The production is not mentioned much in the continuing debate on 'why Shakespeare?' but it has a bearing, particularly in relation to arguments that separate Shakespeare from the world around or that promote relevance while avoiding the present. For me, coming into a new decade out of the restrictive 1950s, the RSC *Lear* was memorable because it undermined deference, questioned the basis of authority and said we are all responsible and must therefore make choices and take responsibility for them. The production made real the idea of Shakespeare our contemporary in a thrilling way that made me believe theatre could confront the world in which I lived with imagination, insight, and elation.

Endnotes

1. 'Awesome', *Daily Telegraph*, 7 November 1962; 'towering', *Stage*, 8 November 1962; 'revolutionary', *Observer*, 11 November 1962
2. Brook shot the film in 1968–9; it was released 1971. John Tydeman directed Scofield in a 2002 radio production of *King Lear* to mark the actor's 80th birthday.
3. Of the national critics, only J.C. Trewin (*Observer*) reviewed Brook's production of *King John*.
4. *New Theatre*, June 1947, p.8
5. Scofield had been expected to return to Stratford in 1960 to lead the first season under Peter Hall's leadership but had pulled out.

6   He twice rejected a knighthood after accepting a CBE in 1956 and was made a Companion of Honour in 2001.
7   Michael Kustow, *Peter Brook: A Biography*, London: Bloomsbury, 2006, p.80
8   Peter Brook, *Threads of Time: A Memoir Biography and Autobiography*, London: Methuen, 1998, p.34
9   Peter Brook, *The Shifting Point: Forty Years of Theatrical Exploration 1946–1987*, London: Methuen, 1988, p.12
10 Ibid., p.12
11 Information on remaking the costumes comes from interviews with the author by Farrah (26 June 2000) and Ann Curtis (10 February 2000).
12 Charles Marowitz, 'Lear Log', in Charles Marowitz and Simon Trussler (eds), *Theatre at Work: Playwrights and Productions in the Modern British Theatre*, London: Methuen, 1967, p.137. The log first appeared in *Encore* and is also reproduced with a postscript in David Williams (compiler), *Peter Brook: A Theatrical Casebook*, London: Methuen, 1988.
13 Brook puts forward the ideas on Shakespeare that are outlined in this paragraph in a number of places and over a number of years, for example, in 'An Open Letter to William Shakespeare, or, As I Don't Like It', *Sunday Times*, 1 September 1957, or 'What is a Shakespeare', in an interview with Ralph Berry for *On Directing Shakespeare: Interviews with Contemporary Directors*, London: Croom Helm, 1977. The quotations can be found in *The Shifting Point*, op. cit., p.75; Shakespeare and the cubism of theatre, 'What About Real Life?', *Crucial Years*, London: Max Reinhardt, 1963, p.21; idea of the play is the play itself, *The Shifting Point*, op. cit., p.48; a Shakespeare play as an object, *The Empty Space*, op. cit., p.102. The *Lear* references come from *The Empty Space*, op. cit., pp.102–6.
14 *Crucial Years*, op. cit., p.21
15 Quoted in David Addenbrooke, *The Royal Shakespeare Company: The Peter Hall Years*, London: William Kimber, 1974, pp.125–6
16 *Crucial Years*, op. cit., p.21
17 *The Empty Space*, op. cit., pp.25–6
18 *Daily Sketch*, 7 November 1962
19 Alexander Leggatt, *King Lear: Shakespeare in Performance*, Manchester: Manchester University Press, 2004, p.10
20 In *Evoking (and Forgetting) Shakespeare*, London: Nick Hern Books, 2002, p.29, Brook says *King Lear* is 'not a bleak existentialist play showing that mankind is a worthless species, nor a naïve expression that all mankind is noble and beautiful'.
21 A good example of the differences between the Quarto and Folio versions is the final scene, in which Lear's last lines are changed and the closing speech is given to a different character (Albany in the Quarto, Edgar the Folio).

22 *The Empty Space*, op. cit., p.43
23 Peter Brook, Preface to Jan Kott, *Shakespeare Our Contemporary*, London: Methuen, 1967 (2nd edition, revised), p.x
24 Ibid., p.96
25 See, for example, *Threads of Time*, op. cit., p.34
26 Ibid., p.32
27 *Flourish* (RSC magazine), vol. 2, no. 1, autumn 1968
28 Hare, *Guardian*, 21 March 2008; Darlington, *Daily Telegraph*, 7 November 1962; Gellert, *New Statesman*, 16 November 1962; Kroll, *Newsweek*, 1 June 1964; O'Connor, *Paul Scofield: The Biography*, London: Sidgwick & Jackson, 2002, p.178; Bratton (ed.) *Plays in Performance: King Lear*, Bristol: Bristol Classical Press, 1987, p.3; Leggatt, *King Lear*, op. cit., p.61
29 *The Empty Space*, op. cit., p.50
30 Richard Eyre, *Utopia and Other Places*, London: Vintage, 1994 (revised edition), p.120

CHAPTER THREE

'I've been Nicked!'[*]:
The Life and Adventures of Nicholas Nickleby by Charles Dickens, adapted for the stage by David Edgar

EDWARD LEWIS

Introduction

One Monday evening in the summer of 1980 I found myself standing in the foyer of the Aldwych Theatre, then the London home of the Royal Shakespeare Company's main house productions. With all the vim and vinegar of youth I sported that decade's uniform of rebellion: leather jacket, political t-shirt, Levi 501s and Converse All-stars, considering myself vastly superior to the suited, booted and twin-setted bourgeoisie who then, as now, made up the majority of the audience for the subsidised national theatre companies, only the clothes being different. Little did I know that the 'four-and-a-half hour passage of the play' that was to follow was to define my future career, academic and creative. That I was in that foyer at all was one of those defining strokes of fortune. A week previously I had met a young actress at a party who told me she was part of the company of *Nicholas Nickleby*. Her enthusiasm for the production had stimulated my interest even though she had said that audiences had up to that point been somewhat disappointing. That ticket sales were slow was confirmed by my ability to get a seat three rows from the front for that and the next night's performance as late as that morning.

I entered the auditorium and was faced with something I had not encountered in the theatre before. Members of the cast were mingling with the audience, a few chatting animatedly with friends who had come to see the show, some answering questions from strangers, others talking amongst

---

*   Publicity slogan on T-shirts sold by the RSC to accompany the production.

35

themselves, all of them in costume but out of character. I also noted a number of familiar faces from stage and television in that audience. As I looked around the theatre, what also became clear was that the layout of the auditorium had been changed. A number of seats in the centre of the front stalls had been removed and a narrow thrust stage built out into the auditorium, reaching to the cross-aisle that divided the front stalls from the rear, on which some of the cast were perched talking to those of us in nearby seats, whilst along the front of the Dress Circle balcony and the boxes either side, overhanging the stalls, a catwalk had been hung from the safety rail, connecting with a scaffolding structure that bridged the entire stage and with ladders to allow direct access to stage left and stage right.

This set appeared to be constructed from the sort of architectural salvage that could be found in skips in those older parts of London that at the time were being subjected to 'gentrification'. Wrought-iron gates and railings, wooden banisters, fire-surrounds, shelving and other Victoriana that was being trashed to make way for through-lounges and central heating in areas such as Islington, Kennington, Wandsworth and Battersea. The overall effect was of an Impressionist interpretation of the engravings of London contemporaneous with Dickens' work. Various props such as chairs were hung from the set, whilst the stage itself had a number of trucks parked upstage and the slightly raked stage included a track on which some of these trucks might move. Costume baskets and clothing racks were dotted around the periphery of the performance space and the upstage wall was clearly visible. Although, as I was to later learn, none of these aspects of the production were particularly innovative in themselves, they did seem to add to the atmosphere of expectation engendered in the audience, which went beyond the normal buzz of conversation experienced in a large auditorium shortly before curtain-up. Despite the fact that the auditorium was not full, there did seem to be a qualitatively different air of expectation amongst the audience.

Although the traditional succession of bells signalling that the performance was about to begin had sounded, the buzz of conversation continued whilst the actors made no attempt to leave the auditorium. As I continued to look around I saw that the theatre doors had been closed and shortly afterwards the band began to play what I later understood to be the main theme tune for the performance. The actors finished their various conversations and using the central catwalk and the balcony 'rat run' made their way quickly to the stage, where they formed an arc some two or three deep across the downstage area somewhat in the manner of a Victorian family photo. As the house-lights dimmed and a general lighting state illuminated the entire stage, an actor, if my memory serves me correctly, Teddy Kempner, not in character, uttered the opening words of the novel and the play:

> There once lived, in a sequestered part of the county of Devonshire, one Mr. Godfrey Nickleby, who, rather late in life, took it into his head to get married.*

Thus, in this somewhat prosaic fashion, were we launched into the life and adventures of our eponymous hero.

What follows in this chapter is a personal response to this original production, tempered with analysis of the conditions of production, the social context of the work and a critical review of its various aspects, performative, literary and scenographic. Like all personal responses it contains a subjective element and may be challenged by others who experienced the production. It is one of the characteristics of live theatre that the performance is essentially transitory and the audience experience, though communal, is intensely personal. It is this inevitable difference in personal response that makes theatre a stimulus for discussion and debate and, like all cultural constructs, a means by which we as individuals make sense of the world. The theatre critic Ken Tynan once opined that every theatre performance, amateur or professional, good, bad or indifferent, was a unique piece of history. This brief study attempts to capture at least an impression of this particular piece of history.

The Social Background to the Staging of *Nicholas Nickleby*

In 1979, the election of a Tory government under Margaret Thatcher with a secure parliamentary majority of 43 enabled her to push her radical right-wing agenda through parliament, despite attracting only 44% of the popular vote (an almost identical percentage as Adolf Hitler received in the last free elections before he became Chancellor). The beginning of 1980 saw a worsening economic recession and the regime's adherence to monetarism led to stringent state spending cuts which, coupled with inflation, had a severe

---

*   Edgar, 1982, Part One, p.13. All script references in this chapter are taken from the Dramatists Play Service Inc. edition published in two volumes in New York in 1982.

effect on the subsidised theatre sector. For Thatcher, companies such as the RSC were seen as a luxury that should be funded on a free-enterprise business model. Her suspicion that subsidised arts organisations and broadcasters such as the BBC were organically left wing in their political orientation led to a determined assault on their funding and organisation over the next decade. When the project that became *Nicholas Nickleby* was first posited, the RSC was in severe financial straits.

Britain in 1980 was very different to Britain today. Higher education was still free, with students receiving a non-repayable grant for maintenance, trade-union membership was high and workers' rights were protected by law. Although Britain was a member of the European Economic Community, the integrated market and its associated social legislation were still some years away, whilst leaving the EEC was still considered a real proposition by die-hards on the right of the Tory party, with whom the Prime Minister had much sympathy. Gas, electricity, the railways, telecommunications and the iron, steel and coal industries all remained in public ownership run for the benefit of the people rather than a handful of private shareholders, whilst the water industry was controlled by local councils and paid for through the rates, as were schools, polytechnics and hospitals. Council housing, as social housing was then called, was often occupied by employed members of the working class, thus ensuring a diversity that militated against the sink estates that social housing has now in the main become.

Television broadcasting remained divided between the BBC and the regional ITV companies, whose ownership was regulated to avoid the dominance of media moguls such as Rupert Murdoch and his ilk. Only three channels were available, BBC 1, BBC 2 and ITV, Channel 4 not coming into being until November 1982. The BBC still followed broadly Reithian principles of educating and entertaining and, as well as producing high-quality popular entertainment, also nurtured new talent through its in-house production process, with only a few, mainly American, series being bought in from outside the Corporation, and its highly regarded training schemes. Although a few independent radio stations existed, the bulk of radio broadcasting was controlled by the BBC which supplemented its regional television services with local radio stations serving individual towns and cities and their surrounds.

The RSC was, of course, not exempt from the harsh economic realities of Thatcher's Britain. By August 1979 the company's deficit was some

£200,000 and projected losses of a further £200,000 by the end of the financial year in April 1981. The Arts Council had indicated that the increase in grant aid for the following year would be in the region of 7% whilst inflation alone was running at a rate of over 15%. The implications for the company were clear, even though some production costs, such as sets for the productions that were to be transferred to the Aldwych Theatre from Stratford had already been covered. New work would have to be kept to a minimum.

Creating *The Life and Adventures of Nicholas Nickleby*

The RSC's main base was at the Royal Shakespeare Theatre in Stratford-upon-Avon, with a small studio space called The Other Place in the same town. Shakespearean productions were generally premiered in the main house, with new plays and some more experimental work premiered at The Other Place. Stratford productions played for a season at their home bases and then were transferred to the company's London bases at the Aldwych, in the case of main-house shows, or The Warehouse, in the case of some studio shows. There were exceptions to this rule, C.P. Taylor's *Good* being premiered at The Warehouse for example, and some popular shows transferred to West End theatres, often with a cast change and subject to a financial agreement with those theatres' commercial managements. Although the programme at Stratford was generally dominated by Shakespeare's plays, the company had a long and honourable record in staging new and often controversial work, Howard Brenton's rewritten *The Churchill Play* being first staged at The Other Place and John Arden's *The Island of the Mighty* at the Aldwych – the latter being the subject of a very public falling out between author and company, leading to Arden himself picketing the production on its first night. In addition the company also undertook a short residency in Newcastle-upon-Tyne each year.

Central to the RSC's artistic policy was an ensemble approach to casting. Actors were contracted to the company for the year, usually from September to September, with a requirement to accompany productions that were transferred to London, and all might be required to play supporting roles in some productions despite taking lead roles in others. This ensemble approach proved crucial to the development of *Nicholas Nickleby* or 'Nick Nick' as it became known in the camp parlance of the British theatre community. Trevor Nunn, faced with the possibility of not being able to finance a full RSC season with multiple productions, decided instead of the usual seasons of new plays and revivals to focus the company's resources on one extended production that would utilise all the actors for the year, although no featured roles were guaranteed to any one actor. According to Leon Rubin, whose 1981 book[*] is the most complete account of the play's original production process, Nunn had long been interested in putting Dickens on stage and had once, on holiday, read the whole of *Little Dorrit* out loud to his wife. He therefore decided that a full-scale production of a Dickens novel would enable the company to utilise its resources as economically as possible and also demonstrate what an ensemble company could achieve. He brought on board as a collaborator John Caird, who co-directed, whilst Leon Rubin's insight into the production comes from his role as Assistant Director.

By the time work began, David Edgar had been added to the production team as writer on the strength of his two stage adaptations, *Mary Barnes* and *The Jail Diary of Albie Sachs*. Edgar, an avowedly left-wing writer, was to have a significant effect on the political alignment of the adaptation. However, the process through which the adaptation was made was probably unique to a major national theatre company at the time, particularly in the ways in which the actors were able to make their mark on the production other than simply through their performances. Once the decision had been made to choose *Nicholas Nickleby* rather than *Hard Times* (which had recently been adapted for television) or another of Dickens' novels, the company were asked to read the entire novel and then, after a series of sessions in which they collectively told the story to each other, either individually or in small groups research aspects of Victorian society and make a presentation to their fellow company members. This was followed by a series of group sessions to dramatise and perform scenes from the novel, many of the ideas from these sessions being incorporated by David Edgar into the script. Throughout the rehearsal period the actors worked and reworked scenes that were provided by Edgar in the morning and then rewritten overnight following meetings with Nunn, Caird and Rubin. At one point these meetings were even taking place at Nunn's bed side after he was laid up with a back problem.

It had been decided that the production would be scheduled in such a way as to enable the audience to choose to watch Parts One and Two on

---

[*] *The Nicholas Nickleby Story – The making of the historic Royal Shakespeare Company production*

separate nights or essay the marathon and watch the whole adaptation on one day. To this end, Part One was performed on Mondays and Thursdays, Part Two on Tuesdays and Fridays and the whole play on Wednesdays and Saturdays, Part One as a matinee and Part Two as an early evening performance, with a break between the two. Part One was finally to come in at approximately four hours in length and was played with one fifteen-minute intermission, whilst Part Two ran at about four-and-a-half hours with two twelve-minute intermissions. Spectators were offered a discount for buying tickets for both parts and a further discount for tickets for both parts played on the same day.

As a result of problems encountered in the latter stages of rehearsal, this performance pattern was not adhered to, Part One being first performed on 6 June 1980* whilst Part Two was not performed to an audience until 11 June. The two parts were finally put together on Saturday 14 June with the Press performance being held on 21 June.

The Performances

One of the characteristics of theatrical performance is its ephemeral nature. In most cases a play is performed and one's memory is all that remains, whether it be as actor, director or audience member. It is possible to attempt a simulacrum of the original production, the success of French's Acting Editions of popular plays, based as they are on the prompt copies of the first productions, being testament to that; but in general it is impossible to recapture the immediacy of a stage performance and the experience of seeing it live and in the company of an audience, large or small. Although film versions of stage plays do exist, they rarely attempt to recapture the theatricality of the original production, Peter Brook's own film of *The Persecution and Assassination of Jean-Paul Marat as Performed by the Inmates of the Asylum at Charenton Under the Direction of the Marquis de Sade*† (understandably usually known as *The Marat/Sade*) being one exception. The RSC do hold video recordings of many of their more recent productions in their archive at the Shakespeare Birthplace Trust's library

---

*   Although the original RSC programme from December 1980 (RSC, 1980) gives the first performance date as '5 June 1980', this is later corrected in the May 1981 edition (RSC, 1981). This error is understandable given the cancellation of the first preview that was schedule for 5 June 1980.
†   Brook, 1967

in Stratford-upon-Avon, but these are videos taken from the control box during the performances and give only a limited idea of what it might have been like to experience the performances. No archive video exists of the 1980 production of *Nicholas Nickleby*, although the archive does hold a video of the 1986 revival. However, following the success of the first run of the show, it was decided to attempt a television version of the full theatrical production. This was filmed in front of a live audience with the original cast immediately after the production closed in the summer of 1981 in The Old Vic Theatre, London, whence the original set was transferred. Under the television direction of Jim Goddard what resulted is an excellent re-creation of the original staging, although the theatrical acting style does initially come over as somewhat stilted. The recording was broadcast on Channel 4 in November 1982 and is currently available on DVD.[*] Of course, the best companion work to the production remains the original novel.[†]

Given the existence of this DVD, what follows is not intended to be a comprehensive narrative description of the production, not least because of its length, but rather to focus on some of the elements that made it such a powerful and influential production. Prior to watching the production, I had some knowledge of the story; however, I had never read the book.

As the performance proper started, I was immediately aware that what I was seeing was not a traditional adaptation. These usually take the form of a stripped-down narrative focussing on the key plotline and ignoring most if not all of the subplots, which in Dickens often contain some of the more interesting characters and dramatic incidents. As Rubin points out,[‡] the novel has effectively two openings: one outlines the recent history of the Nickleby family[§] and the other the inaugural meeting of the United Metropolitan Improved Hot Muffin (and Crumpet) Baking and Punctual Delivery Company, which ends in a public disturbance.[¶] The history of the Nickleby family was delivered by the company as a whole, not in character, sharing lines amongst themselves, with the named characters often stepping out of the group to identify themselves, sometimes delivering lines in character but often being described by other members of the company. This somewhat Brechtian technique, which I later discovered had been pioneered

---

[*]   Goddard, 1982
[†]   Dickens, 2003
[‡]   Rubin, 1981, p.85
[§]   Edgar, 1982, Part One, Act I, Scene 1, pp.13–16
[¶]   Ibid., I.2, pp.16–19

in the genre of adaptation by Mike Alfreds in his time as Artistic Director of Shared Experience (and whose work included an adaptation of *Bleak House* using seven actors to play all the roles and tell the story), was central to the way the production was staged.

One of the problems with adaptations for stage or screen is that often the elements that make the original work remarkable are lost in translation. The plot of *Jane Eyre*, for example, is not far removed from a Mills & Boon romance, but what makes the novel great is the authorial voice. That voice is all too often either lost in adaptations of novels, which rarely consist of more than lifting the plot line and the dialogue to tell the story, or, in the case of film, television and radio versions, reduced to a voice over reminiscent of 1940s American 'film noir'. Nowhere is this more pertinent than in the work of Dickens, whose novels are layered with detailed description. As *Nicholas Nickleby* progressed it became clear that this group narrative technique was essential to the success of the production. This is exemplified by the beginning of Part Two* where the company summarise the events of Part One for the benefit of those who had either missed or forgotten the early performance. Here the artifice of the production was emphasised through exaggerated acting and rapid-fire delivery of the lines where actors often caricatured their own performances in the first part.

The technique was also used to great effect to create an impression of changing locations and to emphasise some of Dickens' social commentary. Although the individual characterisations were generally naturalistic in style, the minimalist nature of the settings meant that Dickens' descriptions, for example, of Nicholas and Smike's arrival in London, were staged not just through the dialogue and physical responses of Roger Rees (Nicholas) and David Threlfall (Smike) but also through non-naturalistic staging by other members of the cast. As Nicolas and Smike are surrounded by the narrators, who burst onto the stage playing different aspects of the London populace, the production emphasises the duality of class relations in the metropolis. Building on ideas devised during the rehearsal period by a group of actors under the leadership of Edward Petherbridge, who played Newman Noggs in the production, the company adopts varying postures of the rich and privileged, eating and drinking. Then after turning a full circle, the same actors become the poor and dispossessed, their noses pressed to

---

*   Edgar, 1982, Part Two, I.1, pp.13–18

the 'one thin sheet of brittle glass" that guards wealth from poverty in the shops and restaurants of Victorian London.

Such collective performance extended beyond mere dramatisation of the authorial voice and also helped to create physical objects. Hanging from hooks attached to the scaffolding of the set were various items that would be utilised by the cast, props, pieces of costume for quick changes (it should be noted that the company consisted of 43 actors playing some 150 parts), and other items that were to be used to create stage props. Perhaps the most spectacular example of this collective creation was the stagecoach on which Nicholas leaves for Yorkshire. As with so many aspects of the production this had grown out of work during the preparatory period. Using a flat truck as its chassis, the coach is quickly assembled as the background to Nicholas's tearful farewell to his family by members of the cast using a table used earlier in the same scene as part of the interior of the coaching inn *The Saracen's Head*, costume baskets and various other items. As Nicholas and the other passengers board the 'coach', it is propelled up-stage and off by cast members. The speed and precision with which the building of the coach and its departure was executed left members of the audience convinced they had seen a stagecoach in The Aldwych Theatre and brought a burst of spontaneous applause.

Amongst other examples of this approach to setting, three particularly stand out. In a street scene, a single actor, carrying a whip, leads six actors in pairs, each holding a chair in front of them, trotting across the stage in an impression of a horse-drawn omnibus, the sound of the horse's hooves being made, quite openly, by someone trotting behind with a pair of coconut shells. Similarly, when Nicholas attacks Sir Mulberry Hawk in his hansom carriage, Bob Peck, playing Hawk, is seated on a dining-room chair and raised onto the shoulders of four actors, whilst the horse, which plunges and rears during the fracas, is created by two other actors, one of whom is holding a pole, with a black cloth thrown over them. The whole atmosphere is intensified by the use of smoke and low-level lighting. The technique extended beyond means of transport. In what was, for me, the most striking use of the method, members of the company created a roulette table simply through posture and the use of a simple prop. Its effectiveness might be judged by the fact that it was only on the third time I saw the scene that I was able to discern how the effect had been created. I had previously sworn that a real roulette table had been brought on stage since I had heard the roulette ball spin round the wheel. In

---

*   Ibid., I.11, p.50

fact a group of actors in a square had stood as if leaning over a table and the 'croupier', after calling the bets, had spun an old-fashioned football rattle to produce the sound of the ball spinning.

This excellence in ensemble work was matched by many of the individual performances whether from older actors such as John Woodvine, Edward Petherbridge, Jane Downs (as Mrs Nickleby) and Lila Kaye (as Mrs Squeers and Mrs Crummles), or younger performers such as David Threlfall or Cathryn Harrison (as Miss Petowker and Phib). The acting style of the production mixed both stylised performance, what would now be called 'physical theatre', and more naturalistic characterisation. Many aspects of the work fitted with Brecht's concept of Epic Theatre, but it would be misleading to describe the production as 'Brechtian', Threlfall's performance for example being fully naturalistic. Given that the company of 40 or so actors was portraying around 150 characters between them, with the exception of Rees and Threlfall all were required to double and treble their roles, including playing the inmates of Dotheboys Hall. Nunn had decided that rather than use real children in the roles with all the problems that would entail, members of the cast, male and female would portray the children. Similarly in group scenes, such as the Mantalini's shop, male as well as female actors would play the girls. Both approaches worked to great effect, to some extent heightening the inherent humour of the Mantalini's whilst not detracting from the pathos of the children's plight. Often non-speaking parts were taken by featured actors and one of the minor pleasures of the production was to spot, for example, Edward Petherbridge playing a non-speaking role as an arrogant, aristocratic rival to Hawk in a break from his major part as the down-trodden Newman Noggs. Characterisation in the doubling and trebling of roles was not always supported by full costume changes and much was achieved by the judicious use of selected costume items over a generic base costume.

Another aspect of the varied acting styles present in the production worthy of note is the use of a Brechtian rehearsal technique in performance. Brecht suggests that on occasions it is informative to ask actors to deliver their lines in the third person in order to develop a more objective approach to the performance. On several occasions in *Nicholas Nickleby*, an amended version of the technique is used to articulate the artifice of adaptation by a character adopting the authorial voice to comment on his or her own actions, whilst in all other respects playing the scene naturalistically. For example, in a scene where Nicholas encounters Fanny Squeers and her friend Tilda Price, he disabuses her of her belief that he is enamoured of her in a particularly forthright way, then, turning out front he declares: 'And waiting to hear no more retreated. *(Nicholas retreats.)*'* This is an effective anti-illusory technique and focuses the audience upon the literary nature of the original work.

It would be inappropriate to conclude this account of the performances without mentioning the contribution of David Edgar, the adaptor. Whilst the original novel contains trenchant social criticism it remains essentially the work of a bourgeois liberal and, as Orwell points out, Dickens' message appears to be 'if men would behave decently the world would be decent.'† Edgar, at the time an avowed Marxist, clearly saw the opportunity to present a critique of the nascent Thatcherism. It has already been noted that the novel had essentially two openings. Edgar was very keen for the second, a satirical representation of corrupt business practices, to be kept. As Rubin points out, Edgar told the *South Bank Show* team, 'I want it because the plot is about money and the main plot of the book is almost all about money and relations between people and their money and I wanted to start with a scene about money.'‡

In the last scene of the production, the final scene of Part Two,§ Edgar inserts an invention of his own to undercut the cosy ending characteristic of Dickens' plots. With Smike by now dead and the various couples happily married, Edgar creates a Dickensian Christmas party with all the principal characters present, upstage, eating and drinking, whilst downstage a ragged boy, left over from the previous scene of the breaking up of Dotheboys Hall and named in the script as 'The New Smike', sits and '*in the loneliness and silence, begins to sing what he can remember of a Christmas carol.*'¶ As the remaining characters deliver their narrative lines, the new Smike begins hesitantly to sing 'God Rest Ye Merry, Gentlemen', quietly and with only a limited memory of the lines. As the scene progresses, the carol is taken up by the remainder of the company who have taken their places about the stage and on the various raised sections of the set. Nicholas turns and notices the boy, breaks from the party '*and picks him up in his arms, looking at his wife and sister*'** and then '*turns to us, and stands there holding*

---

*   Edgar, 1982, Part One, I.17, p.64
†   Orwell, quoted in RSC, 1980
‡   Rubin, 1981, pp.85–6
§   Edgar, 1982, Part Two, III.12, pp.169–72
¶   Ibid., stage direction, p.169
** Ibid., stage direction, p.172

the boy in his arms" as the carol ends and the lighting fades to darkness. It is interesting to note that when I first saw the production, Nicholas' final gesture was a clear challenge to the audience, Rees holding the boy in his arms and offering him to the audience with an angry expression as if saying, 'What are *you* going to do about this?' However, as the production grew in popularity, Rees' posture became more of an embrace implying, 'It's all right *we'll* take of him.' According to Bob Peck,† both Trevor Nunn and David Edgar noticed this change and asked Rees to revert to his original stance, Edgar feeling that he had intended the ending to raise a question rather than provide reassurance for the audience, whilst Rees was unaware of the change that had taken place. This provides an interesting example of the effect an audience can have both on the interpretation of the play and on the individual actor's performance, an issue that Alan Ayckbourn addresses in the structure of his play *Sisterly Feelings*.‡

Edgar's satirical input to *Nicholas Nickleby* extended beyond the political realm and also engaged with theatre itself. In the Crummles Theatre Company's *Romeo and Juliet* section at the end of Part One, a Victorian production of Shakespeare is pastiched by Edgar. As was often the case with Victorian versions of Shakespeare, Edgar gives the play a happy ending with Romeo, Juliet, Mercutio and Paris all coming back to life, the latter marrying Rosaline, and Benvolio (after revealing herself to be a girl, Benvolia), Mercutio.§ However, Edgar and Nunn do not ignore the opportunity offered by the company to make a final political point in the finale of Part One. After the Crummles Company have taken their curtain call, Mrs Crummles comes back on stage dressed as Britannia with helmet and union flag and sings a pastiche patriotic song, *England Arise*.₵ As the song proceeds, other cast members join the Crummles' Company on stage and form a parody of *The British Beehive*** that presents the British class structure with Lord Verisopht, Hawk and Ralph above, representing

---

*   Ibid.
†   Private conversation with author, 1980
‡   Ayckbourn, 1981
§   Edgar, 1982, Part One, II.18, pp.155–63
₵   Edgar, 1982, pp.164–5. Music and lyrics by Stephen Oliver, composer of the original incidental music and lyrics for the production.
** An 1867 cartoon by George Cruikshank, illustrator of a number of Dickens' books, a copy of which forms the title page of the RSC's programme for the production (RSC, 1980 and 1981).

High Society; Kate, Mrs Nickleby and others, the Middle Classes; and the Dotheboys Hall inmates kneeling at the front as the lumpenproletariat. As the song builds to its climax, the irony of the final verse: 'Evermore upon our country God will pour his rich increase: And victorious in war shall be made glorious in peace"* is underscored by the figure of the ragged beggar Brooker, who prowls across the stage staring threateningly at the audience, a forewarning of the havoc his presence will wreak in Part Two.

It has already been noted how aspects of the set and props were used to assist with the doubling of character and the changing of locations. The use of the different levels and the intrusion of elements of the set into the auditorium also aided the breaking of 'the fourth wall'. The 'rat-run' in front of the Dress Circle was used on several occasions for the staging of chase sequences and during the early 'Muffin Company' scene† as a vantage point from which the disgruntled muffin boys whose occupation was threatened by the new company could seek support from the audience and bombard the stage with muffins (and crumpets) in protest. The 'cat-walk' projecting into the stalls also helped integrate the audience into the production. In Part Two the duel that leads to the death of Lord Verisopht‡ took place on that 'cat-walk' and the proximity of audience members to the shots that were fired helped to increase the shock of the events depicted. In the final scene of Part Two, the bridge across the stage proper, which had been used on several occasions as a location for narrators to comment upon the action on stage, as well as the entrance to Miss La Creevy's apartment, allowed members of the cast to scatter 'snow' from buckets upon 'The New Smike' adding to the scene's pathos.

Stephen Oliver's 'incidental' music also became an integral part of the performance, adding to the filmic nature of the production. Scenes rarely had distinct endings or beginnings, but often one began as the other was ending, giving a feeling akin to the cross-fade in a film. In common with film scores, Oliver also devised a series of themes ranging from the lyrical *The Farm* with the bucolic associations of the Nickleby home in Devon, through an up-tempo *London* theme, which also, at a slower pace, served to underscore the dialectical nature of wealth and poverty to a mournful and eerie theme for Smike. Oliver also wrote a pastiche of a Donizetti opera for Sharon Bower, Andrew Hawkins and John Woodvine to perform as

---

*   Edgar, 1982, Part One, II.18, p.165
†   Ibid., I.2, pp.16–19
‡   Ibid., Part Two, II.12, p.119–21

the background to one of Hawk's attempts to seduce Kate Nickleby, as well as the already mentioned 'patriotic' song.* Nowhere is Oliver's music more effective in building atmosphere than in the brief scene following Smike's escape from his recapture in London by Squeers.† Underpinning a melange of voices is a distorted version of the Smike theme and the combination serves to emphasise the nightmare playing in the runaway's head as he attempts to evade capture and return to the safety of his 'only friend', Nicholas.

The combination of all these elements: a full and particularly effective adaptation by Edgar, that engages with contemporary political issues whilst remaining faithful to Dickens' original achievement; an impressionistic set by John Napier, who also designed costumes that added to the period feel without intrusion or inhibiting performances; the music of Stephen Oliver; and focussed and effective acting, in a variety of styles, under the direction of two of Britain's leading theatre directors, Nunn and John Caird, resulted in what was to me one of the most effective pieces of theatre I have ever seen, before or since. The critical response was, however, initially more muted.

The Aftermath

Although *Nicholas Nickleby* was to go on to win some ten awards in Britain and the United States,‡ the initial response of the London theatre critics was at best mixed. Felix Barber of the *Evening News* disliked its length, as

---

* It is interesting to note that, so accurate was Oliver's pastiche, 'England Arise' was included in *Posse Comitatus*, the final episode of Season Three of the American television series *The West Wing*, under the mistaken belief that it was the genuine article. In another connection between *The West Wing* and *Nicholas Nickleby*, Roger Rees, who by then had moved permanently to the United States, was a regular guest artist on the series playing the eccentric Lord John Marbury, expert on the Indian sub-continent and latterly British Ambassador to Washington.

† Edgar, 1982, Part Two, I.24, pp.83–7

‡ 1980 Laurence Olivier Awards (London): Play of the Year; Director of the Year (Trevor Nunn & John Caird); Designer of the Year (John Napier); Actor of the Year in a New Play (Roger Rees); Actor of the Year in a Supporting Role (David Threlfall); Actress of the Year in a Supporting Role (Suzanne Bertish)
1982 Tony Awards (New York): Best Play; Best Performance by a Leading Actor in a Play (Roger Rees)
1982 New York Drama Critics' Circle Award for Best Play

did Francis King in the *Sunday Telegraph* and several other critics. Most scathing was Michael Billington in the *Guardian* who, whilst praising some individual performances, thought the production 'a waste of the RSC's amazing resources'.* There were, however, several champions of the production, amongst them Robert Cushman of the *Observer*, James Fenton of the *Sunday Times* (who described it as 'a marvellous show and a very valuable experiment')† and Ned Chaillet in *The Times*. For a fuller account of the critical response, see Chapter 13 of Rubin's book which gives a detailed summary.

Despite the mixed critical response, the public who had actually seen the production had taken it to their hearts and letters of support poured in to the theatre. Nonetheless, ticket sales remained relatively low until an article by Bernard Levin in *The Times* castigated the negative critical response and assessed the production in 'rich terms of admiration'.‡ The result was an immediate upturn in ticket sales, the production selling out for the rest of its six-week run. More significantly, Levin's article prompted an almost unique occurrence: critics who had previously castigated the production re-viewed it and revised their reviews.

With the demand for tickets continuing and the run concluded, Nunn decided to find a way to extend the production's life. It was impossible, given the existing season, to extend the run immediately and transferring to a commercial theatre (as the subsequent RSC adaptation *Les Miserables* was to do some four years later) was financially and creatively unmanageable. Nunn therefore decided to bring the production back to the Aldwych at the end of the season for a short run. Although the majority of the cast were able to stay with the production, it did require some recasting with Fulton McKay replacing Ben Kingsley as Squeers and Emily Richard returning to the company to play Kate Nickleby. This time the production garnered overwhelmingly positive reviews and a transfer to New York as well as the project being filmed for Channel 4. The theatre world had truly been 'nicked'.

---

* Quoted in Rubin, 1981, p.176
† Quoted in Ibid., p.177
‡ Ibid., p.178

Conclusion

At the start of this chapter I wrote about the effect the production had on me personally and it seems appropriate to recapitulate why I consider *The Life and Adventures of Nicholas Nickleby* worthy of inclusion here. For me, the effect of seeing an audience respond to a live performance in a way I had only previously experienced at rock concerts made me realise that the creation of live theatre was a valuable way to spend one's life. The clear and immediate connection between audience and cast present in the Aldwych Theatre that night and on the other nights that I saw the production convinced me that theatre was the most vibrant and engaging of art forms. That is not to say that I haven't spent some dire evenings and afternoons in the theatre, but I am always optimistic that what I am about to see will be as affecting as *Nicholas Nickleby*.

In the end, great theatre is about great acting. As such it is appropriate to conclude with a brief anecdote about Roger Rees' performance, one that illustrates acting at its most effective. On the second or third time I saw the production, during the interval, Roger Rees was sitting on the edge of the stage a few feet away from me talking with two school children who had been brought to the theatre as part of a school outing. They were clearly enthralled by the performance and were asking Rees the sort of questions all actors regularly get asked: 'How do you remember the lines?', 'Do you like your costume?', 'Did you really hit Squeers?', 'Did it hurt when he hit you?' Sitting there, Rees answered them patiently and chatted with them about their night at the theatre, every inch the thirty-six-year-old RSC actor off duty. The music for the next act began to play, the lights dimmed and I watched entranced as John Woodvine started to come on stage and wondered what would happen next. Rees concluded his chat with the children by saying politely, 'Sorry chaps, but I've got to go back to work.' And as Woodvine delivered his opening line, Rees stood up, turned and in that split second became the eighteen-year-old Nicholas picking up his cue perfectly. For me, that is great acting and the thirty-four hours I spent in the Aldwych watching *Nicholas Nickleby* in its entirety on four separate occasions were worth it for that moment alone. Truly, I had been 'nicked'.

Works Cited

Ayckbourn, Alan (1981) *Sisterly Feelings*, London: Samuel French
Barry, Christopher (dir.) (1977) *Nicholas Nickleby*, British Broadcasting Corporation [on DVD]
Brook, Peter (dir.) (1967) *The Persecution and Assassination of Jean-Paul Marat as Performed by the Inmates of the Asylum at Charenton Under the Direction of the Marquis de Sade*, Marat Sade Productions and Royal Shakespeare Company [on DVD]
Brook, Peter, (dir.) (1968) *Tell Me Lies*, Ronorus
Craft, Joan (dir.) (1968) *Nicholas Nickleby*, British Broadcasting Corporation
Dickens, Charles (2003) *The Life and Adventures of Nicholas Nickleby*, ed. by Mark Ford, London: Penguin Classics
Edgar, David (adaptor) (1982) *The Life and Adventures of Nicholas Nickleby by Charles Dickens*, in two volumes, New York: Dramatists Play Service Inc
Goddard, Jim (dir.) (1982) *The Life and Adventures of Nicholas Nickleby*, based on the original Royal Shakespeare Company production by Trevor Nunn and John Caird, starring Roger Rees, Emily Richard, David Threlfall, John Woodvine, Jane Downs (Richard Price Television Associates in association with Channel Four and RM Productions) [on DVD]
Royal Shakespeare Company (1980) *The Life and Adventures of Nicholas Nickleby by Charles Dickens*, December programme, London: RSC
Royal Shakespeare Company (1981) *The Life and Adventures of Nicholas Nickleby by Charles Dickens*, May programme, London: RSC
Rubin, Leon (1981) *The Nicholas Nickleby Story – The making of the historic Royal Shakespeare Company production*, London: Heinemann

CHAPTER FOUR

Robert Lepage and Théâtre Repère: *Trilogie des Dragons*

JEAN-MARC LARRUE

It is 6 June 1987 and there is nothing attractive about the Old Port of Montreal's Shed No. 9. It hasn't been used for years and is now stuck between two eras – the not-so-distant past when the port was still bustling with activity and the current late twentieth century when everything seems in abeyance. The enormous urban renaissance project that is going to give Montrealers renewed access to *their* river, the St. Lawrence, and make the district a new hub of activity for the city's tourists and cultural life is still only at the draft stage. In 1987, the Old Port is a forlorn no man's land – isolated, sinister looking and poorly maintained, despite the beauty of the river and the magnificent view of the islands. And walking to the river's edge after crossing the similarly deserted railway lines, we could not help but think of the ships that should be there, moored to the quays, and the sailors and stevedores who used to go noisily about their business the full length of this huge shed, which, though built in the early twentieth century, is already such an old relic and almost a ruin.

In fact, we find the inside of this cement and steel structure no more inviting than its exterior, as we're forced to walk along endless dark corridors, punctuated here and there by small windows letting in a few rays of sunlight. We finally come to a huge space in the centre of the shed, where our ears pick up sounds that are very different. It is here that Robert Lepage and Quebec City's Théâtre Repère are giving the premiere of the complete version of *The Dragons' Trilogy*, the marathon, six-hour-long play that is destined to be a turning point not only in the history of Quebec theatre and collective creation, but also in the history of the outstanding troupe performing it and in the career of Robert Lepage, whose name is already beginning to circulate beyond the 'regular' attendees of the closed world of experimental and avant-garde theatre, particularly after his play burst to prominence by winning the Grand Prize at the second edition of the *Festival du théâtre des Amériques* (FTA).

Flashback to the Collective Creation Era

Interestingly, the audience was not put off by the unusual venue, because audiences in those days had become quite accustomed to the most daring experiences in all theatrical spheres, including explorations of new spaces that upset the traditional relationship between audience and stage. Those particular spectators were even less discomfited than others because, since the early 1970s, they had become accustomed to an increasing number of performances in the most unlikely venues by the major theatrical collectives of the time, like the Grand Cirque Ordinaire, Théâtre Euh and the Théâtre du Même Nom (TMN), in what retrospectively appears to be the most eventful period of collective creation in Quebec. As TMN's director and co-founder Jean-Claude Germain recalls, the search for new spaces and a new dynamic between actors and spectators was not only an aesthetic quest, it was also political:

> As actors, we were no longer putting on those mauve Turko-Indian costumes to seduce the audience in its comfortable, perfumed palaces. We proclaimed the emancipation of the actor... We took our leave of those disreputable venues, moving far away from those weird, prison-like houses of ill-repute and into the streets and the world at large.*

This desire to break away from 'those disreputable venues', which motivated the new theatrical troupes to perform outside the traditional, 'bourgeois' theatres, expressed itself in both Brecht's epic theatre and Artaud's 'theatre of cruelty'. Indeed, this movement's great figurehead troupes (The Living Theatre and Bread & Puppet) were still very much part of the scene in 1980 when

---

* (Author's translation.) Julian Beck, *la Vie du théâtre* (translation from English to French by Fanette et Albert Vander), Paris: Gallimard, 1978, p. 38. This book is not the exact French version of Julian Beck's *The Life of the Theatre: the relation of the artist to the struggle of the people* (San Francisco: City Lights Books, 1972) and the paragraph cited above only exists in the French text.

Jacques Lessard founded Théâtre Repère, of which Robert Lepage quickly became the dominant figure.*

Théâtre Repère

After graduating from the Quebec Conservatory of Dramatic Art in Quebec City in 1970, Jacques Lessard took part in Quebec's collective creation movement from the outset. In 1973, he created the *Circuit temporaire*, a collective troupe that remained active until 1976. Although Lessard was convinced of collective creation's potential, his disappointment in its results caused him to move to California where he took classes at Anna Halprin's San Francisco Dancers' Workshop in 1978. It was there he discovered the work of postmodern environmental architect Lawrence Halprin and the cyclical creative approach which he immediately found was more relevant to the requirements of collective work than the prevailing models based on a rational and linear approach to creation. The RSVP (Resources/Scores/Valuaction/Performance) model developed by Halprin was a radical but effective new approach to how a creative group might function. It is cyclical because the participants can – and should – continually return to the previous stages, thereby establishing the basic principle of a work-in-progress – neither the work nor its component parts are ever finished. Unlike standard practice, the 'resource' or starting point is not an idea or theme but rather a palpable and tangible entity that challenges the actor's body in one way or another. This approach to initiating the work places the actor at the heart of the creative process – in fact, the actors truly become author–actors insofar as they are required to participate in the search for these resources and their interpretation, given that a particular resource does not necessarily have the same meaning for all participants.

> The importance of the resource lies in its capacity to generate personal feelings, interpretation, and motivation for the performer. The meaning of the resource is purely in the actor's emotional response: the same resource (physical object, music, visual image, or anecdote) can elicit entirely different responses from other individual performers.†

---

*   Robert Lepage took Jacques Lessard's courses at the same conservatory from 1975 to 1978.

†   Aleksandar Saša Dundjerović, *The Theatricality of Robert Lepage*, Montreal and Kingston: McGill-Queen's University Press, 2007, p.81

The resources are either physical (e.g. a sound or a material object) or emotional (e.g. a memory, story or symbol). Much of the initial resource-based exploration involves improvisation that produces several hypotheses in which all the future show's components, such as dialogue, sound environment (noise, music and voice), props, visual elements, characters and actions, are intermingled. These hypotheses are transcribed as scores, which are then tested, evaluated and, if necessary, validated by the group in onstage performances as part of an 'action' and 'evaluaction' process. The cycle can begin at any moment and it is always possible to go back to what was previously done, evaluated and even validated. The performance thus does not constitute the end of the process and can become a new 'resource' in itself.

This cyclical creation system attracted Lessard because, whereas the collective creation movement advocated eliminating the hierarchical organisation of functions and disciplines within the practice and strove to abolish the historical hegemony of the script over the show's other components, it had not yet developed an adequate *modus operandi* and it was this factor that, in Lessard's view, largely accounted for the ephemeral character of theatrical collectives and their difficulties in creating collectively.* Although the RSVP creation cycles might not be a universal solution, they are, as Lessard points out:

> an extremely valuable work tool that gives artists bearings and tools, without going so far as to inhibit the freedom of their imaginations and sensibilities. The cycles are not explained, but become easier to work with: they do not directly produce talent, but rather facilitate its emergence.†

After returning to Quebec, Jacques Lessard rounded up a few young actors whom he had taught at the Quebec City conservatory and persuaded them to experiment with the RSVP cycles that eventually became the Repère (Ressource/Partition/Évaluation/Représentation) cycles in French.

---

*   Jacques Lessard, 'Vers une communauté de vie (un projet de croissance artistique)' [Towards a life community (an artistic growth project)], *L'Annuaire théâtral*, No. 8, 1990, pp.31–40

†   Irène Roy, *Le Théâtre Repère. Du ludique au poétique dans le théâtre de recherche* [Théâtre Repère: from the playful to the poetic in experimental theatre], Quebec City: Nuit blanche, 1993, pp.33–4

The actors reacted enthusiastically with the result that Théâtre Repère was founded in 1980 with Robert Lepage directing its first public performance the same year.*

The Dragons' Trilogy: Robert Lepage and the Repère Cycles

Robert Lepage remained with Théâtre Repère until 1989. There, he created singly or collectively his first major works in addition to *The Dragons' Trilogy*: *Circulations* (1984), *Vinci* (1986), *Polygraph* (1987) and *Tectonic Plates* (1988). *The Dragons' Trilogy*, which was first performed as a work-in-progress in Quebec City from 12 to 16 November 1985 (i.e. eighteen months before the complete performance in Montreal), marked a high point in this first creative decade. Although this masterly work contains all the foundations of the aesthetics and themes that Robert Lepage cherished, it also bore the imprint of the collective approach to cyclical exploration and creation. Two years after the Montreal performance, Robert Lepage left Théâtre Repère. The break with Jacques Lessard has been deep and irreversible.

> Even though the Repère Cycles are extremely rich in some respects, the method should not dogmatically restrict creators, but rather be an organic tool that can be modified depending on the show concerned.†

In retrospect, *The Dragons' Trilogy* represented both the triumph and limitations of the Repère Cycles.‡

It was thus as a collective creation that Marie Brassard, Jean Casault, Lorraine Côté, Marie Gignac and Marie Michaud, joined by actors Robert

---

*　*L'École, c'est secondaire*, 27 August 1980, Lévis
†　Patrick Caux and Bernard Gilbert, *Ex Machina*, Sillery (Quebec City): Septentrion, 2007, p.17
‡　Indeed, the creative approach that Lepage subsequently adopted in his own company, Ex Machina, is not very different from the Repère Cycles: 1. 'Extract fragments from chaos'; 2. 'Bring out the story's components'; 3. 'Impose structure'; and 4. 'Invite chaos'. This approach is supplemented by a number of other principles: the 'creative actor', the blending of disciplines and the abolition of hierarchies. (See Caux and Gilbert, *op. cit.*, pp.30–45)

Bellefeuille, Richard Fréchette and Yves-Éric Marier, plus Robert Lepage as director, embarked on the *Trilogy* adventure with a series of cyclical improvisations dealing with the theme of the Other interspersed with periods, spaces, memory and hallucination. This 'otherness', as perceived by Francophone Quebecers, possesses many faces – those of the Chinese and Japanese communities in Canada, those of the French (from France) and the English (from England). The work's 'archaeology' gave rise to three generations of characters, whose intersecting destinies constitute the story's dramatic driver. Although some randomness, luck and misfortune are intermingled with these intersections, the fact they take place at all is also due to factors of money, calculation, strategy and personal affinity or incompatibility. The respective psychologies of the characters are not only decisive elements in such circumstances, they are also the basics of Mahjong, a board game played with a set of 152 tiles bearing Chinese characters and symbols. The tiles with the highest value are the famous three dragons – the Red, Green and White Dragons, to which the three major parts or movements of the story are related and dedicated. The Green Dragon's ideogram represents water and spring, evokes childhood, children's games, beginnings and innocence, and its portion of the story takes place in Quebec City between 1910 and 1935; the Red Dragon, representing fire and summer, transports us to adulthood in wartime Toronto from 1940 to 1955; and the White Dragon, representing air and autumn, takes places in the relatively serene environment of Vancouver in the mid-1980s (i.e. the present at the time when the play was first performed).*

The variations between the dragons are not only spatial and temporal, but also organic and structural. The Green Dragon plunges the audience into closed, dark and almost underground spaces (even the parking lot seems covered) where the action evolves linearly. The Red Dragon is composed of two parts: the first is devoted to the meeting between the White Dragon's main characters, Jeanne and Françoise, who are now adults, while the second presents a series of scenes connected with the commemoration of the tenth anniversary of the destruction of Hiroshima by an atomic bomb. During this

---

* In 2003, *The Dragons' Trilogy* was remounted by Ex Machina, the company Robert Lepage founded in 1994. The play then went on to experience a second series of international successes. The main character of *The Blue Dragon*, which was created in 2008 and covers the period from 1985–2008, is Pierre Lamontagne, the son of Françoise, one of the two young girls in the Green Dragon; in this play, Lamontagne lives in Shangai where he has opened a gallery.

part, the pace accelerates and becomes syncopated with spaces and places simultaneously coexisting on stage, colliding with each other and destroying the initial linearity. The White Dragon transports us to the present (1985) and returns us to the rhythm and linearity of the Green Dragon, but this time in a soothing, bright outdoor site (on a mountain) or in sites that open on to the outdoors (an airport) or on to something else (an art gallery). With the passage of 75 years (since 1910), we now view things with more calm and perspective, with the otherness that seemed too disturbing and menacing so many years ago now becoming so ordinary that it is no longer noticeable except in terms of familiar and even attractive, physical features (like those of Youkali, the young Japanese woman from Vancouver).

The intermeshing of all these destinies is part of the three dragons' cycle, which in itself is animated, like ocean tides, by a continual inflow and outflow – between the *yin*, the dark, soft and hidden female side, and the *yang*, the bright, hard and visible male side. This cycle is set within another, more astronomical cycle marked by the appearance of Halley's Comet in 1910 and its return in 1986 in a world where everything is somehow connected by a kind of chaotic determinism.

The Over-simplification of the Simplistic Theory

It is often said of *The Dragons' Trilogy* – as indeed it is often said of all of Robert Lepage's major subsequent creations – that it was based on the simplicity and even the over-simplification of the situations and characters, as well as on clichés, overgeneralisations, predictable storylines, tried-and-true formulas and ideological conformism.

> [The play] has the simplicity of popular entertainment and would lend itself as a scenario for a soap-opera TV series. In a nutshell, the characters are searching for love and find themselves on a journey to overcome personal, socio-cultural, and geographical obstacles to their self-fulfilment.*

Repeating an analogy that originally came from Lorraine Camerlain,† Robert Lepage himself seems to substantiate this argument: 'In the final

---

* Dundjerović, op.cit., p.79
† Lorraine Camerlain, 'O. K. On change!', *Cahiers de théâtre JEU*, No. 45, 1987.4, p.94

analysis, our stories are simply melodramas… *The Dragons' Trilogy*'s is a clever melodrama."*

Therein lies the paradox of these productions and at the same time their incredible evocative power. While the audience never gets lost in the enormous six-hour epic of *The Dragons' Trilogy* (nor in Lepage's other major creations for that matter), it is not because it is simple or simplistic, since the audience would get bored if it were; rather, the audience is mentally prepared for the play, takes an active part in it, and is continually bemused and amazed by it.

The attitude of regarding melodrama and burlesque as simple and minor theatrical genres has been a persistent prejudice from which history and theatrical theory have not yet freed themselves. But this is a double error: not only are these genres not simple, the analogy to *The Dragons' Trilogy* is not tenable either. While the destiny of Jeanne – one of the young girls in *The Green Dragon* – is tragic, this kind of tragedy is not melodramatic and does not cast a melodramatic pallor over the play as a whole. *The Dragons' Trilogy* is not based on the principle of causality or on a fatal chain of events from which the melodrama's hero cannot escape, nor does it aim to melt the audience's heart or aspire to any other objective in terms of realism or illusion. And the same goes for the purported relationship to burlesque, which is similarly tenuous. The fact is that Lepage does not leave any room for ambiguity and doubt: the characters and objects that populate the play's staged universe are clear cut and possess remarkable symbolic clarity, with the result that everything in the play is readily recognisable. On the other hand, thanks to the actions and the dialogue, nothing in the *Trilogy* is fixed – everything is transformed and needs to be continually reinterpreted.

Indeed, Chantal Hébert and Irène Perelli-Contos have written a nuanced analysis of Robert Lepage's theatricality that highlights the tremendous complexity of the procedures and means used during both the creative process and the performance, arguing that it is precisely these elements that guarantee the work's comprehensibility and the audience's sustained interest. For these authors, Robert Lepage is *the* outstanding 'practitioner of complexity'.† And the experience of *The Dragons' Trilogy* proves them right.

---

*   Caux and Gilbert, op. cit., p.24
†   Chantal Hébert and Irène Perelli-Contos's expression appears to be totally justified. (Chantal Hébert and Irène Perelli-Contos, *La Face cachée du théâtre de l'image* [the hidden side of image theatre], Quebec City: Les presses de l'Université Laval, 2001, p.17)

The Audience and its Experience of the Performance Space

Our experience as audience members starts even before the dialogue begins. Unbeknownst to us, the play begins even before the actors appear – we are participating in it as soon as we embark on this unlikely journey to a place that is both familiar (Shed No. 9 in Montreal's Old Port) and intriguing (the structure is normally boarded up and inaccessible). As we approach and enter the venue, we have become part of the story: it is the first act and we are clearly the first character.

As mentioned above, the audience at *The Dragons' Trilogy* premiere was accustomed to such a 'change of scenery' and was thus amused by it without being astonished or blasé. For instance, three years earlier, in 1984, Gilles Maheu of the Carbone 14 group had transformed the Espace Libre's normal stage into a huge railway track by covering the entire floor with stones for his production, *Le Rail*; and in 1986, Jean-Pierre Ronfard was even more daring when he took his audience into an automobile scrap yard in the heart of Montreal to present a stunningly apocalyptic show, *Le Titanic*. There is no doubt that the metonymic value of the railway track and vehicle scrapyard intrigued and fascinated the audience, but did not upset anyone.

However, what *The Dragons' Trilogy* offered was not this type of playful and congenial 'change of scenery'. In the smoky shadows of Shed No. 9's huge, empty and sonorous space, with its amazingly powerful presence, the spectators found their bearings and were able to make out a first fixed, vertical element – a sentry booth. Then, when they lowered their eyes, they realised that the performance area was entirely covered with undulating sand – a pluralistic but intriguing reference to a desert, a sandbox, a vacant lot and solitude… Thus, when the prologue begins, the show has already started.

'I've never been to China', announces a female voice. 'When I was a little girl, there were houses here. This was Chinatown. It's now a parking lot. … If you scrape the earth with your fingernails, you'll find water and motor oil. … And if you dig deeper, you'll end up in China.' The sentry, who has been in his booth throughout the prologue, immediately becomes 'the dragon guarding the gate of immortality'. And the sandbox simultaneously becomes a Quebec City parking lot with traces of its past history, precisely where the city's Chinatown used to stand. End of prologue!

The Art of Relations and Transformations: Another Way of Relating to People and Objects

Two cheerful young girls – Jeanne (Marie Michaud) and Françoise (Marie Gignac) – are playing in a sandbox. They are enjoying themselves, using shoeboxes to create this familiar neighbourhood with its main places and most remarkable residents, like Crawford (Robert Bellefeuille as the adult Crawford and Marie Gignac the young Crawford), who is an immigrant from Britain and a shoe salesman; Wong, a Chinese laundryman and his son, Lee (both played by Yves-Éric Marier); Lépine and Bédard (Jean Casault); and Morin (Richard Fréchette), the barber who is also Jeanne's father. Once separated from the children's playing, these characters become alive in turn under our eyes, drawing us into the intimate details of their lives, and, in turn again, they produce other individuals – Youkali (Marie Brassard), Stella and Sister Marie (Lorraine Côté), soldiers, officers, Pierre the pilot and so on, which give rise to other places and other encounters. The spatial and temporal markers dissolve and are continually transformed as a logic of chaos is established in which we fearlessly immerse ourselves from the first scene onwards. The basic impression is not only one of witnessing something new being born before our eyes, but also to take part in it and physically feel in our gut the very simple truth that objects, like people, are only illusions – moments of time in an enormous system of relations and transformations that we can sense but cannot rationally understand in their entirety. And it is these changing, unpredictable and elusive relations, combined with their unexpected transformations, that are the basis of the *Trilogy*'s dynamic as well as its dramatic and poetic power.

This system of relations and the transformations it entails are created before our eyes. Lorraine Camerlain suggests that, starting with the play's first three scenes:

> its codes are established, the particular rules of an apparently familiar game appear and a chemistry emerges whereby both actors and spectators become the artisans of a common object.[*]

As the choice and use of Shed No. 9 suggests, the conditioning of the audience commences before the play actually begins. In fact, although the spectators understand from Scenes 3 through 21 that they are not watching

---

[*] Lorraine Camerlain, op. cit., p.85

a linear plot, they do not have the same mastery of the play's codes and still have to discover them from scene to scene. The only certainty is that nothing in this play is stable and that the audience needs to rely on its own recollection of the actions and characters. We quickly grasp this principle that mobilises our entire attention, particularly since there are clearly no main actions in the classical sense of the term; at the same time, the play is not a rhizomic or fragmented intrigue.

Furthermore, any summary of this epic play would need to revolve around the respective destinies of the two young girls who appear at the beginning. First, there is the question of Jeanne's destiny, which we know will be tragic (and which, as it happens, is based on the life of a friend of Robert Lepage's mother*). Jeanne's father is Morin, a barber on St. Joseph Street, who is drowning in alcohol and debts. He risks everything he still owns in a game of poker with his neighbour, Wong, the Chinese laundryman. After losing, Morin then stakes his own daughter, who will be given in marriage to Lee, Wong's son, whom she will follow to Toronto. However, Jeanne always remembers her first love, the young Bédard, with whom she later has a daughter, Stella. Afflicted with meningitis, this daughter, whom Lee loves as his own, is severely handicapped and is ultimately committed to an institution in Quebec City where she dies. Jeanne is inconsolable and commits suicide. On the other hand, Françoise, who has joined the army during the war, remains as cheerful as she was when a child. She has a son, Pierre, who leaves to open an art gallery in Vancouver.

Enjoying the Acting

Despite some particularly intense and even painful moments, the spectators' overall impression of the play is one of profound serenity. As Diane Pavlovic points out, the audience abandons itself 'to the *Trilogy*'s calm motion, to the balance between tension and motionlessness that results from a strangely soothing effect. The spectators depart, feeling as if they have been meditating.'† Although all the play's elements – the space, the visual environment (the set design coordinated by Jean-François Couture and Gilles Dubé, and the lighting by Lucie Bazzo, Louis-Marie Lavoie and Robert Lepage) and the sound universe (Robert Caux's live music, the

---

* This memory, which Robert Lepage's mother transmitted to him, is a 'resource'.
† Diane Pavlovic, 'Reconstitution de *la Trilogie*', *Jeu* 45, p.42

mixture of languages, the noises and Shed No. 9's distinctive acoustics) – clearly contribute to this remarkable effect, it is primarily due to the acting.

That is why we need to remember that the *Trilogy*'s actors participated in the various phases of the creative process from start to finish; they were the piece's co-authors, drawing on various aspects of themselves – memories, experiences, knowledge and emotional associations – to create their characters, define the play's situations and imagine its actions. The collective work multiplied not only the artistic themes, but also the various meanings of these themes, since the same resource did not have the same evocative significance for everyone – it became polysemic, and these multiple meanings were largely responsible for the semantic transformation of the onstage objects – the sentry booth that became a laundry, an x-ray machine, a basement, an observatory and an office (where Françoise learns typing), or the white sheet being washed by the Chinese laundryman, which became first a screen, then a ship's sail and, lastly, a shroud. There are countless such examples, and Lepage uses tremendous virtuosity to juggle this polysemy and 'multivision'* in order to punctuate and enliven the whole show with the transformations and changes they inspire.

However, another reason for this overall atmosphere is clearly the contagious enjoyment of the actors in playing the many characters they helped to create. The role of the director, as conceived by Robert Lepage, is also largely responsible for this outcome as well, since it consists in 'making an interesting playground for the actors. ... Creating a piece should include the childish spirit – when people have fun, you feel the warmth of the emotions and the interactions. Then you bring it to the audience and it has to be a playground for them.'† This playful dimension is omnipresent throughout the production and imbues even its most dramatic sequences. Critics unanimously hailed the acting in *The Dragons' Trilogy* with words like 'profound', 'sensitive' and 'generous'. Another important factor is the creative process itself, given that the characters were developed collectively over a long period of time, removed from formal constraints except for those imposed by the place where the action was taking place; as a result, the author–actors were totally free to launch themselves into in-depth artistic explorations. In fact, the *Trilogy*'s dreamlike and theatrical universe was an

---

* The expression comes from Alison Oddey: 'a "multivision" results from the director's integrating of these various views, beliefs, and life experiences into a multiple narrative structure'. (In Dundjerović, op.cit., p.82)

† Cited by Dundjerović, op.cit., p.86

opportunity for the actors to draw on all their acting resources – and they did not hold back. This gave rise to a tremendous variety of scenes, running the full gamut from very poignant to very funny. Indeed, humour at all times is never very far from the action.

Unforgettable Moments

Almost a quarter of a century after its premiere, some unforgettable scenes from *The Dragons' Trilogy* remain engraved on the spectators' memories. One of these is the 'skaters' waltz', which marks the end of the first part of *The Red Dragon*, the time of adulthood and war. The scene is set in Toronto, where the sand in the sandbox is covered with shoes that Jeanne and Françoise have put there to remind themselves of their childhood games. The stage is then transformed to show Jeanne groaning as she gives birth. While Françoise and her lover skate around the stage (on ice skates), the music becomes louder and the lighting becomes stronger. Then a group of parading soldiers arrive, wearing ice skates as well. Jeanne and her daughter, Stella, run from one corner of the stage to the other to get a better view of the parade. However the soldiers' pace changes and the initially playful atmosphere of the outset becomes more sombre and ultimately anguished. The soldiers now brutally pound on the ground with their skate blades. The music gets even louder, the noise of the skates becomes deafening, the moving parade dissolves, and the soldiers end up crossing the stage in genuine chaos, trampling, lacerating and destroying the shoes in the process.

This change of pace and of meaning is combined with the symbolic passage from the metonymy (the skater's skate) to the metaphor – the skate blade becoming a weapon of destruction.

Another powerful moment in the play is Stella's metamorphosis into Sister Marie. This scene takes place at the end of *The Red Dragon*. Jeanne is preparing her handicapped daughter, Stella, for her trip to Quebec City, where she will be placed in an institution and ultimately die. Sister Marie comes to check whether everything is ready for the trip and reassures Jeanne about what will happen to her daughter. As she speaks, Jeanne undresses the nun whose body is transformed as it is undressed to become Stella. The gentleness of the initial gestures, which are both sensual and ritualistic as Sister Marie's clothes are carefully folded and placed in Stella's suitcase, in due course produce a deformed, ugly and mute body. Despite the simplicity of the means used, Lepage later confided that this scene, which is one of the most disturbing, albeit most beautiful, in the play, was necessitated by the circumstances: because Lorraine Côté was playing both characters at the same time and did not have time to change off stage, it was agreed that her change of costume and character would take place in full view of the audience.

Another disturbing scene, which was almost unbearably so but for another reason, is the poker game with Wong, the Chinese laundryman. This scene, in which Morin, the barber, bets his daughter's future, is silent and strictly choreographed. Three characters are playing cards. Every time they play their cards onto a metal barrel, they strike it. As the scene unfolds, the noise of the blows becomes increasingly loud. Morin loses. His barber's chair is then staked and hoisted onto the barrel. Jeanne, his pregnant daughter, is then hoisted as well, perched in a daze on the top of the barrel in the barber's chair, like a ridiculous throne. Although this image might seem to be ridiculous and even ludicrous, its very incongruity and fragility made it very striking.

The scene where Crawford leaves for Hong Kong, hoping to recover a small part of his childhood and of himself, is similarly intense, but in another register, that of infinite poignancy. Both Crawfords, the child and the old man, are on stage when time dissolves and condenses. The old Crawford remembers his past life and acts out his own memories, becoming the hero of his magnified past. This is an emotionally moving scene because it is such a painful experience for Crawford, who no longer thinks he can assuage the pain by returning to the noises and smells of the Hong Kong of his childhood. He slowly sets off towards the other end of the shed, but it is so far away that the spectators see him gradually shrink into the distance for what seems like an eternity. Then the shed's huge door opens onto an infernal din of blows and scraping noises, and six barrels shooting flames appear on the dock against a quiet backdrop of the river at dusk...*

One of the play's most incongruous and humorous scenes is the tribute to Mao by Sister Marie (Lorraine Côté), which occurs at the end of *The Red Dragon*. Bédard, Jeanne's lover, who is a grocery boy who makes his deliveries by bike, is riding his bike around the stage. During this time, Sister Marie, who is at Jeanne's home, has launched into an inflammatory speech on the merits of missionaries and revolutionaries. She becomes so carried away that she gets on the bike while it is still moving (an allusion

---

*   A Chinese junk happened to be passing by on the river at exactly the same moment as the shed door opened, which only added to the scene's magic.

to Mao's intention to carry out the Chinese Revolution on a bike), sits up in its front basket and there continues her speech in an increasingly excited manner. Her words become surrealistic and sing the praises of this 'great nation of god' where everything is mixed indiscriminately. As both a vocal *tour de force* and a balancing act, this scene makes the audience laugh at the same time as it criticises the madness of preachers and revolutionaries.

The Dragons' Trilogy Around the World

After its Montreal premiere, the *Trilogy* went on a long tour that took it to the world's greatest cities and a universally enthusiastic reception. The story of Quebec City's departed Chinatown clearly resonated with every audience. While the play's themes are universal – identity/otherness, war, death, love, art and the fascination with the Orient – its success and effectiveness have been primarily due to the very particular art of creating and staging that Lepage developed on the basis of the Repère Cycles.

In 2007, to celebrate the twentieth anniversary of this memorable premiere, Robert Lepage and his company, Ex Machina, once again remounted *The Dragons' Trilogy* with tremendous success. A new cycle had begun...

Chapter Five

Styx

Anthony Mawson & Ursula Raffalt

1. Introduction

The growth of global networks, with their sophisticated and very expensive marketing machinery and their absolute control over the flow of art works as well as arts funding, has made it increasingly rare to be able to be genuinely surprised by what is promoted as 'great'. The blatant use of the fashion and pop principle of 15-year cycles tends to grey out the arts for many people over thirty, blurring it into the realms of mass culture. That all of the chosen can be seen in all of the major centres in cyclic rotation underlines the suspicion that the 'flavour of the month' contains a blueprint against which all work is judged, by which it is marketed and on which all works aiming to be a part of that cycle must be modelled. Not far in principle from the 'Hollywood formula'.

The cult of celebrity ensures that once a 'name' is found, anything that can be attributed to that name, regardless of quality or content, can be similarly branded so that a large proportion of the work that gets widely seen is often void of both. The insane amounts of money in play allow the 'names' to earn large sums, which then get thrown at any vacuous idea they stumble across, thus buying its status as Art. Nothing impresses more than seven or eight digit numbers. This situation also becomes cyclic, providing an endless line of vacuous jaw droppers.

Occasionally, a truly deep work will slip through this filter providing desperately needed food and bringing a little light into the darkness; but sadly, more often than not, these independent works are regarded as distractions that need to be disappeared. So it is necessary to search far and wide to find any work that is both deeply moving and also seriously challenging.

Finally, it is all but impossible to ignore the hype and view an arts event from a wholly innocent standpoint and particularly rare to be privileged enough to be present at an event that could be said to be truly moving or life altering. But when those occasions do occur, more often than not in the humblest of circumstances, in the quietest of situations and at the least expected of times, they have a greatly enhanced power to surprise and to nourish.

2. Introduction: AM

I trained as a painter and have been working since the late sixties on the construction and use of chance-driven engines for organising, composing and constructing art objects. It very quickly became clear that the canvas was far too small a stage to contain the scope of the work I was trying to address. I had found that it was possible to organise all of the disciplines using the same basic sets of rules and that the whole could be combined to make installations in which every single element was a fully worked out and independent unit, capable of standing alone without losing any of its force. The key to this level of integrity in the component parts of a work was to pay absolute attention to every single detail: an extremely arduous but very rewarding practice.

Parallel to the development of systems for making Art, it was also necessary to develop a philosophical ground for the work through a process of questioning the functions and relevance of Art in twenty-first-century society. It was time to re-assess the function of Art relative to the needs of that century. The use of cheap shock tactics to illustrate, or worse exploit, the evil in our society can only ever be superficial. It is time for more humility, time for the Artist to become less egocentric and more useful. Time to give something to the people that they really need and the one thing that everyone, without exception, needs badly is the possibility to reflect, to take a step back, to take time to rest, to take stock and to generate energy for the next burst of activity.

3. A Ten-minute Text Showing that Lifted My Spirits and Altered My Perception Forever

In 1990, when I was in the transitional phase between the 'apprentice years' (my own definition) and my work proper, I was invited to go to Holland to make a restoration project. I agreed to do it primarily because I felt I was ready to begin my work proper but also felt the need to leave England to find the freedom to do so.

The work in question was to restore a sixteenth-century Dutch town house in Arnhem, providing me with money and a certain degree of technical exercise. The house belonged to a choreographer who was teaching at CNDO (Centre for New Dance Development), a recently formed performance school modelled on the Judson Church period of the birth and development of post-modernist performance.

It was often necessary to go backward and forward to this school in the course of the work and the only entrance to the main building was always guarded by a seated young woman, deep in concentration and feverishly typing at a table which all but blocked the way. She was the unofficial doorkeeper. Although there was no other way round, she was always visibly irritated whenever anyone needed to go in or out of the door as it disturbed her flow… I later discovered that this spot was the only one with access to a power point for the typewriter.

Some weeks later I was invited to attend a series of evening performances in one of the studios in the school. After a handful of short dance/movement works, of which I can now recall no detail, there was a short pause after which the doorkeeper, who had been sitting up to this moment in the audience, stood up, walked forward and after a short period of deeply focused silence launched into a text recital with a microphone which made my spine tingle.

The powerful presence of the performer, the amazing power and focus in the delivery of the text were such that it was impossible to avoid being drawn into this world both strangely intimate and eerily distant at one and the same time. The text, partly in German, but mostly in English, had one particular part that has been deeply imprinted on my memory ever since. She began repeatedly to chant the phrase 'I love you' over and over and over again, for several minutes, whilst simultaneously taking her enthralled audience on a journey through every subtle shade of emotion that could possibly be attached to that phrase. From hatred and anger, through the most tender of whispers, to the most demented of shrieks, those three words rang and sang and whimpered and whispered and caressed and cursed until everyone in the audience was transported into a space where they were convinced that they were the only ones in the room, that they were the subject and the object, each being personally addressed, until finally, and very softly, after a timeless breath of time, the text slid gently and almost unnoticeably into the next phase; and then the ten minutes were over and the performer was once more sitting in the audience, the awed silence a fitting ovation for the magic of that moment.

I am certain that I could safely say that no-one who witnessed that moment would be able, if asked, to remember anything else that happened that evening. It had such a profound effect on me that it altered some aspects of my thinking forever. Before leaving, I learnt that this was a short extract of a much longer work to be performed in full later in that month, that the name of the work was *Styx* and that the name of the performer was Ursula Raffalt. An Austrian by birth, Ursula already had the reputation, within the school, of being both deeply serious about and utterly dedicated to her work.

The following is a series of interviews and conversations that I had with Ursula Raffalt about this phase of her work, about her 'Focus Point Technique', which has been in development since 1989, including an analytical look at the performing arts, with particular emphasis on the components that make a work powerful enough for it to qualify as great.

4. Interview 1

AM: Tell me about the making of the work and your reasons for choosing to make this very reduced showing.

UR: 'Lunch Performances', as these very short performances or excerpts were called, were organised to give students some experience of presenting work at various stages to a very critical audience of their peers as a means of training the act of 'performing'. Anyone could participate but usually I tried to avoid them as I was very deeply involved in my own work. On that day I found it very interesting because I had, since starting work on *Styx*, been making what I called 'out of context' rehearsals. In order to develop the work in as natural a setting as possible, I was making text rehearsals in various odd places and situations. Whilst riding on my bicycle to and from the studio, for example, I could listen to the music in a Walkman and I could rehearse the text. I called these rehearsals 'out of context' because they were not on stage, but they were in fact very contextual performances as the locations and times were carefully chosen for the information and experience they could provide. I was trying to make the boundary between audience and performer, between auditorium and stage and perhaps ultimately between art and life a little more porous, a little less defined.

STYX

I made performance rehearsals in cafes. I would walk in, wait until a round table was free and then I would sit, put on headphones and silently go through the piece with the cafe clientele as a virtual audience. Sometimes, when another person sat at the table I would experiment with trying to keep my distance from them. I worked a lot with closeness and distance, a key condition relating to my perception of the horizontal in the work. The vertical plane was light to dark and the horizontal in the composition was the river Styx. The river was the border between the living and the dead, the physical and the spirit and this is also how the table became integrated into the set.

At first on the diagonal, the table was eventually turned to become frontal with seats for around 30. On it were carefully arranged plates of food, glasses and water for the audience to help themselves to, with arrangements of stones, candles and flowers. These served as bridges between the performer and the audience whilst simultaneously functioning as symbols representing life, energy, the earth and light, welcoming the audience and further weakening the barrier by allowing a two-way communication to pass over the table. Ultimately the table itself became like an embrace opening on to that other world, the virtual world of the performance.

In this way too I also became very strongly concerned with direct eye contact whenever I was close to the table. I could observe and train my reactions to whatever random interference might occur. I could observe how the 'audience' reacted. I was very much concerned with an investigation of the audience–performer relationship, a topic which runs through the whole of my work. I was researching the performance quality of being very close to the audience, then creating distance through projection. The table became a metaphor for the river Styx, it was the transition between the work and the audience.

Finally, I made a detailed study of the compositional layout of Monteverdi's orchestra, which I used to structure the spatial organisation of the sections of text. Each position was marked by a pool of light. I used information like his placement of the violins, where he allowed Orfeo to enter and leave, where was the spirit of Euridice placed, where were the other spirits placed, where the living. Further referenced by a study of the *Art of Memory* by Frances A. Yates, this systematic study gave a very clear layout wherein the most important information of all was the placement of the brass instruments which were very clearly used to announce the entry into Hades.

For this lunch performance, however, I had set myself the task of being both audience and performer. That necessitated making a relatively quick switch from the one state to the other. I gave a colleague a stop-watch and the task of stopping me after exactly ten minutes. I can't remember what the order of showing was but I was last on and until the moment I stood up to go on stage I took everything in from the audience perspective and at the signal to start I stood up and walked straight onto the stage and after only a short pause, made my ten-minute text performance and then sat down again in the audience. I wanted to know how it felt to switch sides from the one state to the other, what adjustments I needed to make to be able to be completely in the performance. I can remember being very pleased that no-one clapped afterwards as I felt that I had woven a spell which applause would have broken too soon.

This was a very important experiment for me as a measure of my progress. Being a performer requires a very deep commitment and an honest involvement in those moments and it is that honesty that conveys the 'truth' of the work. It also has a lot to do with the spirit, because, in order to be a strong performer, the perception, on the one hand, must be extremely highly tuned and the body, on the other, must be very fit. Finally, the performer must be able to become transmitter, receiver and, most important of all, transmuter of all energies present.

5. Interview 2

AM: Could you tell me something about the text, how you came to work with myth and with this particular music?

UR: I know exactly how I came to Monteverdi, it was another strange co-incidence. I had almost become accustomed to having metaphysical experiences in rehearsals of my work but it had started happening even more than usual in this particular process. For instance: I would be about to leave my room to cycle to school but before I left I would unconsciously put an empty cassette into the radio/recorder and then, later that day, when I came home, I switched on the radio and there was a programme about Monteverdi's *L'Orfeo* which I was able instantly to record. So I learned that the premiere of *L'Orfeo* is believed to have taken place in the mirror room in the Palazzo Ducale in Mantua.

I also learned about a book by Klaus Theweleit (*Buch der Koenige I Orpheus und Euridike*). I was trying to find a copy of it for my research but it was out of print. I asked a friend who worked in a bookshop to search for it and she could not find it either; but then, by chance, when she was visiting a tiny village in the North of Austria she found it in a tiny bookshop.

The process continued that way. Whenever a problem came up, the solution seemed to present itself, as if to tell me that I was tuned in to that world and rightly so and everything could just fall into place.

AM: Would you say that *Styx* was a personal response to the Orpheus myth?

UR: I would say that the work was both subjective and objective. Myths are alive. The whole working process is fed by real experience which puts truth into the mix. In a sense I had to become both Female Orfeo and Male Euridice, creator and muse.

AM: Would you say that you were able to remodel the material of the Myth?

UR: In fact what happened is that the whole process guided me to the conclusions that were reached, and this continued long after the *Styx* process was over because that was what brought me later to Dante's *Purgatorio*, my current work.

(**AM:** Interesting too that that also came about because the only English book on a street bookstand in Berlin was *The Divine Comedy Part 2 Purgatory*.)

AM: You made a trip to Mantua to make research: how was that made possible?

UR: My grandmother died and left me some money which I put aside to pay for research into the project. *L'Orfeo* was believed to have been premiered in the mirror room of the Palazzo Ducale. I was able to get permission to work for two weeks in the mirror room and it was a very deep experience during which I felt steeped in the essence of Monteverdi's work and the Renaissance.

But the text came first. It poured out in a burst beginning in Arnhem and completed in Portugal. I did not know where it had come from or why it was entirely in English (the German came later). It was this text that led inevitably to *L'Orfeo* and Monteverdi.

After the Mantua trip I found the courage to edit the music. This was a nightmare even though it felt like a necessary sacrilege. Although the text itself had very clear chapters, it was this editing process that finally gave a very clear structure to the staging of the work.

At first, I rejected the theatre and I felt that even conventional rehearsals were inappropriate – besides which I felt it would have been dangerous to rehearse the piece in a studio setting because it was such extremely deep material. I had to find a way of rehearsing it without being drained, without breaking down. The solution I found was to recite the text whilst travelling to and from the studio and in site-specific locations as already described.

Twilight also became a very important factor. The vertical axis (light and darkness), the horizontal (the table) and the orchestral placement all fused together to form a ritualistic walk into Hades and my deep relationship with the Renaissance provided the final link.

Styx was entirely created and rehearsed in the dawn and dusk times. The central point of the work, Hades, the underworld, the unconscious, was the main topic, a ritualistic walk into Hades, into darkness. I had done six months blindfold training immediately prior to beginning this work and the need for blindfold work evolved very naturally into that process. The most important topic was the transformation of dark and light, the ritualistic walk into a dark space, a tunnel, into black and the blindfold work was a study on the empty space. How can you tune the perception, the senses, in a dark empty space? Where are the darkest spots? Where the lightest areas? It was fascinating.

It got so that I could run through the space, sense the half-metre aura space of the walls and never run into them. If I went into the darkest corners of the space, I perceived them often as the brightest and there were many grey areas. I learned about the energies of the space, the shades from pitch black into grey and then white and then very bright white and I remember one spot was so bright that I ran into the light and nearly fainted. It was fascinating because it was a really transcendental moment. But it was also quite a dangerous process and there had to be someone there to observe you. Of course all of these experiences fed into the work and helped immensely with the search for the black, the white and the grey areas in *Styx* (in Hades), whilst the composition overall was built on a walk into the darkness and out again. Parallel to this, I was also working on the voice, searching for the high points and the low points, and the darkness and light in that. Searching for 'in between' resonance and colour in my voice. It was an incredibly intense process. I found I could use the natural energy of the twilight, which is why I only worked in dusk and dawn light. It was a very important factor. It helped me to tune in deeper.

Monteverdi had also made a very clear division of his stage, left and right, so that the whole ritualistic walk actually passed through the landscape of Monteverdi's music.

AM: How did your text directly affect you and your place in the work?

UR: What was it for me, this Orfeo text? It specifically points out the transformation into female Orfeo and what did that mean? It was the beginning of the creator in me, an awakening and enlightenment of the creative spirit in me, it awoke the artist in me which was why I had to go into this work.

AM: And you had to die, metaphorically speaking, in order for that new flower to be allowed to grow?

UR: Exactly, it was the spur that set it in motion and the food that enabled it to grow. It was an enlightenment of who I am and who speaks in me and through me. There were two interwoven pathways, the conscious and the unconscious and for me personally it provided the key to survival.

It needs two threads to really describe this process. One is the chronological history of the thing, but the other, more important thread connects through the heart. It is the subjective process of the embodiment of the living myth, of female Orfeo and male Euridice.

It was an extremely strange time for me. So much was happening which was foreign and bizarre that I thought I was going mad. Luckily, I met the Portuguese philosopher, Jose Gil, at this time and he was able to teach me how to work my way through the more terrifying parts. Jose is Professor of Philosophy at the University of Lisbon and the Collège International de Philosophie, Paris and he was the first person who was able to explain to me that what I was experiencing was a normal part of a deep creative process. The next step, placing the sections of text in space was important; it played a vital role in the building up of energy fields. The light fields that marked them were circular and I carefully located the recital of specific parts of the text, each with its own pool of light: six scenes, six spots, six lives. My study of the placement of the orchestral elements by Monteverdi had been the main influence in this.

It was incredible to me that the first words I had ever written were in English. As if, in the subconscious, I knew I was going to live my life in English. *Orpheus and Euridice* is about two people, about a couple, about love, but it is also about the one and the multiple. My understanding of the dialogue with Jose Gil was that I was functioning as a medium for the embodiment of the living myth and that all myth is alive and that I must very clearly choose: either to become a creator or to learn to be content with being a dancer, whose function would be to translate the material of others. It is only in rare cases that one person is given the gift where both are fused and this brings an incredible artistic responsibility with it as well as an intensive workload.

6. Conversation 1

This very modest ten-minute showing, in the humblest of settings with the simplest of means, with one single performer and the text was a very profound experience for all who were there, giving very strong indications of the power of theatre to move despite all contextual shortcomings. It was a deeply moving moment of theatre. A profound and deeply felt text delivered with absolute truth by its creator, and yet it was only a short extract from a larger work.

Prior to this time I had worked a little in the theatre world and had seen many performances, plays, dance works, ballet, concerts, opera: I had often gained an energy boost from the exciting newness or the strangeness of some of them but none had truly affected me quite as deeply or as spine-tinglingly as had this short, timeless, ten minutes.

AM: What elements would you say are required for great performance?

UR: The first thing would be to open up towards a deep process, the second would be to take great care to work it completely thoroughly through and the third would be to mature it enough to make it possible for it to transmit a profound experience of the process of familiarising the unfamiliar. A strong performance lives from the authentic embodiment of an example of that experience.

For instance: when I began to work on *Styx* I had no real idea what I was going into. The whole process, which lasted for eight years, was a very difficult one because every day I had to face up to this unfamiliarity and I did not know how I could tackle it. During the process of thoroughly working it through I had first to invent the necessary tools and then I had to invent how to use them. That was one of the main factors that actually helped form and shape my technique, the 'Focus Point Technique', which I have been developing since the late 1980s.

AM: Could you give me a brief outline of that technique and what it entails?

UR: In order to open up to a deep state in a creative process, I need a strong focus to build up a high degree of concentration and to tune all levels of perception. Even when I did not know where I was, I still had to find a compass to help me to find my way in this very unfamiliar situation, a means of holding on to my sanity, of not stopping and that meant that when I actually went through that it was like going through a tunnel where you know that at the end of it you can see light, so then you can focus on that goal and neutralise any negative interference from the outside. That is what you must try to edit out, whilst holding on to any positive interference, which is necessary for the work to grow.

You must deal with new distractions every day and need to be very conscious of how that which is happening all around affects your process. Sometimes you are forced to work passively and if you don't realise that this is a time in the artistic process where you are communicating with your work, exercising on a passive level, from your memory for example. If you don't understand that this is a very important step up the ladder then you will not be able to return to working actively.

That is also how I define my technique in the physical training: I reduce it to very few exercises but those few become so important, so effective because it is not about quantity, it is about capturing the quintessence. You go through a piece of work editing out the unnecessary things, as if you are trying to get rid of this materialistic clothing so that you can find a very deep pure state.

This is what I mean by 'the unfamiliar'. It is very scary, when you suddenly give up all control. You know you cannot manipulate any more, not even in a positive sense. There comes a moment when you know that you have to go into the studio and you must keep faith and know that the process will guide you, that transformation takes time and it is very important for every creator–performer (I am not just a performer, in solo work I am responsible for both) to know that if you want an audience to open up and go deep, you must already have been through and have mastered that depth of experience.

AM: You mean you have to have had that experience in order to be able to function as a guide?

UR: Yes, but it is more than that because every time you go into that performance you will meet a new set of challenges and new unfamiliar territories because you will have a new bundle of energies (the audience) to transform your experience and you have no way of knowing exactly what will come out. You need to have found a tool that will allow you to manage every unfamiliar situation. You will undergo a new experience every time because it is always a new abstraction and the tool that I have that guides me through is the Focus Point Technique.

For great performance it is vital that the audience be endowed with an innocent spirit and that they are capable of suspending their existing knowledge to allow the new in. The venue director must be capable of providing real, in-depth, support for the work through an understanding of its needs. The performer, it needs to be understood, even in a mainstream context, is extremely vulnerable, so a solid support system is essential and even more so when one is dealing with the unfamiliar.

Finally, both audience and direction need to be capable of recognising the importance of the spirit in the work. A great work can't be just a work for the market, it must include a sacred element, it must have a higher purpose. I began to make *Chamberworks* because it is never a matter of how many or who comes. It is always a matter of sharing a profound experience with an individual or a body of individuals.

AM: With those that made the effort to come, be it one hundred or even just one?

UR: Exactly. Also, how can I encourage them to relax into the challenge of the unfamiliar? That is a very difficult question because to be great the work needs also to be challenging. Where is the balance between overwhelming and challenging? But really, I don't need to worry too much about that because the audience is always free to leave but it does still remain my responsibility.

AM: How can you create a situation that is challenging but where the audience don't get damaged?

UR: By just trying to be really caring? What tool do you think I can use?

AM: After the journey you have to be able to bring them back…

UR: How do I do that? This is typical of my work, it is the key element. The very slow timing…

AM: …the long, slow timing and taking great care to close the circle.

UR: First I must focus them and then anchor them before taking them on the cloud walk. Then I must bring them safely down and anchor them again afterwards. That is the Focus Point Technique. It is a very natural, organic process: to lead people into multiple realities whilst allowing them to keep their integrity and their own reality, by not forcing them into anything. You need to be very aware of where they stepped in and where they are when they arrive.

I would say that another key element in the making of a great show would be to be mature enough in the work to be able to give a very clear idea that they are going to go on a journey that is already processed. It is very important to clearly define the beginning of the journey and its end. When I start the show they must already know A and Z, then they can experience the A whilst Z is waiting for them to arrive. A great piece of work, therefore, must be fully resolved. It works in circles or, better, in a figure of eight as the process is a continuum. That was what provided the healing aspect in Mozart's work. You cannot move on to the next cycle until this one is resolved, depth is introduced through multiple circles linking to form the spiral.

The performer must be capable of transmitting a deep abstract understanding drawn from the micro perception (the intuition) as opposed to the macro perception (the intellect). That is the essence of what is passed to an audience and they will either pick it up and run with it or (perhaps only subliminally) find it lacking. When this abstract understanding gets so firmly anchored that the audience is also able to feel it, they will gain confidence enough to be able to relax into the work and what is more, they will be able to draw maximum benefit from it and leave feeling deeply fulfilled/refreshed.

AM: What you say, more or less, is that the process of showing is itself like a feedback loop with the audience, having many new conditions built in on every level that constantly change.

UR: Every performance is a completely new situation. You know the material, but still you must become totally equal to the audience in certain moments (you are on a level regarding understanding where you are in the material) making it a joint venture. You are describing and experiencing completely new territory.

Unfamiliarity is differently defined for every individual but what I am trying to say is that a great performance is one that becomes one omnipotent, all embracing experience of being human. Only then can you walk hand in hand with a body of individuals into something completely new, united in your curiosity.

I would define the purpose of live art as being to open an audience up towards that which they are about to see. You have to let go and become one with the audience, taking care not to miss those first vital seconds. This is why my method is called Focus Point Technique and why most of my work starts in silence. I aim to become one with the audience, I become their guide. To keep them safe I need to have full knowledge of this particular moment in space and time.

7. Conversation 2: On Focus Point and Archetypes

AM: May I suggest that another key to great performance would be its archetypal content, which can, by its very nature, be intuitively understood on one level or another by all?

UR: You were saying that the ten-minute text performance really shook you through: that you felt a tingling in the spine. We agreed that it must have been an archetypal experience because you felt those ten minutes in a very kinaesthetic, sensory way. That type of sensation is often attributed to an experience of the deep past, indicating an archetypal or deep psychological connection. What you actually saw was a highly concentrated vocal performance, only fragments of a text, a snapshot, and a clear embodiment in the gestural movement all linked through a spatial structure. That archetypal experience was transmitted through the voice and gesture and how it was directed.

AM: I would say that the transmitter of that experience was the strong focus and concentration and the carrier was the voice and the body.

UR: Agreed. That is the main function of the Focus Point Technique. Where is it directed? With very clear eye contact, where do I direct my eyes, where do I direct my gesture?

AM: I think that as a member of the audience, what I received connected to something that was already in me and that is what I would define as archetypal and what makes a powerful communication in performance, is when that archetype is allowed. You, as a performer, could not place it there as it is already there, but you would find ways to connect to it and channel it. That would be strengthened by its presence in you too, through your training and your allowing it to be, through the deep concentration, focus and deep sense of being rooted in that moment and through all those collected moments that you achieve through Focus Point Technique.

UR: This is what I would call channelling through the medial body. The body becomes a highly tuned receiver and transmitter for energies present in the room generated or released through the transmission and reception of the material. The performer must connect to those energies and transmute them.

AM: The focus and concentration, or the depth and degree of both are actually magnets to the audience, drawing them in and holding them. After such an experience they have a feeling of fulfilment, that they have been the privileged receivers of something, each on his/her own terms.

UR: I spoke about deep listening, about emptying the body, about the breath, before I move or before I do any exercise: first the preparation, then the embodiment. The preparation is the process of focussing and tuning; how to deal with stillness. Opening up is a complete process, integrated in the physical and vocal training. It plays a huge part in the staging, providing a powerful visual concept for organising space and time. But in order to tune space, time and the perception on all levels, I must first go through a process of preparation which means tuning in to the most subtle of intensities.

For example, before I do voice work, I lie very still on the floor and open up to the sounds in the space, then I shift my focus to the outside and when I am tuned to the sounds of the interior and the exterior, I shift all my focus into my breathing: both inside and outside my body. Once I know where the boundaries are I start to shift the attention from out to in and then I focus on the following breathing exercise. First I rest, and then, when ready, I breathe in sharply and deeply through the nose, hold the breath for a couple of seconds to find a resting point, whilst visualising the in breath as reaching the highest point on the top of a cliff. I let the body drop into the floor but still hold the breath, like a floating balloon. Then comes a natural point where I deeply and very slowly exhale so that the downward stream of air goes down to the deepest point visualised below as the bottom of the ocean. Once there, you rest, at which point there is nothing to be done except just being, then naturally the next destination is upwards again and the breath cycle starts again. Physically I make two different intensities, the inhalation is through the nose and very sharp and the exhalation from the mouth is very slow and gentle. First deep listening, then the physical exercise of the breathing and when that is done I can start with the physical programme but not before I have achieved a tuning of the intensities.

AM: There is also another link to be made, to your route so to speak?

UR: Yes it is silence plus activity that has been established, which is nothing more than tuning plus focus, both of which are physical acts, directing the awareness from diversity into a central reading where the embodiment is the integration of both, the transformation process.

The staging of all of my work is defined in this way. The breathing defines both departure and arrival points, along with the rest positions in between, by placing a memory of the image and of the feeling that is evoked at every stage. I see and I feel. When I arrive, I activate the visualisation process and at the same time I also activate the sensory memory. I repeat the process, first with the focus on the seeing, then on the feeling and with the third cycle I add them together. That needs to be reiterated for both the silence and the activity parts so it is a constant process of balancing the one with the other.

AM: Ultimately there is no difference between them because it is all activity, silence is an activity and activity is silence, they form the figure of eight, infinity.

UR: But they are still different. I imagine each as a circular motion, silence concentric, activity excentric. Silence is the resting part, floating, it is the aura around the pitch in the voice. Silence is a *caesura*, the space in between. In a musical composition it is the moment before you start a phrase, more a holding than a pause, the vibration that comes before and after the phrase. In dramaturgy, Silence is the moment of thinking. Silence is, for me, the invisible world beyond.

The poetic notion is embodied entirely in the Silence, in the resting point, because that is where all tension gets released by working only with the force of gravity. That means, you can lie on the floor, with your legs bent and your arms up and if you find the right angle, gravity will hold your limbs. Gravity is a magnetic force so you do not need any other. The resting point, Silence, is the most natural state of being, a magic state, a complete moment of transformation. The rest is just balance and Focus Point is about balancing out these forces of silence and activity. That is the entire compositional method of Focus Point.

8. The Full Performance

By the time of the full showing of *Styx*, I was completely tuned to receive it. The audience seats were laid out along one side of the table and on the other was a single chair, occupied by the performer, who sat relaxed and smiling and gazing directly at each individual as they came and took their place.

> Layer 1. The music, a basso-continuo, underscoring the text and the movement transitions, weaving in and out of focus, provided the ground for the work.
>
> Layer 2. The long table covered in a white cloth and decked with food and drink; the microphone stand and the pools of light that provided locations for the different elements of the text plus the performer, smiling and warmly welcoming each guest.
>
> Layer 3. The subtleties of the transitions between 'scenes' and the movements between spots.

Layer 4. The very slow timing and gesture and the breathing space that it allowed all those present.

Layer 5. The crown. Woven through all other layers was the voice with its remarkable range of emotion and energy and subtle gradations of level and tone. It was the vehicle that carried the whole mesmeric work.

The audience, comprising students, staff, visitors like myself and interested parties from the local community, was, broadly speaking, an informed one, but every single one of those packed tightly into this small space was completely transported by the sheer power of what they had witnessed. They had gained a glimpse into a world where none of their knowledge counted. They had been given a tour of a completely unfamiliar place and this fact alone put everyone there on an equal footing. Those who 'knew' about theatre and performance had to suspend that knowledge as this work lay outside its ken and those who knew little or nothing were the lucky ones who were able to just take it all in and walk away re-energised with the image conjured by the final lines floating before their eyes.

Hades Decke, voll Schnee, halte den Fruehling zurueck!
[Roof of Hades, covered in snow, hold back the spring!]

CHAPTER SIX

Third World Bunfight's *Ipi Zombi?*

KEVIN J. WETMORE, JR.

S aturday, 4 July 1998 was a day that would ordinarily have been spent at a festive gathering, cooking foods outdoors, playing various games with friends and then settling down to watch fireworks in honor of my nation's birthday. Instead, I found myself in a deserted power station, lit mostly by candles and a bonfire in an oil drum, confronted by zombies, *isangoma* (witches) and a dwarf transvestite lip-syncing a Doris Day song immediately before a group of schoolboys hacked the witches to death. And I would not have been anywhere else for all the fireworks in the world.[1]

The 1998 Standard Bank National Arts Festival in Grahamstown, South Africa was a remarkable event, both in South African culture and personally for me. Killing two birds with one stone, I was an actor appearing in the fringe festival with an American theatre company but also doing research for my dissertation, which was on African theatre. To be acting and working in South Africa was a dream come true. The festival itself had many remarkable theatrical productions packed into ten days: Northwest Arts Drama Company's production of *Not with my Gun* by Aubrey Sekhabi and Mpumelelo Grootboom, directed by Sekhabi (which was also profoundly moving and thought-provoking), the Vusa Dance Company, Reza de Wet's *Yelena*, and the Takeaway Theatre Company's acclaimed production of *King Lear*. It was, in all, a paradise for an American actor–academic who was spending every minute not on stage either in the library of the National English Literary Museum or watching theatre. One piece, however, stood head and shoulders above the others. While all the above mentioned productions were good theatre, only one festival production brought me back to see it two more times, dragging along

87

friends and colleagues to share in the experience. Third World Bunfight's (TWB) *Ipi Zombi?* delighted, amazed, confused and transformed me and it has haunted me ever since. In this chapter I hope to capture both the excitement of the moment of viewing and the understanding of memories of the performance as filtered through subsequent research.

Never having heard of the company, I was nevertheless intrigued by the name of the show (I am a horror fan as well) and by the production's listing in the festival program: 'SEE Stark African realism... a fully authentic township saga... savage dancing... primitive ceremonies... schoolboys track down vicious killer witches in wildest terrain... all from the comfort of your theatre seat.'[2] The language was reminiscent of the advertisements for apartheid-era exploitative productions showcasing supposedly indigenous performances created and staged by white South Africans and yet also suggested a very postmodern post-apartheid theatre. The unquestioned use of the word 'primitive' also struck me as being out of place in post-apartheid South Africa. Also, as an American, I found the term 'township drama' reminded me of the 'stark African realism' of the early dramas of Athol Fugard and wondered if the production would be similar to *Nongogo, No Good Friday* or even *Sizwe Bansi is Dead*.

For me, there was a personal interest in the director as well. I learned that TWB artistic director and *Ipi Zombi?* writer–director–designer Brett Bailey and I were roughly the same age (he is only two years older than I) and, like me[3], he was an artist of European descent working in African diasporan drama. Furthermore, as an artist and scholar interested in syncretic ritual theatre, intercultural fusion performance and how one might successfully blend traditional culture with contemporary theatre in a manner that was neither imperialist nor insensitively culturally appropriative, *Ipi Zombi?* interested me – especially since it raised, critiqued and then transformed neocolonialist expectations. I realized while watching it that even as the play excited me with its exoticism, its unexpected surprises and visceral *mise-en-scene*, it was also placing me in a position where I was sited as a privileged audience member, self-aware of my own culpability in neocolonialism, as already indicated by the program copy that had intrigued me. I wanted to see both 'Stark African realism' and 'primitive ceremonies... all from the comfort of [my] theatre seat.'

Like most Americans interested in South African theatre, I had been educated to see South African theatre as a political theatre. Anti-apartheid drama was a theatre of resistance, best known outside the RSA through the plays of Athol Fugard. Having also studied at the Workshop Theatre at the University of Leeds, however, I had gone much deeper into South African drama than its exports and felt myself fairly knowledgeable about the theatre of South Africa until 1993. In 1998, post-apartheid drama was still taking shape. I remember a remark of Maishe Maponya, who said that with the fall of apartheid, South African actors were now free to be good regardless of political content and the new challenge was to develop a post-apartheid theatre that both demonstrated the challenges to South African society while still being aesthetically and artistically well done.

I found my own preconceptions of contemporary South Africa being challenged simply by being at the National Arts Festival itself and speaking with different artists and audience members and even just folks I met in the street or in line at a food stand. While the festival was celebratory, there was a tension and a variety of different takes on the past, present and future of South Africa that differed from the presentations in the American media (not that I thought the American media was representing anything accurately; but it was still disconcerting to see just how inaccurate a portrayal can be). I heard a good deal of anti-Truth and Reconciliation Committee (TRC) rhetoric from artists and individuals who believed the TRC was whitewashing the past and hiding many of apartheid's sins. I heard from others that the economic situation of blacks and coloureds (as identified under apartheid) had not been improved with the fall of apartheid and the rise of Mandela. I was shocked to hear a young, college-aged girl in the dorm in which my theatre company was staying remark that, 'in order to get a job in government you have to have been in prison and when you've been in for twenty-seven years they make you president.' Perhaps it was naïve of me to believe in uncritical respect for President Mandela; but even to that extent, the ghosts of the past haunted the National Arts Festival.

Hauntings were also a theme of *Ipi Zombi?* which was, in fact, rooted in a series of incidents that took place in rural South Africa three years previously. On Friday, 29 September 1995, a minibus carrying fifteen boys from Carl Malcomess High School crashed twenty-eight kilometers outside of Kokstad.[4] A survivor of the crash claimed that before the bus rolled, fifty naked women were seen by the side of the road. The young men held the women of Bhongweni Township responsible and went on a literal witch hunt. On Friday, 13 October, a mob executed Mrs. Magudu, an elderly woman whose 11-year-old granddaughter claimed she was holding the mutilated souls of the dead boys in her cupboard.[5] The following Sunday, 15 October was to be the mass funeral for the boys, but the mob claimed the bodies had been replaced by 'witchmeat' and a second 'witch', Mrs. Giyose, was killed by a mob of boys. The crowd feared that if the 'witchmeat' was buried, the boys' souls would be lost forever. The mob took the bodies back to the mortuary.

The bodies were stored for six weeks while *sangomas*, traditional diviners and healers among the amaXhosa, amaZulu and Ndebele peoples, attempted to locate the witches, neutralize their evil magic, and reunite the boys' souls with their bodies so that they would no longer be 'zombies'. On Wednesday, 6 December 1995, another funeral was attempted, but a mob of axe-wielding boys attacked the caskets and corpses with *pangas* (machetes) and torches. The police intervened and the bodies were finally buried that day.

Loren Kruger has argued that the boys' 'zeal was in part a response to their own disempowerment as their political authority gained by direct action during the 1980s passed back to older and better educated people in the communities in the 1990s.'[6] Kruger also sees in the play an indictment of the 'scapegoating of women.'[7] In other words, the disempowered and disenfranchised young men used the accusation of witchcraft to strike back against women, and especially socially prominent women. Yet behind the politics is a genuine fear of magic, witches and the fate of the dead. Both Christian ministers and *sangomas* were called in to combat the believed presence of evil magics.

Brett Bailey went to Kokstad and Bhongweni, speaking with those involved and those who lived in the area. Many individuals were still concerned that the boys' bodies were not reunited with their souls and that their souls were still enslaved by witches. Previously, he had spent parts of 1996, 1997 and 1998 studying with *sangomas* in rural and urban parts of the Eastern Cape, undergoing training in, among other things, 'dancing, drumming and singing: a training regimen to deepen the ability of the *sangomas* to enter that zone where they can meet with their ancestors and access the collective wisdom.'[8] As a practitioner interested, as noted above, in the resacralization of theatre, this story represented the type of narrative that appeals to TWB: tradition and modernity in seeming conflict, the disenfranchised of the post-apartheid period in conflict with one another, and an inherent theatricality and rituality.

At the 1996 National Arts Festival, Bailey staged an early version of the play called *Zombi*, which paradoxically featured a larger cast in a smaller play. He then spent the next two years reworking the drama with TWB. He describes his own creative methodology thus:

take township styles and traditions, throw them in the blender with rural performance and ceremony, black evangelism, a handful of Western avant-garde and a dash of showbiz, and flick the switch: THIRD WORLD BUNFIGHT!⁹

The cast worked with *sangomas*, added different elements from their own backgrounds and even spent two weeks rehearsing in mThauleng cave, a site sacred to the Xhosa, in order 'to give that play a charge of vital energy.'¹⁰ The end result was first performed at Grahamstown in the summer of 1998 and subsequently toured the rural areas of South Africa.

I must confess my own delight that the play was published twice: once in the United States in 1999 and in South Africa in 2003.¹¹ Yet the script does not do the experience justice. As Bailey himself observes, the plays 'were never envisioned as pieces of literature separate from the rich and multi-layered non verbal elements which make up the language of living drama: the music, the dramatic form, the spectacle, the ritualistic rhythm, the atmosphere.'¹² Much of what follows here is a combination of my recollection and the actual text from Bailey's 2003 edition.

The production was listed in the program as being performed at 'The Power Station', which was not a traditional festival venue – it literally was an old abandoned electric power station converted into a performance space. The use of space and atmosphere was both formidable and evocative. The abandoned building seemed to press down on the audience while simultaneously soaring up into shadows. It also struck me as the completely appropriate venue: an electricity-generating power plant serves as the metaphor for technology and modernity. It is what allows humanity to transform night into day and yet the building was abandoned, empty, no longer serving its function. The shadows give way to phantoms and phantasms, as a contemporary audience brought there by automobiles and buses sits and watches and listens to tales of zombies, ghosts and witches in a symbol of modernity, technology and the illusion that humanity has 'conquered' nature.

In the middle of the power station, Bailey and TWB drew upon traditional ritual and culture to engage this narrative of tradition and modernity in conflict. As Kruger observes: 'Post-apartheid theatre, by and for local communities, has attempted to combine theatrical performance and religious expression to grapple with the conflicts arising with the falling-away of anti-apartheid certainties in the absence of radical social transformation.'[13] In other words, Bailey and TWB were following a growing trope of combining religious ritual with Western-style theatre, combining Xhosa and Zulu culture with Western culture in order to explore the newly emerging nation's newly emerging identity.

The actual site was several kilometers away from the festival location. In order to make transportation to and from the site easier, TWB provided the 'HEEBIE JEEBIE SHUTTLE', a bus that picked up audience members in front of the history museum on Somerset Street at 18:30, half an hour before showtime. The site was chosen not only for its centrality but also, I suspect, because we were departing from in front of a standard, government-supported history museum to travel to an abandoned industrial site in order to engage in a Xhosa ritual reenactment of a series of contested events from recent history. Bailey was placing the performance of *Ipi Zombi?* as a literal departure from 'official' history to a more folk and spiritually oriented approach.[14] The shuttle returned patrons to the same stop after the show. Thus, even travel to the venue was framed as part of the experience.

When one entered the space, it was not a traditional Euro-American beginning in which audience members find their seats, the houselights dim and the performance begins. The space was already active when the audience was allowed to enter. The production was presented in three-quarters in the abandoned power station. Dried cow dung and straw covered the concrete floor. Sparse electric lights competed with candles, torches and a bonfire in an oil drum to light the space. A tall man with a feathered headdress and skirt of monkey tails threw fragrant herbs into the oil drum, an activity repeated frequently throughout the production, filling the space with a sweet smoke. Surrounding the playing area was the cast, of about a dozen or so, wrapped in blankets and softly singing. I learned later the song was called *Sitsho thina, sifela emathongweni* ('We die in our dreams'). Two drummers beat a slow, hypnotic rhythm in counterpoint to the singing.

Along the back of the performing area was a giant cupboard with a sort of altar in front of it, candles on either side. Sitting on the altar were two performers dressed in schoolboy uniforms whose faces, like those of many of the other performers, appeared to be covered in a chalky white paint of some kind. (They were, in fact, 'covered head to toe in white clay – an indicator of sacred people amongst the amaXhosa'.)[15]

The effect of the white clay was unsettling. At first I wondered if the cast was performing in whiteface, a comment on South African whites. I realized very quickly, however, that it was indicative of something else.

While I thought it may have been some sort of shamanic body painting, it also had the effect of immediately challenging the program's assertion of 'Stark African realism', at least to my American mind.

Upon closer examination, I saw in the program that the full title of the piece was *Intombi 'Nyama and The Natives in 'ipi zombi?'* This full title frames the piece as a form of urban entertainment while also categorizing almost all the performers as 'natives'. It suggests the apartheid-era entertainments for whites that featured black performers in indigenous dress, dancing and singing (see below). Intombi 'Nyama is presented as an urban celebrity, contrasted with 'The Natives', who are rural performers. Viva, the narrator, in fact, introduces many of the dominant themes with the opening lines:

> Hey, we are the pride of the Eastern Cape, we are the pride of this place; we The Natives, we entertainers, we who are telling you this story, this IPI ZOMBI? *sitsho thina*, a story of this country; we who are traveling from village to village, from town to town, while others are afraid, locked up in their houses, believing their televisions, and outside the wild spirits of the forests are possessing the people, killing each and everybody in the streets, in the taverns, even in their beds. Hey, this country is struggling. These are the hungry times: the rich are eating the poor, the dead are eating the living, even the roads are eating the children...[16]

This opening monologue creates a complex construction of the performance about to happen, the relationship between performers and audience, the identity of the performers and even the national identity of the 'New South Africa'. 'The Natives' are both a source of pride for South Africa while defining them using the language of earlier exploitative entertainment.

The opening speech is a celebration of the power of live theatre, of those who 'tell the stories' as opposed to those who 'believe their televisions'. That phrase also indicates a tension between the relatively new media and the power of storytelling and face-to-face communication.[17] Yet behind the words lurks an understanding of the tensions of postmodern, post-apartheid South Africa: 'Hey, this country is struggling.' The end of apartheid's political structures did not entail the end of the economic structures. Although a black middle class has emerged and the country's ruling class has arisen mostly from the ANC, the vast majority of wealth still resides in white hands and the vast majority of blacks are economically disenfranchised.

After Viva's speech, the actors began to move. A box on the altar that had been covered by a sheet was uncovered, revealing the head of Intombi 'Nyama, a dwarf performer presented as a statue, speaking slowly. It was uncanny, to say the least. The brief speech closed with the line, 'I knew it was the end of the world.' Viva threw more herbs on the fire and the room became more smoke filled. The overall effect of the opening was phantasmagorical.

The play then immediately switched modes into a much more realistic scene. The two schoolboys sitting on the altar stood up and began to tell their stories. Though covered in white clay, and thus not particularly naturalistic, the costumes were realistic for two fifteen-year-old high-school students who then told the audience what happened to them in Kokstad. Steve and Krotch spoke back and forth, telling of the fatal crash that killed them. As they mentioned that they were dead, we in the audience realized that they might be the 'zombies' of the title, as they were moving and speaking dead people. At the very least, they were ghosts. Like many theatrical ghosts, from Tantalus in Seneca's *Thyestes* to Hamlet's father to Dou E in the Yuan drama *Snow in Midsummer*, these ghosts were brought back to tell their tale. Unlike those other spirits, however, these two were uncertain of the details or even what happened. One said the driver was drunk, the other said he was sleeping. One did not remember where he was sitting in the vehicle. The other tells him he was unconscious during the crash. Steve asserted: 'Ja, now I'm remembering... as we went off the road I saw fifty females in front of the taxi, just watching, with no clothes on, naked, undressed....'.[18] Krotch was amazed, as he had not seen that. While the stories they told were suggestive of the real world accident, the characters' inabilities to recall details, their disagreements over what happened and the revelation of the fifty naked women seen, while the character says 'now I'm remembering' suggest the unreliability of not only memory but of eyewitness accounts of the event. This is not to suggest the characters are lying, simply that what they stated was not a verifiable, accurate description of the events. History is not written by the victors, it is misremembered by those who lived through it and died during it.

Enter Mambamba, a mother of one of the boys killed, played by a man in drag. She was a comic character of sorts, whom the boys then accused of being a witch. To defend herself against accusations of witchcraft, Mambamba began accusing audience members of being witches. Comic though it was, it also pointed out the culpability of those of us watching.

There is little difference between an audience and an indifferent mob. We both watched the onstage community collapse in paranoia and accusation and found amusement in it.

Sangomas entered and began a divination ritual in order to determine where the witches were and to combat their evil magic. Viva explained what they were doing to the audience and informed us that the *sangomas* found things in people's houses in Bhongweni Township which proved they were witches. 'These things have power for our people,' he proclaimed, 'whether you believe it or not.'[19] This statement struck me as an inversion of the modernist's ordering of traditional culture in the modern world. The 'believer' is not the traditional person but the modern audience member. It was one of the clearest examples of Ngugi's 'moving the centre' on stage that I had ever seen: the West is free to believe in the power of *sangomas* or not, but it is just that: a belief.[20] The amaXhosa know that that power is real for their society and therefore a reality.

Intombi 'Nyama, dressed in a plastic dress, pearls and jewelry in his hair, played the 11-year-old girl who claimed that her grandmother was making zombies. S/he repeated the phrase, 'You know, when my friends were killed it took my breath away' many times and then told the story of her dream, in which she saw 'the boys in the cupboard calling her name.'[21] The men repeat the lines while the women dance. Intombi 'Nyama then broke character and told the audience:

> My friends, hey we are proud to have you here to come and enjoy our performance, to listen to this terrible story. You make us very strong. And we have worked hard to make this drama great for you – we even went to the mountains for two weeks to find the Spirit of this play. You think there is no Spirit, you think we are not working with the Spirit. You think the Spirit of Africa is dead because everyone is wanting the hungry Spirit of America inside them? We are making the Spirit strong, we bringing it to you. So you are not coming here by accident – something, maybe even your ancestor, brought us all together tonight. Also to our sponsors, we thank you very much that you helped us to do this work in these hard times.[22]

I am copying these lines from the text, but I remember sitting in the power station, simply awestruck by them. First, there was the Brechtian moment of breaking character and again elevating the audience to the level of patron. Not only was this break a metatheatrical moment of ritual self-awareness and an assertion of efficacy, it also reframed the audience as outsiders. Combined with the lines that suggest the assertion of amaXhosa reality – the Spirit is real, what you see on your television is not – the audience was framed as the ones who might have power and money but who did not understand the true nature of reality.

What really took *my* breath away was the contrast of Africa with the 'hungry Spirit of America', which had all the power of a metaphor that accurately describes one's world striking one for the first time. And then, to further complicate matters, came the immediate twist – thanking the ancestors and 'our sponsors', Standard Bank, all spoken by a dwarf transvestite playing an 11-year-old girl. There was an acknowledgement that this piece of ritual Xhosa theatre might be construed as entertainment for whites who were essentializing the performers and the world they represented, while also acknowledging that none of this ritualized recreation of the witch and zombie story would have been possible without funding from South Africa's largest bank.

No time was given to reflect upon these issues, however, as a funeral followed, in which a small woman dressed as a cartoonish yet sexy devil emerged from a trapdoor in the altar. With a pair of priests leading the 'congregation' in a call-and-response ceremony, the devil crouched on the coffin and lead the singing. The schoolboys entered and seized the casket, insisting that the congregation not bury 'witchmeat'. Opening it, they found only bird and animal bones, feathers and a shroud.

The boys decided they needed to kill the witches. The devil immediately became a reporter, interviewing Mrs. Magudu, who continued to sing a gospel song: 'Go away, Devil, go away devil go away… Who is knocking at my door? Who is knocking at my door? The devil is knocking at my door,' to which the devil–reporter responded: 'Do you think your mother was a witch?'[23] This moment strikes me as a quintessential TWB moment. Without denying the reality of a devil or Christianity, the play constructs a reporter as the devil (an indictment of the media which also fanned the flames of fear and which, in order to 'get the story' of human misery, must often display callousness and a clear lack of sympathy to that misery), demonstrates the deep Christian faith of the women of Bhongweni Township, and asserts the reality of an evil presence, while it just as quickly undercuts that spirituality, reducing it to cartoonishness.

The boys then entered and bludgeoned Mrs. Magudu to death. Again, TWB's theatricality encompasses a sudden shift on every level. What was playful and fun and complex then is rapidly transformed into something disturbing and real. We laughed at the devil-as-reporter, and then were reminded of the real violence and the actual deaths that inspired the play in the first place. As the audience fell into a shocked silence, the devil opened the cupboard.

Suggesting that the boys were right all along, and witches had captured their friends' souls, five boys emerged from the cupboard. Skeletons were painted on their bodies, elongated white masks covered their faces and heads, and their arms were tied behind their backs. Like vultures, they began to peck at and feed on Mrs. Magudu's corpse, occasionally looking at and threatening nearby audience members. It is one of my strongest memories of the play. Visually, it was stunning. It was also one of the quietest moments of the play, if I remember correctly. The boys entered in silence. The title of the piece was fulfilled, not only literally, but also because this was a moment of pure horror.

What followed was another instant shift and rapid transition of mood and technique. Suddenly, the lights changed and Intombi 'Nyama appeared and began to lip synch to Doris Day's *Shaking the Blues Away*. This moment was beyond surreal. Intombi lead the zombie boys in a dance that eventually took them out of the playing area. The zombies had come out of the cupboard, eaten Mrs. Magudu and then joined in a conga line following the lip-syncing transvestite. It was a moment of theatrical genius.

Viva then returned and told us that the bodies sat in a mortuary for six weeks, but the Sangomas could not bring them back. He cautioned the audience that 'This is a hungry story, this story eats people alive.'[24] As he cautioned the audience, the schoolboys reentered and crouched in a ring around the coffins. The boys began to dance with axes and launched into a manic hacking dance, until one of them stood astride the coffin and screamed as he chopped into the body inside. The others immediately collapsed as the boy continued to hack away. As his axe rose and fell, however, the transformation of the character was startling. From a manic, dangerous young man with a weapon, he suddenly seemed a teenaged boy, crying as he tried to free his friend from what he thought was a fate worse than death. His wails and tears were profoundly moving and they, along with the hit of the axe blade, were the only sounds echoing through the power station for a long minute.

The performers put on the blankets they were wrapped in at the beginning of the play and slowly exited the space, while Viva warned one final time about the 'hungry thing' out there, outside the theatre, then wished the audience a good night and exited, laughing manically. There was no curtain call, though there was tremendous applause. Instead, as we exited the building, there was a gauntlet of the cast, still singing, which we had to walk through to reach the parking lot.

The first night I saw the show, I chose not to ride back in the Heebie Jeebie Shuttle, preferring instead to walk the several kilometers back to town, alone along the desert road with my thoughts and the night sky. The path was well lit by stars and I did not yet want to return to the world of the festival and Grahamstown and the dorm and my company just yet. TWB had taken the audience to someplace remarkable, disturbing and transformative and I needed to hold onto it for a little while longer. This experience was not only theatrical, it was spiritual, in a way I rarely feel in the theatre; and it was also specifically African. Most of what I had seen as an audience member in my life (and in fairness, most of what I had done as an artist) reflected what Bailey calls 'the de-spiritualisation of the West', noting that in the West, 'theatre has largely been reduced to an audio-visual display.'[25] Yet, simultaneously, Bailey did not romanticize precolonial Africa, nor post-apartheid Africa. The production provided no neat, pat answers. Instead, it provided a model for post-apartheid theatre in South Africa.

Beyond the setting, the story and its politics, I was amazed by the sheer theatricality. The production was full of visual surprises: transformations of objects and people: umbrellas held by church choirs became the wings of birds, the young boys who killed an old woman became the spirits of the dead boys they were avenging, a head was revealed and it spoke, telling a story. Unexpected emergences (Intombi emerging from the drum, the devil emerging from the casket, the souls of the dead boys emerging from the cupboard) and strange but fascinating characters, self-aware, metatheatrical and yet highly entertaining, occupied the space. For one of the few times in my life, I truly understood the idea of a liminal experience in a real way, as we had been transported somewhere by the Bunfighters.

A production that had advertised itself as 'stark African realism' was as about as unreal as anything I had ever seen and yet it *was* 'real' – a real story told in a real way by real performers that caused the audience to question their own ideas about 'reality'. While Bailey may decry the 'audio-visual display' of Western theatre, his own theatre is also a theatre of spectacle.

It is also an experiential theatre: music, dancing and drumming changed the environment. The herbs thrown on the fire filled the room with a sweet smoke which transformed a visual experience into a fully sensual one. It was truly an example of resacralized theatre, but a highly entertaining one. It was playful and smart and moving. It was reverent irreverence and irreverent reverence. Bailey wrote in his notebook in February 1998 while working on *Ipi Zombi?*: 'The two realms – showbiz and ritual – can work together: a high-speed show; the whole show is like a tumbling act, one scene flipping to the next, the intensity getting higher and higher.'[26] As Larlham observes, 'Sensory saturation, rhythmically driven exhilaration, and intense interpretive investment have all featured strongly in my own experiences as a spectator at Bunfight productions.'[27] I must agree with this assessment: one does not merely watch a TWB production, one is saturated by it.

Leaving the power station that first night, I was a convert. I confess, as an American somewhat familiar with South African theatre, I had never heard of 'Third World Bunfight' or *Ipi Zombi?*, although the latter seemed like a play on *Ipi Tombi*, which I had heard of. As an American I had no idea what a 'bunfight' was. I subsequently learned it was British slang for both a formal party and a petty squabble. It was only much later that I got the full definition: 'a heated altercation, but one that the describing observer feels is of no importance', rooted in a 'nursery squabble' at teatime.[28] Not as popular in the USA or RSA, the company's name nevertheless frames its identity by being a 'Third World' bunfight – a squabble important to the third world, but of no importance to the first and second worlds, proud in its position in the third world and equally uncaring about the squabbles outside its own context.[29]

As for *Ipi Tombi*, the title is a corruption of 'iph'inzintombi', isiZulu for 'where are the girls'?[30] *Ipi Tombi* was a musical ostensibly based in traditional Zulu and Xhosa culture, created by and benefiting Bertha Egnos and Gail Lakier, the white producers who sent three different touring companies around South Africa and Europe. Loren Kruger describes *Ipi Tombi* as 'us[ing] a "Jim comes to Jo-burg" scenario as an alibi for scantily clad women dancing to canned *mbaqanga* music'.[31] In that play, a young Zulu woman is threatened by an evil witch doctor, but saved by a young man and the power of Christianity. As David Coplan observes, 'Despite producers' claims that, like the government, they were promoting traditional African culture, *Ipi Tombi* showed little respect for it. Ethnic traditions were mixed haphazardly throughout the show for sensational effect.'[32] Shows such as *Ipi*

Tombi generated much condemning criticism from anti-apartheid theatre activists and critics and engendered much anger in the black community.

In naming his play with a reference to such a despised piece of theatre, Bailey seems to be doing several things. The new play's referential title is playful. It directly engages the concerns of a white artist working with indigenous black traditions (again) while simultaneously mocking the original play. It hints at the concerns of the new work while also linking them to that of the old: indigenous culture in a modern world, this time done respectfully (maybe). The title of the piece alone also indicts the mostly white audience (this author included) at the National Arts Festival, 'especially since, as in the earlier play, *Ipi Zombi?* offers a representation of rural black life for urban white entertainment,' as David Graver notes in his introduction to the play.[33] To see *Ipi Zombi?* at Grahamstown was, in a sense, to admit being part of the problem.

Yet, despite some critics' objections, both during the festival (*Cue*, the festival newspaper gave the production a negative review)[34] and in subsequent academic studies of Bailey's work, others, such as Zakes Mda, saw in *Ipi Zombi?* a model for post-apartheid South African drama. Mda called the play 'a work of genius that maps out a path to a new South African theatre that is highly innovative in its use of indigenous performance forms.'[35]

Others, however, have seen Bailey's work as embodying the worst of cultural imperialism.[36] As Judith Rudakoff observed, some South Africans refuse to attend Third World Bunfight productions as we do not 'need to see another white man reinterpreting [black] history or staging folkloric representations of rites he holds sacred'.[37] Coplan would later refer to Bailey as 'brave, but offensive.'[38] Bailey could also be argued as falling into Jerry Mofokeng's category of problematic South African theatre in which whites such as Donald Woods, Athol Fugard and Barney Simon 'become the articulators of our struggles and our aspirations'.[39] And yet, we should not be quick to assign to Bailey the role of white man through whom black struggles are articulated.

It is possible to see Bailey in the tradition of Western interculturalists such as Peter Brook, Richard Schechner and Ariane Mnouchkine, who seek to resacralize theatre by blending contemporary performance practice with traditional culture, but do so as cultural imperialists. Yet to do so is to miss Bailey's own unique position as local, working within, and without, a very specific nation with a wide variety of cultures. Though not Xhosa himself, he works with *sangomas*, embraces all of his African heritage, and seeks to employ South African traditions, history, politics, culture and people to create a theatre that genuinely responds to post-apartheid South Africa. His theatre is self aware.

David Coplan views Bailey's work as unique in that it grows out of the anti-apartheid tradition and the ritual history of South Africa, but it is aimed at multiple constituencies:

> In his determination to move away from what he calls 'message theatre' towards a more savagely entertaining medium he believes more suited to the grotesque ironies and contradictions of contemporary Africa, Bailey indulges raucously in repeating history as farce. More specifically, Bailey says he is interested in patterns of cultural collisions of the spirit between Africa and the West and the chaos they cause.[40]

What struck me that first night in the power station was the eclectic audience. I have subsequently learned that *Ipi Zombi?* has also been performed in urban theatres and rural village centres. It is aimed at the next generation of South Africans who are growing up having not known apartheid, but also those who fought in the struggle. Unlike *Ipi Tombi* and *Sarafina*, which Jerry Mofokeng objects to because they are not 'illuminating of the South African situation',[41] I would argue that *Ipi Zombi?* is very much illuminating of the South African situation. David Graver observes that the play:

> seeks to show the audience the social pressures that lead to witch killings as well as the brutality and uselessness of this behavior for solving the community's problems. None of the characters in the play serve as a moral compass for the audience and none act out of evil intentions. Bailey's play shows how evil can steal upon a community despite the goodwill of all its residents. It asks the audience to understand and confront this danger.[42]

Like the best theatre, it honestly demonstrated the real concerns of the community and offered no solution 'from above'. Instead, it took the concerns of the community seriously and responded to them without presuming to lecture or moralize. Bailey himself states:

> I believe that theatre can be like ritual: an event which incorporates all people involved – performers and audience – and which affects

these people at profound levels of consciousness. Theatre has the potential to be immensely powerful, to stimulate the senses, the intellect, the emotions and the spirit of people; to give us collective access to deep realms of our psyche.[43]

He is correct. *Ipi Zombi?* was powerful, stimulating and worked on many levels; but what it did best was incorporate all involved. I was not and am not South African, nor Xhosa, nor worried about witches. Yet, while in the theatre, all of us were involved. I was not a passive audience member. For that brief period of time, we in the power station were a genuine community, concerned with the larger community of South Africa. Though it was not my history or concerns on the stage, I felt welcomed, encompassed and encouraged to join whatever frisson was happening in that space, more so than in the audience of many American plays I have seen. Perhaps that is Bailey's success: that what happened on stage was a collective access and an act of collective creation. I walked out both moved and connected to what I had just seen.

Like the best theatre pieces I have seen, *Ipi Zombi?* caused me to reflect upon many different things, from the current state of South Africa to the existence of the soul to the challenges of modernity. Like the theatre artists whose work I admire most – Noda Hideki, Declan Donellan, and Matt Walker, among others – Bailey forced me to examine my own theatre practice, gave me something to aspire to and reminded me why I did theatre in the first place – in the hope that something I do as an artist would move and affect others as much as their work had moved and affected me. The poster for *Ipi Zombi?* now hangs on my office wall as a reminder of all that; but it also serves to take me back to the Power Station on that 4 July, a mystical, magical moment of live theatre and a reminder of the interconnectedness of all things.

Endnotes

1   Coincidentally, another of the greatest productions I have ever seen was also on 4 July. In 1992 I was living in the United Kingdom. Feeling homesick for Independence Day, I went to the National Theatre to see Tony Kushner's *Angels in America: Part 1: Millennium Approaches*, knowing nothing about the play but having enjoyed Kushner's adaptation of Corneille's *The Illusion*. The fourth is, seemingly, a very good day to see theatre.

2   From the Standard Bank National Arts Festival (SBNAF) 1998 Program, p.54

3   I was at the festival with an African-American theatre company called Each One Tell One, named after a line in Ola Rotimi's *Hopes of the Living Dead*, playing the sole Euro-American roles in a pair of one acts about African-American life.
4   Background events of the story are taken from Bailey, B. (2003) *The Plays of Miracle and Wonder*, Cape Town: Double Storey, pp.30–1 and the SBNAF 1998 Program, p.55.
5   The actual age of the girl is in question. Bailey states she was ten (op. cit., p.31), the SBNAF 1998 program states she was eleven (op. cit., p.55).
6   Kruger, L. (1999) *The Drama of South Africa: Plays, Pageants and Publics since 1910*, London: Routledge, p.137
7   Ibid., p.202
8   Bailey, 2003, pp.16 and 19
9   Ibid., p.3
10 Ibid., p.99
11 The script for *Ipi Zombi?* is in *Drama for a New South Africa* (Graver, D. (ed.), Bloomington: Indiana University Press, 1999) and Bailey (2003). The reader is warned, however, that the script fails to capture the actual experience of being at a Third World Bunfight performance.
12 Bailey, 2003, p.10
13 Kruger, 1999, p.21
14 Bailey also dealt with the recovery of African items from European museums in his next play, *iMumbo Jumbo*, which dramatized the quest of Chief Gcaleka to recover the skull of an ancestor from Scotland. Bailey himself wrote, 'In the display cases and back rooms of museums in probably all the ex-colonial powers lie the bones and the royal and religious artifacts of the nations they conquered in their heyday. Delegations have been sent from several of their former colonies to attempt to retrieve these. Because they contain the essential power of the nations of their origins, there is something almost magical about spiriting away such items and reducing them to trophies, souvenirs and trinkets: he who holds these things also possesses their power.' (Bailey, 2003, pp.109–10) It seems that by starting the bus trip in front of one of these museums and taking the audience to an abandoned power plant where a ritual drama about witches and *sangomas* was set, Bailey was reversing this journey. The power was returned from the museum to the indigenous community.
15 Bailey, 2003, p.40
16 Ibid., p.44
17 Although the Internet has become widely accessible in South Africa since 1998, at that time television was still the dominant mass media, having only been introduced in 1976.

18 Bailey, 2003, p.46
19 Ibid., p.53
20 Ngũgĩ wa Thiong'o (1993) *Moving the Centre*, London: James Currey
21 Bailey, 2003, p.55
22 Ibid., pp.56–7
23 Ibid., p.68
24 Ibid., p.74
25 Ibid., p.203; Bailey, B. (1998) 'Performing so the spirit may speak', *South African Theatre Journal* 12.1&2: 191–202, p.191
26 Bailey, 2003, p.37
27 Larlham, D. (2009) 'Brett Bailey and Third World Bunfight: Journeys into the South African Pschye', *Theater* 39.1: 6–27, p.16
28 Quinion, M. (27 December 2003) 'World Wide Words: Bunfight', <http://www.worldwidewords.org/qu/ga-bun2.htm> accessed 27 November 2010
29 For more information on the company, see their website: 'Third World Bunfight: All African Performance Company', <http://www.thirdworldbunfight.co.za/site.html> accessed 5 December 2010
30 Coplan, D.B. (2008) *In Township Tonight! South Africa's Black City Music and Theatre*, Chicago: University of Chicago Press, p.280
31 Kruger, 1999, p.137
32 Coplan, 2008
33 Graver, D. (1999) 'Introduction' in *Drama for a New South Africa*, Graver, D. (ed.), Bloomington: Indiana University Press, p.18
34 Zaheda, M., 'Cheap Tricks and White Lies', *Cue*, 6 July 1998, p.3. As the title suggests, at least part of the reviewer's objection to the piece was Bailey's ethnicity.
35 Quoted in Graver, D. (1999) '*Ipi Zombi?*: Introduction', *Drama for a New South Africa*, Graver, D. (ed.), Bloomington: Indiana University Press, p.201
36 For a summary of the criticisms leveled at Bailey and TWB, see Larlham, 2009, op. cit.
37 Rudakoff, J. (2004) 'Why Did the Chicken Cross the Cultural Divide?', *The Drama Review* 48.2: 80–90, p.82
38 Coplan, 2008, p.377
39 Mofokeng, J. (1996) 'Theatre for Export: The Commercialization of the Black People's Struggle in South African Export Musicals' in Paris, G.V. and Fuchs, A. (eds), *Theatre and Change in South Africa*, Amsterdam: Harwood, p.86
40 Coplan, 2008, p.378
41 Mofokeng, 1996, p.85
42 Graver, 1999, p.9
43 Bailey, 1998, p.191

Chapter Seven

Performing Nation: The Opening Ceremony of the Sydney 2000 Olympic Games

Peter Snow

The land of milk and honey. Not the promised land, nor Australia, but the title of a most interesting performance I went to at Performer Stammtisch in Berlin in October while I was writing this chapter. Standing behind a table, in the middle of the small white room as we went in, was a bare-breasted woman in nondescript trousers and a Russian hat with the earflaps down so that her hair was completely covered. She was in bare feet and completely naked from the waist up. On each of her nipples was stuck a small sticker saying 'Bio' – the kind you see on vegetables and fruit in the local stores.

When we were seated, in three rows in a horse-shoe formation around the table, the performance artist, Dovrat Ana Meron, explained to us in simple spoken English – there was little rhetorical flourish – this was performance art after all – that the title of the first part of the performance was 'the land of milk and honey' and that in each of the four bowls in front of her on the table was a different kind of milk – biological milk, ordinary milk, mother's milk and soya milk. She invited people in the audience to come up, take a straw, sample each of the milks, decide which was which and register their opinion by marking the table grid she had prepared and stuck on the wall. This grid had been drawn up simply, almost crudely. Again, no attempt at flourish.

My companion was first up and, facing 'up-stage' away from the audience, she started to sample one of the bowls. She was immediately asked by the artist to come around to the other side of the table, so she would be facing the audience. Others followed, one by one, including a nursing mother carrying her baby in her arms. There was quite a bit of interest amongst those watching – tittering, *sotto voce* conversations, excited guessing and so on. After several people had sipped and guessed, the artist removed the table, while telling us that she would announce at the end of the performance which milk was which. There had not been uniform opinion among those who had tried. I did not have a go. I am not sure whether I regret that. I did have a keen sense of what each should taste like, the sweet watery taste of mother's milk and so on, and I participated imaginatively as each person sucked on their straws, mulled it over, and deliberated their choice. We were told that if we had not tried because we had been too shy or whatever, we could do so later.

The artist then proceeded to the second part of the performance, which she told us was called 'get it while you can'. Firstly she tied a black bra by its straps to poles on either side of the room, so that the bra stretched horizontally across the room with the cups pointing downwards. She then filled the cups with sand which she took out of an old plastic bag. No beautifully made stage props here. She cut holes in the top of each cup which meant that the sand poured down onto two piles on the floor. As the sand poured out she kept re-filling the cups. It was a strangely beautiful image echoing the release of milk which had been prefigured in the previous segment. She then replaced each of the Bio stickers on her nipples with an image of an eye cut out from a magazine. She covered her own eyes and moved around in front of the audience standing briefly in front of people. This was repeated with several different configurations of eyes.

Finally the artist moved to the third part. She read out a list of instructions to herself and then proceeded to perform those actions. They included doing a handstand, running, skipping and so on. For each of them she stuffed her breasts into a tiny bra or taped her breasts with gladwrap, which of course emphasised their size and how difficult it was to manage them. And finally, in a wonderfully cheeky and clever final image, she burnt one of the bras. As it was synthetic it flared into life with a rush and burned fiercely before being dropped into a bucket with sand. The incorporation of an image referring back to the history or performance art, including the art of performance protest, is a key feature of performance art. As it is, I might say, with all theatre genres.

Indeed, despite the radical nature of the content and the self-conscious anti-theatricality of aspects of the performance, this was quite a traditional dramaturgy. There was a very clear structure – three distinct acts constituting a beginning, a middle and an end – there was a very clear narrative and so on. I am sure that the performance artist would not agree with me about this, fiercely opposed as such artists usually are to theatre, to its fictions, to its virtuosity and to the smooth seamlessness of its productions. However, that is not really the issue. What *is* the issue – and I imagine you are wondering about this too – is what this has got to do with the Opening Ceremony of the Sydney 2000 Olympics Games.

Well, for one thing I was struck by the almost absolute contrast between the two events. A single performer in a tiny room in a central European city on a very cool night in front of maybe thirty people, compared to sixty thousand spectators and more than three billion television viewers watching three thousand performers on a balmy night in an open air stadium on the opposite side of the world. But there were also many similarities. Among them, a knowing and self-conscious dramaturgy, a highly politicised aesthetic, a very appreciative audience who were clearly 'in the know', a focus on the experience of women, a ceremonial dimension and lots of questions. Some of these nuanced similarities, and indeed differences, will become more apparent as we proceed.

The opening ceremony of the 2000 Games occasioned great pride amongst most people in Australia. One newspaper critic called it 'an international show stopper'. (Gilbert & Lo, 2007, p.1) Juan Antonio Samaranch, the then apparently eternal President of the International Olympic Committee, said it was the most beautiful opening ceremony ever. Quite an accolade. But maybe he says that to all the hosts. Two of Australia's leading theatre scholars, Helen Gilbert and Jacqueline Lo, make the following claim in the opening sentences of their recent *Performance and Cosmopolitics*:

> On 15 September 2000, Australians from all walks of life joined with the performing arts community to stage what is undoubtedly the most spectacular theatrical event in the nation's history: the Opening Ceremony of the Sydney Olympic Games.
>
> (Ibid.)

They go on to declare that 'the utopian vision of the opening ceremony could not be all show', (Ibid., p.2) before contrasting the vision with the reality of race riots on Sydney's eastern beaches some months later. But for the ceremony itself, there has been nothing but praise. In fact it is hard to find a dissenting voice.

So popular and well liked was the Opening Ceremony, and indeed still is, that the DVD has long been unavailable and has to be purchased on ebay for a considerably higher price than when first released. In the end I paid eighty dollars rather than thirty. One of my sons helped me: I am hopeless technologically and always need help, even with setting a mobile phone. For those of you who have never had the joy of attempting an ebay purchase, I can assure you it is a very dramatic event, especially if the stakes are so high that you just have to have the article, rather than simply desiring it. All the characteristics are present: a live event with a beginning, a middle and an end; a constrained time; a defined place; a strong, clear narrative; suspense, as we don't know really how it will turn out; and living breathing engaged bodies, to whom it all matters. Just like the land of milk and honey. Or indeed, an opening ceremony.

It is a beautifully structured event, an opening ceremony, and also very complex. In the case of Sydney, it encompassed a welcoming fanfare, a national anthem, a grand performance, a parade of athletes, songs by local superstars, official welcomes by Head of State and President of the IOC, another song, the raising of the Olympic flag, solemn oaths taken by a representative athlete and judge, a further song, the final lap of the torch relay, the lighting of the flame and a rousing finale. And all the announcements linking the segments are in two languages. The many diverse sections appear to flow seamlessly into one another and the drive through to the conclusion seems inevitable. To my mind it rivals the catholic mass for shape and purpose.

The opening ceremonies of Olympic Games have been, in recent times, opportunities for nations to strut their finest on the world stage. Sydney 2000 was no exception. From lip-synching pop stars to hat-clad horsemen it was all on display. Or was it? At the centre of the performance, within a millennial demonstration of the optimism of the new world and its relation to its own old world, was a relation between an Aboriginal man and a young white girl replete with sun cream on her nose. But what was in the shadows?

On the surface, the Opening Ceremony of the Sydney Games was a brilliant millennial display of the optimism of the new world and its relation to its own old world. The event was certainly sparkling. One of the striking images that has stayed with me is the continually twinkling stars of the flashes of thousands of photographs being taken throughout. In fact great chunks of the performance have remained vividly in my memory. Although seeing the DVD did make me recall one or two things, I realised while watching that I had carried most of the images with me for ten years. I don't think I am alone in this.

Two features of the performance struck me forcefully at the time and have remained with me strongly ever since. One concerns the narrative structure, the other the central relationship of the Indigenous man and the young white girl – in other words, action and character, which have been known since Aristotle to be the key features of a theatrical event. (Aristotle, 1951) First, the narrative. The opening image of the performance was of mounted stockmen and women riding into the stadium and sweeping up and down the sandy coloured arena. They were dressed in Australian Akubra hats and Driza-Bone raincoats and carried Australian flags. It was a rousing image, displaying courage and skill, and of course denoted ownership of the arena, here standing in for the continent. They immediately created, as we say in the theatre, 'a world', what philosopher Edward Casey might call 'a place world'. (2001) For Casey, a place world is a ground of embodiment and of being. He claims there is no place without bodies and no bodies without place. In this way implacement and embodiment are co-constitutive of being.

Watching the DVD of the Opening Ceremony, I was reminded that the shape of the Sydney Olympic Stadium is almost like a boat, uncannily recapitulating an inverted configuration of the Sydney Harbour Bridge: boat, container, continent, white settlers. So far so good. Then out of the flurry emerged a young blond white girl in a sundress with a beach bag. After skipping to the centre of the arena, she lay her towel down in the middle of the arena as on a beach and applied sunscreen to her nose. It was a marvellous physical action, focused, cute and resonant. Thoroughly sentimental. You could hear a pin drop. She went to sleep, perchance to dream, and the deep blue sea enveloped her. Then an Indigenous songman emerged to guide her, along with many Indigenous peoples from over two hundred and fifty clans, all dressed traditionally, on her journey.

Indigenous Australian director and choreographer Stephen Page, who directed the Indigenous segment, notes that Indigenous people had discussed boycotting the Opening Ceremony but later agreed to participate. (Page, 2003) It was important to them, he notes, that many were involved. He claims that he and they ultimately had pride in what they did and what it signified, namely that many Indigenous groups came together to celebrate their culture and that reconciliation is possible. Page emphasises the importance for Indigenous people of connection to tradition as a ground of culture and for Indigenous artists of tradition as a ground of contemporary art making. (See also Glow & Johanson, 2009) He also observes that, although the IOC has intellectual property rights over the Opening Ceremony, a fact reinforced strongly in the opening segment of the DVD, in a notable agreement, the Indigenous communities retained the rights over the Indigenous segment of the performance.

Subsequently there were many segments, all charting the history of Australian white settlement in a kind of little girl's dreaming. Some were witty – jumping sheep turned into suburban lawnmowers; some were colourful – giant fish swept through the heavens; some were boisterous – thousands of volunteer tap dancers rattled on tin sheets; some were startling – swarms of Ned Kellies in iconic black helmets fired their guns. The sequence of images purported to be a chronology of settlement. But if that was so, why in the narrative did the Indigenous man appear after the horse riders? It worked theatrically. After the storm, the quiet solo appears. But historically? Imagine if it had been the other way round. We would first have seen the Indigenous man and tribes, and then the charging horses obliterating the previous traces. That would have been historically accurate. And just as dramatically powerful. But the message? It simply would not have been done. Not in the political climate of the time under Prime Minister Howard. (Brisbane, 2003) His lengthy period of office was, after all, distinguished by three resounding 'no's: 'no' to a republic, 'no' to reconciliation with Indigenous people and 'no' to refugees seeking asylum in Australia. Though it has to be acknowledged that the 'no's were balanced by two formidable 'yes's: 'yes' to a new goods and services tax and 'yes' to an overseas war.

Now, what about the central relation between the Indigenous songman, Djakapurra Munyarryun, and the young girl, Nikki Webster? This was a clever theatrical device – and it worked. He appeared to guide her through an initiation into the wonders of Australia – its fauna, its flora, its tribal cultures and its history. I was reminded of Virgil showing Dante around the wonders of the nether world – or, more prosaically, Dorothy getting a tour of Oz. But why and how does an image like this work? Well for one thing, relationality is always at the heart of performance, as I will argue below. For another, the performance, which is always partly a rite of passage, enshrined at its heart a neophyte's rite of passage which was mapped onto a rite of passage for a country. Again, more of this below.

But before that, let me dwell on each of the images. Firstly, the little girl. On the surface she is a sign of innocence, in this case of Anglo-Celtic innocence – blond hair and fair skin, which in the harsh light of Australia needs sunscreen, or was that also mozzie screen? In that sense it is partly a true sign. True in the sense that it does convey the recent nature of white settlement in Australia, along with the recent advent of nationhood, and even the recent assertion of national identity or identities. But what is it with this obsession for 'little girls' as a performative signal of nationhood? Admittedly it was not only Sydney that indulged. Beijing carried it on in 2004, though perhaps there it was an aping of an Occidental festive icon.

The fascination for girls plays out in certain women's sports, typically those that receive points from judges, like diving and gymnastics, where the criteria for worth are relative and can be set and reset culturally. The current criteria in these sports are able only to be satisfied it seems by pre-pubescent girls. Dexterity, flexibility, cuteness and precocity are highly valued. And the liminal border between sexuality and asexuality is teasingly asserted. Grown women in these sports are consigned to being judges or coaches or commentators.

So what else does the little girl stand for, other than a culture not yet grown? Deleuze and Guattari in *Anti-Oedipus* (1983) discuss the 'little girl'. It is a puzzling image. In my view they propose the figure of the little girl – in contradistinction to the grown man of Freud as the key sign of psycho-sexual maturation – as a very different kind of 'organisation', or in their terms 'disorganisation'. The little girl is a line of flight of desire untrammelled by social organisation. The line of flight goes where it will, led only by its own desire. To become what? A grown woman? To that extent the image of the little girl is provocative, as an intimation of anti-structure, and yet strangely safe, harbouring a feeling of planned order.

In this Sydney Opening Ceremony, which claimed to celebrate one hundred years of women participating in the Olympic Games, the runners who performed the final lap with the torch were mature women – former superstars of track and pool. For most Australians, they are household names. Betty Cuthbert pushed in her wheelchair by Raelene Boyle, Dawn Fraser, Shirley Strickland, Shane Gould and Debbie Flintoff. Transporting the flame from Olympia to the Olympic Stadium of the host city was inaugurated in the Berlin Olympics of 1936. In Sydney 2000 it culminated in Cathy Freeman lighting the flame. This final image, while stirring, was also sadly comforting. On one hand, an Indigenous person was placed firmly in the centre of the Australian and world stages. On the other hand, it allowed us to say, 'Look at that Aboriginal superstar. They are all so talented. If only they tried as hard as she did. They would all be brilliant.' And we could content ourselves with this striking example of brilliance, never mind the shameful statistics of inequality and disadvantage that still plague Australia today. After all, the figures for disease, for life-span, for infant mortality and for incarceration of Indigenous peoples are all appalling compared to those for non-Indigenous Australians.

The Indigenous songman was a somewhat different image. He was clearly, on the surface, a sign of tradition. Of a mythic past extending into the present and, by implication, into the future. This, unlike the figure of the girl, was not a figure of everyday life. Most Australians do not see Indigenous people like this in their daily lives, if they see them at all. This was a ceremonial body, clothed (or rather unclothed), marked and carrying 'traditional' instruments. It was an image quite unlike that of the little girl carrying everyday beach paraphernalia. Hers was not a ceremonial body. His plainly was. But both were participants in the social drama of cultural estrangement and rapprochement which, in my view, is at the paradoxical heart of Australian identity.

How real is this kind of relation? Not very, I venture to suggest. It is an unmistakably utopian vision, perhaps even a fantasy. Stephen Page (2003) claims that the hand-in-hand image of songman and girl was not created by him and looks romanticised, which raises the spectre of the overall arbiter of the performance. A New South Wales Government Minister was assigned the Olympics portfolio and given the title of President of Sydney 2000. When I saw the relation I was reminded of Indigenous theatre director Wesley Enoch's triple challenge to non-Indigenous Australians, which he articulated to me in 2000 during a conversation about his production of *Stolen.* (1998) Do you know a black person? Have you been to a black person's house? Have you had a black person to dinner at your house?

Why do we yoke an image of unsullied innocence with one of mythic tradition? What does each image gain from the other? Is it that one earns a future and the other a past? What does the combined image speak for that each alone does not? Well at one level, we are invited to believe in a purported relation. But such relations are largely non-existent in Australian society, are they not? Where else are they celebrated other than in certain kinds of films and in ceremonies like this? It is a wished-for image rather than an image of reality. It is an image of hopefulness – of a desire to be fully grown up and to be together.

And yet 'we' recognise it instantly and glory in it. 'Yes, that is "us"', we chorus, 'that is who "we" are.' A non-existent relation is invoked to bolster a temporary sense of well-being and a marketable cultural identity, which is replaced with other relations once the ceremony is over. I wondered at the time, what if the image had been reversed? But the little Indigenous boy and the grown white woman came with Baz Luhrmann's *Australia* in 2008. I also wondered at the time what if their costumes had been reversed. Would the Indigenous man have been in jeans, boots and cowboy hat? Like the image of the 'western no-name' portrayed and parodied by Trevor Jamieson in Marrugeku's striking production of *Burning Daylight* set in Broome, the West Australian town which embodies several strands of Australian colonisation. (Dennis, 2009) And the little girl? How would she have been dressed? There is simply no answer to that. So what was her mythic status? Or was that already captured in her curly blond hair? Was she a golden princess sent by the gods to bring us, or at least some of us, good fortune?

Speaking of fortune, what is the purpose of an event such as this? At one level, the answer is obvious. It ushers in a sporting spectacle, an international event of staggering size and reach, an Olympic Games, the biggest festival on the planet. It also celebrates the possibility of athletic greatness, of overcoming all odds to triumph. To go faster, higher, stronger, than any have gone before. But at a deeper level? To respond to that, let me pose another query. What is the cultural purpose of performance? There have been a number of responses to this and I will mention only a couple. For Jeffrey Alexander, performance is a potential fusion of social groups and it is in fusion that societies really advance. (Alexander & Mast, 2006) For Peggy Phelan, a performance is a healing, overcoming fracture. (1998) While Herbert Blau claims that the gap between actors and audience replicates the psycho-analytic and physical gap between infant and mother at the stage when the infant recognises she is separate and yearns to be reunited – hence the audience longs to be at one with the performers, desiring re-unification and completeness. (1990)

Artists typically give a different kind of answer. For Stanislavski, performance uplifts the human spirit. For Brecht it embodies the possibility of bringing about social change. Butoh dancer Ushio Amagatsu says performance embodies the gestures hidden in the heart of the race. (Viala & Masson-Sekine, 1988) Australian opera and theatre director Neil Armfield speaks of a community of souls. (2003) But the common thread is clear. Oneness, togetherness, completeness.

I have a different perspective. For me, performance and performances actually bring culture into being. (Snow, 2010) In my view – and this is the theoretical framework of this chapter – the ground of culture is performance, the ground of performance is embodied being and the ground of being is relationality. We are always and everywhere constituted by our relations: our relations to one another, to ourselves, and to the world in all its domains. These latter relations includes those to the imagined future and to the posited past. Further, it could be the case that the ground of relationality is stillness and silence. And it could be that stillness and silence are grounded in the duality of continual living and dying. We know that we are living and dying every moment. Every breath in and out is to inspire and to expire. As with culture: it too is living and dying continuously. I believe that it is precisely this relation of moment-by-moment existence to culture that performance embodies and thrives on. Only performance has such a relation to culture. For that reason it bears the weight of bringing culture into being.

A performance such as the Sydney Games Opening Ceremony professes to perform and thereby celebrate the nation – and indeed it does. But it does more. In the sense of performance I have just proposed, a show like this actually attempts to bring the culture, or cultures, of the nation into being. It is not only a performative embodiment of a utopian vision. It is an imagined and enacted promised land – but if not of milk and honey, then of what? We could also ask, in addition to why we have these ceremonial events, just what kind of events are they? What is this Opening Ceremony? For Gilbert and Lo, as above, it is a spectacular theatrical event. Well it is evidently theatrical. And it is certainly a spectacle. But it is also a ceremony. That is what it is called after all. But what is a ceremony?

A ceremony shares some of the features of a performance art work, a piece of theatre, a concert and a ritual. But is it any more than this? According to the *Oxford English Dictionary*, a ceremony is 'a formal religious or public occasion, especially one celebrating a particular event, achievement, or anniversary'. It thus involves 'an act or series of acts performed according to a traditional or prescribed form'. 'Ceremony' also connotes 'the ritual observances and procedures required or performed at grand and formal occasions', thus implicating 'formal polite behaviour'. It has its origin in late Middle English, from the Old French *ceremonie* or the Latin *caerimoni* denoting religious worship and ritual observances.'Ceremony' therefore clearly invokes the resonance of a rite, more specifically of a rite of passage. Rites de passage were described and analysed by the Belgian anthropologist Arnold van Gennep more than a century ago as key events in the life of a culture. For van Gennep, a rite of passage typically has three parts. (1960) Briefly, they are a separation from the community, a transformation, and a re-aggregation into the community. The Games Opening Ceremony then is a rite of passage, not only for the athletes but for all those who participate. It is also and perhaps even more importantly a rite of passage for a city, in this case Sydney. I remember the street party that broke out when Sydney was announced as the 2000 host city. It was as if everyone was wanting, and waiting for, a chance for their city to strut its finest on the world stage.

Van Gennep's view of ritual has been very influential on subsequent anthropological thinking, especially so in the case of Victor Turner, one of the co-founders of the deliberately hybrid discipline of performance studies. Turner elaborated Van Gennep's structure into a four-part model, adding a new phase to emphasise the crisis, the drama, the social drama, which he claimed to be at the heart of the process. (1987) These social dramas usher in a liminal phase of anti-structure. In this phase things are for the moment upside down, rules and taboos are held at bay and transformation potentially occurs. It is in this phase that the experience of communitas or potential oneness with the group takes place. The relation to theatre and performance is obvious. Turner also pointed out that the crisis can be a schism, which in some cases is resolved, while sometimes it remains permanent, such as, for example, in a divorce. In larger scale, heterogeneous societies like ours, according to Turner, there is not true liminality, but rather liminal-like or liminoid phenomena. (1969) So on this view, the Opening Ceremony would be seen as a mode of anti-structure. It ushers in an extended liminoid period of transition in which all sorts of transformations and becomings (including comings of age) can and do take place.

It certainly seemed to me that the period of the Sydney Games was an example of a liminoid phenomenon. I had never felt the city like this before and have not felt it like that since. Barriers did appear to be, at least partly, broken down. There was for many a palpable feeling of community, on the streets, at events, everywhere it seemed. People mentioned this to one another. I heard it on the ferry across to Manly when we saw by chance the conclusion of one of the yachting finals. I heard it on Anzac Bridge when we gathered to watch the women's marathon and witnessed tiny heroic bodies running past faster than I could sprint. I heard it at the cycling road race near Bondi as we walked the circuit hoping for a better view and saw stony-faced riders flash past in what is virtually a contact sport. And I heard it at the Olympic Stadium at a night session of the athletics when we saw Maurice Greene sprint into glory. And it was for many people their experience of the Opening Ceremony itself.

But to look back at the Opening Ceremony of the Sydney Games is to discern several key contexts. There are obviously many, as with all large-scale public events. In the first place, there are other opening ceremonies. Barcelona's flaming arrow and Atlanta's Muhammad Ali spring immediately to mind as indelible images. As does the striking massed synchrony of Zhang Yimou's Beijing Opening. Each of these performs a vision of its culture in its own way. Everyone seems to have an investment in an Opening Ceremony. Everybody speculates on what it will involve, especially the lighting of the lamp. How will the flame be lit? Who will light it? It is the suspenseful end of the narrative, held secret until the night of the performance. It is also the high point, the apotheosis of the ceremony. The sacred moment. It is when the group nature of the event crystallises into a 'solo' performance and an 'individual' performs 'on behalf of' the nation. To describe it in this way appears to undermine the notion of relationality posited above. Until we recall that at the moment of the lighting of the flame, neither Freeman nor Ali nor the Barcelona archer is really an 'I' but rather a 'we'. Everyone watching is doing it too. It is a classic moment of fusion, of oneness, of communion.

Although in Sydney it nearly didn't happen. Watching, I was struck by the image of a black woman in a white costume mounting a temple-like structure carrying a sacred flame, then standing in water, a sacred element, waiting for a sacred cauldron to rise. All to the sound of sacred music. Only it didn't rise. Freeman had the good sense and grace to stand there while we all waited. And waited. Apparently a computer glitch had to be manually overridden. Isn't that the thing with live performance? We know it is live because something always goes wrong. Some little thing breaks the magic and it dies, or almost dies. That is another characteristic of a ceremony. It purports to invoke the sacred. And nothing in Australia is as sacred as sport. The fact that Australia has hosted two Olympic Games in fifty years, and is by far the smallest population to have done so in that time, speaks for itself. But the relation of sport and therefore the performance of games to the Australian pysche is quite another topic.

There were myriad other performances that took place during the 2000 Games. I will describe two of them. Sydney and Australia have a very funny and beloved comic duo who call themselves 'Roy and H.G.', short for Rampaging Roy Slaven and H.G. Nelson (not their real names of course, which are much more prosaic). Roy and H.G. are cult figures who made their name with irreverent commentaries on major sporting events, such as the Grand Final of the National Rugby League competition. They went on to host similarly irreverent television programmes during several Olympic and Commonwealth Games. In Sydney they were in their element and became more celebrated than many of the events. In what is both a celebration and a parody of a key feature of Australian linguistic life, Roy and H.G. use witty and often crude euphemisms for the names of sports people and what they do. People were particularly taken with their commentary on the men's gymnastics. When the men rotated on the floor on their backsides the action was described as 'spinning dates' and when the men lay on their backs and lifted their legs in the air, opening them in a V, this was called by Roy and H.G. 'hello boys'. I wonder where else in the world commentators would get away with such sacrilegious banter on national television – perhaps only in a place where everything is ripe for taking down, including the sacred, which of course in Australia includes sport.

But it was not only on small screens that the Games were omnipresent. On large public screens around the city, which have since become ubiquitous at large-scale sporting events, the public could gather and watch key events. One such was the final of the women's 400 metres, which everyone hoped Freeman would win. And she did. And we all breathed a sigh of relief and celebrated our good fortune. In 'her race' Freeman ran in a hooded bodysuit in the Australian sporting colours of green and yellow. But when she did her victory lap she carried two flags: one the colonial Australian of Southern Cross with British Union Jack in the corner, the other the unofficial Aboriginal flag of red, black and yellow. I noticed that no-one called Freeman the golden girl, as they had called the white Australian women athletes and swimmers who carried the torch into the arena. Though she was called 'Cathy' in that irritating way in which commentators often call sportswomen by their first names and refer them to as 'girls'.

We were at one such public screen at Circular Quay down at the edge of Sydney Harbour. While we waited for the running of the race we noticed heightened activity on the top of a very tall building nearby, the Immigration

Building. Several people, who were cast in light, were throwing ropes off the top and down the side. They were clearly preparing to abseil down. As we watched, and it was transfixing, we saw several figures simply climb over the edge from this incredible height and make their way down like ants. We found out later the performers were from Australian physical theatre company *Legs on the Wall*. To climb down the side of the Immigration Building struck me as a wonderfully apposite metaphor for Sydney Cove. Everything in Sydney seems to flow to the water, to the harbour. To Sydney Cove.

Another watery context. In 1988, Australia celebrated its Bicentennial. Or rather some people celebrated. It had been two hundred years since white settlement was initiated with the arrival of the first fleet in Sydney Cove. Well, it was either settlement or invasion, depending on your point of view. Unlike the Games, the Bicentennial was a controversial event. Not surprisingly. Many Indigenous people boycotted it. In the midst of the re-enactment of the landing at Circular Quay, near the Opera House, with tall ships, sailors in period costumes and so on, an Australian performance artist called Mike Mullins staged his own one-man performance protest, which he called somewhat ironically *Lone Anzac*. He dressed himself in an army uniform modelled on that of his uncle, a First World War ANZAC.

I do not have time to explain the sacred nature of this image in Australasia, but it bites at many levels in Australia and New Zealand. Throughout both countries, from city to small town, there are war memorials to the dead of the First and Second World Wars. They are very moving. Often you will see, in a village or small town, several with the same name. Generations of men from the same families were wiped out. My grandfather, though half Chinese, volunteered at seventeen to go from New Zealand on a European adventure. France! Twice his mother went to rescue him, the third time she let him go. He was invalided lying under one of his mates when they were shelled – they took it in turns to lie on one another in no man's land to protect themselves from the shells. He was lucky and survived. I note in passing that these wars in foreign fields, so often depicted as the growing up of Australia, were not part of the Opening Ceremony performance. And yet not so long after the Games we were at it again, fighting on foreign soil.

As well as a costume, Mullins also made himself a flag. He took out the Union Jack and changed the deep blue colour to what he called the light blue of an Australian sky, though he might have said of the eureka stockade flag, of white Australia's first and only republican revolution. And finally he swathed his face in white bandages and took up a position on the harbour front among the arriving costumed sailors and onlookers. He was almost inconspicuous. The grainy video record shows a few interested spectators. But after some time he was arrested by the police and taken away. It was something of a *cause célèbre* at the time, as no-one was sure what he was being charged with. In the end it was 'causing an affray'. At the subsequent court case Mullins turned up in his uniform and stood silently while his lawyer defended him, part of which included explaining his costume. He was acquitted.

There was one boat in the Games Ceremony. It was a large cleverly built contraption on wheels with a flag and a British naval captain with a telescope, representing presumably Captain Cook. That at least was how the narrator described it. But it was a fleeting image and not one that has endured. I asked myself at the time, where are the boats in the Opening Ceremony performance? There was plenty of water and images of fish... but no boats. To be fair, there was a strong image at one moment of peoples from all over the globe running onto the arena but this was rather subsumed under the colours of the Olympic rings. And no boats. No indication of the repeated waves of immigration, mostly by boat, which have populated Australia for two centuries and probably more.

Not long after the Olympic Games, another Mike, Australian performance and visual artist Mike Parr, staged another solo protest performance. *Aussie Aussie Aussie Oi Oi Oi (Democratic Torture)* was a bold and uncompromising work that had a number of incarnations, although typically for performance art it was seen by few people and has become better known in the re-telling. The title echoes the irritating call that some Australians use at major sporting events as a kind of rattling battle cry and it became a signature of the Sydney Games. (Scheer, 2008) Whenever crowds were gathered waiting to enter a stadium or a train, one of the volunteers – who, it has to be said, were wonderfully pleasant, engaging and welcoming and a feature of the games experience for everyone – would strike up this awful cry, 'Aussie Aussie Aussie, Oi Oi Oi'. I have to say I find it nauseating and I am both proud and embarrassed to say that one time while we were waiting for a train and a volunteer called out, 'Let's do Aussie Aussie Aussie', I called out, 'No let's not. Please'. People laughed and clapped. Perhaps they were sick of it too. In his performance, Parr sat on a chair in the middle of an open room with an Australia flag stuck into the stump of his left arm – he had a childhood accident which left him with only one arm – and had electric shocks administered to him in a random sequence. These left him visibly shaken. But the performance went on for quite some time. Apparently Parr was concerned enough before the show to update his will. (Scheer, 2008)

Endurance is a feature of some kinds of performance art as it is of sport. It emphasises actual bodies, often experiencing and overcoming pain, in real places, over real durations of time. Just like sport! Parr's performance was clearly a protest at the mandatory detention of refugees and asylum seekers in Australia, which for some years now has been a deeply divisive and controversial part of our culture. He had also sewn up his mouth and face with thread. This was an unmistakable reference to a group of asylum seekers who had sewn up their mouths to protest their lack of voice at their lengthy and unconstitutional confinement in Australian detention centres, which were more like prisons. Parr was obviously drawing attention to Australia's non-welcome in contrast to the myth of friendly Australians. The sort so proudly celebrated in the Opening Ceremony. I remember that early in the performance a huge banner unfurled which said simply, under an image of the Harbour Bridge, 'G'DAY'. The crowd loved it. As they did when Samaranch said 'Guday Sydney, Guday Australia' at the beginning of his speech. But to whom was this lively example of the Australian vernacular delivered?

For the Bicentenary, in a wonderful display of continued colonial deference, Sydney imported a large-scale theatre production from London – the Royal Court Theatre's production of *Our Country's Good* by Timberlake Wertenbaker, directed by Max Stafford-Clark. (1988) Wertenbaker had based her playtext on Australian author Thomas Keneally's novel *The Playmaker*. (1987) And Keneally had enshrined at the centre of his work a production of George Farquhar's *The Recruiting Officer*. According to Keneally, the first theatre performance in white settler Australia was a production in Sydney Cove, the place of the first settlement, very close to the current site of the Sydney Opera House, of *The Recruiting Officer*. It seems that this Restoration playtext was produced and performed by the officers and convicts together. Whether accurate or not, it is a lovely pretext. A social drama becomes theatricalised. Keneally's and Wertenbaker's texts reprise the making and performing of *The Recruiting Officer* within the political power plays of the fledgling settlement at Sydney Cove. Making a performance becomes a metaphor for the making of a 'new' culture.

Who is allowed to perform? Who not? Who directs? Who watches? Who disapproves? Who transgresses? Who pays?

It seems that Wertenbaker was not so much interested in Australia but rather in prisons and prisoners, and she found the idea of a country as prison fascinating. In the work, there is a lone Aboriginal person, watching at the beginning as the sails of a great bird descend on his sacred country. After that, it is all white people's business. Stephen Page muses about another possible encounter of whites and blacks. What if, he asks, Captain Cook had attempted to speak an Aboriginal language with the native inhabitants of Australia and all subsequent settlers had learned to speak similarly? We would all be Aboriginal and speaking a shared language. (2003) It is a utopian fantasy, but perhaps no more so than that reconciliation is as easy as an Olympic ceremony.

In another historical work, *A Commonwealth of Thieves: The Improbable Birth of Australia* (2005), Keneally writes an account of the landing of the first fleet at Sydney Cove and the early days of the settlement. It's a lovely title isn't it? 'Commonwealth' asks just whose wealth is being held in common, and among whom? And 'thieves' reminds us that many convicts were transported for thieving, only to be directed by their masters to thieve someone else's country as their penance. And both found redemption in stealing it for good. Where is the redemption for the Indigenous peoples of Australia? Where and when is this to be celebrated?

Keneally points out that unlike the captains of the slavers, who were paid on the number of live bodies they delivered, the captains of the convict ships were paid on the numbers who embarked. There was patently little incentive to keep their charges alive. There were no convicts in the Opening Ceremony, despite the fact that we have witnessed recently a nascent inversion of social status regarding convict ancestry. Where once it was unspeakable, it is now quite a coup to claim a convict in the family tree. Will there be a time when it is cool to claim part-Indigenous ancestry? This has started already in New Zealand. My guess is that it is only a matter of time before it occurs in Australia. But for the moment, white Australia maintains a colonial relation with Indigenous Australia within a continuing colonial relation to Britain.

The performance context that affected me most at the time of the Sydney Games was a research project I was conducting on the relations between actors and spectators in two Melbourne theatres, Playbox (as it then was; it is now Malthouse) and Theatreworks. I wanted to find out whether the ideas regarding Australian culture that artists embodied and communicated in their productions correlated with what audiences thought the productions were about. The methodology was simple. I asked theatre artists what they hoped to communicate in their productions and I asked groups of spectators, in interviews immediately after the performance, what they had noticed. Then I compared the sets of responses. Somewhat surprisingly, this has been rarely studied, if at all, and certainly not in Australia, despite theatre artists readily acknowledging that it is the key to the whole operation of putting on shows for audiences.

Perhaps unsurprisingly we confirmed what you might suspect. There is considerable concordance between what artists and spectators think is going on. Especially about storyline and characters – and as above we know these to be the critical features of a performance, from Aristotle – but also about thematic ideas. Spectators are much less forthcoming about production elements such as sound, lighting and props, though they will say a little about set and costumes. Of course this varies across genres. Dance and physical theatre is a little harder for spectators but there is still a lot of concordance. Although this was not an unexpected finding it was interesting, especially as it was for the first time, and also because in the days of post-modern theorising about multiple audience responses, the prevailing view had come to be, albeit with only anecdotal evidence, that there was always a wide variety in audience responses and little concordance.

The productions we studied ranged from *Stolen* (1998) to Neil Armfield's production of an adaptation of Tim Winton's *Cloudstreet* (1999). *Cloudstreet* depicts several generations of a white working-class family in Perth who come to realise that in their home on *Cloudstreet* they are standing on the blood of their Indigenous predecessors. While Jane Harrison's *Stolen*, written in association with the Ilbijerri Theatre Company, concerns the generations of Indigenous children who were taken away without consent from their families to be raised in orphanages or in white families for their own good. Cathy Freeman's mother was one of the stolen generations. The dreadful shame is that this was official government policy for many decades, until as recently as the nineteen fifties. The report of the Commission of Inquiry makes harrowing reading, but few of its recommendations have been acted on. (Wilson, 1997)

I have moved some way from the Opening Ceremony. It was certainly a landmark social drama. And it was to be some years before another magnificent social drama would be seen in Australia in another landmark opening ceremony. I am referring to the national apology to the stolen generations in the House of Representatives in the Federal Parliament in Canberra on the opening session of the new Labor Government on 13 February 2008, where we heard perhaps the most significant performative utterances spoken in Australia in recent times. Prime Minister Kevin Rudd said repeatedly 'I am sorry' for the pain and anguish that had been suffered by Indigenous peoples of the stolen generations. It certainly beat 'I declare these games open'. But was it an apology for more than the stolen generations? Was it for being here at all? For being strung out in a small suburban thread around the edge of the continent with a great mythical centre at our back ready to escape in boats if something goes wrong, when the red, or is that the black, heart threatens to usurp us.

As I reflect on the Opening Ceremony of the Sydney 2000 Olympic Games and on its multiple contexts, several of which I have outlined above, I wonder about Indigenous ceremony. Was there a first Indigenous performance in Australia? It doesn't really make sense as a question does it? Unless one invokes the spirit dreaming, in which the mythic ancestors, often totemic animals, travelled the country bringing the land and its features into being. Interesting that. Performance bringing culture into being.

Works Cited

Alexander, J. & J. Mast (2006) 'Introduction', in J. Alexander, B. Giesen & J. Mast (eds), *Social Performance: Symbolic Action, Cultural Pragmatics and Ritual*, Cambridge: Cambridge University Press

Aristotle (1951) *Theory of Poetry and Fine Art Poetics*, trans. S.H. Butcher, New York: Dover Publications Inc.

Armfield, N. (2003) 'Australian Culture: Creating It and Losing It', in K. Brisbane (ed.), *The Parsons Lectures: The Philip Parsons Memorial Lectures on the Performing Arts 1993–2003*, Sydney: Currency House

Blau, H. (1990) *The Audience*, Baltimore: The Johns Hopkins University Press

Brisbane, K. (2003) 'Yesterday the World, Tomorrow Australia', in K. Brisbane (ed.), *The Parsons Lectures: The Philip Parsons Memorial Lectures on the Performing Arts 1993–2003*, Sydney: Currency House

Casey, E. (2001) 'Between Geography and Philosophy: What Does It Mean to Be in the Place World?', *Annals of the Association of American Geographers*, 91(4), pp.683–93

Deleuze, G. & F. Guattari (1983) *Anti-Oedipus: Capitalism and Schizophrenia*, trans. R Hurley, M. Seem & H.R. Lane, Minneapolis: University of Minnesota Press

Dennis, R. (ed.) (2009) *Marrugeku: Place, history and community*, Sydney: Stalker Theatre Company

Enright, N. & J. Monjo (1999) *Cloudstreet*, adapted from the novel by Tim Winton, Sydney: Currency Press, in association with Company B. Belvoir and Black Swan Theatre

Farquhar, G. (1995) *The Recruiting Officer and Other Plays*, Oxford & New York: Oxford University Press

Gilbert, H. & J. Lo (2007) *Performance and Cosmopolitics: Cross-Cultural Transactions in Australasia*, Basingstoke: Palgrave Macmillan

Glow, H. & K. Johanson (2009) *Your Genre is Black: Indigenous Performing Arts and Policy*, Sydney: Currency House Inc.

Harrison, J. (1998) *Stolen*, Sydney: Currency Press in association with Playbox Theatre Centre, Melbourne

Keneally, T. (1987) *The Playmaker*, Sydney: Hodder & Stoughton

Keneally, T. (2005) *A Commonwealth of Thieves: The Improbable Birth of Australia*, NSW: Random House Australia

Page, S. (2003) 'Kinship and Creativity', in K. Brisbane (ed.) *The Parsons Lectures: The Philip Parsons Memorial Lectures on the Performing Arts 1993–2003*, Sydney: Currency House

Phelan, P. (1998) 'Introduction', in P. Phelan & J. Lane (eds) *Ends of Performance*, New York: New York University Press

Scheer, E. (2008) 'Australia's Post-Olympic Apocalypse?', *PAJ (Performing Arts Journal)*, 88, pp.42–56

Snow, P. (2010) 'Performing Society', *Thesis 11*, November 2010, 103: *pp.78–87*

Turner, V. (1969) *The Ritual Process: Structure and Anti-structure*, Chicago: Aldine Pub. Co.

Turner, V. (1987) *Anthropology of Performance*, New York: PAJ Publications

Van Gennep, A. (1960, 1st ed. 1908) *The Rites of Passage*, trans. M.B. Vizedom & G.L. Caffee, Chicago: Chicago University Press

Viala, J. & N. Masson-Sekine (1988) *Butoh: Shades of Darkness*, Tokyo: Shufunotomo

Wertenbaker, T. (1988) *Our Country's Good: based on* The Playmaker *a novel by Thomas Keneally*, London: Methuen in association with the Royal Court Theatre

Wilson, R. (1997) *Bringing Them Back Home: Report of the National Inquiry into the Separation of Aboriginal and Torres Strait Islander Children from Their Families*, Commissioner: Ronald Wilson, Sydney: Human Rights and Equal Opportunity Commission

CHAPTER EIGHT

Pilgrim: Taichi-kikaku

ALLAN OWENS

This chapter is based on my memories of the original 2001 production of Pilgrim *in Tokyo, journal entries written afterwards, company documentation, reviews of the work in Japan and three interviews with the company, conducted nearly a decade later as they toured Finland in August 2010.*

The Japanese contribution to theatre 'is one of the richest and most original in the world' even though a relative latecomer when compared to Greek tragedy and comedy, the Sanskrit Dramas of India and the courtly performances of China. (Ortolani, 1995) Whether staging plays downtown in the small Tiny Alice venue, the Tokyo Metropolitan Theatre or in the centre of a village in the Ivory Coast, Taichi-kikaku bring a rich mixture of Ki energy and silence with them; 'Pilgrims' en route, encountering others, moving towards a destination that resists fixity.

Pilgrim was created in response to the question the company asked in 1999, 'How is mankind to move into the new millennium?' The first performance was given in that year with the express intention of travelling with the production from 1999, through 2000 and into 2001. *Pilgrim* deserves a place as one of the greatest shows on earth because it connected uniquely with audiences across cultures without recourse to words in profoundly hopeful ways about the lonely togetherness of everyday life.

The performance was given in fourteen chapters and I use these to form the spine of this chapter.

125

1 Circle of Time

A thin circle of dark shiny synthetic material taped to the floor defines the performance space, a flat merry-go-round on which pieces of white and red cloth are placed at four points. The space is gently lit by the projected film of a soft blue full moon in a deep blue sky gently pulling indigo waves below. This huge swathe of backcloth drops along the full length and sides of the Open Digital Space. The audience sit in a long strip, facing end on with eyes at the level of the wide and deep stage area. The sound of waves breaking on a shore is heard as the recording of a Tokyo lounge love song fades in suggesting that all is right with the world. Text is projected on to the moonlit sea:

> People meet and kill each other
> People meet and dance a waltz
> I will certainly come just to dance a waltz with you
> I will surely come

A silhouetted figure of a woman, bare footed and wearing a summer cotton dress and long-sleeved cardigan, walks slowly and easily across the space as though along a beach. At the edge of the stage she sits to drop down the metre or so to the front row of the audience where in the half-light she takes off the cardigan and gives it to a member of the audience. Climbing back on to the stage she walks to the circle and begins to skip softly around its inner side, smiling and skipping against time in an anti-clockwise big-stepped joyous motion as the lights fade to black.

Since their first overseas performance in Paris in 1988 the three performers that are Taichi-kikaku – Rumiko Morimura, Yosuke Ohashi and Asahi Yoshida – plus the documentary-film maker Eisei Tabuchi, have performed for an extremely wide range of international audiences 'seeking to overcome barriers of race, culture and language'. (Morimura, 2006) Their aspiration is 'to travel through life together creating a form of theatre that allows for universal communication between people, for a sharing and celebration of existence'. As I interview director Morimura in 2010, she recognises that this is an idealistic aspiration but also a firmly held conviction.

As in much Japanese performance, the emphasis in *Pilgrim* is on beauty, myth and the ritualistic. As with many other traditional theatre forms throughout Asia this involves integration of dance, music and lyrical narrative. 'Japanese theatre artists have always practised the fine art of holding on to established forms whilst simultaneously living in an evolving contemporary world. Old and new are balanced in various ways'. (Mizuki, 2009) The complex interpenetration of time and tradition in *Pilgrim* are in this way typical of modern Japanese theatre.

Morimura's dramaturgical approach starts with poetry; Taichi-kikaku present her inner spiritual world to the audience. When she wakes she writes poetry, awake but in the marginal, semi-unconscious time where everyday life and the dreaming world are close together. It is in this way that dream is the source of *Pilgrim*, which the company entreat the audience to 'Watch as a dream' and not to search for meaning within. Ohashi views the work as 'a constellation that allows the performance to touch the audience, each constructs their own story in this dream.' (Morimura & Ohashi, 2010)

Taichi-kikaku are guided by the belief that materialism dominated and deadened lives the world over in the twentieth century. They are in search of what they call 'new–ancient ways of being' and view the act of performance as central to this. The new–ancient Japanese sensibility involves experiencing the material world, not looking for a blind accepting religious faith but instead for an intellectual, critical spirituality. For Taichi-kikaku this involves the creation of 'art spiritual theatre'. (Morimura & Ohashi, 2010)

2 Blue Moon and a Candle

Tabuchi's film shows the moon high in the sky, calm waves below. Three figures lie still on the circle which now looks like seaweed washed up on the shore. The same three figures come into shot in the bottom-left-hand corner of the film, stood on the edge of the beach looking up, contented, paddling in the waves. The song 'Have Yourself a Merry Little Christmas' fades in.

> Have yourself a merry little Christmas
> From now on your troubles will be out of sight
> Have yourself a merry little Christmas
> Paint the Yule tide gay
> From now on your troubles will be miles away
> Here we are, happy golden days of yore
> Through the years we all will be together
> That's if the fates they allow
> Hang your star upon the highest bough
> And have yourself a merry little Christmas now
> (Martin, 1944)

These lyrics play for the first time beginning the formation of a thread through *Pilgrim*. Later in the performance, I realise that the ironic effect of playing Christmas lyrics on this hot night in Tokyo is wrapped inextricably in with the company members' aspiration to 'be together/that's if the fates allow'. Tabuchi's documentary films of the three performers 'being together' in different locations over the years, looking younger as they throw stones into the sea by some Hawaiian shore or ride bikes around Hanoi; looking older as they gaze out of rooftop windows in Paris. In 2010, director Morimura tells me of times growing up in her parental home when the record would be played again and again and came to represent 'golden times' with 'troubles out of sight'.

The selection of 'Have Yourself a Merry Little Christmas' says much about the form and feel of *Pilgrim*. Recorded by more than 500 singers – including Frank Sinatra, Christina Aguilera, Ella Fitzgerald, Whitney Houston, the Jackson 5 and Lou Rawls – the version used in *Pilgrim* is by Lou Rawls. Composed as part of the score to the 1944 musical *Meet Me in St. Louis*, the sentimental setting of the tune led Judy Garland, the original performer, to criticise it as depressing and Hugh Martin the composer (1924–2011) made several changes to make the song more upbeat. The performance of *Pilgrim* plays with this sentimentality and that of the American musical, drawing on the slapstick traditions of early Hollywood with the careful life observations and humour of Chaplin and Keaton.

Wrapped inextricably in with these recognisably American forms are the traditions of the Noh stage, where the actors provide the contact point between the everyday world in which the audience sits and the other/outer world of the spirits. At the moments when the audience is reminiscing on happy times past or enjoying the pause after laughter, the mood is ruptured, torn apart by death, departure and separation. We anticipate the 'knock of death' but then after a while forget, enjoy the moment of being together, until again, it sounds.

The projection cuts to four candles flickering. One by one they are blown out. In the silence, the miniscule size of the figures in the face of the huge blue shimmering sea and moonlit sky film gives a feeling of vulnerability. Three friends together, 'if the fates they do allow.' Nature and the human figure are framed together, the juxtaposition of the song, candlelight and moonlight taking the audience back to the opening titles, killing and dancing. The actors are bringing something with them, 'a spiritual gift', says Morimura. (Morimura & Ohashi, 2010)

The moment highlights the preciousness and transience of such times, melancholia, reminiscent in my Western frame of reference of Keats' notion of negative capability (1818, in Forman, 1935), of living in a state where there is no irritable reaching after thought or reason to explain why things are as they are, but an intense understanding that they are brief moments of beauty where we experience what it is to be human.

> The full moon in *Pilgrim* is a very important symbol of peace, the moon is very changeable, fickle, but the full moon is only for one day. It symbolises the ephemeral, people reaching for the moon, transient hope, need and desire.
> (Morimura & Ohashi, 2010)

3 Lonely Restaurant

A 1940s-café-style single hanging light emerges from the blackout. One bulb throws a light on the two male performers naked from the waist upwards, joined by a white sheet, two-as-one, staring upstage with backs to the audience. They raise a glass to those we cannot see, wave, greet, receive applause and reach out to the light. They are separate but as one, united in loneliness, a pool of white in the blackness.

In silence they drop the sheet to reveal themselves, each wearing a skirt of cloth. The moonlight shines as they step through the café door. Moonlight is shining down, each gazes up separately. Movements are synchronised as they open the window shutter, step into the light and look up. They are transfixed, something beyond words, the universe, light from so many miles away, there is a peace, each is alone, but together they bathe in moonlight as it fades to black, burning this image of intense lonely togetherness into the retina.

This image is rooted in the company's early work in Paris. Morimura would spend hours in cafés in Paris watching people. Though music was playing and there was talk and laughter, people would often come in on their own, often sad. She reasoned that if they bought their own wine to drink at home it would be much cheaper and asked why they came in spite of this. Her conclusion was that they wanted to be with others.

> This is very human. People want people, why do they come? In the heart or mind of people there are a lot of desires… to be

> with others is one of them. I have experiences of cosy, interactive communication, but I have also seen violence. Before this happened I would often feel the dark and fury Ki energy. Feeling happy or lonely, each person radiates and emits their own Ki energy which operates at a level both deeper and beyond the emotional; a radiation of the vital energy from the core each person's life.
>
> (Morimura & Ohashi, 2010)

In *Pilgrim*, Taichi-kikaku use Ki energy to communicate directly with the audience on a subconscious level without sign or subtitle in a way that is universally accessible.

> The more we harness Ki energy more effectively we can exchange our emotions, feelings and thoughts with the audience. When we use these, certain words are produced. When we use the mind, emotion along with imagination is produced. At a much deeper level than words and emotion, at the deepest level, Ki exists. Ki comes from the core which radiates vital energy.
>
> (Ohashi, 2007)

Taichi-kikaku work in the form they have created, Shintaishi, translated into English as 'Body Poetry'. One of the only groups to have been allowed to perform on the Umewaka Noh Stage in Tokyo, the company's creation of 'art spiritual' acknowledge roots in ancient Japanese sensibility and primordiality such as Noh play, haiku and Tanka poetry forms. At the same time their post-industrial concern with alternatives to materialism and post-modern dramaturgical treatment acknowledge the influence of contemporary global performance practices.

> 1995 was the year we went to the International Experimental Theatre Festival in Cairo, Egypt and said good bye to the Japanese theatre world in which the main motivation is often either the exploration of social problems or working within forms such as physical theatre. The Shintaishi form is a rejection of the national commercial model and instead embraces the international and intercultural. Eight international judges awarded Yosuke Ohashi the Best Actor award at the Cairo festival, we saw the audience connected with our performance and it gave us the confidence to experiment further.
>
> (Morimura & Ohashi, 2010)

4 Golden Tray

A small golden orb appears to be floating in the darkness. As the lights come up Morimura appears to be holding a golden circle of light, waist high, cradling it to her stomach. She starts to move gently on the spot giving the illusion that she is running towards the audience. She holds the orb in front of her stomach, then high above her head, on her toes pushing as high as she can reach, teetering, the sun at midday, then drops it down to waist height suddenly turning it to the horizontal. Golden light beams powerfully up, washing her neck, shoulders and face, a reflection sunlight off water at midday, then takes it slowly to the ground, the orb becoming a tray, round and full of sunlight. She washes in it, gently bathing, her arms, face, neck; the golden light shines up.

She is suddenly aware of something outside this circle of activity, stops bathing and holds out the golden tray; she looks at it happily, then stops as though a shadow has fallen across her; something is wrong, she looks around. Throughout the whole of this chapter there has been silence but at this point it becomes overwhelming. She watches an invisible figure walk by then catches sight of a red piece of material stage left on the track of the big circle. The dream unfolds, she is holding a body, breathing life into it, another moment of sadness on her face and the same sequence begins again. Tabuchi's film is deep midday blue which slowly turns deeper until the stars are out – it is night.

Morimura steps into the golden tray and her hands start to circle from the wrist, feeling the air as she turns around, feeling atoms. This sequence takes time, endless time. There is a happiness and sense of focused purpose in this Ki-energy generation, silence with one figure, slowly moving in light finally fading into black. We are drawn into the heart of Keats' sense of negative capability, of intense beauty and loss, connection and loneliness. This is the touchstone of art spiritual. The film projects dark blue, time has passed in this theatre and the Tokyo night into which the audience will step after the performance.

5 Passion on an Uninhabited Island

Ohashi stands in a red skirt against a matt-grey backcloth, stripped from the waist upward save for red beaded necklace on which hangs a silver whistle. He lets go of a red balloon tied to the back of his skirt, it rises vertically then stops mid-air held tautly by the string tied to the back of the dress, a floating red full stop a metre above his head. Breathing in he looks around in the silence. Removing his red skirt, he stands still in a pair of white shorts with a high waistband.

The red skirt becomes a bull fighter's cape and music fades in – 1920s Hollywood film slapstick ukulele. The bull fighter advances, but not to a bull as he makes the yapping sound of a small dog which he swiftly kicks out of the circle into the audience waving it goodbye, smiling at the conquering of this fear. He turns as a huge force knocks him violently to the ground where he is hit repeatedly and the violence of this is extraordinary. Spanish classical guitar plays, something grabs his leg, pulling him in, he breaks free to run out of the circle and discovers the balloon, holds it in front of him and runs back into the circle.

Now he is an actor, happily shaking hands after a performance, bowing upstage after a very successful show. He jumps with joy 'Bravo! Bravo! Bravo!' again and again until this effusive acceptance of audience applause turns into a total frenzy taking huge amounts of energy when he stops, sees something – the audience. Arms outstretched, he slowly waves to us before stopping again. One outstretched arm deflates, he feels something between two fingers and the whole theatre watches, his other arm deflates and both appear to hang in the air. Each leg deflates and is pumped up again.

Shouting 'Bravo' he is thrown flat against the floor where he crouches in the darkness silently. The moonlight has returned. He looks up, stands and waves, blows on the whistle as a lonesome railway-engine whistle sounds out. He is a figure in the desert far from anywhere: the life of the performer, the attraction and terror of performance, failure and moments of wild joy and success, then doubt, always life passing, always finally alone, waving to the moon, to others who have gone that way, to the way all will go.

The literal translation of Taichi-kikaku is centre (tai), pole (chi), project (kikaku) – Centre Pole Project. The intention is to convey the idea that the centre is omnipresent in the universe. The concept of the centre is rooted in primitive art, in creation, in the one starting point where 'the one becomes two, the two becomes three and the three becomes all things' (Lao Tzu, 6 BC – Wilhelm & Tze, 1985, p.30), existence, creation and Ki energy.

> Existence consists of physical gesture (expression of face and body), the voice (rather than words) and being itself (including creatures). We creatures make much of our communication with each other through the exchange of Ki energy (invisible and spiritual) radiated between each other's existence.
>
> (Morimura, 2006)

The company do not treat Ki as a metaphor, but as the actual life-process that sustains living beings. The etymological root found in the ideogram for Ki is 'steam rising from rice', in the West perhaps 'breath on a cold day'. This corresponds to Western notions of humours on one level but on the philosophical level moves in a different direction and is found in many Asian belief systems. When vital energy dissipates there is death. In the Noh tradition in which Taichi-kikaku's work sits, the stage is the place where the 'real world 'meets 'the other world' of spirits through the performers. For the company, life and death breath and stillness are ever present in the performance space.

6 Printemps

Yoshida is in the circle which is lit to look like the froth of small waves. He is wearing a slouchy white beret, brown Parisian artisans' shirt, knee-length shorts, high socks and sensible shoes. We are back with the lone artist creating work. The self-referential nature of Taichi-kikaku's work is pronounced: they are humans, alone but travelling together trying to make art spiritual, drawing attention to the process of creation, of performance, critiquing what they themselves are attempting to do and aware of the failure. There is no irony, but nor is there self-aggrandised seriousness: they puncture their own aspirations, undercutting continually by reference to the act of acting itself.

Yoshida plays the stereotypical nineteenth-century genius–artist, looking ahead with an intense, mad fixity, asking the imaginary life-drawing figure in front of him to move, drawing but never once looking at the paper. Echoing the crazed energy of the previous chapter he uses two hands in frenzy before finally looking down to see what he has created. Pleasure spreads across his face and he turns the pad to the audience – a page of black and red scribble. He looks at it again, but the pleasure is visibly draining away until he realises it is nothing and lets it drop to the floor. What had possessed him totally, now holds no interest whatsoever.

A lounge version of 'Blue Moon' fades in. A silent comedy sequence starts as he wiggles in a wave motion, wraps a towel around his head, then holds a balance with arms strangely framing his face whilst stood on one leg presenting a ludicrous figure, bored in front of a mirror. When this sequence feels as though it should finish it continues, he turns his back to the audience and shimmies, one leg out, he moves and dances, sticks the other leg out then wiggles, all quite out of kilter, awkward and uncomfortable, pushing at the absurdity of human behaviour.

Just when this absurd but all-consuming world of individual hope and aspiration has its own momentum, there is the sound of a knock on the door. For Morimura, this is an important symbol. 'Beyond the door is the inner world, the opening of which signifies a welcoming into the mind, not only the positive and the good, but also the difficult and the bad.' (Morimura & Ohashi, 2010) The evil person is also the good person, when she or he meets others they can kill or dance.

The artist, freezes, looks at his drawing then runs to open the door, staring as if into a void. 'Blue Moon, I saw you standing alone' plays. Turning to the audience the void recedes and there is interest and hope again. He takes a lipstick from his long socks, paints his lips, contorts his face before again starting to move to the music and then stopping in silence. Nothing is happening, he starts to draw again but is very worried, starts whimpering, crying he is terrified. Once again he turns the pad to the audience who read the word 'Death' as the chapter fades to black.

Ohashi's character in the previous chapter wants to be a hero, to fight bulls, stage revolutions. Yoshida's character wants to be a genius–painter. They live in the same neighbourhood, do not know each other, but share a solitude.

> I wanted to express the concept of re-incarnation through this pairing of character changes. Ohashi and Yoshida express the other side of their selves as Jungian actors on a journey to the soul that Jung called self-realization, the journey in this sense being one of the archetypal Asian metaphors.
>
> (Morimura & Ohashi, 2010)

7 Into the Night

Tabuchi's film shows celebratory fireworks exploding in the night sky as Morimura walks round the circle in the semi-dark. The film cuts to a city, perhaps Hanoi. Ohashi, Yoshida and Morimura are on small motor cycles, oncoming car headlights and rickshaws pass by capturing the excitement of early evening in the city. Then she is alone, still in the silence, peering into the dark, remembering. In the early years of their international touring work, critics referred to Taichi-kikaku's form as 'play beyond words'.

> The Shintashi form is concerned with 'theatre-able existence'. It took some time before we realised that one secret of Ki energy performance is that Ki is radiated most effectively when the performer is static.
> (Morimura & Ohashi, 2010)

The word 'static' itself conveys this possibility, suggesting as it does the build-up of electricity through friction – movement through life, 'rubbing-along', 'scraping-by' and then a discharge and flow of energy through connection. This is related to another distinguishing feature in many forms of Asian theatre, 'ma', perhaps best translated as a 'pregnant pause'. More than just silence, ma is the space that interrupts musical notes or words and is used to intensify the power of play, of the dramatic moment.

> In the course of their daily life people do not often live existentially. Shintaishi form is intended to allow both actor and audience to enter into existential communion. In order to create Shintaishi expression we as actors have to purify our mind in a similar tradition to that of Noh Theatre. We simplify and universalise our action and movement in order to engage on the level of Ki energy with the audience.
> (Morimura & Ohashi, 2010)

Shintaishi has been developed through a process of trial and error as the company travelled through life and overseas together. Amongst the characters we meet, with the possibility to be intimate, the bullfighter and genius–artist are two people who meet under the moonlight and make friends. They have a wonderful time, waiting for the waiter, singing happy birthday, perhaps the best time of their lives in these small moments. I ask Morimura ten years after the *Pilgrim* performance if the company will always be together.

> We will never dissolve, our unity is most important. In the 1970s many new experimental theatre groups were born in Japan. With the move into the 1990s many dissolved and only a few of the original groups such as Taichi-kikaku now exist. We are a small communion, soul-mates travelling through time together into the future. We do not travel for the purpose of performance but as art, always documented by Tabuchi and we use this film in the new performance. We will travel until we die, it is the best education we can have, learning directly from people.
> (Morimura & Ohashi, 2010)

8 Queen

Dressed in a night dress and with his long hair brushed around his face, Ohashi stands as a queen on a chair stroking a piece of fur, until we have a sense of it as a cat. At the moment this is established he gets bored and loses interest in it. Momentarily fearful he reaches inside a bag and puts on a half mask. The queen becomes a lover running to a ball. When she arrives at a door she takes the handle, opens it and peers into the void. Someone has called her, a lover who she listens to and then in a fun-loving way runs for what he wants, brings back wine and they celebrate together. The wine runs out and she goes for more, the sequence is repeated, good company and wine and conversation.

Suddenly she is caught between need for this pleasure to continue and the pain that now starts to be inflicted on her from somewhere, from someone. She keeps opening doors, turning a key, holding the handle, looking, seeing nothing, closing the door and putting the key away.

Finally she drops to the floor and bunny hops upstage to un-wrap a Javanese rod puppet. Holding it at arm's length, she falls asleep, waking suddenly with a start when her arm brings the puppet close to her face. She pushes it away with her other arm and sleeps, but the fear returns as the puppet comes close once more as she pushes away her fear, again and again. The acting is mesmerising and the symbol of the other us stark, the other world, knowing that we are living and that we will die.

The puppet hits her, but as it goes to leave she calls it back, asking it to stay. Ohashi takes the countess mask off and dances with the puppet, no music, all is deadly silent. The first bars of 'Blue Moon' fade in and they waltz together in the moonlight: 'You knew just what I was there for'. I think back to Yoshida dancing, this pleasure cannot last, the puppet grabs her hair after a while they kiss each other and dance again.

Suddenly the puppet dies, horror spreads on the face of the queen, it pops up again, then the knock at the door and all goes dark. She takes a deep breath, the two of them in the dark, she kisses puppet goodbye and opens a door, puppet in hand. The desolation spreads slowly over her face, there is nothing, she looks to the audience, silence, the puppet looks at her slowly she touches its face then plucks its head off and throws it away. Ohashi and the puppet, the queen and her lover, a couple, any two people who meet and spend time together.

We work with fragments of the imagination and memory, a constellation of ideas and motifs, specific pieces of recurring action. The key is travelling. When we travel we find the new 'real' thing which in turn becomes a fragment of the memory, both the past and the new thing. Travelling has always been an inspiration for Japanese poets. Taneda Santoka (1882–1940) said that when he coughs he remembers the solitude of travelling alone in Japan, through this simple action he thinks and finds out through the body. Santoka wanted to find reality in creation and what inspires creation. When he wrote poems he did not think at a desk, his travelling was his experimental work.

(Morimura & Ohashi, 2010)

In *Pilgrim*, Morimura's fragments lead to the collective memory, the subconscious. Contrast and montages are central in the Haiku and Tanka forms and in *Pilgrim*.

> One lady sleeps alone
> She looks at the long tailed bird flying

Long tail means long nights alone. The contrast is a montage and it is in this way that Matso Basho (1664–1694) always held two things in contrast, something which Morimura aspires to in performance. For her, Japanese art is primordial. Manyo Shu, one of the earliest Japanese poets, explores this lonely togetherness as one of the central feelings and tensions of life.

9 Crying Woman

Yoshida has a large magnifying glass connected to a transparent plastic cup by a silver wire. Wearing striped tracksuit bottoms he peers at it, looks to the audience and then starts to squeeze and crack the cup as he moves around the circle. The more he scrunches the more he gets excited. He takes off his trousers and puts them on his head, makes a skirt out of his top, parts the two trouser legs as two bunches of a woman's long flowing hair and squeezes one of them dry. Continuing to get ready, moving like a model preparing for the evening, conscious of the beauty of her body.

There is something sharp in her leg and she pulls it out, barbs, one, two, three four, she puts them in a drawer but it will not close, pulls something else out which grows. Arms outstretched she balances on one leg sneezes and is blown to the floor where she tries to sweep the things that are causing her pain together. She is cold and then sneezes, tries to manage with these small pains, capturing then and then letting them go and washing her hair. She sits and waits, time passes.

Yoshida reaches down to pick up a plastic bag taking out a bunch of bananas and eating one as though it is the best food he has ever tasted. He shakes his head slowly from side to side with pleasure, then eats another then another, five in all. His appetite for pleasure is not waning at all and when all are eaten he ties bag and screams 'NO! NO! NO!' Running around the circle screaming he suddenly stops and ties the trouser legs around his neck strangling himself, then goes to the stool crying. Moonlight falls and he pauses slowly looking up at the moon.

> 'Crying bitterly in agony' – you will always recognise this scene in our performances, when we have to face the reality that we cannot accept, when we have to accept death, the agony, we have to face it, when we have lost a person who we love and who loves. It is possible to go directly and deeply into the spiritual world, and this can give courage. Theatre in this form exists as a primitive primordial art it has always had this function.
> (Morimura & Ohashi, 2010)

Morimura's view is that in Japanese people are often open to spiritual feeling, but also able to laugh at their own spirituality.

> If we were dominated by one religion we would feel the seriousness of the postmodern taking all from us, instead we seek to find a native sense, to return to a native culture. A new start is possible, a new–ancient Japanese, a new–ancient world 'new native'. The post-'80s economic depression in Japan marked the start of the process. The postmodern turn often leads inwardly to cynicism to Ki energy negative. We work from ancient Japanese, the positive, generous life, Ki energy positive.
> (Morimura & Ohashi, 2010)

Japanese critics Eisuke Shichiji and Nishido Kojin said of Taichi-kikaku, 'We have to disarm our minds when we meet their creation, it is very pure, people's cynicism and defences melt.' (Morimura & Ohashi, 2010) Critics have also pointed out that 'pureness cannot overcome reality, pureness does not have a strategy to overcome or transform.' Morimura's answer is that the company 'chooses to tell' and that this has its own resonance in the world.

10 Blue Moon

As Yoshida stares up, his figure fades and the moon is revealed in Tabuchi's film, on a deep indigo sky with wisps of white. There is no sound until eventually we hear a train whistle in the distance and the moon gets smaller and smaller until it fades, to blackness out of which a note sounds out, 'Aaaarh', then the same cry but a higher note. All three performers are now on stage together for first time. Sat on three stools they are trying to attract the attention of someone or something at first in the audience then all around. They call out waving at things only they can see.

Pilgrim has its roots in time Taichi-kikaku spent in Croatia. Morimura met a member of the audience from Sarajevo who watched their performance of 'When comes the day to Die' in Zagreb and said that the company must bring it to Sarejevo. She imagined the destroyer, the knock at the door, as the war. The woman talked of the wretchedness and horror of that time and, soon after, work began in Paris which would become *Pilgrim*, be taken Sarajevo and then back to Tokyo.

Whilst in Sarajevo, the company was walking near the old town on a hill which was found to be full of graves. Reading the names and ages they realised that:

> Most were in their 20s, many others were teenagers buried with desires, dreams and hopes, perhaps to be a singer, actor, get married, live a happy life. This was the start of the creation of *Pilgrim*. The full moon symbolises not only hope but having been in Sarajevo and also symbolises the peace. While doing the performance in Sarajevo we realised another factor in its creation: why Ohashi had acted the revolutionary, the bullfighter and the countess lover, why Yoshida the genius–painter, because they all are waiting with hopes and dreams, but all are destroyed by the knocking. The young people of Sarajevo had been forced to fight and kill each other. Performance opens the door and looks outside, facing the evil, wanting to watch, trying to see the evil thing but realising that it is endless, trying to catch the limitless.
>
> (Morimura & Ohashi, 2010)

11 Light of Four Moons

The three performers sit on stools as though on a wall at the roadside. Ohashi tries to attract the attention of passing motorists by raising the hem line of his cream dress; Yoshida calls to someone passing; then all three call to one person with hopeful thumbs up, manically using all their energy to clap someone or something towards them before all falls quiet. Yoshida finds a banana in pocket which they all celebrate before he unceremoniously throws it out of the circle and they wait again. Morimura slumps, losing all energy, quickly followed by Ohashi, then they clap each other back to life – 'Bravo!' Ohashi as the Queen gets them things to eat, wine and the most wonderful food in the world. Eyes closed, they enjoy this with every ounce of their bodies – 'Nastrovia!' Black out.

In the darkness, they start a live soundtrack of animals, cats, beasts, dogs and a cuckoo. Using torches underneath their faces they become spirits, funny and terrifying by turns. Yoshida emits a deep throaty 'Huh, Huh' to Ohashi's small animal noise; then there's running and for a moment all is silence again. Five candles have been lit within the circle which is now a large golden orb. Silence for a long time when finally they sing 'Happy birthday to you' and in the same breath blow the out the candles. 'Blue moon, you saw me standing alone without anything to live for' plays as Morimura once more radiates Ki energy positives and Ohashi and Yoshida are repeatedly knocked off their stools by some unseen force. Blackness and silence once again.

> My idea is rooted in primitive art, in creation devoted to a universal God without religious meaning. Like Steiner, we intend to express this spiritual science as art, a performance of prayer radiating pure Ki energy continually re-creating. So our answer to the question 'What is Shintashi?' after a long journey is that it is the embodiment of a prayer, to directly communicate with the people around the world with vivid love.
>
> (Morimura & Ohashi, 2010)

12 Shining Journey

Tabuchi's film of the big blue moon floods the stage to reveal Morimura again washing herself in the golden orb, shoulders exposed, holding her dress close, looking up before turning to join Ohashi and Yoshida, who are joined at the waist by a single white sheet. She slips into the place between them letting her dress drop as the three, with their backs to the audience, hold their arms high in the air, swaying gently to:

> Have yourself a merry little Christmas…
> Here we are as in olden days
> Happy golden days of yore
> Through the years we all will be together
> That's if the fates they will allow
> Hang your shining star upon the highest bough
> And have yourself a…

There is a knock, Ohashi and Yoshida have heard but Morimura has not. They raise the sheet slightly as she goes under, covering her in a white shroud.

Ohashi takes out a key and opens a door looking at Yoshida, both faces full of fear as they take unsteady steps backwards. Looking down at their friend, they let earth fall from their hands onto the grave in silence. They turn and walk across the circle and then each turn to go their separate ways around. Black out on their separate journeys.

Morimura stands slowly and the shroud drops. She looks at the cloths on the circle. Time is passing, we are dying. She looks ahead, not knowing what to do, how to go on, trying to make sense of what is happening, not moving; then she slowly looks up towards the moon, turns her back and steps into the light shining on the golden orb on the floor and for the second time steps into it. Head down in silence, then her arms moving, feeling the molecules, the energy and huge sadness of loss, total loss, then Ki energy upwards into the light, Morimura's fingers winding upwards, just hands and swaying, an expression of total absorption.

The other two figures lie as dead. She is wearing a calico pink grey dress and hears something we cannot hear and again looks up and 'Arrghhh' screams as in the earlier chapter, sounding like a mournful train whistle. She waves as the whistle becomes louder and pan-pipe Celtic-type music plays and she tries to communicate with what is above, she screams again and goes down like a bird flying down towards the golden tray.

The music plays louder and the train whistle sounds as Yoshida and Ohashi try to lift themselves up, finally managing to get to their feet. Staggering as the whistle blows again and again, they start to dance around the stage running, striking the air in a cumbersome, clumsy, ugly way as Yoshida falls, then Ohashi, and all the time the whistle and the Celtic panpipes sound. They are running in a frenzy when the music cuts to silence and they resume their journeys around the circle in opposite directions. The lights come up as they turn to each other; pain and fear on their faces, they walk to each other. Black out. We do not know if they fight or dance.

13 Departure for the Year 2001

Tabuchi's film of a blue night sky with a train as it moves through countryside, filmed from inside a carriage. We see another twelve figures moving round the circle, some in stylish coats, some holding themselves in pain, others in ordinary clothes as the film cuts to Morimura, Ohashi and Yoshida, in what looks like Vietnam, on a river, the sun in the sky. 'Have Yourself a Merry Little Christmas' plays as they look down from the screen at the figures on the circle travelling on their journeys. A live video screening of the figures is projected on to the backcloth which fades into the image of the blue moon reflecting on the water. We are back to the opening chapters of the performance but now the image of the figures on their journey is refracted, the circles of travelling figures are huge, infinite circles repeated and repeated, journeying pilgrims.

> In contrast to ancient Japanese theatre, European theatre is city based with the citizen as the centre, a horizontal dramaturgical world view based largely on the Greek model. Ancient Japanese theatre is best viewed as two circles, one signifying the world of our everyday lived life and another the 'other world' – the theatre being located where these two separate worlds meet. The performer takes the audience into the other world and then out to the everyday world, a very ancient Asian conception. For example, in Noh theatre the stage is like an island with a long thin bridge leading to it, back stage is other world and the stage is the place of dream. Around stage is river of white pebbles, a river separating the real world and the other world (back stage), actors and actresses appear from the other world to the audience and appear on stage as the dream world.
>
> (Ohashi, 2007)

Taichi-kikaku's work acknowledges this structure, always a circle on the floor of the stage, every performance like an island, a dreaming place both new and ancient.

We want to integrate the ancient Japanese world with that of the contemporary citizen. Japanese theatre is often not based on a definitively finished text or dramaturgical score but on symbolic form and response to this. We integrate Ki-energy-based theatre and the modern European theatre form using the poems written by Morimura in conjunction with video text of our lived lives.

(Ohashi, 2007)

14 Prayer

The three performers wear full, white dresses as they slip off the stage into the audience. Each holds out their hands to a member of the audience and gently waltzes with them in the aisles. Tabuchi's film shows Morimura, Ohashi and Yoshida dancing in the same way with people all around the world: France, Poland, Italy, Greece, Hong Kong, Cote d'Ivoire, Egypt, Israel, Vietnam, Rumania, Bulgaria, Bosnia and Herzegovina, Croatia, Hungary, Japan, Senegal, the UK, Finland. On the screen, Ohashi and Yoshida look down on the dancing below from two moonlit windows in what looks like a European city, perhaps Paris. Morimura takes back her cardigan from the audience member she left it with at the start of the performance and puts it on.

Looking directly at the audience, the three performers slowly back away, all the time gently waving. They climb back onto the stage and as the lights come up they bow, hold still, then raise themselves and clap the audience members before backing off, waving hands in small gestures, smiling. Ohashi and Morimura look on the figures in the moonlight and at the sparkling sea. There is no end, the circle remains on the floor, the audience looks at the two figures looking at others.

> Art spiritual is still a new thing in Japan. 9/11/2001 shook people's minds around the world. We believe that there is need for a new form of critical spirituality that might provide an alternative way forward.
>
> (Morimura & Ohashi, 2010)

Works Cited

Bashō, M. (2005) *Bashō's Journey: Selected Literary Prose by Matsuo Bashō*, trans. David Landis Barnhill, Albany, NY: State University of New York Press

Brandon, J. (1985) 'Time and Tradition in Modern Japanese Theatre', *Asian Theatre Journal*, Vol. 2, No. 1, Spring, University of Hawaii Press

Forman, M. (1935) *The Letters of John Keats*, Oxford: Oxford University Press

Martin, H. (1944) 'Have Yourself a Merry Little Christmas'

Mizuki, M. (2009) 'Traditional Japanese Theatre Overview', *Time Out Tokyo*, September

Morimura, R. (2006) *What is Shintashi/Body Poetry?*, trans. Y. Ohashi, company documentation, unpublished

Morimura, R. & Y. Ohashi (2010) Series of three interviews in Helsinki, Espoo and Kokola, Finland, 4–12 August 2010

Ohashi, Y. (2007) *Ki Energy and Ma*, company documentation, unpublished

Ortolani, B. (1995) *The Japanese Theatre: from shamanistic ritual to contemporary pluralism*, USA: Princeton University Press

Wilhelm, R.R. (trans.) and Tze, L. (1985) *Tao Te Ching by Lao Tzu*, London: Arkana

CHAPTER NINE

O ACHAMENTO DO BRASIL, Foco Musical

GUILHERME MENDONÇA

In the following chapter I will be writing on the 2004 production of O ACHAMENTO DO BRASIL* by Foco Musical – a Portuguese company whose mission has been the dissemination of erudite music for young audiences. As an opera that narrates the 'finding' of Brazil by the Portuguese discoverer Pedro Álvares Cabral, O ACHAMENTO is one of Foco Musical's repertoire pieces. The score was composed by Jorge Salgueiro and the libretto was written by Risoleta Pinto Pedro. Foco Musical has four pieces in its repertoire,† each of them corresponding to a musical paradigm.‡ The shows are presented in rotation, so that each show is repeated every four years. The 2004 edition of O ACHAMENTO had the musical direction of Jorge Salgueiro; I provided the stage direction.

Rather than circumscribing myself to a show I have ended up transforming the work of the company in the main axis of this text; I have put much emphasis on the personality of the founder of the company, Miguel Pernes, who is, as fortune has it, a good friend of mine; and I have purposely adopted a tonal mix of the informal with the academic. Considering my overt disrespect for such commonsense rules for the writing of a critical work (having been involved in the production, being good friends with the company director, etc.) the reader might ask in what capacity am I writing?

---

* I will refer to the show merely as O ACHAMENTO.
† A fifth work was added very recently, A Menina de Pedra, a ballet. A sixth piece is in preparation.
‡ A symphonic fable, Quinta da Amizade; a suite, A Floresta d'Água; an opera, O ACHAMENTO; and a cantata, O Conquistador.

How can I preserve any objectivity? Why should this be of any interest to any constituency of readers?

I should like to say a few words on the why. Foco's shows are pedagogical events developed throughout extensive periods in collaboration with schools. The nature of the project is so plural that it is impossible to regard the show as the sole object of analysis. What is at the centre of Foco's work is not any particular show but the company–audience relational model – the centre of the analysis is a strategy not a show. This is also the reason why I think much attention should be devoted to the founder and director of the company. It is true that much of what Foco is today is a direct result of the work of its creative teams. But creative teams come and go and develop similar creative work with other companies. What is unique about Foco is the molding of that creative work to the specific interactional and pedagogical strategy that was developed by Miguel Pernes throughout the years. Finally, a book called *The Greatest Shows on Earth* lends itself to some subjectivity – it is, after all, about what one particular writer feels is the 'greatest show on earth' and that, of necessity, must have a personal element. My hope is that by including some admittedly subjective experience I would be able to better explain what it has been like to produce artistic work in Lisbon in recent years and to give some sense of the relevance of particular work in its context. What I am aiming at is a workable distinction between the subjective aspects and what can be regarded as objective, without excluding any. Hopefully, this will become apparent as the reader moves through the text.

Foco Musical works both as a music school and as a producing house (though with a very specific object). The method used by Foco is what can be described as the Active Music Listening (AML) method. I will subsequently explain Foco's particular of approach to AML in more detail. For now it suffices to say that AML designates a large number of music teaching strategies, in concert, that involve having some kind of activity within the audience.* What is specific to Foco is the duration, continuity and preparation of the projects.

The strategy of Foco is the creation of purposely designed musical events in integration with a teaching programme. What this means is that Foco invites a composer† to create a score within the given paradigm – in the

---

*   This is generally rehearsed in concert with no previous preparation.
†   Jorge Salgueiro has been the composer of most of Foco's pieces.

case of O ACHAMENTO, an opera. Parts of the score are written with the future participation of the audience in view: there will be sections that can be accompanied either with instruments, voice or movement routines. The format followed by Foco includes pre-recordings of the music and score extracts.

A number of teachers, either coming from Foco or trained by Foco for this specific event, will begin a series of workshops with children from schools that have a protocol with Foco. This will include learning a number of routines for the show. Younger children might learn simple choreography, body percussion or miming; older children might learn choral parts or elements that have been specifically composed for particular instruments. The workshops are held throughout the academic year.

In March/April (the dates vary from year to year) Foco prepares the production of the event. The event is prepared like a normal musical or theatrical production – singers, actors and musicians are contracted for the particular show, there are rehearsals, fittings, technical rehearsals, a dress rehearsal and an opening morning.* The show runs for a few weeks – a sufficient number of days to guarantee the presence of all the associated schools.

What distinguishes this from most other musical events for children is that at Foco's shows all children will be familiar with the whole score: they will enter the concert hall with a thorough understanding of the piece to which they are about to listen. They will also, if experience stands as evidence, be eager to do so and keen to take part in the show.

Typically, a show by Foco will be assisted by a number of teachers and local staff. The teachers will come from the schools where the preparation for the show has taken place. The staff will have several origins: they might be people from the city hall, the house technicians, and sometimes people from interested parties and collaborators such as the Fonoteca Municipal. Additionally, Foco has established a number of protocols with higher education institutions – these will be students finishing their BA or HED in the cultural animation area, which utilise Foco's team for their final apprenticeship placement. In 2004 a protocol had been established with EPED, a cultural animation school near Lisbon.

---

*   There are many independent musicians that constitute the Orquestra Didáctica Foco Musical. Other collaborators, singers and actors, tend to be regular too.

What is required of assistants in shows, generally, is that they help with the co-ordination of entrances and exits of children and that they do a part of the audience musical conduction. The youngest children, notwithstanding the preparation they might have had, invariably need some assistance with the timing. Each assistant will be responsible for a number of children, standing in strategic positions in order to prompt the audience at the right moments.

The students from EPED were supposed to be not merely the assistants but also to play smaller parts. I had, in the previous two months, met twice a week with the EPED students. With them I had organised a workshop so that they were engaged with the performing aspect of the play too – there were a few parts that required considerable performance skills. In 2004 we were still experimenting with the degree of permeability between audience and stage. Miguel had been insistent on this point and, during rehearsals, we had been looking for strategies to improve that permeability. What is meant here by 'permeability' is that the performance must be held in such a way that at given points the focus of attention is exclusively in the audience – singers and actors must be able to prompt children to sing; sometimes the audience will be lit; the sound levels in the audience will be higher than the orchestra. This is not a problem – it is what is specific to a show that is performed significantly by the audience as well as on-stage performers.

With each new production, Foco publishes a guide to the plays in comic-book form. This book is intended to be simultaneously a fun book and a pedagogical guide. Within it, the materials needed to be a part of the concert are included. The narrative is interspersed with the scores and there are clear indications in the drawings of the kinds of instruments that are being played. There is also a CD on which can be found a recording of the whole piece and discreet demonstrations of each instrument and its range.

Foco Musical began in 1996, after a preparatory period of some years. Miguel started his career as a musician and I was curious to understand how he had leaped on to musicology and the foundation of Foco. I first met Miguel when we were in the army, which for our age group in Portugal was still compulsory. Through the years that followed our military service we met occasionally, on a social basis, and I confess I had very little idea of what he was up to until the turn of the century when I was invited to direct O ACHAMENTO. At this point, I tried to understand what set of conditions and intentions had led Miguel to produce music performance for and with children.

The interview transcribed here was held at Foco's headquarter in late October 2010.

>Guilherme Mendonça – Was this what you thought FOCO would become? Can you go back a few years now and tell me: when you started FOCO you were not yet 30...
>
>Miguel Pernes – 25
>
>GM – You are, what, now 39. You had left music school (conservatoire). You had a band – I think it was called *Caganisso* – you were doing Musicology at Universidade Nova...
>
>MP – A rock band.
>
>GM – So what happened? I remember we were in the army together – you use to take the classical Portuguese guitar and play it in the barracks with the rest of the guys... so your background was in, well... music, all kinds: not just popular or erudite. My question is: why not become a musician or a teacher, why did your career go this way?
>
>MP – As a musician, I realised immediately I wasn't made for it. I was dead scared each time I stepped on a stage. So I knew it wasn't for me. And, as I began to study musicology, that part of music that has to do with history, composition and acoustics, I dived into a fascinating world. And I began to understand a bit better. It is what I call the world of music as art, as opposed to the world of music as entertainment. I fell in love with those aspects of music, and kind of detached myself from other kinds of music; and all this was organic you know. Sometimes I look back and I feel no identification with the kinds of things I used to do. it's kind of... natural.

I had had myself a difficult relationship with the military. Yet I had managed to pass unnoticed in the compulsory service. Miguel was less lucky. I have never met anyone quite so averse to the military etiquette, so gawky with guns, so distrustful of pointless physical exercise. His congenial nature and his love of music guaranteed him a special place within the group. It was Miguel that prompted singing when the garrison was in transit to field maneuvers. Often soldiers gathered around Miguel late at night to hear him play the classical guitar. I remember his moaning as we returned from long nocturnal night drills, hungry and covered in mud. If that memory is vivid, so is my certainty that there was no other twenty-eight-year-old, in the late 1990s, in Lisbon, who produced an articulate defence of communism, drove a Porsche, sold his own property to produce classical music shows for kids and loved boxing, erudite music, bullfighting, politics and musicology.

Technically of middle-class extraction, Pernes, the younger of two sons of a family of psychiatric nurses, defied what might be regarded as his social destiny. A career in business or public service would have been more likely. I do not want to fall in to the social mobility commonplace of poor boy becomes producer: it really does not fit this story and, for sure, it does not fit Miguel Pernes. This is a story of successful intellectual entrepreneurship and persistence. My point is to emphasise how someone coming from a family with no musical tradition became so intensely interested in that universe.

> MP – Many things are also a matter of chance… everything in life. When I was doing my BA I was working at a Jet Service warehouse. As loader, during the night, just to get some money. Meanwhile, because of the training I was getting in musicology, I was invited to teach a module – I started it just for survival but I ended up loving it: the kids, and the experience. I was integrated in the AEC*, so I came into the City Hall Project and became musicology consultant. And I got in touch with this paradigm – the Active Music Listening (AML) – even though we were working with recorded music and not live music: with the work of José Carlos Godinho whom I think was the father of AML in Portugal.
>
> GM – This is what: late 1990s?
>
> MP – Yes, about '96, '97. And suddenly that worked as a way of bringing kids closer to erudite music. Why? Well, kids just fell for the music. It was fun, bringing fun to erudite music. You see, this is what pop music gives to kids, but we could do it with music that

---

* *Actividades de Enriquecimento Cultural* is a programme implemented in Portugal, in the '90s, aiming at creating a flexible platform for cultural activities within communities.

was intrinsically very rich. Kids don't necessarily like 'easier' music – it is just a matter of approach.

GM – That brings a whole world of new questions. Why kids and not adults? Is it going to happen with adults? This wasn't predictable: you had kids quite late in life, you were about 35. Nothing made this predictable. So what is it: just science? An interest in children and pedagogy?

MP – Well, I identify with the little guys. They are receptive. We're speaking here of primary school kids, and kindergarten, they just show such openness and lack of prejudice. These will disappear later on, as teenagers, high-school. But now they are open to everything. They will assimilate Mozart, or Bach as well as they will get Stravinsky or Boulez.

GM – Are you telling me there is no great difference between the kinds of music for them?

MP – It's all about the approach. For sure, the child's personal taste is part of the equation.

My interest in characterising Pernes is not just incidental: his lively temperament is at the heart of what Foco Musical is today. We know at the start of a new project that Miguel will be thinking big. He will be imagining 80-strong symphonic orchestras, he will be adamant in hiring celebrities for the promotion of shows; he will have imagined sets with complex machinery and lighting effects, all of the musicians in thematic clothing. This, as the finance manager, Marco Mendes, knows, is not always possible and it has many times been a source of financial agony. I do not know how many times Pernes has bargained private property for the survival of Foco – I suspect quite often – and I cannot recall a single production prior to which Marco Mendes hasn't voiced deep concerns for the survival of Foco. But it is also a fact that the company has managed to survive: it is a fact that it produces shows for large orchestras; that for some shows musicians have dedicated thematic costumes; that the company has managed to extend its activity to Spain in at least one project; that the publication of a comic-book guide and CD has extended to all of Foco's projects.

Pernes became a much better communicator in recent years, managing to keep his ambition high but becoming a little more realistic. The company has grown and people have grown in the company. It is no longer a group of twenty-year-old music enthusiasts trying to change the panorama of music teaching and listening in Portugal. There is a permanent team of teachers and musicians, a faithful and permanent group of collaborators, headquarters in Lisbon and Oporto, a permanent management and artistic directing team. Above all, there is regularity in production and an increased knowledge and specialisation.

There had been some discussion in newspapers and magazines about kids and music: fairly popular stuff like the 'Mozart effect'. I wondered what someone in the business would say, and I knew there was a political twist there.

> GM – So what about the 'Mozart effect', the commonsense idea that kids respond to Mozart. Would you say that it is not true?
>
> MP – Absolutely.
>
> GM – It's false then?
>
> MP – It's false. For sure it is easier with older kids: they have a trained ear – from the point of view of tonality – the classicism will be easier, from the melodic point of view too, it is all balanced, music tends to be tonal... the baroque too. Of course there are challenges in all kinds of music – timbre in baroque music. But they are totally open
>
> GM – A side question – just out of curiosity: do you think there are innate musical structures?
>
> MP – No. No. It is just about access. And we are lucky, access is improving at earlier ages. The sooner you access richer and more diverse language, in whatever field – be it music, or spoken language – the easier it will be for the child to understand that language. You will develop complex understanding of models if you are exposed to them. If you go back to Piaget and Vygotsky, the association of thought and language as they showed: the correlation between the verbalisation and reasoning. It is the same thing with sound – with the art of organising sound. The richer

the environment in a given language, the easier to understand that
kind of language... to understand intrinsically. The idea that music
is universal... there is nothing universal about music.

GM – It is cultural, then?

MP – Absolutely. The earlier the contact the better. I am referring
to Western erudite music, for sure... but the same will be valid to
other traditions... It is to do with contact with that language at the
right time.

O ACHAMENTO, like many shows by Foco, had a programme of
decentralisation and went to a number of venues around the country. I
felt this was quite a big concern for Pernes: a political concern with access.
I knew touring was tried for quite a long time at Foco but the company
moved into locating their performances in a few venues around great
centres. I asked Pernes about this:

> GM – It seems to me that most companies, at least in theatre,
> think it is not worth it to decentralise... I mean weighing the
> expenses and the kind of support...
>
> MP – Yes but we do it with the 'ensembles'* – it is the schools that
> are involved in the project... Gondomar, Gaia, S. Tirso, Loures,
> Amadora, Oeiras, Cascais, Barreiro, Almada...
>
> GM – Still those are all regions located around big urban centres.
> I suppose it is a matter of finding the right venues and equipment
> too? The ensembles are also much cheaper to produce.
>
> MP – We were faced with that problem and we concluded, when
> we first tried decentralising, you will remember, we went to
> Montemor and many other places.
>
> GM – Yes, with ACHAMENTO in 2008.

---

* The 'ensembles' are smaller concerts available to number of entities throughout the country, city halls, schools, companies.

MP – And it was great. We went to Fatima and Montemor, as well as Oporto and Lisbon which we always do. But it was an overstretch for us. It was a great time, and we were very pleased with it, but when we got back to our bookkeeping and accountancy we realised there was no point. We had no more audience because of decentralisation. The same people will come to our shows in Lisbon and Oporto, and getting out was not financially worth it. The fact is that there are a lot of schools that will complain they get no shows visiting them, but then when we try we will have those and a few more people.

GM – But do you think people, throughout the rural areas, are eager for cultural offerings?

MP – They might be, but they are not enough to make the project viable… even more so when we are speaking of structures that have no financial support. We do now*… but let's see if this will endure or if it will be just this year. The box office must support all the costs. Outside Lisbon and Oporto it is even more difficult to find a paying audience, and tickets need to be cheap because these are shows for schools. 8.5 Euros a ticket… venues of 500 or 600 seats, four sessions: that's not enough to cover the production cost. We had to recentralise. This was a great pity for us, but inevitable.

One of the difficulties we had in 2004 was the adaptation of the set design to the shallow stage. The design had been done with mobility in mind: it consisted of a number of large differently shaped vertical printed pieces that reproduced the drawings in the comic book. The idea was to create some kind of transversal aesthetic unity.

Forum Lisboa, where the first and final sessions were held, is a cinema venue located in the new area of town. Stage depth is about five metres and there is but one stage exit, stage left. One specific aspect of Foco's shows, particularly with the operas, is that, contrary to what will happen in a strictly commercial opera, the orchestra must be in view. All aspects are subservient to the active listening strategy. The show is not about the action taking place on stage but the articulation of elements needed for the production of a musical piece. All the elements need to be visible so that the

---

* The Portuguese Ministry of Culture started supporting Foco Musical through the Direcção Geral das Artes.

child mentally relates instruments, their instrument families, the sound, the conduction and the action on stage.

Because Forum Lisboa is a film-dedicated venue, a large area is left free between the first rows and the avant-scene. The space is, still, considerably low and we were able to squeeze in a full orchestra. We had to create a very agile system of entrances and exits – the narrator and the lighting were sometimes used to cover scene changes that would otherwise be made through the wings; but on the whole, because of the predicted difficulties, Forum Lisboa ended up being the sprightliest of performances. The season started and ended at that venue and by the last performances a considerable improvement in performance agility was noticeable. The interaction between extras, assistants, actors and singers was quick and tuned with the audience's response.

Concerts for children have been a common practice from the beginning of the twentieth century. The best known of these concerts are, of course, Prokofiev's *Peter and the Wolf* and the TV concert/programme *Marsalis on Music*.[*] It is fair to say that a considerable and successful share of the market is dedicated to children in several artistic fields. In Portugal alone, there has been an increase in offerings of theatre and music for children – the *Dias da Música* programme at Centro Cultural de Belém has included, since its foundation, a number of events for children and there has also been a growing offering of music for babies[†] or children's concerts in general.

Many of these approaches work on the specific modes of presentation of music for children or on the kinds of repertoire, so that they are not specifically aimed at linking an in-depth pedagogical approach and concert experience – their specificity is the production of adequate music formats for children.

> MP – I think we are talking of access to the idea of beauty too. It is also that which makes it so interesting to work with children. People tend to underestimate the ability of children to understand and even to produce music – I mean to interpret. They can do everything: you put on a project and you realise in the end that

---

[*] I am purposely mixing very different objects in order to illustrate the array of children-dedicated music events.

[†] The list of these in Portugal is extensive. Some examples: the *Concertos para Bebés*; there are also the events at Oceanário de Lisboa (baby concerts at the oceanarium); Concertos para Bebés e Famílias, at Casa da Música.

you are in fact conducting on orchestra. Sometimes I hear people saying 'they are too small' – it is not about the children generally. It is not them. The problem is that we are not able to conduct them... but they can. Studies say that from about nine years old children can improve from the point of view of interpretation, but not in terms of his ability to construct music. This is highly debatable though.

GM – Oliver Sacks says in *Musicophilia* that music structures are stored deeply in your brain – in some part of your most primitive brain. Can you relate to this in your work? Do you have any thoughts about this? My thought is that for sure painting cannot do this... just from the point of view of co-ordination.

MP – Yes, well; lots of issues there. One of the specificities of music is the fact that it is 'temporal'. In painting when you look at a given point in a picture, your eye will perceive, also, the context in which that point is inserted. This is not the case when you hear music. If you listen to a new piece you will not know what comes and probably – because there is so much in music that is simultaneous – you will not remember what passed before. This is one of the difficulties children have with erudite music, and this is why we speak about making erudite music fun. I don't mean any fun, or fun for 'fun's sake'. I mean fun that is planned so that it facilitates the taking in of the values of the music – there are criteria that need to be met in this kind of work, so that the musical work is understood as a whole, namely the formal structure of music. So when this formal structure is understood – with no need for abstractions: 'this is A-B-A form' or something of the kind. Children will not abstract the form in such a way. So when this formal structure is understood, it will stay. They will understand the piece from top to bottom and its internal logic. So, when they get it, they start taking pleasure from the piece in new ways. I am not sure this is what you were aiming at... in terms of structures... not sure.... As to primary emotions, from what I remember from reading, for example, Damásio – when we get that shiver while listening to some piece – be it music or something else, when music gets under our skin – it seems we are going back to primary emotion. So, what is strange, or at least very hard to explain, is that an art that requires training to be understood, an art that relies on very cerebral processes while you are learning it, is then experienced in a way that is very similar to the way you experience your primary emotions. It's a fact. If you are not told how Messiaen builds his 'transposition modes' you will not get the kind of thought that is behind the music – but if you are, then you will be able to take pleasure from it. After an intellectual exercise, the thing will get under your skin.

The Associazione Lirica e Concertistica Italiana, through its Opera Domani (OD),[*] seems to be doing similar work to that of Foco Musical, though using well-known scores instead of dedicated compositions. The programme has existed since 1997 (Foco was founded in 1998) and it involves the community and schools in their concerts. The Opera Domani has been very effective in promoting its materials and making them available. Like Foco, it produces graphic material, scores (in several simplified formats), historical information and partial lyric transcriptions, which are published on the Internet.

The *Orquesta Filarmónica de Gran Canaria* (OFGC)[†] too has a programme dedicated to schools and families that involves activities prior to the concerts and promotes a number of concerts with its juvenile orchestras and choruses. Through its Servicio Pedagogico, founded in 1992 the OFGC has been running workshops for teachers and educators in music, storytelling,[‡] the production of plays in school context, preparatory constitution of musical groups in school context, a number active music listening events and the promotion of active links with the Red de Organizadores de Conciertos Educativos (ROCE).[§]

One aspect most children will not be familiar with is the constitution of the orchestra. They will have heard about orchestras in their workshops, they might have heard recordings, they will have worked on transcriptions of the themes to piano, recorder or to electronic synthesiser, but they will only rarely know what an orchestra looks like in real life. A great deal of Foco's shows is the presentation of the instruments. This will take a good twenty minutes: instruments and instrument families are introduced by a game. Typically the cicerone will get the names of instruments wrong and

---

[*]   http://www.operadomani.org/
[†]   http://www.ofgrancanaria.com/index.php/es/programacion/conciertos-escolares-y-en-familia
[‡]   They call it 'narradores' by which is meant an array of narrations within shows, so not exclusively story telling.
[§]   Educational Concert Promoter Network

he will prompt the audience to provide the right names. By this simple and informal game, children are put in a state of excitement and in a participatory position.

Having a visible orchestra can be technically challenging. In 2004, in venues where it was not possible to have the orchestra in view, in front of the acting area, we had to resort to having an elevated orchestra upstage on a raised deck. This was in some ways a beautiful arrangement but it posed immense technical problems. There is a reason for placing the orchestra and conductor in their traditional positions. Having the conductor behind the set design forces the inversion of the position of the orchestra and makes it very difficult for the singers to see the conductor, unless they turn their back to the audience. This was finally settled in rehearsal by changing slightly the action on stage so that in the required moments the singers could be sideways and follow the music. But it was not easy and, for sure, it was not free of problems.

I am not aware of the full music strategy of OD or OFGC or indeed of other companies but it is worth mentioning a subdivision within the Audição Musical Activa (active music listening) between the mimicking techniques and the participatory techniques. The former implies some kind of imitation process but not necessarily the practice with an instrument and the latter implies sonorous interference* (generally voice or body percussion).† The specificity of Foco's approach is to do with its holistic view of music appreciation. It is all about preparation for the concert. The shows cannot be seen as mere concerts but as long events involving preparation in class, study, instrument practice and concerts. The concerts are the visible part of the show.

> MP – There are a number of issues in what concerns music teaching at least in the Western world. This is not just a Portuguese problem. I think teaching is too centred on imitation

---

* 'Sonorous' rather than 'musical'. Considering the age groups and the difficulties a given group might have it is more inclusive to call it 'sonorous'. Any kind of activity participation may be welcomed.

† Miguel Pernes in *Audição Musical Participada ao Vivo: Aprendizagens significativas no 1.º ciclo do ensino básico* produces the following distinctions: Active Listening (Escuta Activa) implies concentrated listening; Active Music Listening (Audição Musical Activa) implies music synchronous movement; Active Participated Music Listening (Audição Musical Participada) involves sonorous interference.

– one is tempted to say on playing but it isn't, it's on imitation. The teacher will do something and the children will copy. This is the existing paradigm. This is not what we do at Foco. The centering of the teaching on the way you listen and the creation of new audiences, which is what we do, requires the work to be done in long-run projects. This is why we need public presentations. That is how it works – it is how it works, if you want listeners that are open to a certain kind of music you must have them listening to live music in the first place. It is not enough to play a CD. Okay, now this kind of approach wasn't invented by us. We knew of events and circumstances when this kind of approach had been used – I mean some kind of 'active listening'.

GM – Here in Portugal?

MP – Yes, in Portugal too, even though this kind of work was circumscribed to brief moments in a given presentation – there was no 'active-listening-oriented approach' – it was kind of a fun thing people used every now and then, in an event. In the project I was just telling you about, the Municipal AECs. There was this AML program we had been working here at Foco, but at the time using recorded music, and we managed to persuade the Orquestra Metropolitana de Lisboa to include it in their repertory. And so one bit of AML was tried in the middle of a concert. And what happened was that suddenly, in a concert that had extraordinary levels of noise, a lot of difficult kids, and schools, from socially neglected areas... suddenly there was a moment of silence – the kids had this movement score happening on top of erudite music, and there was silence, and after that: the noise came back again, complete disaster – kids talking and shouting on top of each other. As I was observing all this, not just with kids that were in my class, but kids from different areas... I was thinking 'why not do the whole concert like that?' because that was quite a surprising moment in the middle of the concert. So when we started the work with our orchestra, we said, okay, we must forget our existing repertoire, and we began conceiving a new repertoire, a special repertoire that is composed with a new group of instruments in mind: the audience. Because with kids that age, the concert will work if they become a part of the show. You see they are listeners, amongst many other competences that are being addressed in the training (I want to say that our project is not reducing its mission to the idea of creating listeners – this is very important – but because we are talking specifically about O ACHAMENTO I want to emphasise that aspect) so they are listening to music and they are part of the show too. Also we are working specific areas that would be approached in music classes, so we might as well prepare for a specific context – that of a concert. This is what we understand as 'project oriented work' – kids will be starting instrument lessons, generally the recorder, or they will be working on rhythm schemes; or canon, or chorus, initiation to recorder… stuff they could be doing with no connection, but within a project – and it is also relevant because we tend to use episodes from Portugal's history (at least in the case of O ACHAMENTO) so we try to integrate that too. So, kids are taking possession of a narrative that will transform the way they receive the show. It is not just because of the routines but also because of the story. Sometimes the problem of the symphonic fable is this… the narrator speaks and then comes a piece of music or the showing of a musical instrument and when the narrator comes back again the kids are lost in the story. So, with all the preparation we do, even if the kids get distracted for a few seconds – sometimes you hear some background burble in the concerts: they are talking about the show itself, they are not distracted – but, anyway, when they come back to the action on stage they will know in which part of the concert they are. What I am saying is that what could be otherwise an ephemeral experience becomes relevant and long lasting, or so we hope. This is why we think it works: we integrate the work done in class with the concert experience rather than providing music exercises in isolation.

I directed the 2004 *O ACHAMENTO* with very little notion of what was in fact implied by the actual performance. My previous directions had been regular theatre shows for adults where no surprises are expected apart from those that might occur on stage and I directed it as such. For *O ACHAMENTO* I was lucky in that the professional singers and actors and the assistants that were also playing extras had bonded quite well – this created a certain feeling of security. I knew also that shows would involve between 800 and 1,500 children, in disparate and often poorly equipped venues around Portugal, and that this would necessarily involve some degree of adaptation.

The first unusual thing about the shows of Foco, assuming a readership that has never seen one, is the introduction of the instruments. Nobody had told me that there would be a long introduction to the orchestra – there was this show before the show happening almost spontaneously on the spot – no matter if children are still getting into their seats. School buses in Portugal will often run late, so there is always a class arriving and being seated while the introduction is going on. This is one of the functions of the introduction – to give a bit of leeway to latecomers – you just can't send a group of late three-year-olds home after they have been preparing a show for months.

There is, so to say, an improvisational tone about the concerts and the team is used to that. One has to accommodate all that is not expected in the show. The speed of the audience, the entrance of groups, children crying, teachers moving around taking children to the toilet, repositioning them or just helping with the choreography. Lights need to be kept at some level of luminosity – three-year-old children tend to panic if lights are turned down suddenly, or even completely. Consequently, there are no absolute blackouts.

Then something overwhelming happens, there is this moment, in which all the children suddenly start singing at the same time. And this is what makes Foco's shows absolutely spectacular – the sight of 1,500 children of varied ages accompanying a symphonic orchestra from their seats, producing coherent sound, singing, dancing and, most of all, having fun with classical music.

And what makes it such a great show is not how the show is presented by the artistic team, but the way children become such a central part of it.

> M.P. – Of course, when we started this was just a matter of belief – we were confident that this would work – and later on I could verify that it really works. For my Master's dissertation I had to produce a number of statistics that suggested that it worked. That the kids that had been in the programme were more responsive in the concerts in several fields: cognitive, musical, visual. There are a few companies, like Opera Domani that do similar work, preparing kids in the classroom and involving teachers – the difference is that they work only with known operas, Verdi, Mozart etc., and they centre the work on the arias… they centre their work on the performance, we moved away from the show and concentrated on the integration with the classroom. What needs to be understood is that for us, the work done on the stage is subservient to the work done in class, not the other way around.

Chapter Ten

Faustian Fears: *Dr. Atomic*, National Anxiety and J. Robert Oppenheimer

David Jortner

> We have had the bomb on our minds since 1945. It was first our weaponry and then our diplomacy, and now it's our economy. How can we suppose that something so monstrously powerful would not, after forty years, compose our identity? The great golem we have made against our enemies is our culture, our bomb culture – its logic, its faith, its vision.
> E.L. Doctorow

> Could we have started the atomic age/with clean hands?
> *Richard Paul Fink as Edward Teller in* Doctor Atomic

At the end of the first act of John Adams and Peter Sellars' opera *Doctor Atomic*, Gerald Finley, the actor playing J. Robert Oppenheimer, the nuclear scientist and ostensible title character, stands in front of a white sheet. Behind the sheet, casting an ominous shadow, the 'gadget', the first atomic bomb, hangs suspended in the air. Alone, Oppenheimer sings 'a poem of almost unbearable self-awareness, an agonistic struggle between good and evil, darkness and light'. (May, 2006b, p.224) Singing John Donne's Holy Sonnet XIV, Oppenheimer begs, 'Batter my heart, three personed God, for you/As yet but knock, breathe, shine and seek to mend;/That I may rise, and stand, o'erthrow me, and bend/Your force to break, blow, burn and make me new.' (Adams & Sellars, 2005b, p.19) Oppenheimer struggles with issues of ethics, science and his own actions and here we can see a moment of *anagnorisis* for the character – a recognition that the scientific knowledge he has created may have become too great for him to control.

The issue of science, ethics and social responsibility is not new to the stage, with historical figures as diverse as Galileo, Darwin, Heisenberg and Feynman serving as inspiration for theatrical presentation. In addition, the literary canon has seen notable archetypal scientists take on cultural lives of their own: certainly Drs Faustus, Frankenstein and Strangelove have all become a part of the American collective unconscious. *Doctor Atomic* takes part in this literary tradition as well, for it connects Oppenheimer with Faustus in numerous ways. Primarily – importantly – it uses the Faustian connection to explore issues of scientific ethics, inquiry and responsibility. While the opera is a political play in some respects, it is a political play about the limitations of knowledge, the ethics of action and the rejection of moral absolutism. *Doctor Atomic* positions the physicist as a synecdoche to connect Cold War fears of sudden annihilation to current concerns about terrorism, destruction and national ideologies in the post-Iraq, post-9/11 world.

The genesis of *Doctor Atomic* began in 2002 with conversations between composer John Adams and Pamela Rosenberg, the general director of the San Francisco Opera. Adams, in an interview with Thomas May, related that he 'didn't start work on the opera until January 2004... [and] finished the full score in June of 2005'. (May, 2006b, p.219) Peter Sellars, the noted theatre and opera director, provided the libretto as well as directing the production. The opera premiered on 1 October 2005 at the San Francisco Opera. This Adams and Sellars piece had great success from its opening and has subsequently been played in Chicago, New York, London and Amsterdam. The opera has also been shown on national television (TBS) and featured on national radio (NPR).

Creating historically based work was not a new endeavor for Adams. Perhaps best known for his 1987 opera *Nixon in China*, he has also written operas and music pieces about the hijacking of the cruise ship Achille Lauro (*The Death of Klinghoffer*, 1991), California earthquakes (*I was Looking at the Ceiling and then I Saw the Sky*, 1995) and 9/11 (*On the Transmigration of Souls*, 2002). Despite the assertions of several critics, Adams does not see his work as overtly 'political'. For instance, he has said 'I [do not] like it when people use the term "political" [in reference to me], as in "Mr. Adams is fond of political themes in his stage works". All life is political. Does one say the same thing about Mozart or Verdi, who wrote operas about the struggle of one person's will against another's?' (May, 2006b, p.229)

While Adams eschews being labeled as a 'political writer', his works are often intrinsically linked with historical events, lending them a political dimension regardless of his intention or desire. Examining Adams' work closely, one has to acknowledge that he is deeply interested in the political, exploring the intersections of personal figures within politically charged moments. Emulating Benjamin's *Angelus Novus*, he examines the actions of individuals caught in whirlwind of history. In fact, it may even be better to consider Adams as a composer deeply concerned with American history and identity. Critic Alan Rich gets close to this when he writes, 'The office of composer laureate does not yet exist; if it did, John Adams would be the hands down choice for occupant. In the quarter century since his works reached their first thunderstruck cheering audiences he has found within his soul the appropriate music for a swath of American history'. (Rich, 2006a, p.63)

Doctor Atomic certainly fits within this category of the personal–political drama. Like most of Adams' operas, the work is less narrative than impressionistic. The work begins with a chorus illustrating the hope and progression of science, as they say, 'All problems are believed/to have been solved/at least well enough/to make a bomb practicable'. (Adams & Sellars, 2005b, p.1) The scene then shifts to the lab at Los Alamos, as Oppenheimer, Teller and others struggle with the scientific, political and ethical conundrums of the 'Gadget'. The opera then has a scene of domesticity between Oppenheimer and Kitty, including a long aria where Oppenheimer expresses his love of his wife's hair. The final scene of the first act finds Oppenheimer and the scientists preparing for the Trinity test at Almagordo and the act ends with Oppenheimer singing an aria of John Donne's *Holy Sonnet XIV*. The second act is entirely focused on the night of the Trinity test; there are scenes between Kitty and her Native American maid, Pasqualita, as well as dance sequences and scenes of the anxiety of the men before the test. The final two scenes of the opera, entitled 'Countdown', follow the final minutes before the test. The opera ends with the cast silent and music counting down to the atomic explosion, signified musically by a low rumble and theatrically by a wash of green light across the stage. As the cast is bathed in this eerie green glow, Japanese voices echo in the theatre, asking for water, help and aid in finding loved ones.

Sellar's libretto was created mainly from primary and secondary sources. According to Adams they

> were dealing with information from all sorts of sources: firsthand accounts, memoirs, journalistic narratives, declassified government

> documents, and, in one case, a detailed description of the construction of the plutonium sphere I'd found on an Internet [sic] site, and which I'd set for a women's chorus. And then, of course, there was the poetry, verses that Oppenheimer, an immensely literate individual, loved: Baudelaire, Donne and the *Bhagavad Gita*.
> (May, 2006b, p.222)

From this source material Sellars composed the libretto by blending quotations and snippets of information from the above sources. The video documentary of the process of creating *Doctor Atomic*, entitled *Wonders Are Many*, actually shows Sellars cutting and pasting text together. This process caused Adams some concern. He said, 'I was worried by how this method of libretto creation would work... In an opera you need that personal interaction, clashes of will, strong emotions, anger, discord, love, hate... the last thing we would want was something historically accurate but emotionally frozen'. (Ibid., p.223) These apprehensions would prove unfounded: later in the interview Adams claimed that Sellars 'did a brilliant job of solving that challenge. I think the dialogue in *Doctor Atomic*, particularly in the first act, virtually crackles with the high energy of human interaction'. (Ibid.) According to Adams, then, the political discourses of the atomic bomb project were made into a personally affecting narrative. Despite his aversion to political theatre, Adams' work on *Doctor Atomic* shows his penchant for exploring the personal side of historical events – a task that could never be accomplished without delving into areas of politics.

Sellars and Adams' use of a scientist – in this case J. Robert Oppenheimer – who becomes wrapped up in a politically charged historical moment is not all that surprising. The stage has long employed scientists and scientific themes to examine sociopolitical issues. As dramatic characters, scientists allow playwrights to explore issues of genius, ethics, morality, knowledge and humanity. Kristin Shepherd-Barr, in her study *Science on Stage*, notes, 'There is something very appealing in the quest of the scientist; audiences are drawn to the lone crusader's neoromantic pursuit of truth, knowledge, and beauty'. (Shepherd-Barr, 2006, p.3) Science plays also allow us to confront and debate issues in our collective history. As Shepherd-Barr writes, 'So many science plays dramatise events that profoundly shaped our lives, from Galileo's discoveries and recantation to the race to develop the atomic bomb. They delve into the genesis of these events, as well as their repercussions, and the bridge to the difficult science is our common humanity and the need to understand our history'. (Ibid., pp.12–13) Shepherd-Barr suggests that 'Physics plays make up the bulk of science plays and one can understand why. The subject is innately dramatic; it entails conflict and controversy, the threat of mass destruction, and the possibility of vast unifying theories unlocking the "secrets of nature"'. (Ibid., p.61) Physicists, perhaps more so than other scientists, simultaneously engage and frighten audiences with the potential of their knowledge; we both desire and fear knowing the intimate secrets of the universe.

The popularity of the scientist as a dramatic and literary figure has led to the development of specific archetypal characters. In her work *From Faust to Strangelove: Representations of the Scientist in Western Literature*, Rosalynn Haynes identifies several archetypal scientist characters which appear and reappear in literature. Haynes proclaims that the study of the scientist in literature begins with the development of alchemy as a profession and as such the alchemist is the first of the scientific literary archetypes she explores. (Haynes, 1994, p.9) In the mind of the medieval European populace, the alchemist connected the unrestricted and secretive quest for knowledge with magical/supernatural abilities. The alchemist figure is, according to Haynes, 'Driven to pursue an arcane intellectual goal that carries a suggestion of ideological evil'. (Ibid., p.3) Despite this sense of 'evil', the primary icon of the alchemist is Doctor Faustus, a character who has 'attained the moral status of a tragic hero'. (Ibid., p.18) Haynes claims that Faust, despite his dealings with the Devil, 'may be seen as embodying the noblest desire of man to transcend the limitations of the human condition and to extend his powers, for good as much for evil, a Promethean figure who asserts the rights of man over a tyrannical order that seeks to enslave him'. (Ibid., p.19) What is fascinating to consider here is that, as a scientific archetype, Haynes (and others) are less interested in Faustus' metaphysical interactions – that is, his deal with the devil – choosing instead to see the archetype as one whose desire for knowledge is, while to some degree abstract, nonetheless thought of as for the good of humanity. While Faustus may demonstrate the Greek concept of hubris, Haynes' analysis suggests that audiences still respond positively to his quest for knowledge and an understanding of the universe.

Certainly, this idea is one of the keys to understanding audiences' longstanding relationship with Marlowe's protagonist, as well as the intertextual popularity of the character. Much like *Doctor Atomic* centuries later, Marlowe's play explores both political and personal discourses in the alchemist's quest for knowledge. Faustus, despite the deal he makes with

Mephistopheles, is not all evil, nor is his plight for knowledge malevolent. His construction, his impulse for greater understanding and control over the sociopolitical situation, is one to which many people can relate. Likewise, it is a situation in which many stage scientists find themselves. 'It is not difficult to see how much of the popular image of the scientist derives from the alchemist tradition' claims Haynes. (1994, p.22) She continues, 'The aspiration to know more than others about the causes of natural processes is inevitably associated with the desire for power over nature and hence with the attempts to manipulate or modify some aspect of nature for one's own convenience'. (Ibid.) Herein lies the dramatic seed found in so many other characters, including Adams and Sellars' Oppenheimer.

A brief examination of *Doctor Faustus* illustrates the Elizabethan concern with the nature of knowledge and scientific inquiry. Likewise, it demonstrates how this particular alchemist straddles the border between the political and personal, allowing him to function as a synecdoche for nationalist anxieties. Faust makes a deal with the devil. There is no doubt in that. Yet his fall from grace and/or what we might call legitimate, established or accepted scientific endeavors begins before he ever even meets Mephistopheles. He gives up law because he finds that it is filled with simple drudgery, and gives up divinity because he does not want to contemplate how all men are sinful and thus must 'die an everlasting death'. (Marlowe, 2005, p.46) Each of these books – areas of study – he discards one by one. What he turns to is magic: for, as he says, within 'lines, circles, scenes, letters, and characters… [exists] a world of profit and delight,/Of power, and honor, of omnipotence'. (Ibid., pp.51–3) He turns to this field despite the warnings of his friends, the good angel and even Mephistopheles. Faust's flaw – his fall from grace – is his desire to know more than is natural. His desire for extraordinary power, knowledge and scholarly fame is what drives him to destruction.

The original story of *Doctor Faustus* came from a German legend and, in the script, Faustus is German. Yet this character is tied to English subjects and English national anxieties as well. An Englishman wrote the script (Marlowe); a highly esteemed acting troop – the Admiral's Men – put on the play twenty-five times in only three years (1594–7); and one of the most revered English actors played the title character (Edward Alleyn). For a few decades England had been swept up (as was most of Europe) in a wave of new learning. The printing press was in its beginning stages and English subjects might have heard of this German advance. Progress was being made in astronomy by scientists such as Thomas Digges and Thomas

Harriot. William Gilbert was studying and publishing on magnetism and the world seemed to grow infinitely larger as Sir Frances Drake completed his circumnavigation of the globe. Some scientists even devoted themselves to the study of magic.

Yet not all areas of study were open to the legitimate scientist/subject. The Elizabethan court, for example, made a very clear delineation between black and white magic – or, as we might rephrase it today, between ethical and unethical science. While the Witchcraft Act of 1562 made all witchcraft illegal, several variations of so called 'good' or 'white' magic were still practised, albeit not as openly as before. These included visits to healers, who used medicinal herbs and such, and visits to the Court Astrologer in order to determine precipitous dates for events of national importance. In contrast, 'black' or 'dark' magic was seen as in league with the devil and one which transgressed both divine and human law.

Black magic had another negative connotation. It was heavily associated in Elizabethan England with Continental Europe. Riggs states, 'English scholars learned to operate demons from Continental books on Magic, from John Dee's *Preparatory Teachings* and *Hieroglyphic Monad* and works by the Italian immigrant Giordano Bruno, especially his *Expulsion of the Triumphant Beast*'. (Riggs, 2004, p.177) The connection between occultism and Continental (read predominantly Catholic) Europe created a sense of fear for the audiences watching *Doctor Faustus*. At the time of production, Queen Elizabeth was trying to maintain a sensitive balance between the Protestants and the Catholics in her nation. Despite her delicate treatment, Catholicism was looked on with greater scepticism every day. One can even see an anti-Catholic vein running through *Doctor Faustus*. When Mephistopheles first appears, for example, Faust tells him to 'return and change thy shape;/Thou art too ugly to attend on me. Go, and return an old Franciscan friar;/That holy shape becomes a devil best'. (Marlowe, 2005, pp.23–6) Later, too, Faust and Mephistopheles play tricks on the Pope and even physically assault him on stage. Despite Faust's performance of anti-Catholic gags and tricks, when he turns to black magic – when he stays in 'a Franciscan friar's company' and goes in league with him – in addition to selling his soul to the Devil, Faust may have been acting as a traitor to his nation.

The uncertainty of Faust's alliance may account for some of the key re-writes between the A and B texts of the play. Andrew Sofer notes, 'Both versions lurch between comedy and tragedy, with the B-text's additions accentuating slapstick, theatricality, and Protestant nationalism at the price of diluting the A-text's focus on Faust's psychology'. (Sofer, 2009, p.10) Sofer also notes David Bevington's assertions that the B text becomes more 'theatrical' compared to the A text's 'authorial' vision. For the purposes of this study, this shift from the authorial/psychological into the theatrical is seen as a move from the realm of the private into that of the public; issues of Faust's damnation are no longer the sole concern of the individual but rather have involved the metaphysical soul of the entire nation.

Faustian references and overtones pervade *Doctor Atomic*. Critic John Davidson writes 'Oppenheimer… is as sharply sketched a Faustian character as any in operatic literature'. (Davidson, 2006, p.380) Alan Rich cites Pamela Rosenberg, saying, 'Rosenberg speaks of the opera as the last she has produced in the shadow of the Faust legend' (Rich, 2006b, p.384) and Adams has claimed the title is in part an homage to Thomas Mann's *Doctor Faustus*. (Davidson, 2006, pp.225–6) Yet it is important to note which Faustus is aligned with the work. When Thomas May mentions the American adaptations of the metaphysical Faust myth, Adams critiques him, claiming 'I didn't want *Doctor Atomic* to be launched as an "American Faust"'. (Ibid., p.229) Speaking of the scientists, Adams states, 'I don't see a close analogy here. These physicists working overtime to build the bomb thought they were in a race to protect us from the Nazis… I don't see anything Faustian about that endeavor at all: I think it was a race to save civilization'. (Ibid., p.230)

It is important to note that Adams refers to the metaphysical Faust here as opposed to Haynes' Faustian archetypal scientist. Adams sees Oppenheimer not as one who makes a deal with the Devil but as one whose quest for knowledge leads, inexorably, to tragic endings. He states, 'You can also say – and this is an unknowable thing, but also human nature – that if the bomb had not been used by us then and there it inevitably would have been used by someone, if not by us, then by the Russians later on. It's just like one of those terrible Greek myths of self-discovery: the weapon is there, we built it, and somebody is going to use it just to see what it's like'. (Ibid., p.232) The connection to the 'Greek myths of self-destruction' links Adams' vision of Oppenheimer with the tragic overtones mentioned in Haynes' discussion of the Faust archetype. These tragic concerns deal less with metaphysical matters than with the intersection of the personal and the political; Oppenheimer's moral flaw is ambivalence as to the uses of his creation.

There is little doubt that Adams and Sellars are clearly utilising the alchemist/Faustus archetype in their construction of Oppenheimer. Immediately after the choral opening, Teller expresses moral concerns over the creation of the bomb saying, 'First of all, let me say/that I have no hope/of clearing my conscience./The things we are working on/are so terrible/that no amount of protesting/or fiddling with politics/will save our souls'. (Adams & Sellars, 2005b, p.2) Oppenheimer's response is a curt dismissal of the use of emotion. Quoting Baudelaire from *Les Spleen du Paris*, Oppenheimer says, 'The soul is a thing so impalpable/so often useless/and sometimes so embarrassing/that at this loss I felt/only a little more emotion/than if, during a walk,/I had lost my visiting card'. (Ibid.) Like the archetypical alchemist, Oppenheimer is seen as having no use for emotion; in his view, it appears to have no value other than to interfere with scientific, logical research. Like Faust, Oppenheimer wants only to further his knowledge, to reach his goal.

Oppenheimer also confronts those scientists who want to use their position to raise concerns about the risks of nuclear power. Oppenheimer tells the assembled scientists, 'I'd like to persuade you/not to have it./I feel that such a discussion in the lab/in the technical area,/is quite inconsistent with what/we talk about there. ...Isn't it better that I have/a voice within the government?' (Adams & Sellars, 2005b, p.6) Note how Sellars has Oppenheimer emphasise that 'the technical area', the laboratory, is not the place for moral discussion, thus further increasing his connection to the alchemist archetype.

The first act of the opera concludes with Oppenheimer standing in front of a shadow of the bomb as he sings an aria consisting of Donne's *Holy Sonnet XIV*. The historical Oppenheimer, of course, claimed he named the Almagordo test site 'Trinity' after the Donne poem. Adams and Sellars extend meaning to this gesture, connecting the poem with the loss of faith. The sonnet, with its invocation for God to enter the soul of the individual, also connects Oppenheimer's work with a lack of morality. The poem invites the divine to 'Batter my heart, three person'd God/That I may rise, and stand, o'erthrow me, and bend/Your force, to break, blow, break, blow, break, blow/burn and make new'. (Adams & Sellars, 2005b, p.19) The repetition of 'break, blow', which does not occur in Donne's work, connects the desire to be with God to the action of the bomb. In addition, Adams and Sellars have Oppenheimer sing the latter half of the sonnet, where he says 'But I am betroth'd to your enemy,/

Divorce me untie, or break that knot again/Take me to you'. (Ibid., p.20) Traditional readings of this sonnet connect 'betroth'd to your enemy' as an allegiance or connection with the devil; however, this could also been seen as Oppenheimer's privileging of science over divinity and of unrestrained research over ethical considerations. Essentially, Oppenheimer's scene at the end of this act, in front of 'the gadget' (one wonders if he is singing to the divine or to the bomb at times), allows Adams and Sellars to highlight the scientist's awareness of the dangerous areas his research has led to, as well as his inability to stop himself from continuing on that path.

J. Robert Oppenheimer's career was long, much longer than the opera would make it seem. Born of Jewish parents in New York in 1904, Oppenheimer was educated in the humanist tradition at the Ethical Culture Society School and attended Harvard in 1922. Graduating *summa cum laude* in Physics in only three years, Oppenheimer continued his education, studying theoretical physics with Max Born and receiving his PhD in 1926 from the University of Göttingen. Oppenheimer taught at both UC Berkeley and Caltech, commuting between both institutions in the 1930s. In 1940 he married Katherine 'Kitty' Harrison, a UC student known for her radical leftist political activities.

With America's entry into the Second World War, Oppenheimer became involved in the efforts to build an atomic bomb and was eventually asked by General Leslie Groves (in 1942) to oversee what became known as the Manhattan Project. Oppenheimer selected the site of Los Alamos, New Mexico and eventually worked with over 3,000 people developing a nuclear device. The first successful test of a nuclear bomb occurred in the New Mexico desert on 16 July 1945. The explosions in Hiroshima and Nagasaki occurred less than a month later.

After the war, Oppenheimer served as both the chairman of the Atomic Energy Committee (1947–52) and director of Princeton's Institute for Advanced Study. In addition, Oppenheimer became a leading anti-nuclear protester and was vociferous in his opposition to the development of the so called 'super', a hydrogen bomb. In 1953, at the height of the McCarthyism, Oppenheimer was stripped of his security clearance for his alleged communist sympathies in what was seen as an overtly political decision. He retired from Princeton in 1966 and died of throat cancer in 1967.

Doctor Atomic, unlike other biographical dramas about Oppenheimer, depicts only the time when he was involved with the Manhattan Project. In fact, one could argue that it shows even less than that, for the majority of the play focuses on the day of the bomb test. Snippets of time from before the test are hinted at in Act One, but the entirety of Act Two takes place on the one day – the day of the test. *Doctor Atomic*, in other words, highlights only two days in Oppenheimer's long career. Adams and Sellars' choice to focus on this brief time period reinforces the Faustian construction of Oppenheimer. Most biographical work about Oppenheimer focuses on two areas: the creation of the bomb and the removal of his security clearance in 1953 for his opposition to the hydrogen bomb. According to the record of the San Francisco Opera, originally the opera was to include a greater sense of his life, but it was cut on 1 September 2003. The Opera's website states, 'The scope of the opera has dramatically changed and the timeframe telescoped. Decisions have been made not to include the development of the hydrogen bomb or the confrontation between Teller and Oppenheimer in the 1950s'. (San Francisco Opera website) The 1953 security clearance hearing was widely regarded as a political witch hunt; Oppenheimer himself called the affair 'a farce'. (*Time*, 1964, p.70) However, in terms of audience reception, any deviation into an examination of the security treaty affair moves Oppenheimer from the alchemist/Faustian archetype into a more traditional, heroic mode. Therefore, the decision of Sellars et al. to excise the material in many ways forces the audience to see Oppenheimer in his Faustian construction.

Surprisingly, in the past ten years there has been an enormous growth of interest in Oppenheimer's biography and the events of his life. Several major new biographies have been written, including Bird and Sherman's *American Prometheus: The Triumph and Tragedy of J. Robert Oppenheimer* (2005), David Cassidy's *J. Robert Oppenheimer and the American Century* (2004), Priscilla McMillan's *The Ruin of J. Robert Oppenheimer and the Birth of the Modern Arms Race* (2005), Jennet Conant's *109 East Palace: Robert Oppenheimer and the Secret City of Los Alamos* (2006), *Oppenheimer: Portrait of an Enigma* by Jeremy Bernstein (2005), Charles Thorpe's *Oppenheimer; The Tragic Intellect* (2006), Pais and Crease's *J. Robert Oppenheimer: A Life* (2007) and Gregg Herken's *Brotherhood of the Bomb: The Tangled Lives and Loyalties of Robert Oppenheimer, Ernest Lawrence and Edward Teller* (2003).

Moreover, a statistically large number of plays featured Oppenheimer in the 2000s. *Doctor Atomic*, of course, came out in 2005. Carson Kreitzer's *Love Song of J. Robert Oppenheimer* premiered in 2003 at the Cincinnati Playhouse in the Park and the International WOW Company's *The Bomb* emerged in 2002. Thus, there appears to be a historicist question. If Adams and Sellars wanted to write a play about scientists going to extremes there are any number of possible candidates for a biographical opera: even Edward Teller, for example, who continued to advocate nuclear weaponry and was the designer of the hydrogen bomb, would have been a more appropriate candidate. This growth in interest, both biographical and theatrical, can be understood through the connections between national anxieties and fears during the height of the Cold War and in the present post-9/11 American landscape. Oppenheimer – because of his unique biography and presence within the American national memory – presents Adams and Sellars with an excellent figure to explore the ambiguity and confusion surrounding the 11 September 2001 attacks and the invasion of Iraq by the United States in March 2003.

The early 2000s were filled with national anxiety. A war unlike any other was waged on U.S. soil on 11 September 2001 and the resulting Iraq War made many Americans worry about their personal and national safety. Haynes Johnson, in *The Age of Anxiety: McCarthyism to Terrorism*, states that the attacks of 11 September 'shattered the nation's sense of invulnerability, initiated a global war on terrorism and spawned a wave of apprehension and fear'. (Johnson, 2005, p.xi) Numerous cultural critics have made the connections between the attacks of 11 September 2001 and the atomic anxieties of the Cold War. Una Chaudhuri, in a special issue of the *Theatre Journal* on tragedy put out in the wake of the 9/11 attacks, claimed 'September 11th thrust us back into that Cold War imagination'. (Chaudhuri, 2002, p.98) The ideas of the Cold War – preparedness, watch lists, subversive activities, un-Americanism and civil defence – have now become once again become a part of the American lexicon. As a result, classic Cold War anxieties of destruction and annihilation have also recurred.

The Cold War fear of annihilation, as well as its connection with 9/11, is perhaps best seen in testimony by sociologist Robert Jay Lifton at the United States' House of Representatives in 1983:

> The fact that we die is one of the difficult lessons of early childhood. The capacity to learn that lesson, which we all succeed at only imperfectly, depends upon death having some appropriateness: the idea that one dies after a good deal of living; that old people die rather than young ones. But now death has become associated with massive, grotesque extermination that consumes the young, as well as the old, those who have not yet

lived their lives, as well as those who have. Inevitable individual
death becomes confused with unacceptable meaningless
annihilation.

(Lifton & Humphrey, 1984, p.91)

Lifton's description of 'unacceptable meaningless annihilation', whilst referring to nuclear war in 1983, could just as easily apply to fears of terrorism in the post-9/11 landscape. The fears Americans felt during the Cold War are connected to similar anxieties after the 11 September attacks: one could die a meaningless death with numerous unlucky others who happened to be in the same time and place.

This type of fear leads to a desire for preparedness. This move was seen in the 1960s 'duck and cover' bomb drills as well as in the current environment. Tracy Davis notes the connection in her work *States of Emergency: Cold War Nuclear Civil Defense*:

> During the Cold War, citizens' perception that the effects of
> nuclear bombing could be mitigated led to judicious preparation
> and coordinated campaigns of rehearsal. We now execute our part
> in the new protocols of defense – presenting laptop computers
> for scanning at airport security, passing through metal detectors
> in federal buildings, and scrutinizing our neighbors' behavior in
> response to the latest warnings of terrorism – and thus provide
> continuity with Cold War practices. No longer merely an arcane
> by-product of the Cold War... civil defense is resurrected as
> homeland security.

(Davis, 2007, p.1)

The connection between the Cold War and the post-9/11 landscape is not limited to the national security sphere: as in the Cold War, there is a concern with fifth-column subversives. Johnson notes:

> During the McCarthy era, the profiling of people perceived as
> national security threats became commonplace. Then, suspected
> communists were profiled – artists, Jewish scientists and intellectuals,
> and foreigners – and subjected to imprisonment or blacklisting.
> Today, another type – Muslim males – has been subjected to
> profiling, resulting in massive detention 'sweeps' eerily similar to the
> dragnet arrests that grew out of the Great Red Scare hysteria.

(Johnson, 2005, p.467)

Johnson and Davis present excellent examples of the re-emergence of Cold War actions under the post 9/11 paradigm. Anxieties spawned by 9/11 and national responses to the attack (among them the Iraq War) resound with imagery, reactions and impulses similar to those seen during the Cold War.

Theatre has responded to these renewed Cold War anxieties. Numerous works have addressed the events of 9/11, both directly and obliquely. Andrea Nouryeh, in her article 'Reflections in a Pool: Mary Zimmerman's *Metamorphosis* and Post-9/11 New York City', claims that postmodern artists 'look to the past for icons and stories that they copy and reinvent for contemporary purposes' in order to try to bring healing to the audience/nation. (Nouryeh, 2007, pp.267–8) Finally, then, it is important to look at *Doctor Atomic* to see how Adams and Sellars use the Faustian construction of Oppenheimer to address the difficulty of action when confronted by events such as 9/11 and the Iraq invasion of 2003.

When asked about creating an opera about Oppenheimer, Sellars made the following remarks:

> This [The Second World War] was a human struggle which is almost unimaginable in our very comfortable time. While even most of the world is at war right now we do this very comfortably, pushing buttons, calling in airstrikes, creating a kind of war that has been automated. That war was prepared by the firebombing of Japan... that was the first time that a kind of computer printout of destruction with arches and parabolas was prepared by young Robert McNamara who eventually perfected creating war as a giant mathematical equation for Vietnam.
>
> (Sellars, 2005)

This sense of war as a science, of science in league with the military, is in many ways the subject of *Doctor Atomic*. Sellars and Adams at one point have General Groves, played by Eric Owen, threaten a meteorologist, saying, 'The test will proceed as scheduled/with full weather compliance/or you will spend the rest of your life behind bars/Mister Meteorologist!' (Adams & Sellars, 2005b, p.14) General Groves believes that he can actually change the laws of nature. He believes that nature must bend to the will of science. Here he too is like Oppenheimer. He will not relent in his pursuit. He will even put an innocent man in jail in order to test the bomb.

Examples such as this demonstrate the dangers and fears of the Faustian archetype. As the soldiers and scientists prepare for the detonation, Nolan warns General Groves that fallout could hit and affect everyone at Los Alamos. While they debate feverishly, Oppenheimer sings the following lines from the *Bhagavad Gita*: 'A serene spirit accepts pleasure and pain/ with an even mind,/and is unmoved by either./He alone is worthy of immortality'. (Ibid., p.17) Oppenheimer, at this point in the opera, is now willing to forsake all for the greater gain of knowledge and, by extension, immortality, again echoing Marlowe's alchemist.

In discussing the search for 'absolutes' whether in science or in warfare, Sellars states, 'The strange thing of course is that we didn't exactly win the war in Japan, because of the bomb, in a way that felt good, felt right, and the subsequent history of America's firepower in Korea, Vietnam, Cuba, El Salvador and Nicaragua, right now in Iraq and Afghanistan strangely fails to win a war. This sense that you're invincible is not a good way to live, to be, to imagine yourself'. (Sellars, 2005) Adams and Sellars allow the audience to witness the effects of this sense of invincibility in the final moments of the opera: the haunting green light and Japanese voices crying for water serve as an indictment of the results of Oppenheimer's quest for knowledge.

In the great tragic Faustian tradition, though, Sellars clearly has some empathy with his hero:

> One of the things that I think operates in all of our lives is that we're living in a time of enormous historical forces which no one individual can really oppose and I think a lot of the operas in opera history are about this sense, this atmosphere of an historical moment. Robert Oppenheimer could have at a certain point said I resign from this atomic bomb project but he would not have collected a paycheck and the project would have continued. I mean there is something so large that it could not be stopped and it's very much what we feel as American right now watching our country in a kind of historical momentum with very profound self-destructive elements as well.
>
> (Sellars, 2005)

Oppenheimer is, for Adams and Sellars, a perfect synecdoche for the nation: in an ambitious drive for knowledge he has unleashed forces with their own momentum and he now is helpless before his own invention. In the same way, Sellars seems to say, Americans still reeling from the violence of the 9/11 attacks find themselves confused as they watch their nation invade Iraq, unsure of what actions can or should be taken. *Doctor Atomic*, then, at least allows the audience to act by bearing witness and completing the story in their own minds, bringing themselves from the dawn of the atomic age to the present day.

Adams' operas often engage in dialogue between the individual and history; doing so allows him to explore different elements of national identity. Writing an opera about Oppenheimer allowed him to explore issues of the scientific ethics, discovery and responsibility. By constructing Oppenheimer as a Faustian figure, he and Sellars are able to connect with the audience's knowledge of the scientific archetype; moreover, this specific archetype has clear historical connections to issues of national identity. Finally, by going back to the father of the atom bomb and the birth of the atomic age, Adams and Sellars have created Oppenheimer as a synecdoche for American post-Iraq, post-9/11 fears of sudden death, destruction and the direction and ideology of the nation. In *Doctor Atomic*, the audience can both witness and empathise with Oppenheimer, admiring the Faustian desire for knowledge while simultaneously condemning and bearing witness to the results of that desire.

Works Cited

Adams, J. & P. Sellars (2005a) *Doctor Atomic* (video recording), Amsterdam, De Nederlandse Opera

Adams, J. & P. Sellars (2005b) *Doctor Atomic: Libretto Drawn from Original Sources*, Hendon Music, [PDF file online] available at: http://www.metoperafamily.org/metupload/DoctorAtomic_libretto.pdf

Chaudhuri, U. (2002) 'Forum on Tragedy', *Theatre Journal*, vol. 54, no. 1, pp.97–9

Davidson, J. (2006) 'History's Unholy Trinity' in *The John Adams Reader*, ed. T. May, Pompton Plains, NJ: Amadeus Press

Davis, T. (2007) *States of Emergency: Cold War Nuclear Civil Defense*, Durham, NC: Duke University Press

Haynes, R. (1994) *From Faust to Strangelove: Representations of the Scientist in Western Literature*, Baltimore, MD: Johns Hopkins University Press

Johnson, H. (2005) *The Age of Anxiety: McCarthyism to Terrorism*, Orlando, FL: Harcourt

Lifton, R. J. & N. Humphrey (eds) (1984) *In a Dark Time*, Cambridge, MA: Harvard University Press

Marlowe, C. (2005) *Doctor Faustus*, ed. David Scott Kastan, New York, NY: W.W. Norton and Company

May, T. (ed.) (2006a) *The John Adams Reader*, Pompton Plains, NJ: Amadeus Press

May, T. (2006b) 'John Adams on *Doctor Atomic*: Interview by Thomas May' in *The John Adams Reader*, ed. T. May, Pompton Plains, NJ: Amadeus Press

Nouryeh, A. (2007) 'Reflections in a pool: Mary Zimmerman's *Metamorphosis* and Post-9/11 New York City' in *Interrogating America through Theatre and Performance*, eds W. DeMastes & I. Smith Fischer, New York, NY: Palgrave McMillan

Rich, A. (2006a) 'Learning to Love the Bomb' in *The John Adams Reader*, ed. T. May, Pompton Plains, NJ: Amadeus Press

Rich, A. (2006b) 'Life as Music: John Adams goes Public' in *The John Adams Reader*, ed. T. May, Pompton Plains, NJ: Amadeus Press

Riggs, D. (2004) *The World of Christopher Marlowe*, New York, NY: Henry Holt

San Francisco Opera, *Doctor Atomic* website, available at http://www.doctoratomic.com

Sellars, P. (2005) 'Interview', *Doctor Atomic* (videorecording), Amsterdam, De Nederlandse Opera

Shepherd-Barr, K. (2006) *Science on Stage: From Doctor Faustus to Copenhagen*, Princeton, NJ: Princeton University Press

Sofer, A. (2009) 'How to Do Things with Demons: Conjuring Performatives in *Doctor Faustus*', *Theatre Journal*, vol. 61, no. 1, pp.1–21

Time (1964) 'Theater Abroad: the Character Speaks Out', *Time*, 20 November 1964, 70

Wonders are Many: The Making of Doctor Atomic (videorecording) (2007) Docudrama films

CHAPTER ELEVEN

Odalan Bali: An Offering of Music and Dance by Gamelan Çudamani

KATHY FOLEY

This chapter considers the work of the Balinese performance group Gamelan Çudamani [Sanskrit 'crest Jewel'*], led by founding director I Dewa Putu Berata, associate artistic director Emiko Saraswati Susilo and choreographer I Nyoman Cerita, with specific emphasis on *Odalan Bali: An Offering of Music and Dance* (2005–9). This presentation theatricalises a temple anniversary, held every 210 days and helping cement Balinese religious and social structure via group participation in the community performance event. As the programme notes, a festival aims to create 'harmony and balance between the three worlds: the divine, the human, the natural'.† (Çudamani, 2007, p.7) To discuss how Çudamani prepares a major performance, I will reference *Bamboo to Bronze* (2010) rehearsals to show how this top *sanggar* (group) of internationally savvy artists constructs contemporary Balinese performance for diverse viewers. Audiences include local Balinese, either in the group's home village of Pengosekan in the Ubud area, or at the island-wide Bali events; pan-Indonesian audiences from across the archipelago present; international viewers such as the group at the University of California Davis on 17 November 2007; and the inhabitants of the three worlds (natural, human, divine) which the piece both addresses and reflects.

---

*   'Çudamani' is related to seeing through illusion and achieving divine potential.
†   The cosmos is made of *tri hita karana* (three worlds). On temple festivals, see Belo (1966) and Dibia (1985).

Çudamani's work relates to performance as *ngayah* (offering, devotion) and the stated intention of the creators is to contribute performance as spiritual and social practice in their village.* However, the piece is also created for international viewers who operate in a secular system, with minimal understanding of Bali. For example, a *legong* (traditional female dance by small girls) traditionally would have run considerably longer than this one and, of course, a real temple festival evolves over leisurely hours and days with important moments dictated by the readiness of the priest to perform ritual actions. Periods of intense performance are spelled by lulls; events are not always sequential, but overlap; and audience members are not spatially divorced from playing spaces, but move around and through one performance to access another occurring at the same time. While some sections of a festival do attract relatively focused audiences, others seem to run along with no particular viewership, and the performers of one presentation are peripheral viewers of another taking place simultaneously. The whole event is multitudinous, where no one viewer can, or is meant to absorb the whole. In contrast of course, the American audience at Davis expected separation of dances, sequential ordering, predictable intermissions and clear signals about what to look at when. Balinese audiences often prefer the atmosphere to be *ramai* – full of action, sound, movement and people. Western audiences in contrast may often value what to a Balinese would be rather *sepi* (empty, cool). Therefore, in addition to Çudamani's local vision in constructing a performance, it has a global outlook – different viewers, literally and philosophically.

After discussing the performance and the troupe, I will consider the 1930 Paris Colonial Exposition ensemble from Peliatan, Ubud, Gianyar which was influenced by German artist–impresario Walter Spies and which enthused Antonin Artaud (Artaud, 1976; Savarese, 1997 and 2001) as a conceptual 'ancestor' to *Odalan Bali*. But Çudamani represents another step away from colonial models of interchange between Bali and the West which have had important cross-cultural impact in the last century. Contextualising *Odalan Bali* illuminates both the individual performance and on-going trans-global flows.

---

* 'Çudamani maintains that the vitality of Balinese arts relies on the connection of performance to the religious and social life of the village'. (Çudamani, 2009)

The Performance

This piece of theatre is simple yet infinitely self-reflexive: it is 'a performance about a performance that includes performance'.* (Vitale, 2007) The narrative is simple and the piece uses movement, mime, lighting and juxtapositions of groups or representative types rather than focusing on specific characters or language (mantras, sung verses and the casual conversations of performers are not translated).

While spoken formulas may be significant religiously or emotively to a Balinese, interpretations of words would not really give deep insight to the international viewer. Most Balinese will only dimly understand the Kawi (Old Javanese) formulas or *kidung* verses in Middle Javanese, which are voiced in a Balinese festival context. These languages, which are used to communicate with the ancestral, are obscure to most of the living. One reviewer, Allan Ulrich (2005) complained: 'This realist will note that much of this presentation was given in a language very few of us comprehend (and no supertitles were provided).' But another embraced the non-comprehension, recalling his Catholic childhood, where he heard Latin, which he did not yet know. (Parish, 2005)

Earlier international tours, such as the 1930 or 1952 Peliatan groups, might borrow Balinese dances presented as part of temple celebrations and move them out of the ritual context for sharing as entertainment on a proscenium stage. By contrast, in *Odalan Bali* artists use dance theatre conventions to revision the sacred; placing pieces where they might sit in temple events, but adopting atmospheric lighting, and ordering scenes from the natural to the human, to the entertaining. These 'scenes' are set chronologically moving from dawn to night, as the performers translated the rhythms and reciprocities of an *odalan* within a village context. Forms that in earlier Balinese touring shows would be recast as secular entertainment were here reinscribed in performative frames which allude to ritual origins.

---

* Wayne Vitale: 'The music, movement, conception, and execution are on such a high level, as to be almost indescribable… Any thirty seconds of the piece… would provide material for several Ph.D. theses… One of the most perfect performances I've ever seen.' Vitale's one criticism was the need for an audience. 'To *ngayah* in an *odalan* is one of the few iterations of heaven on earth. I mean that literally: We play and dance as direct affirmation and offering to the divine with no need for audience or applause and with one musician sliding in mid-piece without a break to replace another'. (Vitale, 2007)

Viewers are embedded in an *odalan*, Pengosekan-style, a presentation which was generated in consultation with temple officials and their imprimatur for international tour. (Mitoma, 2011)

While details remain obscure to those not versed in Balinese culture and though the particulars of the festival are representative of only this one village, this method allows Western viewers access to a Balinese temple festival's larger patterns. Debra Jowitt of *Village Voice* wrote: 'Not many New York dance performances begin with the sound of frogs, stray birdcalls, and the swish of grass brooms against the floor... [But] the piece's artful combination of naturalism and stylization works magically from the outset'. (Jowitt, 2007) Paul Parish, who compared the Kawi [Old Javanese] to Catholic Latin, found the performance reached him at a visceral level: 'I realized it had gently gotten under my skin in haunting ways and that I was experiencing something much deeper than entertainment or cross-cultural exchange... I had an experience resembling Proust's with the Madeleine... Except that these rituals were not those of MY childhood, and yet they were essentially so much the same... For whatever reasons you may bring to Çudamani yourself, the appeal of the show is going to be universal'. (Parish, 2005)

The lighting by Eileen Cooley goes slowly from black to the dawn's early light.[*] These sounds prefigure the gamelan's gong chimes, melding diverse patterns played by individual musicians into an interlocking melody on a set of bronze instruments. The group use a Semarandana[†] gamelan, an ensemble created in the 1980s with seven tones as opposed to the normative five, which allows inclusion of tunes from older repertoires. (Çudamani, 2007, p.9) The chorus transports listeners toward a Balinese village locale, where amphibians sing nightly in the *sawah* (rice fields). These natural interlocks prepare listeners for the music to come. By starting with the animal world sonically, the group focuses attention on a worldview where nature, human and superhuman are believed to intertwine and 'fit together' in related patterns.

A woman (Emiko Susilo) emerges to sweep and put out offerings. The *kukul* (slit drum) invites the village to rise. Triangular-shaped headdresses of the male *baris* (warrior) dancers, adorned with mother of pearl shells (*cukli*), are now visible centre stage, giving the first half of the programme a

---

* Soundscape by Wayne Vitale of San Francisco's Gamelan Sekar Jaya.
† Named after BhataraSemara, the god of love.

stronger 'male' focus. In 'Mebat: Preparing Offerings' women prepare palm fronds and pound rice for the festival while men cut and dice, as if preparing the meat offerings for lower spirits. The sounds start randomly, quickly moving to an ostinato. Now we are in the realm of humans preparing for a service. The males and females, in gender specific yet reciprocal work, create the mesh that is needed for the success of the festival.

Rice pounding is anachronistic in contemporary Indonesian villages, where new strains of rice and modern technology have replaced the old rice-pounding block (*lesung*). Rice pounding has always carried some sexual overtones with its phallic rod and the waiting opening, and the music associated with this activity remains an important source of traditional village poetry and playfulness throughout Southeast Asia.*

As the females and males sing, the Balinese idea of gender interdependence which understruts this programme is introduced: the female side is allocated the more *manis* (refined) tasks, while males take on all things *keras* (coarse, strong). The women deal here with Dewi Sri the goddess of rice making up offerings to gods, meanwhile men's chopping references the meat offerings for *bhuta kala* (demons) from the lower world. A Balinese festival is an environment where the demonic and the divine hunger for human attention and each gets its due. Demonic needs are also met by men dancing *Baris Gede* ('large warrior/line dance')† in a piece called *Mecaru: Appeasing the Playful Earth Spirits* while the women move around the perimeter sprinkling holy water. Given the gender imbalance in the troupe (twenty-two men and six women), the male voices predominate here. Indeed, male energy prevails through the first half of the programme. But after the intermission, females become featured dancers whose movement is offered as devotion to the world of the gods.

Rwa bhinneda, the 'two in one' idea, here represented in its gender dynamics, runs through all Balinese and much of Southeast Asian thinking. The world is full of pairs: male–female, day–night, life–death, black–white, mountain–sea, demon–divine, etc. Two together make up perfection – the oneness that sits behind in the unmanifest world from which all these

---

* Rice pounding songs, where male and female voices alternate, are traditionally part of village courtship.

† 'Baris Gede' is danced during rituals. Dibia and Ballinger note: 'It probably originated as a symbol of soldiers protecting the king in his palace'. (2004, p.80)

dualities emerge. Two-ness leads us toward the unitary source and festivals are a time when we can see the pairings clearly.

The action on stage is never identical to actual ritual, but the choices are inventively allusive. The interlocking vocal chant associated with *kecak* ('monkey chant') brings in the *baris* warriors – four men who play hand-held slit drums as they dance full of male power and protection, wearing the headdresses which have waited centre stage. Next *wayang* shadow figures, the clown (Twalen) and *pandita* (hermit), reference a puppet show, a mandatory part of a festival. The clanging of the *balaganjur* ('to excite an army') marching gamelan brings the first half to a climax. This ensemble is sometimes called *gamelan kalaganjur* ('to excite demons') and it pounds fast and furious. One easily believes that all in the worlds above and below can hear, since no one in this world can miss it! The first half is full of images that are 'male', 'lower world' and 'demonic'. Hence, they are fun, loud, and dramatic. Foreigners, who, like demons, tend to think in straight lines, are able to 'get it' with the lightning fast playing, electrifying rhythms and transparent theatricality.*

As the second half begins, the soundscape has changed to the inner temple. The female headdresses (*susuhunan*) of *legong's* replace the male headpieces, signalling refinement. The head as the top of the body is sacred. Headdresses of the young female dancers who, in *sanghyang dedari* (the antecedent of *legong*), go into trance are considered potent in helping the divine descend into the world. The *barong*, the mythical lion, is also onstage. This figure is probably a Buddhist remnant in Balinese culture and connotes divine protection. The beneficent mask is trotted out during the Balinese New Year (*Nyepi-Galungan*) in a way analogous to lions featured in the Chinese and Japanese New Year celebrations. But if Bali's *barong* began as a Buddhist icon, he has become fully indigenised over the centuries. The mask, when blessed by appropriate vigils, is the repository of important powers which protect the village. *Barong* represents the Forest Spirit (Banaspati Raja): a symbol of the afterbirth, the oldest and strongest of four spirit siblings (water, blood, umbilicus, afterbirth) which accompany each human at birth and guard through life. (Mershon, 1971, pp.55–9) Both the *legong* headdresses and the *barong* let the viewer know this second

---

*   Demons think/move in straight lines, so their music and dances are relatively simple. Balinese temple gates demand a curvilinear path, so the demonic cannot enter.

part of the programme will deal with things divine. The next musical piece 'Çudamani' reinforces the protective feeling with mantras, a priest's bell (*genta*), narrative chanting (*kidung*), slit drum and gamelan: sounds evoke a temple ceremony with its full aural overload. But what in a real ceremony would be disordered chaos is transformed. Sounds are layered so one need not be a Brahma with four heads and eight ears to hear the whole.

A woman's-style dance (*rerejangan*) is performed.* This type of group sacred dance offering is done by local women at a temple festival and is believed to represent the descent of *bidadari* (goddesses). (Dibia and Ballinger, 2004, p.56) The slow dance, with deep plies and flowing arms, is the counterbalance for *baris*, with raised male legs and strong angles. The choreography moves us from subduing nature and lower forces toward the ethereal. 'Tajen' however comes first: a music-mime that captures the essence of a Balinese cockfight, where status, manhood and village rivalries are played out in the confrontation of two birds. (Geertz, 1973) *Kecak* vocal interlocks of the males placing bets and the clash of the *balaganjur* orchestra make for the excitement of a Balinese cockpit. The hands of betting men stretch in full diagonals extending from feet to the tips of fingers. The overwhelming energy of the two groups pours forth in opposing waves of excitement, pounding against one other as they follow the fight. Though there are no birds and the division in the village is merely who appears to be betting against whom, the vocal and visual interlocks of the groups makes sides and stakes more visible than a real cockfight, which is included in temple festival to insure the *bhuta kala* demons get their shot of blood.

Now the performance is ready to soar: 'Legong Gering' is an aesthetization of a *sanghyang* trance dance of little girls.† Two of the adolescent female dancers (Ni Wayan Febri Lestari and Gusti Ayu Suryani) donned the *legong* headdresses as the lightning fast *gamelan kebyar* ('sun burst of flames') took off. Sounds of flutes from *gambuh*, traditional court music, infused something old. Priest bells sounded to let the *wali* (sacred) begin: the music sounded old but the combination was new.

---

*   Susilo writes, 'It is not a "real" *rejang*, but "in the style"… We specifically did not use "sacred" *rejang* dances and prefer to save those for the gods: Pak Cerita created a piece that is so close in spirit that… we have used it in temple ceremonies… [so] though created for the secular world, is now sometimes performed for the divine'. (Susilo, 2011)

†   Dibia and Ballinger (2004, p.76) and Bandem and deBoer (1995, pp.70–1) discuss *legong* and *sanghyang*.

> In the right angles of arms extended from the torso, elbow arching down from the upper arm, hands bent back at the wrist, and in the moves from a now full-frontal position to a precise ninety degree turn to the side, each body seemed a conductor of energy that came from outside the actual young women. Suddenly the music stopped and the dancers continue moving in unison to perfect silence.
>
> Like the gap between inspiration and expiration, the moment melded perfect stillness with frenetic movement – a visualization of how the divine (silent and unseen) and the manifest (moving and material) are juxtaposed in the same instant. This is course what the whole performance was about – how that which is 'in' time [*kala*, the demonic] and that which is 'out' of time [*niskala*, the divine] exist at the same time. Cooperation and small adjustments of each participant [using the methodology of art] …can nudge the cacophony of sounds into its interlock [music]. Mundane movements, through the use of dance, can be superimposed on and reveal the cosmic, still, constant.
>
> (Foley, 2008, p.377)*

The next number was drawn from the secular repertoire, 'Truna Gandrung' (Young Male in Love, danced by the female Dewa Ayu Eka Putri). This sexually ambiguous dance is *bebancihan* (cross-gender, androgynous), a genre of the secular *kebyar* repertoire.† The preference for cross-dressed dancers – whether it be a male playing the Rangda or a female playing a refined male role as in this dance – is a pan-Indonesian tendency,

---

*   Trance is a significant feature of Balinese dance. (See Belo, 1960) While I found this piece breathtaking, a major dancer expressed ambivalence: 'I feel sad to see them presenting whatever people want to do. What are they doing? But I just kept talking. Accepting it, saying, "This is creativity meant to present something new".' The anonymous interviewee noted the dance was not 'sacred', but followed a recognizable sequence. For debates on sacred dance and divisions into sacred (*wali*), *bebali* (semi- ritual), and *bali-balihan* (secular) see Dibia and Ballinger (2004, p.10).

†   Males historically performed these dances and the refined character is male, but women usually present now. While part of a *tari lepas* (secular solo dance) repertoire – *kebyar* dances often enter temple ceremonies since they involve top artists. This particular dance was based on the style of I Gede Manik about 1952 with music by I Wayan Gandera of Peliatan.

relating to finding more power in the 'both–and'-ness of things rather than in the bifurcation that gender imposes. The female–male (or male–female) is a point of power, because she–he has both genders, a resolution of duality into ideal oneness.

This dance also shows the correlation of movement and music that is part of the genre. As ethnomusicologist Colin McPhee notes of Balinese dance technique:

> The rhythm of the body, the halting of the hands, even the last movement of the eyes – all coincide to the last fraction of a second with the syncopated accents of the music. The dancer *is* the music made visible… [Dance] fits the music like a glove.
> (McPhee, 1991, p.125)

The superb musicianship and arrivals of hand–head–body together on the gong note made sound sensible.

The final dance was the *barong*, a representation of Siwa as protector. The *barong* is nature but in the divine form of Banaspati Raja. The head manipulator in this two-man body puppet used the jaw as percussive instrument, playing complex patterns, leading and echoing the main drum's position as ensemble conductor. The mythical animal was *dalang* (puppetmaster) for this number.* As the childlike *barong* danced over the stage, the complex mirror work, inset in the unruly whitish hair of the majestic figure, created shafts of light that irradiated the theatre. The *barong* guarantees protection from all that is dark and ungovernable. In the beams that shone on each who watched, viewers were made safe – even perhaps for the next 210 days.

In this complex, intricate and carefully theorised performance, the parts of the cosmos (day–night, male–female, demon–divine, etc.) were given their moment on the stage; then all vanished as the headdresses, *barong*, and energies were packed away.

> This performance was not an *odalan*, not a ritual. But it playfully gave us insight into the essence of a temple festival. The female and the male trade off… to get the work done. There are places you give up your own autonomy to fit in with the group. You wait for a pause in the music or until you are wearing the right mask or

---

* The shadow puppeteer similarly uses a wooden knocker to lead music.

costume to be featured and let your own voice be fully tapped. But something profound is gained by this sub-structural coordination. As the male and female *pedana* (priests) cover the *barong* to allow the audience to return to the everyday, viewers left the auditorium. Three quarters of the audience probably did not understand what hit them. Was that boy or a girl who danced?... Why didn't the creators, as an American might, show us the birds fighting or the temple itself? But people were moved, without necessarily knowing why... The real audience of the work were the performers who used the excuse of the performance to pull apart a well-known event, a temple festival, and put it back together in a way that is new.

(Foley, 2008, pp.378–9)

The Troupe

Çudamani was founded in 1997 in Pengosakan on the outskirts of Ubud, Gianyar district, an area of Bali which, due to the important political/cultural courts of the past, has a legacy of performance that gives it an edge in the on-going politics of Balinese arts. The website of the Çudamani details particularly a history of growing touristic performance as a threat to local heritage:

> By the '90s most of the musicians of Ubud were playing for tourists in lieu of the needs of the community, and members were hired and fired depending on their technical ability. The youth of Pengosekan often found themselves working in this system – experiencing the financial benefits of tourism while also being keenly aware of the artistic and cultural dangers of this 'professional' arrangement...
>
> The group sees itself as an activist community that responds to the philosophical, practical and problematic issues that face Balinese artists today.
>
> (Çudamani, 2009)

The aim is:

> Not for financial profit or individual gain, the group sets the highest artistic standards in the service of the temple and the community. Members of Çudamani work to achieve a balance of being active creative artists while also preserving ancient and rare

forms of Balinese music and dance. The group invites older master artists to Pengosekan [to teach, and members] ...also compose new music.

(Çudamani, 2009)

The themes on the website are reflected in programme choices: reviving older works, supporting creation that grows from tradition; and performing as a community service. This old–new mix to build community is reiterated in the company's *Bamboo to Bronze* programme notes, which state that art 'reflects members' approach to life as they comingle the ancient and modern, spirituality and globalization'. (Çudamani, 2010b, p.20) They see reconstructed choreography as 'so old it's new'. (Çudamani, 2010a, p.2)

The linking of restoration and innovation is understandable. I Dewa Putu Berata, I Nyoman Cerita and I Made Arnawa (*Bamboo to Bronze* co-composer) have been students and, the last two, teachers in the national academy where faculty and students have been funded by the government to reconstruct older forms, and Emiko Susilo has a graduate degree from the University of Hawaii where she wrote on the history and reconstruction of traditional *gambuh* dance drama in contemporary Bali. (Susilo, 1997)* In the same era that reconstruction has been emphasised, creativity has been valued and students, as their graduation projects, do *kreasi baru* (new creations). Recuperation of earlier forms lead to modern extension.

The group does not work quickly. Performances take a year of conceptualisation and another of rehearsals. Putting a programme together is 'creating a relationship between the parts'. (Susilo, 2010) Older pieces must be inset so themes intellectually cohere.

A strong sense of place is always evident – Pengosekan. Personnel live or have worked here consistently. The aim is to develop Pengosekan's young as top international artists, who can move seamlessly from tours abroad to local temple festivals. Musical choices stem from artistic director I Dewa

---

*   For example, during the tenure of I Made Bandem as rector (1981–97) at the institution in Denpasar which was earlier ASTI (Akademi Seni Tari Indonesia [Indonesian Academy of Dance]) and is now known as ISI (Institut Seni Indonesia [Indonesian Institute of Art]), faculty became deeply involved in reviving *gambuh* court dance drama. Though this was a revival project, as with our baroque dance and music revivals, work may result in newly realised performances.

Putu Berata, his brother I Dewa Ketut Alit and I Made Arnawa. Sound is the driving force in the work. All three represent the best in musical modernization. The dancers ride upon the wave of music that is created by these artists coming out of the very strong nexus of Pengosekan-Ubud musicianship, then trained in the academy, and now diving back into the local *sanggars*. 'For us, the arts are not simply the final product on stage, but about creating a life and world that is full of joy, friendship, and harmony'. (Çudamani, 2010a, p.3)*

'Closing – Or "What Really Happens at Rehearsal"', a piece I observed in rehearsal, shows how tradition is extended. Aspects of monkey chant (*kecak*), body percussion, traditional dance and diverse musical influences were incorporated. Male ensemble players moved and made music with their vocal interlocks and body stomps. They stripped off their costumes, revealing T-shirts and jeans underneath, emulating a jazz-improv structure in which each artist got his 'solo' in chant-dance as the group carried on supporting rhythms. The composers push them: 'Musicians have to own it... [and are] best when it is *really difficult*'. (Dewa Berata, 2010)

Dance is overseen by I Nyoman Cerita.† However, the repertoire can include pieces from other older dancers such as I Ketut Kantor (son of famed *topeng* mask dancer I Nyoman Kakul), I Ketut Wirtawan (Kakul's grandson), or the female dance experts Ni Ketut Alit Arini and Gusti Ayu Raku Rasmin.

---

*   Dewa Berata states that the founding was 'for us... to contribute to the art and the needs of the village... to bridge from the older generation, ...an offering more than a business.' To teach children music and dance is to *'melestarikan'* (preserve) and provide 'the link from generation to generation'. (Dewa Berata, 2010) While attending ASTI, Dewa Berata collaborate with San Francisco area artist Keith Terry on *Body Cak* and, later, with Larry Reed on *Wayang Listrik* (large screen *wayang* which uses shadow dancers). Dewa Barata is music director of Gamelan Sekar Jaya through 2012.

†   Cerita trained in his family and by thirteen taught to supplement family income after his father's death. Due to his fine *baris* (male/warrior dance), he was hired by Anak Agung, Ubud's aristocrat-patron, and met young Dewa Berata by the 1970s. The pair reunited in 1988 for a Festival of Gong Kebyar. Cerita taught at Holy Cross College and Gamelan Sekar Jaya. He received his MFA from UCLA under Professor Judy Mitoma and is head of the dance programme at ISI in Denpasar.

Pak Cerita explained his motivation:

> I don't seek money, but want to teach the small children and teens, so they will avoid drugs. I never felt I had a childhood since my father died when I was seven, so I want to show them that this is old... but being an artist gives you a spirit to face life. You can... calm your soul. In other places they make it pretty on the outside; at Çudamani they make the inside first. Here is not just 'perform and it's over.' ...Ubud is haunted by money; ...here [Pengosekan] the feeling and process are different – we keep on developing.
> (Cerita, 2010)

Emiko Saraswati Susilo, who is married to Dewa Berata, is associate artistic director and production supervisor.* She is the daughter of Javanese musician Hardja Susilo, who received his MA from UCLA in the 1960s and taught gamelan many years at the University of Hawaii. Her mother is Japanese American dancer and arts producer Judy Mitoma, who taught dance and world cultures at UCLA and acts as American producer for the group. Emiko Susilo is administrator of the troupe, writes grants (seven years of Ford Foundation support since 2001) and coordinates international programmes which bring Western students to learn Balinese arts each summer. Funding earned touring or teaching allows the group to train local students. The group plays for free or token compensation at temple festivals and other Balinese events.

Producing the international tours and sponsoring academic activities though UCLA is overseen by Mitoma, who suggested the programme concepts for *Odalan* and *Bamboo to Bronze*. Dewa Berata participated in the Asian Pacific Performance Exchange (APPEX) at UCLA, was supported by the Ford and Rockefeller Foundations, Asian Cultural Council etc. on Mitoma's grants. She sponsored Cerita's MFA at UCLA. Emiko Susilo's early encounters with Bali came through her mother's work there. Mitoma sought to create a level playing field where international artists could explore. Mitoma noted:

---

* Emiko began training at fourteen under noted Javanese dance master KRT Sasmintadipura and studied with Balinese dancer Ni Made Wiratini at UCLA among others. Susilo's Javanese vocals often add a calming energy in the musical mix. Susilo is director of Gamelan Sekar Jaya though 2012.

> We do not ask them [international students] to imitate our values, aesthetics and techniques... Exchange begins as people teach each other, then collaborate and create together, all along the way learning about their differences and similarities. Intercultural collaborative exchange gets at the core issues of culture and has a clarifying and empowering effect for artists.
>
> (Hutchenson, 2001)

This model introduces a new level of interculturalism that revises past tours' models.

Background of *Odalan Bali*

In Indonesia, the home of intricate shadow plays, it is never enough to talk about what is visible. Art manifests the unseen macrocosmic forces or ancestors' spirits. Here I argue this innovative group is part of a larger transculturation, marking a colonial (Paris Colonial Exposition 1930), to post-colonial (Dancers of Bali, 1952–3) to post-post-colonial (Çudamani) shift in Indonesian performing arts. In discussing the face of *Odalan Bali* before it was born, I cite UCLA programmes which were affected by earlier cultural brokers* who translated Bali to the West, including Walter Spies (1895–1942), Colin McPhee (1900–64) and John Coast (1916–89).

Peliatan Gamelan and the 1930s

By 1930, perhaps a hundred Europeans a year were arriving in Bali and Walter Spies, the charming artist, musician and filmmaker (see Rhodius, 1965; Rhodius & Darling, 1980; Spruit, 1997, pp.55–77; Vickers, 1989, pp.105–24), became the culture broker par excellence. Spies helped the emergence of modern painting and became widely conversant in music, dance and theatre. He was able to respond to the cultural efflorescence of the island and history has prized his impact. But, given his formation in the post First World War German avant-garde where dark imagery, sexual openness (he was homosexual), and

---

* 'Representations of peoples, cultures, and institutions do not just happen. They are mediated, negotiated, and, yes, brokered through often complex process and myriad challenges and constraints imposed by those involved, all of whom have their own interests and concerns... Like other forms of brokerage, cultural dealings rely on an extensive base of knowledge, formal and experiential, but they are, in the end, an art'. (Kurin, 1997, p.13)

dreams of idyllic south-sea islands were widespread, Spies may have tended to highlight aspects of Balinese culture that would appeal to European sensibilities as exotic, erotic or magically charged.* Spies' major book is *Dance in Bali* (deZoete & Spies, 1973) – Beryl deZoete did much of the writing – yet Spies was the go-to person on all things Balinese from the late 1920s until his arrest during a homosexual witch-hunt in 1938–9 that sent his circle fleeing. He was interned by the Dutch in the Second World War and died in 1942 when the ship transporting prisoners was targeted by the Japanese.†

Spies consulted for the Paris Colonial Exposition, chose art and advised on that performance that signalled through the flames‡ to Artaud who wrote (somewhat wrong-mindedly) about its meaning.§ (See Foley, 1992

---

*   Spies as early as 1917 was dreaming of world travels. He lived with the openly gay film director Friedrich Wilhelm Murnau (1888–1931) painting and assisting him in the German film industry. While they were a couple, Murnau's work included *Nosferatu, a Symphony of Horror* (1922) an early Dracula film with erotic and, arguably, homoerotic imagery. Murnau's *Tabu* was made in Tahiti while the director was supposedly sailing to meet Spies in Bali. *Tabu's* depiction of 'beautiful bodies diving into the deep for pearls, darting canoes, languid and yearning limbs stretched out or embracing' includes an ominous tone which make it 'a companion film to *Nosferatu*'. (Elsaesser, 2007)

†   In *Blackberry Winter*, Margaret Mead avoided discussing the witch hunts and remembered the Balinese years as ideal: 'I think it is a good thing to have had such a model, once, of what anthropological field work can be like, even if the model includes the kind of extra intensity in which a lifetime is condensed into a few short years'. (1972, p.240) Mead of course was bisexual and had a sometime lesbian relationship with Ruth Benedict and her collection of erotic and Freudian interpretations of *barong* and Rangda meant she was questioned though she was not arrested. Anthropologist Jane Belo's later descent into mental illness may have been prompted in part by the trauma of the witch-hunt; estranged husband, Colin McPhee was part of the gay community but had left. Rich fieldwork and unhappy love made Bali a hothouse for the researchers.

‡   The pavilion where performers lived and presented was burnt on 28 June and Spies' exhibit was destroyed. Musician I Made Lebah recalled the horror (Oja, 1990, p.302), but the display was rebuilt. (Saravase, 2001) The fourteen women and thirty-seven men were not paid. Anak Agung Mandera complained 'The Dutch kept us Balinese apart, like serfs, and we saw little of Paris or foreigners'. (Coast, 2004, p.34)

§   Artaud was using Balinese dance to attack French theatre and make it more visceral.

and Savarese, 2001, pp.51–77) This exposition helped fuel myths of the island paradise full of magical performance. Harsher critics have read Spies work as perpetuating a colonialist agenda.* (Vickers, 1989, pp.105–24; Yamashita, 2003, pp.29–40)

This Paris performance drew considerable attention to Bali in the West, including Canadian composer Colin McPhee, who met Spies through the Paris group, (Belo, 1970, pp.xvii–xxvii; Covarrubias, 1937), was oriented in Balinese music (McPhee 1966 and 1970) and took over music research. McPhee settled in Sayan near Ubud. I Sampih, a young boy whose dance training became a focal point of McPhee's *House in Bali*, was eight in 1932 and became the object of McPhee's affection.† I Made Lebah, from the Peliatan gamelan, helped train the boy and became McPhee's field assistant and Sampih did *kebyar*-style dance with the Peliatan Gunung Sari. This formed the core of Coast's 1950s tour. In 1960, McPhee taught at UCLA and brought I Wayan Gandera, the son of Lebah, to teach (1960–2). McPhee helped forge the lasting Indonesia–America connection that ran though UCLA and which Mitoma would continue.

When John Coast went to Bali shortly after the Second World War, he dreamed of an international tour with support by then Indonesian president, Sukarno. (Coast, 2004) This visit of Balinese artists allowed backstage photo opportunities with composer Richard Rodgers of *South Pacific* for the girl dancers of a real 'Bali Hai' and allowed them to appear in *The Road to Bali* with Hope, Crosby and Lamour.‡ (Coast, 2004, p.203

---

* Spies' film collaborations included *Goona-Goona* (Black Magic, 1930) directed by Andre Roosevelt and Armand Dennis and *The Island of Demons* (1933) by Viktor von Plessen, for which Spies and Rose Covarrubias arranged a *Ramayana*-based *kecak*. (See Chin, 2001 and Spruitt, 1997, p.61) Both films are melodramas of magic that obstructs true love. Spies popularised (rather than invented, as is sometimes claimed) *kecak*.

† Oja, in discussing McPhee's failure to include his wife in his autobiography, notes their growing disaffection: 'I [MCPhee] was in love at the time with a Balinese, which she knew, and to have him continually around was too much for her vanity.' (Oja, 1990, p.142) There is some speculation that McPhee and Sampih are reflected in Benjamin Britten's *Death in Venice*, since Britten, McPhee, and Leonard Bernstein were housemates in New York. A 2009 opera by Evan Ziporyn on McPhee, *House in Bali*, involved I Dewa Ketut Alit, a composer for *Odalan Bali*. (See 'Opera Meets Gamelan in Ubud-Bali', 2009)

‡ See Coast's film connections. (Chin, 2001)

and Coast, n.d.) Coast found Indonesian dance as a prisoner of war building the Japanese Thai–Burma railway and stage-managed Javanese performance for camp entertainments. He came to Indonesia as President Sukarno was innovating using arts in cultural diplomacy. In Bali, Coast debuted his career as an international producer for the likes of Pavarotti and Ravi Shankar.

Odalan Bali distinguishes itself from the 1930s and 1950s performances in that it abjures separate virtuosic 'numbers', but uses a temple festival scenario which takes us from dawn to night. However, dances presented draw on earlier tours' choices and, in some cases, actually reconstruct them; but the result is not the mystical Bali of Spies and Artaud. Nor is it Coast's amazing children and strong men of a new nation. Çudamani marks the new stage and grows out of intercultural blending related to a Peliatan–UCLA connection forged in the 1960s at the beginning of American world music and arts. This link unites Pengosekan back to interactions of the 1950s and 1930s. Writing in 1997, Emiko Susilo noted the future of Balinese performers was unclear: 'Televisions, movie theatres, discothèques, and music videos are easily accessible not only physically but mentally... The challenge that faces them is to maintain, once again the powerful ties of history and spirituality in the Balinese performing arts and respond to the changing world'. (1997: 13) Since writing those words, Susilo herself has become a force in moulding the future for the artists of Pengosekan.

Choreographer Cerita states:

> In Peliatan they always just do the classic and the tourists will always see the same thing, but Çudamani is different. *Odalan* was pioneering... We have classic and traditional materials; they are the ground. But once they are strong then we add the new. The technique is classical but the feeling is different.
>
> (Cerita, 2010)

These Balinese artists know Bali and the world. The American collaborators have lived lives practising Indonesian arts. Balinese and Americans are working together to figure out the next sound, steps, stories in Balinese intercultural arts. Çudamani is dancing for all the audiences they address: past and present, local and global, human and divine.

Works Cited

Arnawa, I Made (2010) personal interview, Pengosekan, 24 August
Artaud, Antonin (1976) 'On the Balinese Theatre (1931)' in *Antonin Artaud: Selected Writings*, ed. Susan Sontag, 215–27, N.Y.: Farrar, Stauss, Giroux, Noonday Press
Bandem, I Made & Fredrik deBoer (1995) [1981] *Balinese Dance in Transition: Kaja and Kelod*, 2nd edition, Kuala Lumpur, Singapore, Oxford, New York: Oxford University Press
Belo, Jane (1960) *Trance and Dance in Bali*, New York: Columbia Univ. Press
— ed. (1966) [1953] *Bali: Temple Festival*, Monographs of the American Ethnological Society 22, ed. Esther Goldfrank, Seattle and London: University of Washington Press
— ed. (1970) *Traditional Balinese Culture*, New York: Columbia University Press
Cerita, I Nyoman (2010) personal interview, Pengosekan, 23 August
Chin, Michele (2001) 'Bali in Film: From the Documentary Films of Sanghyang and Kecak Dance (1926) to Bali Hai in Hollywood's South Pacific (1958),' *Bali Echo* http://www.michellechin.net/writings/04.html, accessed 20 February 2010
Coast, John (2004) [1954] *Dancing out of Bali*, Periplus: Singapore
Covarrubias, Miguel (1937) [1936] *Island of Bali*, Photos by Rose Covarrubias, New York: Alfred Knopf
Çudamani (2007) 'Odalan Bali: An Offering of Music and Dance', Catch it Live at the Mondavi Center 07–08 Programme, 4 (November–December): 5–11
— (2009) 'Çudamani' [website], http://www.Çudamani.org/2009/about.html, accessed 11 February 2010
— (2010a) *Bamboo to Bronze* Programme Stanford Memorial Auditorium, 7 November
— (2010b) 'Gamelan Çudamani, Programme *Bamboo to Bronze*', *Stanford Lively Arts Magazine* (November–December): 17–21
Dewa Berata, I (2010) personal interview, Pengosekan, 23 August
deZoete, Beryl & Walter Spies (1973) [1938] *Dance and Drama in Bali*, Kuala Lumpur: Oxford University Press
Dibia, I Wayan (1985) '*Odalan* of Hindu Bali: A Religious Festival, a Social Occasion, and a Theatrical Event', *Asian Theatre Journal* 2, 1: 61–5
— & Rucina Ballinger (2004) *Balinese Dance, Drama, and Music*, il. Barbara Anello, Singapore: Periplus
Elsaesser, Thomas (2007) 'No end to Nosferatu', http://eurekavideo.co.uk/moc/catalogue/nosferatu/essay, accessed 11 March 2011
Foley, Kathy (1992) 'Trading Art(s): Artaud, Spies and Current Indonesian/American Artistic Exchange and Collaboration', *Modern Drama* 35: 10–19
— (2008) 'Odalan Bali' (Review), *Asian Theatre Journal* 25, 2: 373–80

Geertz, Clifford (1973) 'Deep Play: Notes on the Balinese Cockfight' in *The Interpretation of Cultures*, 412–44, New York: Basic Books

Harnish, David (1997) 'In Memoriam: I Made Lebah (1905?–1996)', *Ethnomusicology* 41, 2: 261–4

Heimarck, Brita Renee (2003) *Balinese Discourses on Music and Modernization; Village Voices and Urban Views*, New York, London: Routledge

Herbst, Edward (2007) [2006] 'Dancers of Bali from Peliatan, 1952 Liner Notes', *World Arbiter 2007, Dancers of Bali Gamelan of Peliatan, 1952* http:www.arbiterrecords.com/notes/2007notes.html

Hough, Brett (1999) 'Education for the Performing Arts: Contesting and Mediating Identity in Contemporary Bali' in *Staying Local in the Global Village*, ed. Raechelle Rubinstein and Linda Connor, 231–64, Honolulu: Univ. of Hawaii Press

Hutchenson, Reed (2001) 'Judy Mitoma, World Arts and Cultures', 1 Aug, http://www.spotlight.ucla.edu/faculty/judy-mitoma_arts/, accessed 11 March

Jowitt, Debra (2007) 'Sweeping it Clean: A Balinese Company Transforms the New York Stage', *Village Voice*, http://www.villagevoice.com/2007-10-30/dance/sweeping-it-clean/, accessed 20 February 2011

Kurin, Richard (1997) *Reflections of a Cultural Broker: A View from the Smithsonian*, Washington: Smithsonian Press

McCrae, Graeme (1999) 'Acting Global Staying Local in a Balinese Tourist Town' in *Staying Local in the Global Village*, ed. Raechelle Rubinstein and Linda Connor, 123–54, Honolulu: Univ. of Hawaii Press

McGraw, Andrew Clay (2005) '*Musik Kontemporer*: Experimental Music by Balinese Composers', PhD dissertation, Wesleyan University

McPhee, Colin (1966) *Music in Bali*, New Haven: Yale University Press

—— (1970) 'The Balinese Wayang Kulit and its Music' in *Traditional Balinese Culture*, ed. Jane Belo, 146–98, NY: Columbia University Press

—— (1991) [1944] *A House in Bali*, Singapore: Oxford University Press

Mershon, Katharine (1971) *Seven Plus Seven: Mysterious Life-Rituals in Bali*, NY: Vantage Press

Mead, Margaret (1972) *Blackberry Winter: My Earlier Years*, NY, Tokyo, London: Kodansha International

Mitoma, Judy (2011) phone interview, 18 February

Oja, Carol (1990) *Colin McPhee: Composer in Two Worlds*, Washington: Smithsonian

'Opera Meets Gamelan in Ubud-Bali' (2009) http://balitrips.net/news_27_Opera-Meets-Gamelan-in-Ubud-Bali-.html, 16 June, accessed 13 March 2011

Parish, Paul (2005) 'O Quam Gloriosam: Çudamani: *Odalan Bali: An Offering of Music and Dance*', *Dance View Times: Writers on Dancing* http://archives.danceviewtimes.com/2005/Spring/01/Çudamani.htm, accessed 20 February 2011

Picard, Michel (1996) *Bali: Cultural Tourism and Touristic Culture*, trans. Diana Darling, Singapore: Archipelago Press (1999) 'The Discourse of Kebalian: Transcultural Constructions of Balinese Identity' in *Staying Local in a Balinese Tourist Town*, ed. Raechelle Rubinstein and Linda Connor, Hawaii: University of Hawaii

Rhodius, Hans (1965) *Schonheit und Reichtum des Lebens: Walter Spies (Maler und Muskier auf Bali 1895-1942)*, Den Haag: L.J. C. Boucher & John Darling (1980) *Walter Spies and Balinese Art*, ed. John Stowell, Amsterdam: Tropical Museum (Terra Zutphen)

Savarese, Nicola (1997) *Parigi/Artaud/Bali: Antonin Artaud vede il teatro balinese all'Esposizione Coloniale di Parisgi del 1931, Conferenza-spettaculo*, Rome: Textus (2001) '1931 Antonin Artaud Sees Balinese Theatre at the Paris Colonial Exposition', *TDR The Drama Review* 45, 3 (T 171): 51–77

Spruit, Ruud (1997) [1995] *Artists on Bali*, Amsterdam, Kuala Lumpur: Pepin Press

Susilo, Emiko Saraswati (1997) 'Gambuh: A Dance-Drama of the Balinese Courts. Continuity and Change in the Spiritual and Political Power of Balinese Performing Arts', *Explorations in Southeast Asian Studies: A Journal of the Southeast Asian Studies Student Association* 1, http://www.hawaii.edu/cseas/pubs/explore/v1n2-art5.html, accessed 17 February 2011
(2010) personal interview, 22 August
(2011) email, 22 March

Tenzer, Michael (2005) 'Review Essay: Wayan Gandera and the Hidden Story of Gamelan *Gong Kebyar*', *Asian Music* 36, 1:109–22

Ulrich, Allan (2005) '[C]udumani: *Odalan Bali, an Offering of Music and Dance*', April 4, http://www.voiceofdance.com/v1/features.cfm/1017/Dance-Review-yudumani-Odalan-Bali-An-Offering-of-Music-and-Dance017.html, accessed 11 February 2010

Vitale, Waye (2007) personal letter [to Emiko Susilo and Judy Mitoma], 17 November

Vickers, Adrian (1989) *Bali; A Paradise Created*, Berkeley, Singapore: Periplus

Yamashita, Shinji (2003) *Bali and Beyond: Exploration in the Anthropology of Tourism*, trans. J.S. Eades, NY: Berhahn Books

CHAPTER TWELVE

Silviu Purcărete's *Faust*: an Encyclopedia of the Emotional

CONSTANTIN CHIRIAC

'I'd sell my soul to see this again'
Elian Ferguson, Observer, 23 August 2009

Faust – Myth, Mystery, Miracle

Every day hundreds of performances are born all around the world: a huge diversity of cultural events that no-one could ever know about or experience in its entirety. If we take this magnitude into consideration, we are faced with an important question: how could anybody single out for greatness that one, unique performance from thousands of productions presented to the public each year? What could the selection criteria possibly be? And how might any such unique show face the judgment of time? I believe the only dimension that makes the difference is the miracle: the miracle of essential discoveries, the miracle of revelations, of the encounters with love, with the conception of life, with God and Death. But 'if youth only knew; if only age could'.

In order to do some justice to these questions, this chapter shall move straight into the fabulous journey of Silviu Purcărete's[1] mega-production, *Faust*, produced by the National Theatre Radu Stanca, Sibiu, Romania, after Johann Wolfgang von Goethe's masterpiece. This production fits perfectly my personally held prototype of the miracle-show. Firstly, the chapter must make mention of the premises that led to the creation of this performance, with a special focus on its difficult conception, before exploring the ways in which the work has been exploited at home, as well as for festivals. The presentation of the show requires special attention, as well as the outline of the spectacular happenings that saved the project from an untimely death: to this end, some significant reviews from British newspapers complete the chapter.

> **The Production:** *Faust* after Johann Wolfgang von Goethe
> **Producer:** The National Theatre Radu Stanca Sibiu
> **Opening Date:** 20 September 2007
> **Script and Direction:** Silviu Purcărete
> **Translation into Romanian:** Ștefan Augustin Doinaș
> **Set & Light Design:** Helmut Stürmer[2]
> **Costumes:** Lia Manțoc
> **Music Composed by:** Vasile Șirli[3]
> **Music Arranged by:** Doru Apreotesei
> **Video:** Andu Dumitrescu
> **Set Assistant:** Daniel Răduță
> **Leading Roles: Faust:** Ilie Gheorghe
> **Mephistopheles:** Ofelia Popii

The Premises

In order better to understand Purcărete's *Faust*, and to engage with the scale of the production, it is necessary to emphasise both the space and place that made the work possible.

Spatial co-ordinates:

Our journey starts in Sibiu, a city with a population of approximately 155,000 and situated in the centre of Transylvania, Romania. Sibiu is a place with a strong sense of history: 1191 is the year of the first documentary mentioning of the fortress built by the Saxon colonists, who came here at the demand of King Geza the Second. In 2007, Sibiu became, together with Luxembourg, the European Capital of Culture. Visitors to Sibiu find themselves in a multi-ethnic, multi-religious urban centre, where one can discover seven churches and places of worship of different religions and rites which have been coexisting over the centuries without any conflicts, all on the same street, Mitropoliei, and within 1.5 kilometers of each other. Sibiu is clearly a city of tolerance, having one of the most beautiful historical sites in Central and Eastern Europe and two museum centres, Brukenthal and Astra, which are acknowledged as unique. Sibiu is the place where the first homeopathic laboratory in the world and the first paper factory from the current territory of Romania were opened. It is the place of birth of Conrad Haas, the father of the rocket. The city of Sibiu is also recognised internationally for its commitment to a dynamic and diverse cultural agenda, one that is exemplified by the Sibiu International Theatre Festival (SITF).

Place of acting:

The mega-production *Faust* was realised at the Simerom Halls, formerly known as the Mechanical Factories, a 'jewel' of Romanian communist industry, where, according to the typical megalomania of the dictator Nicolae Ceaușescu, the biggest and the strongest presses in the world were produced. On the eve of the December 1989 Revolution, the number of workers on these platforms was around ten thousand. In 2006 when The National Theatre Radu Stanca entered the desolate halls there were fewer than three hundred workers employed in the whole complex and these were due to lose their jobs soon after. Subsequently, the country's financial crisis affected the plans to demolish these buildings. Instead of the commercial spaces that were supposed to be built, there is now only a waste land and a part of the old communist halls haunted by night birds and the ghosts of great expectations.

Involved structures:

The production has benefitted from a joint effort. The National Theatre Radu Stanca worked with the Lucian Blaga University of Sibiu (represented by the department of Drama and Theatre Studies and Cultural Management of the Faculty of Letters and Arts) and the Simerom Halls (through Simerom SA) – the venue where the project came to life and lived for a year.[4] The performance was supported by the City Council of Sibiu, the Democracy through Culture Foundation,[5] Culture 2007, the Ministry of Culture, Cults and National Heritage of Romania (which financed the project as the main event of the programme: *Sibiu – European Capital of Culture 2007*).

The Story Behind the Story

The idea of creating a performance after Goethe's masterpiece *Faust* – an initiative that has been carried out all around the world in an overwhelming diversity of projects from one-man shows to puppet shows, non-verbal performances to Peter Stein's anthological 22-hour *Faust* – has never been realised in an approach of such dimensions as Silviu Purcărete's *tour de force*. Since 1988 – the year before the fall of the communist system in Romania – *Faust* and the possibility of creating a performance after Goethe's work had returned obsessively in my mind during the constant meetings that I had with Silviu Purcărete. We started the project wanting to initiate a series of stories that we would then bring to life in the fortresses of Transylvania and around the world. Two of our previous ideas for *Faust* had already become shows: one *Faust* in France, at Chalon-sur-Saone, as a street show with Silviu Purcărete's company; and another *Faust* in Romania, as a workshop with the theatre schools in the Cisnădioara fortress. We could also add the success of obtaining the title of European Capital of Culture for Sibiu. All these fortunate circumstances motivated me to propose this *Faust* project to Silviu Purcărete which, because of its expected dimensions, huge costs and number of people involved, could not have been realised elsewhere. Thus, at the beginning of 2006, the production team was created.

The obsession of a giant space had haunted Silviu Purcărete since his first legendary production, *The Danaides*.[6] That which could not materialise at that time could, through *Faust*, become reality: the Simerom Hall that we chose for the project was 85 metres long, 27 metres wide and 25 metres high.

The venue had two slide bridges, each of which was capable of carrying up to two hundred tonnes. There was also a railway that split the hall in two and it was this that allowed us to transfer the sets. The location was equipped with water and electricity supplies but the roof was deteriorated and the windows broken… all in all, it was a thoroughly abandoned hall, through which the wind blew freely. Our rehabilitation work started in the summer of 2006.

The first proposal regarding the cast had two men for the roles of Faust and Mephistopheles. We had in mind Ștefan Iordache and Gheorghe Dinică, two colossal Romanian actors. They both had – they are no longer among us – matchless careers in theatre, film and television, but they had never worked together as partners on stage. Therefore it was a great challenge and a wonderful dream. The initial project started from the premises that both Faust and Mephistopheles were two individuals who 'aged in evil'. The idea was beautiful as both actors were, in the spirit of old school theatre, legendary drinkers and each completed the other very well.

If Ștefan Iordache, a great whisky lover, was a handsome man, a charmer who embodied throughout his career countless heroes, Gheorghe Dinică, a spritz drinker, was best known for his diabolical film roles, as well as essaying the legendary main character in the *Rameau's Nephew* directed by David Esrig in 1968.

If in Europe or any other part of the world the use of industrial sites became a common practice for theatre producers, *Faust* was the first experiment of this kind in Romania, gathering at the same time a record number of participants, one hundred and forty people (actors and technicians) who were directly involved in the performance and some other hundreds who have worked for at least one year on this project.

The actual work with all one hundred and forty actors, musicians, children, circus artists and technicians started in September 2006. Unfortunately, after a stay of only four days in Sibiu, Gheorghe Dinică, one of the most envied and feared Romanian actors, confessed to Silviu Purcărete and myself, with tears in his eyes: 'Fellows, you are fabulous, I love you, but you came too late. You belong to a different world, I envy you. Unfortunately, I cannot continue anymore.' With these words, he left the production.

So, in order to keep his concept foundation from falling apart, Silviu Purcărete invited Coca Bloos to play the role of Mephistopheles. She is an actress heart-warmingly devoted to Purcărete, having starred in some of his finest works. Fortunately, the actress belonged to the same generation as Ștefan Iordache and things started to get back on track. Two months of work followed: a time of toil and torment, because none of us who accepted the adventure of this project had the necessary experience of assuming and transforming such a huge space in a suitable location for the emergence of the miracle. We were fumbling. We were constantly adapting and learning by doing. It was getting colder as winter was rushing in, and the winters in Sibiu are extremely biting. Furthermore, we had not been able to isolate the immense hall as we had hoped. The specially designed heating systems were short of power and by the end of November, after three months of effort when we fully felt the heritage of the master Manole,[7] we were forced to cease work.

The main objective for 2007 was to carry out this performance on a scale unachieved by any other theatre production in Europe – it was also some sort of megalomania, which had lingered in us subconsciously since Ceaușescu's epoch, and it was being postponed *sine die*. As the producer,

I lived through one of the most difficult times of my life. The contracts with the Ministry of Culture, an important financial supporter, had not been signed by then. A year's effort appeared to be in vain and the show's conception and execution doomed. As if all these had not been enough, Coca Bloos, after a crisis of faith and a long inner battle, told me with tears in her eyes, that she could no longer impersonate Satan. The news confused us all – she was after all the actress that, years before, had distinguished herself as the androgynous Danaus, a role she had created in Purcărete's *The Danaides*. The meeting that followed with all the producers of the show was one of the roughest, because, despite the obvious fact that the project was compromised, I stubbornly wanted to believe in it and I had no intention of giving up hope. I asked the team members for their promise that after having done the project with *Metamorphoses*[8] in Luxembourg, where the same creation team and a part of the Sibiu National Theatre's actors were involved and which was going to be performed at the former Neumünster Abby, that we would continue our work with *Faust*. Meanwhile, the technical team was about to finalise what I thought to be the 'details'. But this was all still in the year 2006. The last piece of news that completed the dimension of our tragedy was Ștefan Iordache's announcement that he was leaving the project. He had made a huge effort to work continuously for three months in Sibiu, trying to speed up things. In hindsight, I think he was feeling his death approaching. Thus, I concluded with Silviu Purcărete that, despite the work done so far, the project had to be completely changed.

In the end it proved to be a fortuitous decision, not endangering the Ovid's *Metamorphoses* project, which represented the biggest event for the Luxembourg European Capital of Culture in 2007. Now *Metamorphoses* lives its second youth as a performance of the National Theatre Radu Stanca.

During the first six months of 2007 we came back to reality only to realise how much work there was still to be done with *Faust*. But, paradoxically, this period of respiro was favourable as it confirmed, after all the sufferings, the idea of an androgynous Mephisto, equally powerful as a man and as a woman. It also gave us the chance to arrange one of the most beautiful spaces imaginable in the world for a theatre performance. The set designer Helmut Stürmer had the time, the patience but most of all the talent and knowledge of gathering a team to produce a magnificent set design, of such richness, power and detail that one needs to see several performances in a row in order to notice a small part of its dimension. In order to cover completely the partition wall built to isolate the hall of the performance from the other halls in drawings, we set a partnership between the Art High School from Sibiu and the Visual Arts University from Cluj. We didn't take any steps to contact the *Guinness Book of Records*, but the total coverage of the vast space with black and white drawings – work that took dozens of young artists working on scaffolds several weeks – would definitely be worthy of inclusion.

For the choir of seventy people conducted by Vasile Șirli to sing the music he had composed live, two streetcar trailers were shifted with cranes and installed in one of the halls to serve as cabins. Ilie Gheorghe, an actor who had interpreted a great many leading roles in Silviu Purcărete's works since the '90s, was invited at the beginning of 2007 to perform as Faust. Gheorge had been invited also in the previous year, but had turned the role down because of his mother's serious illness. Meanwhile, fate confronted him from another angle, with the death of his wife. In many ways it was the nature of Gheorge's struggle with his personal grief that determined him to come and wrestle with Goethe's huge character. Ofelia Popii, a young actress from Sibiu who had already played some parts directed by Purcărete, was given the opportunity of embodying Mephisto. Popii's talent and ambition were rewarded with several important prizes, both in Romania and internationally. Among those prizes, the best actress in a leading part in Romania 2007 and Herald Angels at the Edinburgh International Festival in 2009.

The rehearsals took place on several levels photographically documented by Mihaela Marin. This was a period of maximum intensity. The leading actors, Ofelia Popii and Ilie Gheorghe, had been working separately on their parts all this time. Purcărete was rehearsing twelve hours a day: four with the choir and the overall motion and six hours with the leading actors. At night, after finishing the rehearsals, the technical team would start working. Vasile Șirli was rehearsing the music he composed in the space of the performance. For the accuracy of the sound, an extremely sophisticated surround system had been built. The hog masks necessary for the performance were ordered from Budapest by the scenographer Lia Manțoc. For the performers' make-up two weeks were needed to work with a make-up artist from Bucharest. A number of props had been gathered by set design assistant Daniel Răduță from the Saxon-influenced villages. It was a research period, filled with field work, but the efforts were rewarded: a lot of the props (for example Margaret's iron bed) are, in fact, precious patrimony objects.

Faust – Sibiu's Heritage Performance

Certain dimensions of this production were well captured by Mircea Dinescu,[9] one of the greatest Romanian contemporary poets, in the foreword of the album dedicated to *Faust*:

> Twelve years ago, a former candidate to the United States' presidency, the republican senator Bob Dole, was invited to give a lecture about the ins and outs of the concrete at the Goethe Institute in Berlin.
>
> Mister Dole apologised in a letter saying that due to the election campaign he could not attend but that he would be delighted if Mr and Mrs Goethe visit him at his Arkansas farm.
>
> With an air of innocence, the Institute employees sent the senator the following urgent telegram:
>
> 'Dear Bob, since both I and my beloved wife are departed for more than one hundred years we will not be able to admire your farm cows. But we are impatiently waiting for you to come to us.'
>
> Signed: Wolfgang Amadeus Goethe
>
> I remembered this true story while seeing Purcărete's brilliant *Faust*. Purcărete had grafted elements of circus onto the stem of the dramatic theatre inside an old industrial hall in Sibiu and in so doing took the Inferno's tenant from the Academy's prison and brought him into the twenty-first century.
>
> What was denied to the American statesman was given to the Romanian director, since Goethe could not resist the temptation to re-emerge in Sibiu, where the whale of art swallows from the first moment the spectators leaving them (and even the gantry's technicians) in something of a collective trance when the curtain drops. It is testament to the skills of Purcărete that I had for a moment the feeling that Federico Fellini himself whispered in my ear the *Elegy from Marienbad*.[10]

Faust has been living in Sibiu for the past four years and now enters his fifth year of existence. It is a permanently sold-out show. The reactions that this performance produces are astonishing. We can now really talk about what Jean Vilar was dreaming when he created the Festival of Avignon: the conception of a popular performance that would gather all the possible dimensions, from the accessibility of any kind of audience to the dimension of an art theatre, the foreshadowing of the visionary and research theatre, all melted down in a pot of emotions that gives birth to a miracle. During the five years of its run there are spectators from Sibiu who have seen the show twenty times in a row, alongside an impressive number of tourists that have come from all over the world to enjoy the unique richness of this performance. Due to the events of the European Capital of Culture, since 2007 the number of tourists to Sibiu has continued to rise every year. This is the most edifying example of rehabilitating an urban and in many ways isolated community through culture.

Silviu Purcărete worked on *Faust* using the brilliant translation of Ştefan Augustin Doinaş,[11] a poet of genius, who brought with his Romanian translation a rare beauty to the poetry and Goethe's philosophical thought. Doinaş succeeded in maintaining the text's qualities: the musicality of the lyrics, the depth of the poetry, the perfume of old age that surrounds Faust, as a taster of beauty not as a drinker. Starting from this translation, the director created an extremely unified personal script, leaving one with the feeling that nothing is missing, where we find ourselves transported to a close universe, round, dense, with a solid, integrated vision of Goethe's tale.

Faust or the Appetite for the Burlesque

As for its formula, *Faust* begins like an ordinary performance on an Italian stage. Faust's apprentices are seated upstage on old desks; spectators are placed on chairs raked for view. On first impression it can seem as though we have been taken to a hall that is simply imitating a theatre auditorium. The temptation to ask 'but why have we been moved here?' might exist among spectators, but not for long. Within ten minutes a real dog appears on stage and suddenly changes itself into Mephistopheles: a hallucinatory scene, in which Faust is convinced to sign the famous pact. No sooner has this moment ended than the audience is confronted with a richness of signs and actions undertaken at breakneck speed and with a stunning shift of rhythm by so many performers that the effect is overwhelming. Fire miraculously destroys a door, the sets fall apart, everything glides;

instead of one Margaret there are suddenly seven, according to the ideas of interchangeability that guide the production. These characters pick flowers from the stage as an army of hogs invites the public to take part in the Walpurgis Night. The set leaves on the iron rails, the bridges slide and reveal the witches flying above spectators' heads, fires burn and the inferno blends with circus acts that in turn unleash orgies and mysterious celebrations. All this comes together with an insane beat that overpowers the senses. Leaving the production, it is common to hear spectators vowing to return one day to catch the multitude of details that the eye misses in performance and only begins to see with hindsight. After this installation-like experience, the audience is brought back to their comfortable and safe seats only to see how the one that rules everything with a magical and terrible force arranges Faust (after having said the magical formula: 'Moment, stay!') into a far too small coffin. Mephistopheles, the one who pawned Faust's soul, becomes human, as he is falling in love. It is a dance of joy and love which, however late it might come, saves Faust. It is maybe also a late song that comforts – like hope does – the creator of this performance.

The main quality of the show is the fact that it can interact with any type of audience. The meanings can be peeled as one peels an onion. They are hidden one inside another according to the principle of the Matryoshka and can be decoded according to the intellectual capacities and the cultural landmarks of the viewers. Impressed by what he saw on stage, the critic George Banu wrote:

> At the beginning of this atypical *Faust*, the alchemist philosopher declines his fears while in the back of his workshop, the hardworking disciples nervously type on the keyboard of their computers: on one side, the scepticism of the master, on the other hand the effort lacking the awareness of the tragedy of the disciples! Out of the contrast generated by this universe appears Mephistopheles, an androgynous being, neither a man, nor a woman, the source of temptations and weaknesses... as we all dream of him! To dare to get lost, what a victory! ... This is how the journey of self-forgetfulness starts only to be reborn again... a journey placed by Purcărete and his team under the mark of carnival celebrations pervaded with memories from Bosch and Breughel. We relive the joy of living that fascinated a Faust overwhelmed by his own desires, a Faust who, after indulging in debauchery of pleasure on the background of the exaltation of

theatrical powers, peacefully resigns himself to coil up in a child's coffin. He shaped on a circle of life; thus, even though we do not want and cannot say like he does: 'Moment, stay!' we do know that something old ends, only to make space for something new.[12]

Bridges between Orient and Occident: Kabuki and *Faust*

It is worth mentioning that this big theatre project created a real dialogue between cultures: during the rehearsals for *Faust*, I was carrying out negotiations with one of the greatest Kabuki companies from Japan, Kanzaburo Nakamura-Za, for their participation in the Sibiu International Theatre Festival. After long discussions taken over six years, the company agreed to send the director and the international project manager to Sibiu. It was an approach apparently doomed, as the presence of the Japanese company, which is part of the Japanese cultural heritage and under the high-ranked protection of the Emperor, involves costs of approximately five million Euros. To put that into context, a similar figure represents the yearly budget needed for the entire Festival, involving some 350 performances from 70 different countries in 66 different locations. The representatives of the Japanese company attended the official opening of *Faust*, followed by a high-class reception at the Hotel Împăratul Romanilor. After the performance, the two representatives of the Japanese company asked for permission to stay for a longer period in the hall in order to have a closer look at the technical mechanisms and to understand the way in which this space had been used to create the miracle. After approximately two hours, while other friends from all over the world, including the director of the Edinburgh International Festival, Jonathan Mills, and I were planning future projects, the two Japanese guests appeared transfigured and asked for a five-minute meeting with me. I was expecting them to talk about the performance, to react as Europeans do or as our friends from across the Atlantic do, but their first question was: 'Could we have a performance of the Nakamura-Za company in this hall?' Of course, I was not expecting such a question and probably only the enthusiasm of our success made me quickly answer 'yes', but with the condition that the fundraising will be done in Japan. They replied as sweepingly, that they would give me their answer in a week's time. After three days, I received the invitation to go to Japan for a press conference, which had gathered some of the biggest Japanese companies and significant mass-media representatives, in order to announce the tour and the signing of the contract. On arrival in Japan, I saw a logo conceived for attracting financiers: 'For the first time in Europe. Kanzaburo Nakamura-Za in Transylvania, in Sibiu, in an old communist factory'.

I have mentioned this moment, apparently unconnected to the *Faust* project, only to show that nothing happens by chance. I had promised the Japanese company that they would have their Kabuki performance in the 2008 edition of the Festival, in *Faust*'s hall. Meanwhile, the owner of the Simerom SA spaces announced to me that the halls in question were going to be demolished and on the land the biggest commercial centre in Romania would be built, with multiple foreign investments, alongside a residential area with green spaces. For an entire week I fought so that the action would not begin earlier than the end of the 2008 edition of SITF, in order to honour the promise I had made. At the same time I came back to reality when I realised that the *Faust* sets could not be unfolded, that *Faust* and the hall were complete, the space being furnished especially for this performance. Hence I negotiated with the Japanese to have their act in another hall. I was thus obliged to start on a new venture of arranging a different industrial space for the Japanese company. Fortunately for us, Sibiu is not short of abandoned spaces, due to the post-communism collapse. An equally difficult period followed, perhaps even tougher than the one for arranging the hall for *Faust*, because we had only two months to finish the work. But what a huge chance: the arrival of this company was an unrepeatable event made possible because of *Faust*. Immediately after the 2008 edition of Sibiu International Theatre Festival, the demolition of the Simerom Hall was carried out. This was a painful and bitter experience. Hundreds of people witnessed the demolition with their eyes half opened, blurred by tears.

Despite all of this, the space that came to life due to the Kabuki performance in the Balanța Hall became, as a counterpart of the hospitality given by *Faust* to the Japanese guest performances, the house where *Faust* can live on. The oriental veils created a fortunate bridge between *Faust* and Kabuki. Without the investment made by the Japanese in the Balanța Hall, without the speed of changing the second hall into a technically superior space, *Faust* would have died. Today, after almost five years, the Balanța Hall has become a place of pilgrimage. This is a key point for what cultural tourism means both in Romania and in Europe. Paradoxically, in order to get to the Balanța Hall, one has to follow the road that starts in the centre of the city, passes by the National Theatre Radu Stanca, and before reaching its destination, passes by the waste land where the Simerom Hall used to be. The financial crisis cancelled the investment into the conceitedly designed malls and resident spaces and from the height of the bridge that crosses the railways one can see the piles of rubble that bury now the clouds of applause, tears and sweat.

Faust Abroad: the Frankfurt Goethe Festival and the Edinburgh International Festival

Given the countless difficulties that we encountered, the production's huge costs and especially the gigantic dimensions of this project, I have never imagined that *Faust* could ever go touring. Despite this, the performance was invited in 2008 to the Frankfurt Goethe Festival, where it was performed in a heritage space, the Bockenheimer Depot, the streetcars' depot changed by Peter Brook's set designer, Jean Guy Lecat, into a magnificent performance hall. In the same year, the director of the Edinburgh International Festival came and saw *Faust* in Sibiu, but he was also present in Frankfurt to see the reactions of the German public. Thus, the most important adventure of the Romanian theatre was born, presenting this show as the *main event* of the Edinburgh International Festival in 2009. Following this tour, in five months' time, 79 front-page articles favourable to the image of Romania were published – a fact unmatched so far by any other event. I would very much like this example to be the drop of energy that would trigger, at the European Union level, among the communities and especially for the decision makers of the 27 state members, the resolution that, at least starting with 2020, culture would become a priority of European policies. There has to be a rapid partnership of the cultural operators and of all the visionary Europeans who understand that through a cultural act a community can be radically changed and that the healthiest and the safest investment is in the cultural field.

When I decided together with Jonathan Mills to bring this show, apparently impossible to move, to the Edinburgh International Festival in the Lowland Hall, the idea of this project seemed utopian. The total costs had risen to 2,100,000 Euros. With an intelligent fundraising policy and a constant pressure upon the politicians and the potential sponsors, this miracle became possible. Two weeks before the beginning of the event, *Faust* was the only sold-out performance. There were five shows, with hundreds of people on the waiting list for the possibility of an extra ticket for each night. Even with confirmation that twelve performances would have been sold-out as well, Jonathan Mills preferred not to take this risk. Even so, the triumph of *Faust* was incredible.

Time for Drawing the Line

At the end of this chapter, I would like to offer a selection of critics' opinions of *Faust* as it was performed at this festival:

> It's hard not to be blown away by the Edinburgh International Festival's staging of *Faust*. A production so huge, it has to be staged at the Lowland Hall in Ingliston, it leaves you after two and half hours of unrelenting spectacle, feeling slightly exhausted and a little overwhelmed. From the chalk-faced students behind Victorian desks in a giant classroom full of newspaper, to the pig headed creatures in white coats and pulsating bodies moving in time to the sniggers of Mephistopheles, it's one visual feast after another.[13]

> If you are staging a festival about the Enlightenment, then the tragedy of Faust – the restless and arrogant scholar who sells his soul to the devil – must form part of the picture. And now, it comes to Edinburgh in a version by Romanian director Silviu Purcărete, and his Theatre Radu Stanca of Sibiu, that must be one of the most breathtaking shows ever staged by the official Edinburgh Festival. But it also offers a serious 21st century reinterpretation of the story, in which the devil Mephistopheles is finally defeated by forces of innocence and faith that lie beyond his control.[14]

> Ofelia Popii delivers a tour-de-force as a gender bending Mephistopheles who seems like a man at first, then strips off her costume to reveal both female breasts and a bulging codpiece. Her croaky voice, disconcerting shape-shifting and sheer charisma all combine to create a genuinely disconcerting figure who might really have arrived from some infernal world.[15]

> So ravishing that you're almost prepared to sell your soul to the devil to keep the succession of lush images coming, Silviu Purcărete's version of Goethe's Faust is such a seductive visual fantasia that you might not notice it has sold its own soul to spectacle. But what a mighty spectacle it is, with a series of eye-

popping illusions and conjuring tricks… In Purcărete's vision, hell is so much more exciting than heaven.[16]

I have not seen such a complex, phenomenal staging since Janusz Wisniewski brought his *The End of Europe* to the Fringe here in 1985, half my lifetime ago, and Purcărete's *Faust* has a wealth of intellectual content to match its visceral impact. (After all that, it even manages to bring off Faust's ultimate redemption.) This production by the Radu Stanca National Theatre of Sibiu has already sold out, but I fervently advise anyone within striking distance of Edinburgh to call in every favour they can think of in order to secure a ticket.[17]

Striking and storming, this *Faust* is a spectacle. From start to finish director Purcărete's play, adapted from Goethe's drama, is disturbing. Helmut Stürmer's set design plays an integral part in creating this atmosphere as the play opens in Faust's cold and pale classroom. The production becomes a mind-bending experience in which disturbing characters, costume design and eerie music continually unsettle the audience… Among the cast of 120 actors, Ofelia Popii stands out. Popii's powerful and awesome portrayal of Mephistopheles is world class. Her overwhelming voice and movement means her presence is always felt on stage, even when she lurks in the shadows.[18]

Quite the most blisteringly stunning theatrical experience of this (or, appropriately enough, any other) life, *Faust* (Ingliston Lowland Hall) seared and stuck like hot tar on bare skin. This Romanian production, in a hangar of a shed near the airport, left most of us mesmerised and enthralled, and left me saddened only in one perverse way: I may never see a grander, more *theatrical* event in my life.[19]

Summing up, I have to say that this adventure marked us all in a profound way, the transformation being, this chapter notwithstanding, beyond words. It is an experience that stained us as the waters carve the land, as time carves faces. Throughout this confession about some men who chose a unique way to make a performance, the key word always on our lips was *miracle*. For those of us involved in the production, and for the many thousands who have seen it, *Faust* was indeed a miracle.

Endnotes

1. Silviu Purcărete is one of the best-known of Romanian directors. He studied at the Theatre Academy in Bucharest and soon after his graduation started working with the theatres in Piatra Neamț and Constanța, before moving to the Small Theatre in Bucharest. He has also taught at the Theatre Academy. His 1986 staging of Goldoni's *Il Campiello* won the National Theatre Award, bringing him also the position of Artistic Director at the Bulandra Theatre in Bucharest in 1992. During the early 1990s he directed three productions at the National Theatre of Craiova which were to achieve international recognition: *Ubu Rex with Scenes from Macbeth*, *Titus Andronicus* and *Phaedra*. In 1996 he was appointed Director of Théâtre de l'Union at the Centre Dramatique du Limousin in France, a year later founding the Theatre Academy for training young actors. Purcărete founded his own company in 2002. His theatre productions include *The Tempest* (Porto National Theatre and Nottingham Playhouse), *The Danaides* (the Festival of Avignon, before playing venues in Europe and New York), *A Midsummer Night's Dream* in Oslo, *The Bacchae* in Vienna, Ionesco's adaptation of *Macbeth* for the Royal Shakespeare Company and, in 2007, an extravagant staging of Ovid's *Metamorphoses* which marked the year of Sibiu and Luxembourg and the Greater Region as European Capitals of Culture. Purcărete has also directed opera, including *Roberto Devereux* (Vienna State Opera), *Parsifal* (Welsh National Opera, Scottish Opera) and, in Bonn, *Satyagraha*, *Castor and Pollux*, *Eugene Onegin*, *A Midsummer Night's Dream* and *Lucia di Lammermoor*. He has been appointed a Chevalier des Arts et des Lettres in France and a Commander of the Order of the Star in Romania.

2. Helmut Stürmer, set designer, was born in Timișoara and, following his graduation from the Nicolae Grigorescu Fine Arts Institute of Bucharest in 1967, worked at the State Theatre in Sibiu and the Bulandra Theatre in Bucharest. He also worked at other theatres throughout Romania and as a production designer for films, including Dan Pița's *The Stone Wedding*, *Gold Fever* and *Tănase Scatiu*. Helmut Stürmer was invited to Cologne to work with the director David Esrig on *And the Light Shines in Darkness* and with Roberto Ciulli on *The Italian Straw Hat*, and subsequently on Gorky's *The Lower Depths*, directed by Liviu Ciulei in Munich and Sydney. Since settling in Germany in 1977 he has designed, among much else, *The Master and Margarita* directed by Andrei Șerban in Paris, *Troilus and Cressida* directed by Leander Haussmann in Hamburg, and productions throughout Germany and in other European cities, including *The Trojan Women*, *The Cherry Orchard* and *Hamlet* directed by Vlad Mugur; *Baal*, *Lulu* and *The Sorrows of Young Werther* directed by Konstanze Lauterbach; *The Bacchae*, *The Oresteia*, *Three Sisters*, *The Winter's Tale* and a multi-award-winning production of *Troilus and Cressida* (in Budapest), all directed by Silviu Purcărete. Stürmer

also designed sets for Wagner's *The Flying Dutchman* at the Karlsruhe Opera and Britten's *A Midsummer Night's Dream* in Bonn.

3   Vasile Şirli, composer, was born in Variaş and has been settled in Paris since 1986. Studying in Timişoara but also at the Music Academy of Bucharest, Vasile Şirli dedicates his work to theatre, cinema, dance and music, making good use of any opportunities to express his art in different musical styles: not only pop/rock songs, contemporary symphonic music, but also jazz, ethno and romantic music. He has received many national and international music prizes. He was a publisher at the Romanian Music Publishing Company for eight years and, for four years, Artistic Director for the Romanian National Recording Company. Şirli composed and produced music for theatre directors such as Lucian Pintilie (*The Seagull* and *Arden from Faversham*), Petrika Ionesco (*The Blue Monster*), Dan Micu (*The Brothers Karamazov* and *As You Like It*), Silviu Purcărete (*Richard III, Il Campiello, The Tempest, A Midsummer Night's Dream* (2 versions), *Don Juan, De Sade, The Woman who loses her jumpers, Pilafs and Mule Scent* (inspired by *The Book of the 1001 Nights*), *The Winter's Tale, The Oresteia, Pantagruel's Sister-in-Law, Twelfth Night* and *Scapino, the Trickster, Troilus and Cressida* and *Macbeth*. An accomplished composer for movies, Şirli worked for Mircea Daneliuc (*Glissando*), Nicu Stan (*Singapore*), Constantin Chelba (*Astfel*), and the list goes on. In France, Şirli composes music for TV shows and theatres. He is still a music publisher and producer for the music recording industry. Since December 1990, he has been the Music Director for the Disneyland Resort Paris.

4   The halls were demolished in 2008 and the production was transferred to the Balanţa Hall, the space where *Faust* is currently performed.

5   The Foundation that developed the 'Goethe in Transylvania' project.

6   *The Danaides*, production that traveled around the world. It was created in 1994 together with the Festival of Avignon, the Holland Festival, the Paris Autumn Festival, the Reggio Parma Festival and the Wiener Festwochen.

7   The story goes back to an ancient Romanian popular legend of the birth of the Argeşului Monastery. Because of a curse, all that the Master built during the day would fall down at night. A beauty sacrifice was needed: the craftsman Manole's wife herself had to be built into the wall of the church so it could stand for centuries.

8   An atypical performance of extreme difficulty that takes place in an outside pool, adaptable to big public squares.

9   Mircea Dinescu, considered a symbol of dissidence in the communist period, is the poet who, during the 1989 Revolution, gave the official message on the national television channel of the end of the dictator Nicolae Ceauşescu.

10 Dinescu, M. (2008) 'Purcărete in Weimar, Goethe in Sibiu', in Marin, M., *Album 'Faust'*, Bucureşti: Nemira

11 There are some Romanian translations of *Faust*, among them one signed by Ion Gorun and one by Lucian Blaga.
12 Banu, G. (2011) 'Aus der Nähe – aus der Ferne – zwanzig Jahre später', in Mazilu, A., Weident, M. and Wolf, I. (eds) *Das rumänische Theater nach 1989. Seine Beziehungen zum deutschsprachigen Raum*, Berlin: Frank & Timme
13 McLean, P., 'Descent to Hell', *BBC*, 19 August 2009
14 McMillan, J., 'Purcărete's *Faust* is a breathtaking reinterpretation of the triumph over evil', *Scotsman*, 19 August 2009
15 Spencer, C., '*Faust* is full of sound and fury, but signifies remarkably little', *Telegraph*, 19 August 2009
16 Gardner, L., 'Luscious view of hell that leaves a hangover', *Guardian*, 20 August 2009
17 Shuttleworth, I., '*Faust*, Lowland Hall, Ingliston, Edinburgh', *Financial Times*, 20 August 2009
18 Cromarty, A., '*Faust*: Lowland Hall, Ingliston', *Herald*, 22 August 2009
19 Ferguson, E., 'I'd sell my soul to see this again', *Observer*, 23 August 2009

CHAPTER THIRTEEN

Life is a Cigarette: *Isabella's Room*, Jan Lauwers and Needcompany

JOHN FREEMAN

Like many of the events discussed in this book, *Isabella's Room* resists easy categorisation. On one level the work is dance theatre; on another it is displaced autobiography writ large; on another it is a work with a distinctly linear narrative; and on another level still it is about as fragmented, disrupted and postmodern-smart as those so inclined could wish for. Arnd Wesemann has described the Brussels-based Needcompany as a troupe that utilises film, theatre, dance and poetry, whilst not measuring itself against of these forms (in Stalpaert et al., 2007, p.261) and his is a description that holds true. As with the company's back catalogue of work since 1986, *Isabella's Room* plays with surface and depth as much as with truth and lies. The writer and director, Jan Lauwers, too white-suited to be described as a shadowy figure, floats around the edges of the stage observing actions with a not-quite-Kantoresque presence. Like a cultural anthropologist, Lauwers participates directly at times but never so much that his presence drives any of the scenes. He is at once the personification of his own father and the son who crafts a tale of embellishment and romance, of love and affirmation in the face of life's twentieth-century tales. And as ghost and first narrator, Lauwers makes work here that is as relentlessly European as the cigarette smoke that swirls from Isabella's lips.

But this is to get ahead of ourselves. To lose ourselves in a work before it has been described. As Needcompany blends truths and lies, facts and imaginings, words and movement, so the words of this chapter will blend description and analysis, documentary information and guesswork, the swept-along with some semblance of critical distance; and the words will not follow a smooth narrative line. For how else could memory work but in fits and starts, in the overlap between how things were and how things might have been, in the space between the then of watching and the now of recall?

Isabella's Room tells a story about Jan Lauwers' father through the life of an imagined woman, Isabella Morandi, named after Giorgio Morandi, the Italian painter of still lives: a painter whose work features heavily in Fellini's 1960 film, *La Dolce Vita*. Isabella, played by the *nonpareil* Viviane De Muynck, is seated centre stage in a position from which she will appear only rarely to move. 'Appear' is a necessary word here because subsequent viewings of the work show that De Muynck roams, strips and sashays all over the playing space and yet gives the impression of a woman who dominates the production through stillness. The piece begins with a prologue spoken conversationally and engagingly by Lauwers himself. Members of the cast enter the space and at the front of the stage Lauwers tells spectators the origins of the work, introducing the performers and their roles in a casual, cool and confident manner, before Misha Downey takes over the role of narrator as well as embodying Isabella's erogenous zones. As such, Downey is in for a busy night. If my responses can be couched in the language of the communal for a moment, I can say that we know from Lauwers' preamble that the performance we are watching will amount to some kind of contemporary, personal ritual, rooted in the last hundred years. We know too that the work will somehow tell the story of his late father, Felix, who lived to see too little of the twenty-first century, and of a collection of nearly 6,000 ethnological and archaeological objects, the bulk of which Jan Lauwers had grown up amongst and many of which have been placed on stage. We know that these are not objects purchased as props and this knowledge matters. We see space, wide and flat enough for dance and we see performers who look like they can move; their bodies muscled and lithe, dynamic even in repose and younger than their years. We get the feeling too that shades of Wilson, LeCompte, Fabre, Bausch and Brecht will be as much a part of the next two hours as the ethnographic objects that decorate the stage; that we are firmly in the world of postmodern performance.

We know this despite the fact that postmodern performance lacks anything close to precise definition. Jean-Francois Lyotard has argued tellingly that postmodern artists and writers work without rules 'in order to establish the rules for what will have been made' (Lyotard, 1992, p.15) and Dave Robinson suggests that nobody really knows what the term means

– that it is little more than a 'convenient label for a set of attitudes, values, beliefs and feelings about what it means to be living in the late twentieth century'. (Robinson, 1999, p.35) Elinor Fuchs agrees, feeling that the sooner we can articulate those methods of postmodern theatre that have eradicated plot and killed off all notions of character we will be 'immediately at a better vantage point from which to view what used to be called "avant-garde" theatre.' (Fuchs, 1996, p.171) If this is so then it follows that all theatre produced in this climate is innately postmodern and that all of the problematising of representation we see in *Isabella's Room* is a feature of its time as much as any textual or directorial imperative. Notwithstanding the fact that *Isabella's Room* thrives on character and plot, a great number of the recognisably postmodern features are here and they are about to be deployed to mesmeric effect, developing notions of pastiche, pluralism and simultaneity (the old postmodern standby of de-centring) through merging sharp structural experimentation with the too-cool-for-school taboo of musical theatre. When Brecht told us that 'The Theatre can stage anything (because) it theatres it all' (quoted in Williams, 1969, p.280) he might have been dreaming a dream of Isabella.

We learn almost immediately that Isabella is blind, the reason for her sunglasses, which allow the images in her brain to be projected on a screen. We learn too that as this is no more than a theatrically descriptive conceit we will need to imagine the images her brain projects. Isabella grows up on a lighthouse with her mother, Anna (Anneke Bonnema), and a drunken father, Arthur, played pitch perfectly by Benoît Gob. It is Arthur who tells Isabella that he is not in fact her father and that she was born to a desert prince who disappeared on an African expedition. Following the death of Anna and Arthur, Isabella takes up residence in a room in Paris and it is from this room, expansive, white floored, white lit and white tabled, surrounded by items torn from their cultural roots, that Isabella's story of life from 1910 unfolds. We discover her love of Africa as a mythical land, as a continent she will visit once and then only briefly. We discover her long-term love affair with Alexander (Hans Petter Dahl) and her brief paid-for-by-the-night liaison with a black man called Friday who can ejaculate at will. At this point I catch myself looking at other spectators to see if we have stepped here into a cliché too far. To see if the references to Africa and extraordinary penises are causing any consternation. To determine if the mere mention of Africa in this context, scripted by a white European and being spoken by non-black performers, is an issue. I saw the work first in Sarajevo, then in Madrid and then again in Poznan, and on none of these occasions did I feel that stirring in the air that comes with audience discomfort. Later, in conversation, Lauwers would comment on the fact that at certain North American venues questions of race and of racism were raised and perhaps, had I seen the work as part of an audience mass in Los Angeles or Brooklyn, I might have felt differently. Who knows? Lauwers has often said that he wants people to think and then to think twice, and that he wants his theatre to make provocative statements, to place conflict on stage. More power to him for that. Better that theatre can say the unsayable than that it is forced to unsay the things we would rather not hear.

The acting power of De Muynck is immediately apparent. On this stage filled with dancers' bodies she inhabits her own skin with swagger, grace and majestic seniority. In the role of a protagonist who knows that we live best by reaching out for what we can hold, De Muynck's performance is as epic as the sweep of Lauwers' text. Were this a straight play, Isabella Morandi would be in the Mother Courage, Nora and Medea mould: a must-play part, but with a bigger and a hungrier heart than any other classic role – a woman who is more honest and less judgemental than the rest. This is a role of great strength and subtlety, both in text and performance, because, for all the seventy-plus lovers and the affair with her own grandson, Franky (Maarten Seghers), Lauwers and De Munynck tell us an emphatically moral tale. Moral because love given freely knows no guilt and because a life lived with an open heart knows no shame. Somewhere in the two hours' traffic of the stage we learn that the past is carried with us and the best we can do is learn the story that it tells, because it is our histories that will whisper our futures. Whether this is a lesson learned or remembered makes little difference. The result is work that drags postmodernism out of cynicism and contemporary performance out of its non-narrative grave. We buy the story Lauwers tells because it is a story we need to hear, see and share. This is theatre without a moment's negativity and it shows, like no other innovative performance I have ever seen, that the baby of story has not quite yet been thrown out with the bathwater of modernism.

Blind as she is, Isabella cannot see the summer as it wanes, only a life that brings her closer to her desert prince, Felix. And we see Julien Fauré dance his thrilling emergence as the real fulcrum of the tale as the sur-text gives the birth and death dates of Felix Lauwers. That this synthesis is played out as the cast reprise *Song for Budhanton*, with its lyrics of life going on and a musical loop that draws spectators in, makes for perhaps the most satisfying end to any performance around. In each of the three versions I have seen, in very different countries and contexts, the standing ovation was immediate and sustained. A standing ovation can differ in kind. Often, a few people will get to their feet and others will follow, until everybody stands. At other times spectators rise to their feet as one. Sometimes the manner in which a company takes a bow, half-leaving the stage before running back on with a blend of genuine pleasure and mock surprise, has its own impact and the rhythm of clapping pulls people to their feet. Sometimes we are shamed to our feet by the people around us, as though a failure to stand is testament to rudeness, or worse, a failure to have fully understood. Sometimes we know that work deserves an ovation, which we simply will not give because we are too studied to show those around us that we like anything that much. Sometimes too the greatness of a work does not fully hit us until much later and we find that theatre we thought merely good got under our skin for life. With *Isabella's Room* the applause was not only in response to highly skilled theatricality and the company's knowing use of community singing – of the right songs, at the right time, sung to us in a way that made the theatre feel like a place of (whisper it soft) emotionally charged worship; it was also a celebration of an audience's own humanity and a way of thanking the cast for providing an injection of hope in dark times. We know well that conventional theatre can pull these strings, for we know that sentiment is a short cut to emotion and sentimentality is what happens when we seek familiar responses to familiar stimuli. *Isabella's Room* does none of this. The performers turn what might have been sentimentality into optimism and they do this without missing a beat. Other beats are there, but these I miss: it becomes slowly apparent for example and only fully in hindsight, that Julien Fauré, who represents the desert prince/Felix Lauwers is utterly central to the work whilst having barely spoken at all. Proof, if any such were needed, that actions speak louder than words, in *Isabella's Room*, as in performance, as in life.

What we subsequently learn about theatrical events changes the way we remember what we saw. The story of Franky's death in Africa is rooted in the real. The character is inspired by Wim Van Boxelaer, a young man Lauwers knew when each was in his early twenties. Leaving the theatre in order to work with the Red Cross, Van Boxelaer was killed, along with his bodyguards, by a warlord in Mogadishu. Discovering this, some time after seeing the work for the second time added a layer of comprehension that I find impossible now to ignore. There is a spirit of selective eclecticism at work in *Isabella's Room* that renders the real and the fictional equal – but equally what? Equally valuable? Equally ephemeral? Lauwers wonders how, when we watch death in Africa on television and then one-minute later an advert for a holiday in Africa, we don't kill ourselves. He responds to his own question by musing that we are used to switching between sensibilities as swiftly as we can switch channels on television. And maybe that is where equality lies. Not in inherent value, but through the sensibilities we bring to experience. And in inviting us to switch between sensibilities in *Isabella's Room*, the work becomes a holiday from hopelessness. If this woman can live through all that, then surely we can live through all of this?

In 1827 a completely blind traveller, Lieutenant James Holman, set sail from England for Africa. He stayed abroad for five years, experiencing through non-visual senses a world that few sighted men would ever know, stating simply that the absence of sight was succeeded by an increased desire for locomotion. (Roberts, 2006) The immediacy of his experiences denied any sense of depression and, in essence, we can say that Holman travelled in order to feel fully alive. Somewhere between the shadows thrown by an unsighted explorer and the truism that love is blind, *Isabella's Room* deals with the loss of loved ones and the atrocities of the twentieth century. Along the way, the work leads to a consideration of the relationship between art and entertainment. And this makes for a troubling experience. Steeped as many of us are in the melancholic cynicism of much contemporary theatre, where laughter is rarely licensed other than through irony and where work is often endured rather than enjoyed, I find myself, initially at least, a little at sea amidst all of this feel-good performance. I sit and wonder whether theatre becomes entertainment when people laugh, and at what point entertainment became a dirty word in the narrow world of Performance Studies. I find no satisfying answers and so drift back to our good guide Brecht, who had a great deal to say on the subject of entertainment, not least on the necessary role that it plays in the effectiveness of theatrical events. And watching *Isabella's Room* it seems that Brecht's criticisms of 'culinary theatre', of work that sees entertainment as both means and end, have been too easily, too *lazily* translated into sound bites that equate audience pleasure with some kind of social or intellectual disengagement. Where entertainment has come to be regarded as the merely diversionary, we do well to remember its etymology as a word that means entering into possession of a state of being. Pleasure draws us into *Isabella's Room* on many levels – from the scopophilic delights of seeing beautiful dancers who can out-act most actors to the foot-tapping poppiness of the songs we hear – and yet none of this makes us switch off. Switch off from what? The work is the work, and the better we like it the closer we watch.

Lauwers' background is in conceptual art, where lightness and emotion were tacitly forbidden and where Joseph Beuys was something of a mentor; so it is fair to assume that the road from confrontational art to celebratory performance was not smooth. Yet it was Beuys' own practice that pointed the way, inasmuch as when the great man of angst began to cry to order in his work he segued from the concrete qualities of performance into the rehearsed illusions of theatre. And *Isabella's Room* plays as quirkily with rehearsal as the Wooster Group's *L.S.D.* of 1984 – a production that had a lasting impact on Lauwers. On one (in)famous occasion, the Wooster Group cast rehearsed *L.S.D.* whilst under the watchful gaze of the director Elizabeth LeCompte and the influence of hallucinogenic drugs; the subsequent performance saw the detailed acting out of the seemingly unstructured in a way that showed the group at their most brilliantly disciplined. In *Isabella's Room* the tightest acting comes at those moments where we are half tricked into believing that we are seeing unrehearsed moments, such as Benoît Gob's too-clumsy-to-be-true collision with the synthesiser that sounds out each year of the work's narrative at the same time as we know, as we *must know*, that this is a show with no margin for this type of error and no room for the haphazard. Seeing the work on three occasions only confirms this belief: the performances are nuanced slightly differently, but you could set your watch by the length of each scene.

Isabella recounts the story of her life's adventures and so do those whose roles have shaped that life. Whilst Isabella's telling is mostly in prose, the rest of the cast burst regularly into song in ways that at once interrupt and deepen the narrative. In fact, there is more overt emotion in the delivery of the songs than in the acting, which is largely cool, dispassionate even – a retelling of events that makes no attempt at clumsy stage realism. Speaking of his work with the New York City Players, Richard Maxwell says that he never wants his actors to try to make his words sound 'real'. What reality exists is in the fact that the work is already real: 'It's not another reality that you're trying to create. You're seeing what happens in the moment, which is, for me, the highest reality.' (Quoted in Pogrebin, 2000, p.1) Whereas Maxwell instructs his actors to 'say the lines and not move too much' (ibid.) and Lauwers so clearly licences movement, the directors share a distrust of the pursuit of mimetic performance à la Stanislavski. Where a mainstream theatre perspective locates Chekhov and Ibsen as the fathers of modern practice, Lauwers draws on a different twentieth-century tradition: one that starts with Duchamp and which asks not 'what theatre can we do?' but 'what can we do with theatre?' These different paradigms inevitably lead to the following of different creative paths and in this sense all roads lead through Tadeusz Kantor's Cricot 2 and the Wooster Group. (See Witts, 2009; Kobialka, 2009; Savran, 1989; and Quick, 2007) Where watching *L.S.D.* stoked a fire in Lauwers that had been ignited by Kantor's production of *The Dead Class*, Maxwell's period as an intern with the Wooster Group took him from sweeping the stage and not spilling the coffee to making work which has earned its own international kudos. *The Dead Class*, whilst not theatrically structured like *Isabella's Room*, has certain thematic overlaps. In *The Dead Class*, Kantor's onstage director presides over a class filled with supposedly dead characters who encounter mannequins representing their younger selves; in *Isabella's Room* Lauwers introduces and observes a stage filled with the dead, the drowned and the crazy surrounded by objects representing Isabella's desire to see Africa and Lauwers' own desire to fashion the loss of his father into art. As a director, Kantor was a hugely significant part of the neo-avant-garde of mid- to late-twentieth-century performance and, as with Lauwers, he came to theatre from a background as a visual artist – as a painter who needed the company of players.

Discussions of authorial honesty invoke ideas of memory over invention despite the fact that every memory is always also a fiction of sorts. Memory is to theatre as the still life was to Morandi's art and from Williams' *The Glass Menagerie*, Fugard's *The Fitful Muse*, Pinter's *Landscape* to pretty much anything by Beckett, theatre thrives on an agenda of rediscovering and destabilising identities, and of making cultural memory into an in-the-present restorative. The recent drift towards performance with a focus on personal narratives that explore the writer/performers' experience of life and on the current obsession with self-as-subject celebrity is but the latest in a line that reaches back to the sixteenth century: to Michel de Montaigne's 'I am myself the matter of my book' (Montaigne, 1958, p.2) and to Giulio Camillo's sixteenth-century *Memory Theatre*, a structure which allowed one or two people at a time to enter into its interior. (See Yates, 1966) Once inside, these spectators/participants/observers were able to view seven sections, each filled with a variety of images, figures and ornaments. The connecting line between this and much of what passes itself off as contemporary installation shows how little things have changed in 500 years. A popular phenomenon of the sixteenth and seventeenth century was the wonder cabinet, consisting of tableaux where various items of science and art were placed alongside religious artefacts and exotic New World objects. Even at a time like ours, when the juxtaposition of the old and the new, the domestic and the foreign and high art with low has become as commonplace as it has, seeing Isabella taking a cheap plastic lighter suspended from a possibly fake gold chain wrapped around an oversized and ancient stone penis creates a paradox of perception that forces us to look and look again. On one level Isabella's use of this particular penis is no different to her use of a petrified whale's phallus as a behind-the-door burglar deterrent or her use of Friday's member as a source of physical rather than merely visual pleasure. Without meaning, beauty becomes meaningless and without function a beautiful object is just something old that ends up coated with Parisian dust.

Like the focus of this book, theatre is then always in some ways about memory. The notion of rehearsal to the point of seeming spontaneity reminds us that the art of acting is itself the craft of memory. The idea of emotion memory as described by Stanislavski has done much to harness common ideas of actors drawing on past experiences in present performance to the relatively modern language of psychological realism; and yet we know that actors have always used their pasts in the creation of roles. Just as we cannot imagine that which we do not first remember, so creativity is also a type of rumination on memory. When Walter Benjamin wrote that theatre was the medium of past experience he reconnected contemporary thought and theatre to the ancient Greeks, who knew that Mnemosyne, the mother of the nine muses and the personification of memory, was also the inventor of language and words, preserving the past through its re-telling – and you cannot get much more 'theatre' than that. At the same time as Benjamin took us back to the Greeks, he laid the foundations for Marvin Carlson's 2001 book, *The Haunted Stage: Theatre as Memory Machine*, which expertly articulates the phenomenon of ghosts of previous productions haunting all work that we see. In positioning theatre as the stimulation of memory, Carlson suggests a relationship between the memory of the spectator and the way that work is received that situates who we are and where we have been as no less important than the words of the play or the production's *mise en scene*. If the art of memory makes possible the health of one's existence in ways that allow remembered loss to become a form of nourishment, translating sadness and pain into pleasure, then the memories of death that haunt this production – the loss to Isabella and Lauwers of Franky, and the loss of Felix Lauwers – find, in my watching, echoes of the death of my own father. Reading Benjamin and Carlson casts critical light on the reality we all instinctively and emotionally understand: that like actors bringing aspects of who they once were to who they are now meant to play, we carry the ghosts of our other, non-spectating, smiling/grieving selves with us when we hand in our tickets and take to our seats.

Common wisdom has it that sons experience particularly acute sadness when their fathers die. Maybe this is not common wisdom at all: maybe it is just that I am the son of a dead father and that placing my experience within an apparently universal frame serves to contextualise my emotional indulgence. Maybe common wisdom is no more than pointing to the examples that best serve our ends. No matter. People deal with loss in different ways: some through a focus on significant actions that consciously connect a son with the memory of his father. For an artist like Lauwers, the most significant action that can be created is to create an act of signification: to make a performance. For those of us who do not possess the creative wherewithal to make significant art, or whose sense of self is not dependent upon adopting the title of 'artist' with no justification other than whimsy, our ways of dealing with loss are often mediated through other people's art. So it is that *Isabella's Room* became to my spectating self a type of eulogy. My father was no bearded desert prince, nor yet a doctor, nor collector of artefacts, but as I watch Lauwers' thinly veiled tribute as part of an audience, I realise that I am not just paying tribute to my ocean-going knave of a father, I am working through a credo of sorts, a legend of who he was and who memory has turned him into, in a way that keeps him always half alive. And as a father myself, and one whose absence has been perhaps more significant than his presence, I find myself mourning loss from two sides, feeling the loss of a father to the child and the loss of the child to a father.

It is hard to adopt a position of critical distance when every second of the work draws me in as closely as this; but perhaps critical distance is itself no more than the myth of objectivity... the idea that emotional involvement is antithetical to intellectual engagement. Like the theatre history books that see John Osborne's *Look back in Anger* as the watershed moment of 1956 Britain, perhaps objectivity is something we are taught to believe in by rote, remembering rather than deciding our rules of response. Nietzsche defined happiness as the ability to forget, or, as he stated it, the capacity to feel unhistorically during its duration (Nietzsche, 1998, p.126) because he felt that the past 'returns as a ghost and disturbs the peace of a later moment'. (Ibid.) For Nietzsche, too much of the past is not a good thing, auguring as it does against development and happiness, those greatest of goals. Nietzsche was no man of the theatre, a position he made clear in his statement that 'theatre is a form of demolatry in matters of taste; the theatre is a revolt of the masses, a plebiscite against good taste', (quoted in Kaufman, 1976, p.183) a place and form in which an audience of commoners worships its own mirror image. The extreme nature of Nietzsche's contempt may not mean that we can blithely disregard his views, but it does suggest that he was marching to the beat of a different type of drum: one markedly different from those who are likely to be reading this book.

Most of us mellow as we age. For those of us who make our living picking at the bones of theatre, offering prejudice dressed up as insights and making our often-spurious claims from the safety of the lecture hall, this mellowing might show in the way we ease slowly away from a second-hand attachment to ideas of 'performance' rather than 'theatre'. That some of us are shifting from a particularly empty type of anger to an acceptance that 'theatre' is not an illicit word might strike some others as strange: for isn't theatre the very thing that university departments carrying that name teach? Well, yes, and well, no. In our collective efforts to be recognised as a stand-alone academic subject, ideas of theatre seemed just a little too close for comfort to English Literature. Richard Schechner's spirited and addictive arguments towards 'Performance' as an inclusive and empowering term had much to do with the drift that prioritised ritualistic, physical behaviour over written text and spoken language; but perhaps this coincided with the darker and more secret fear that if BA Theatre could be taught by English Literature specialists then what good were the rest of us? Perhaps then mellowing comes not with age so much as confidence. For Lauwers this confidence is demonstrated through work that is not too knowing to tell a story and not too shackled by the tropes of postmodernism to create characters we care about. Where contemporary theatre can sometimes feel like an exercise in absence, so that the work gives us little by way of skills to applaud, *Isabella's Room* is theatre with all the bells and whistles and with nothing taken away. In this sense, the experience of seeing the work is not unlike walking into a gallery of Old Masters after a self-enforced diet of Damien Hirst, Jeff Koons and Tracey Emin. *Isabella's Room* shows Lauwers at the top of his game and his cast at the very top of theirs. If all theatre were as wonderful as this then we would unplug our televisions and leave cinemas to rot. The work really is that good. And that feels strange to write, because, unlike Lauwers, I am not quite yet confident enough in my own (rather than my borrowed) judgement, especially when it is as unsettled as seeing this work has made it.

After a long experience of being personally disappointed by theatre, of seeing greatness so seldom that I have become more attuned to criticism than celebration, the cynical seen-it-all-before of arch postmodernism has all but snuffed out any vestige of hope, romanticism and joy. After years of this, the language of attack is much more familiar than words of praise and watching theatre that achieves the very things I have spent a career either deriding or denying is a glorious if profoundly curious experience. I find myself lingering in the auditorium long after the performers have left the stage, realising that I am, for the first and, who knows, perhaps the only time in my life, an absolutely satisfied spectator. Satisfied by form, content and verve but also by something more: for if this is the skilfully told story of Isabella, wrought from a son's last respects, it is also the story of the world, of all that we can live through and all that we can love. As far removed from the fakers' safety net of 'it can mean whatever you want it to mean' as from those other fakers' finger-wagging, pamphlet-waving didacticism: this is theatre not as a lesson but as a light.

Truth in art is like truth in love: we know it when it is seen and felt but it is not subject to taxonomical categorisation. And like the loves we have known that did not necessarily last but which were nevertheless true, we cannot measure honesty in performance by the autobiographer's promise, the playwright's search for universality or the critic's purple praise. Before *Isabella's Room* treats us to an extended blast of *Rock 'n' Roll Suicide*, complete with Lauwers on electric guitar, we are reminded by Maarten Seghers that the singer is at once Ziggy Stardust *and* David Bowie: both and neither, identities overlapping seamlessly, folding in on each other so that we cannot separate the singer's persona from the singer nor the singer from the song. Nor even Bowie from Hans Petter Dahl, his ultra-louche doppelgänger if ever there was one, so alike that front-row spectators start checking Dahl's eyes for signs of Bowie's anisocoria. It's a theatre-smart synopsis of simulacrum and it sneaks into the work like a telling footnote, an in-joke that plays so well it makes performative sense of Baudrillard's thoughts. For those who recognise the roots of Manuel Machado's poem *Chants Andalou* in Bowie's 'Time takes a cigarette', the original lines 'Life is a cigarette/Cinder, ash and fire/Some smoke it in a hurry/Others savour it' is an accurate snapshot of Isabella that combines with Bowie's 'You're too old to lose it/Too young to choose it' to create a paean to age that is as evocative as it raucous. The varied repetition of 'You're not alone… Oh no love! You're not alone… Just turn on with me and you're not alone… Let's turn on and be not alone' likewise sets the musical and emotional scene for the reprise of *Song for Budhanton*'s 'We are the people/Who never stop/We just go on and on and on and on' so that, when we hear the song for the second time, it is an entirely different experience, the borrowed informing the bespoke, the million-selling track rubbing shoulders with the art-house score with no fake hierarchy of 'truth'.

The idea of truth having currency in a world of greasepaint and well-rehearsed lines has always been something of a misnomer, more at home in an award-acceptance speech than in the heat of performance, and despite the reverential language we adopt when we talk about theatre, ultimately, it matters not a jot to most of us where the words the performer speaks have come from, nor how painstakingly they were wrought. The current obsession with autoethnography has added its own layer of self-orientation, turning theatres into confession booths, yet it is usually through the lies we tell that we reveal most closely who we are. Where Camillo's aim was to construct artificial memories stemming from truth, Lauwers' is to tap into real memories through fiction. In this way, Lauwers' fictional protagonist tells us what matters at the same time as we know that what matters here to Lauwers is to keep us watching, listening and thinking. *Isabella's Room* honours Felix Lauwers because it is theatre that works as well as it does; and it pays its respects to the dead through its constant celebration of life. Jan Lauwers' memories might inform the narrative (and just as often they might not) but it is the invented memories of Isabella that we come to care about. The only reality in performance is spectators watching performers and excellence does not make theatre more honest – it just makes the lies more thrilling to hear.

The recent focus of much performance has been on diasporic and fractured identities but *Isabella's Room* is having none of this. Life's adventures have not fractured the core of who Isabella is, they have created it; and rather than being in endless exile she is always absolutely where she needs to be, as comfortable in her inherited apartment as she is in her own sense of self. Lauwers casts the same new light on post-colonialism that he brings to postmodernism, taking us out of a set of shackling paradigms towards a sense of old-style community for a new-style audience. Lauwers' belief that art cannot provoke anymore because the world has become too provocative denies the fact that one only has to think of Fabre, Vandekeybus and De Keersmaeker to know that the Flemish theatre of which Needcompany is such a strong part has been responsible for some of the most provocative aesthetic moments of the past twenty-five years. Lauwers may feel that the only connection is that these practitioners are all Flemish but there is more to it than this: not least the fact that Flemish performance makers have to be international precisely because their home audience is so small and that a generous policy of subsidy makes touring a realistic pattern of life. The existence of numerous theatres in Belgium also provides space for experimental work to take root. Nationality may be an accident, something inherited rather than earned, and those of us who luxuriate in our small worlds of near-borderless travel may feel like unfixed internationalists; but it is clear that Flemish theatre *is* unique, something valued without its artists or audiences being precious about it… the opposite of the British situation, where theatre is usually precious whilst only very rarely valued. Needcompany is about as internationally eclectic as it is possible to be and the working process is both open and inclusive, but this is performance making filtered through a sensibility that is more indicative of nationality than Lauwers might care to admit. *Op uw gezondheid.*

Isabella's is a life touched but not defined by sadness that forces the ego to suffer a reduction in self-regard; by the melancholia that leads a father to drink and a mother's heart to burst from the holding back of too many secrets. Like the histories of the Europe she inhabits, much that has happened to Isabella has not been a cause for pride, yet Isabella's European perspective is as central to who she is as her gender. Isabella is a woman who has lived and loved and lost everything that matters. Everything except the myth of a father never known. Everything except the love of a life given once; a life, which, whilst not quite something one would ever describe as sweet, is transformed by De Muynck into its own *La Dolce Vita*. And because of this she is much more than a woman with a past. We look at her and see a woman who holds onto life because she loves it as much as she does and who is not quite yet ready for the curtain to fall. *Isabella's Room* has a focus on the past, but Isabella is a woman with a future. Resolute as she is, the character could not be less like the image of an aged woman experiencing life as an endless waiting for death's escape. If Lauwers and his cast show us great theatre here, they show us too that theatre can still be great; that being in the same time and space as performers telling the story of a wonderful woman and of a woman telling us a wonderful tale can amount to more than the sum of its already excellent parts. Rare as it is, this is what makes *Isabella's Room* an event both for and of our time and it is this that makes the work just about as good as it is possible for twenty-first-century theatre to get.

Works Cited

Bennett, S. (1997) *Theatre Audiences: A Theory of Production and Reception*, second edition, London and New York: Routledge

Carlson, M. (2001) *The Haunted Stage: Theatre as Memory Machine*, Michigan: University of Michigan Press

Fuchs, E. (1996) *Death of the Character*, Bloomington: Indiana University Press

Kobialka, M. (2009) *Further on, Nothing: Tadeusz Kantor's Theatre*, University of Minnesota Press

Lyotard, J.F. (1992) *The Postmodern Explained*, Sydney: Power Publications

Montaigne, M. de (1958) *The Complete Essays of Montaigne*, California: Stanford University Press

Nietzsche, F. (1998) *On the Genealogy of Morals: A Polemic*, New York: Oxford University Press, USA

Pearson, K.A. & Large, D. (2006) *The Nietzsche Reader*, Oxford: Blackwell

Pogrebin, R. (2000) 'A Playwright Who Creates People, Not Roles', *New York Times*, 25 September 2000, pp.1–4

Quick, A. (2007) *The Wooster Group Work Book*, London & New York: Routledge

Roberts, J. (2006) *A Sense of the World: How a Blind Man Became History's Greatest Traveller*, London: Harper Collins

Robinson, D. (1999) *Nietzsche and Postmodernism*, London: Icon Books

Savran, D. (1989) *Breaking the Rules: The Wooster Group*, Theatre Communications Group, Inc.

Stalpaert, C., F. Le Roy & S. Bousset (2007) *No Beauty For Me There Where Human Life is Rare*, Amsterdam: International Theatre & Film Books

ten Cate, R. (1996) *Man Looking for Words*, Amsterdam: Theater Insitut Nederland

Williams, R. (1969) *Drama from Ibsen to Brecht*, New York: Oxford University Press

Witts, N. (2009) *Tadeusz Kantor*, London: Routledge

Yates, F.A. (1966) *The Art of Memory*, London: Pimlico Press

CHAPTER FOURTEEN

Impromptu XL: Tg STAN
Theatre as a Memory Machine

ANNE PELLOIS

'Il faut que je vous dise un impromptu, pierre de touche de l'esprit'.[*]
Damiaan de Schrijver, Les Egotistes, *from* Poquelin

Memory machine/sweet salt sour bitter/repertoire/cross-fertilisations/
old and new plays/everything mixed up/new alliances/party.
Impromptu XL's *programme*

Saturday, 19 December 2009, noon, Théâtre de la Bastille, Paris. *Impromptu XL* by the Tg STAN is starting and will last until midnight. This twelve-hour theatrical marathon, bringing together roughly thirty-five artists,[†] plus the four founder members of the Flemish collective, celebrates the twentieth anniversary of the troupe. The day and the evening at the Théâtre de la Bastille is the last stop of this celebration. The

---

[*] 'I have to tell you an impromptu, which is the touchstone of the wit'.
[†] In random order: Nico Sturm, Damiaan De Schrijver, Frank Vercruyssen, Natali Broods, Jolente De Keersmaeker, Sara De Roo, Aka Moon, Fabrizio Cassol, Stéphane Galland, Michel Hatzigeorgiou, Stijn Bettens, Erwin Sampermans, Peter Verhaegen, Alano Gruarin, Tine Embrechts, Alix Eynaudi, Federica Porello, Liz Kinoshita, Tiago Rodrigues, An D'Huys, Jef Lambrecht, Koen Augustijnen, Jakub Truskowski, Alma Palacios, Vedis Kjartansdottir, Filip Jordens, Claire Dumas, Judith Davis, Mélanie Bestel, Cathy Verney, Simon Bahkouche, Nadir Legrand, Boy Raaijmakers, Paul De Clerck, Erik Morel, Kuno Bakker, Peter Van den Eede, Matthias de Koning e.a.

Impromptu has been played previously in Anvers, its place of creation, and in Bruxelles, in an XXL version entitled *Toestand** in Dutch, with no fewer than ninety artists, and in a very short version lasting four hours, at the Théâtre Garonne in Toulouse, with a dozen guests.[†]

The Tg STAN is a Flemish collective of actors, playing their works either in Dutch, French or English: the collective is free from a director or any form of fixed staging. Tg stands for 'Toneelspelersgezelschap', which means literally 'company of theatre players', whilst STAN stems from 'Stop Thinking About Names', an acronym which highlights the collective nature of the group and their work. The company was founded in 1989 by Frank Vercruyssen, Sara de Roo, Jolente de Keersmaeker and Damiaan de Schrijver. The *Impromptu XL* seems to be a comprehensive offering of the collective's work, past and present, reflecting a whole dramaturgic and theatrical universe in one extraordinary performance event.

The show was performed in a space in which one is free to move around – on the stage side, because there was no neat distinction between stage and wings, and on the audience's side, because everyone could come in and out of the theatre whenever they chose. Therefore, it was composed of a succession of elements that were at first sight markedly disparate, but which in the end formed a coherent ensemble: extracts of plays previously performed by the STAN, with or without the collaboration of other companies, weaving a shared universe of references with the spectators[‡] and composing a 'best of' effect, which is rare in the theatre. Parts were danced by associated companies; concerts performed by artists who had collaborated with or influenced the collective in one way or another; alongside various speeches or readings of literary texts and statements. There were altogether at least forty performances or performance elements that followed on from each other without any break for twelve solid hours.

---

* In Dutch, *Toestand* means state, condition or situation. We will get back to that.

† The premiere took place at the Kaaitheater in Brussels, on 16 and 17 October 2009, from 8 p.m. to 8 p.m. the next day; another performance took place at the Monty, Antwerp, on 30 and 31 October, also from 8 p.m. to 8 p.m. the next day. A four-hour version was performed at the Théâtre Garonne in Toulouse, on 21 November, from 7 p.m. to 11 p.m.

‡ Most of us spectators were familiar with the work of the STAN. Few people would indeed venture into a twelve-hour show without knowing a bit about the collective's work…

From the most serious statement by Jef Lambrecht about the urgent need for ethical journalism to the most hilarious sketch by the duo Damiaan de Schrijver and Peter van den Eede. From violin solos by Paul de Clerck to the jazz set by the group AKA Moon, including songs by a Jacques Brel reincarnation (Filip Jordens), a dance solo on a Glenn Gould interview and the Goldberg variations by Federica Porello. From collaborative episodes with other troupes (L'Avantage du doute, de Koe, Maatschappij Discordia, Rosas) and of course extracts of previous STAN shows, such as *Poquelin*,[*] *My Dinner with Andre*,[†] *In real Time*,[‡] *Sauve qui peut, pas mal comme titre*[§] and *Tout est calme*.[¶]

The number of performers, the lack of interruptions, the continuity of the show, its fragmentation, the variety of the performances, the multiplicity of the emotions and universes explored both by the actors and spectators all contributed to make this show one of the greatest shows I have seen so far, transforming

---

[*] *Poquelin*, created in Dutch on 21 May 2003, in Kaaitheater/KunstenFESTIVALdesArts, Brussels, and in French on 1 October 2004, at the Théâtre Garonne, Toulouse. The show was made with rewritten fragments of plays by Molière: *Dom Juan, L'Avare, La Comtesse d'Estrabagnas, La Critique de l'Ecole des Femmes, Le Malade imaginaire, Le Médecin malgré lui, Les Femmes savantes, les Précieuses ridicules, Sganarelle ou le cocu imaginaire, Psyché.*

[†] *My Dinner with André* was created in Dutch on 17 September 1998, in Het Toneelhuis in Antwerp, and in French on 11 October 2005, in Théâtre Garonne in Toulouse. The play is an adaptation of the film by Louis Malle, *My Diner with André*. The original scenario is a dialogue between Wallace Shawn, theatre actor and author and André Gregory, a famous stage director in decline, written by Shawn and played, in the film, by Shawn and Gregory. The conversation is almost exclusively about theatre.

[‡] *In Real Time*, created in English at the Théâtre de la Monnaie in Brussels, on 18 May 2000. The texts were mostly by Gerardjan Rijnders, the choreography by Anne Teresa De Keersmaeker. With the participation of Rosas and AKA Moon.

[§] *Sauve qui peut, pas mal comme titre*, created in Dutch on 16 February 2005, at the Kaaitheater in Brussels, in French on 17 October 2007 at the Théâtre de la Bastille. The play is based on *Les Dramuscules* by Thomas Bernhard (*Glaces, Un Mort, Match, Acquittement* and *Le Mois de Marie*). With the participation of Matthias de Koning.

[¶] *Tout est calme*, created in Dutch on 12 May 1999, at Minard Schouwburg/Vooruit, in Ghent, and in French on 9 October 2001, at the Théâtre des Bernardines, in Marseille. Text by Thomas Bernhard.

the performance into a real theatrical feast. One that celebrated not only the theatrical universe of the STAN, but also theatre itself as live art, freed from everything that could *fix* it in one way or another. With this show, we, spectators, have been invited to a real 'celebration of live performance',* in an atmosphere made all the more relaxed by each spectator's freedom to move around and the peculiar relationship established between the audience and the stage.

It is difficult to describe such a show without taking the risk of falling into a tedious catalogue, or worse, of betraying the spirit of the show, its impromptu aspect, by fixing it in a form that would be mummified into analysis. I will therefore try to give an account of why this show stands out as one of the greatest shows, in my experience as a spectator, based on my memory of the event and some materials I had at my disposal: notes taken on the night of the show, a live radio show broadcast on France Culture from 8 p.m. to midnight,† an interview with Frank Vercruyssen about the show and various papers I had previously written on other plays by the STAN.‡

The titanic nature of the show enabled the spectators to complete a journey through the whole set of theatrical practices of the STAN, here given as an anthology. But the greatness of the show lay not in the 'best of' or 'anthology' effect which might be induced by the re-run of previous shows but in a 'summa' effect, understood here as a succession of summaries of all the parts of the STAN's work and world. By the very choice of the impromptu form, the Tg STAN affirms a way of making theatre which is open to all sorts of propositions and accidents.

At the same time, the memorial and durative dimension of the show induces a questioning of shared temporality: contemporary times, the time of

---

* The expression (in French, 'fête du live') is from Frank Vercruyssen, who kindly agreed to be interviewed in Lyon on 2 December 2010.

† 'Drôle de drame', broadcast live on 9 December 2009, from the Théâtre de la Bastille, from 8 p.m. to midnight.

‡ Anne Pellois, 'Les intermittences du je(u), à propos du Tg STAN', in *Autofictions scéniques ou l'auto-figuration au théâtre: L'auteur de soi à soi?*, joint publication soon to be published at the Presses Universitaires de Dijon; 'En Quête du Tg STAN: Spectateur en monologues pour acteur polyphonique', in *Le Monologue contre le drame?*, joint publication soon to be published at the Presses Universitaires de Rennes; 'L'acteur déjà là', contribution to a two-day workshop about 'l'entrée en scène' organised by the ENS de Lyon and the University of Lyon II, 29 and 30 May 2009.

the performance, commonly shared memories. Far from being the personal celebration of a troupe which refuses the domination of one name in any way,* this show is a real celebration of theatre itself, tackling the political aspects of the question of men and women living and feeling together.

Impromptu XL: from Form to Material

Impromptu XL, for and despite its size, the number of artists involved and the variety of its forms and themes, proposes a kind of summary, something like an anthology of the collective's work. The 'best of' effect points the way to the previous creations, whereas the various artists invited and the very impromptu form of the event propose an immersion in the whole universe of the STAN to the spectator and give access to everything that feeds the collective's work. The *Impromptu* works as a sum, without burying the show into the grave reserved for complete works. Entitled 'state' or 'situation' in Dutch, this show could be understood as a sort of overview, in a form that exposes the collective's unrehearsed way of performing and the whole dramaturgic context of their creations. The whole thing made from influences, collaborations and various sources, juxtaposed with former productions: 'This is our work', says Sara de Roo about the *Impromptu XL*. 'It's very pure in an impromptu. People see how we work. We allow them to watch us in our kitchen, the kitchen of theatre makers, what do you say again? Actors'.†

The Dramaturgic Contextualisation

The *Impromptu XL* is a kind of dramaturgic landscape, highlighting the multiplicity of influences and materials that give shape to their shows, just as much as the process of collaboration that prevails in the work of the STAN. In the list of invited artists, there are of course the fellow travellers: Peter van den Eede from de Koe, Matthias de Koning from Maatschappij Discordia but also the collective's former teacher at the Conservatoire in Anvers, members of the French collective L'Avantage du doute they met in 2005, members of Rosas, Anna Teresa de Keersmaeker's company, and the jazz band Aka Moon

---

*   As in 'Stop Thinking About Names'
†   'C'est notre travail. C'est très pur dans un impromptu. On voit comment nous faisons notre travail. On fait regarder dans notre cuisine, celle des faiseurs de théâtre, comment dit-on, des comédiens'. Interview on France Culture, at the time the show was in Paris.

who took part in the show *In real Time* in 2000. Other artists who have not necessarily played with the STAN but had an influence on them were there too. The whole panel of artists proposes a poetic crossing of the STAN universe, something like a cartography of influence.

More than that, the fragmented form of the show underlines the aesthetics of montage, of various materials or media that govern the STAN's way of working. In the *Impromptu XL* the textual material is predominant, but also extremely varied: ranging from dramatic texts from Shakespeare, Molière, Oscar Wilde, Thomas Bernhard, Harold Pinter, Howard Barker, Martin Crimp, Botho Strauss and Lars Noren to letters written by Büchner,[*] via some of La Rochefoucault's Maxims (handed out to the public), Diderot's text about the *Paradoxe* and a poem by Jacques Prévert. These literary texts are bundled together with non-literary texts, such as the statement by Jef Lambrecht who announces on stage his decision to quit his job as a journalist.[†]

To all of this are added different musical horizons: the violinist Paul de Clerck, the jazz band Aka Moon, the saxophonist Erik Morel, the hilarious trumpet solo by Jolente de Keersmaeker, the voices of Filip Jordens singing Brel, of Sara de Roo doing slam poetry to Aka Moon music. Some dance, solo or duo, with or without the participation of actors, to words or to music. And finally some excursions through video, particularly during the Tank Man Tango Dance, a choreography based on the pictures of the Tiananmen Square events in 1989.

All these materials are both a source of inspiration and building material for the shows. The spectator is placed here in front of a huge think tank, there for everyone to see, forming on stage a cheerful mess. And this mess was part of the charm of the day and evening. Spectators have varying degrees of familiarity with the STAN's work, but the feeling is the same: we feel like we have been invited to see the other side of the scenery, in the theatre factory, on the other side of the mirror, without losing the pleasure of attending the show. For the STAN,

---

[*] April 1833 and February 1834.

[†] A well-known journalist who is appreciated by the STAN, Lambrecht specialised for a long time in the Middle-East. One of the plays by Frank Vercruyssen, *C'est la nouvelle Lune et il commence à faire froid*, takes its title directly from a sentence by Lambrecht. This play denounces the activities of the American army during the first Gulf War in 1991. This is the first constituent of a triptych composed of two other shows: *One 2 life* in 1996, about the life of the American activist George L. Jackson, and *En Quête* in 2003 (*Questioning*), about the second Gulf War.

it does not make any difference. The show brings together two stages that are traditionally apart in time, the conception of the show and its representation.

The Impromptu as a Style

Without explicitly referring to the *Impromptu de Versailles* by Molière, *Impromptu XL* cannot be studied without referring to this particular form, which refers simultaneously to music, poetry, and theatre. Defined as an 'improvisation on a fixed subject',[*] the impromptu form matches exactly what we feel during the show, whose form is only fixed in its structure (how the different events are sequenced together and succeed each other) and performed on the spot. The impromptu reflects the major creative process of the STAN,[†] well known for not rehearsing on stage but only 'sitting down' for preparatory work. The actors dissect the text and decide on what they call 'the traffic',[‡] that is to say the framework of the show, without agreeing on the details of the staging. All of this so that they can keep a certain element of freshness in their performances:

> Duplicating the same movements in an expected manner, without any surprise, deprives them of their liveliness. That's why we just define a staging framework, *the traffic*: we can decide that in the first act we will be mostly standing, and in the second act we will try and make sure we sit down. Onto these preliminary indications, we superimpose our natural choreography.[§]

---

[*] Georges Forestier defines the impromptu as 'une improvisation sur un thème donné', article 'Impromptu', in *Dictionnaire du Théâtre*, Michel Corvin (dir.), Paris, Bordas, 1995, p.452.

[†] In November 2005, the Tg STAN gave a show entitled *Impromptu*, at the Théâtre de la Bastille. These nights were built on exactly the same premises: the evening's program was not known in advance but only posted at the theatre entrance just before the beginning of the show. The members of the company had invited several artists, musicians, actors, etc., to participate. The texts were by Thomas Bernhard, Bertolt Brecht, Molière, Harold Pinter and others.

[‡] 'Anvers et contre tout', interview by Catherine Firmin-Didot in *Télérama*, 9 November 2005. Interview available on the Tg STAN's web site: www.stan.be

[§] 'Reproduire les mêmes gestes de manière attendue, sans imprévu, les dépouille de toute vivacité. Aussi nous définissons juste une trame de mise en scène, qu'on appelle le trafic: on peut décider qu'au premier acte nous nous tiendrons plutôt debout, qu'au deuxième on tentera de s'asseoir. A ces indications préalables, nous superposerons chacun notre chorégraphie naturelle'. (Ibid.)

The première of the show is therefore a real première in the sense that the show does not exist on stage before the encounter with the audience. The show can only exist in its scenic form in front of the spectators. The sequence of events of the *Impromptu XL*, even if it was not known by the spectators, had been very precisely set in the succession of its different parts beforehand. However, what was *inside* the sequences had not been fixed at all. The acting might get flustered, the installation might take a lot of time, but in any case, the acting style, between incarnation and distancing effects,* was preserved, giving the feeling of a type of acting that is never completely fixed, what Jean-François Sivadier calls a 'writing on sight'† of the show. These characteristics explain the frequent moments of complicity between the artists, who refuse to hide behind their characters, who burst into laughter, accepting without any problem occasional lapses of memory, the loss of an entire text, an error of intonation, all leading to delightful moments for the spectators. We see this in the staging of an extract of Molière with Tine Embrechts, Sara de Roo, Damiaan de Schrijver and Natali Broods. One of the parts was given to Tiago Rodrigues, who was not part of the initial show. And so the actor is *thrown* on to the stage without the text, without any text whatsoever (Frank Vercruyssen confiscated it) and without any indications concerning how and where he should move.

These kinds of moments reveal a strong wish to disclose everything to the spectators. There is a total absence of space where 'secrets are woven', as Patrice Chéreau puts it.‡ The 'outside' of theatre does not exist since the show can only exist in the presence of spectators, 'inside'. Likewise, the partition between stage and backstage is only theoretical. The set is made up of wooden panels forming a stud wall and a big veil at the back of the stage that does not reach the floor, so that it is possible to see the artists' feet moving between stage right and stage left.

---

* 'Nous sommes les enfants de Brecht et de Stanislavski'/'We are the children of Brecht and Stanislavski'. In 'Le Jeu mis à nu', interview of Jolente de Keersmaeker and Frank Vercruyssen by Gwénola David, in *Mouvement*, October 2001. Interview available on the Tg STAN's web site.

† 'écriture à vue du spectacle', comments made during the France Culture show.

‡ Anne-Françoise Benhamou, 'organiser le secret: Patrice Chéreau, le texte et l'acteur', in *Brûler les planches, crever l'écran, la présence de l'acteur*, Gérard-Denis Farcy et René Prédal (dir.), Editions l'Entretemps, coll. 'Les Voies de l'acteur', Saint-Jean de Védas, 2001, pp. 69–78.

On stage, the sound mixing turntable is visible, as is the text that is put there for the prompt. Because of the lack of interruptions the placing of the actors onstage is carried out within view of the spectators and it is not unusual to hear them communicate in Dutch, some to ask if they are in the right place, some to report a lost accessory, before slipping into the character of Viola or the messenger in *Twelfth Night*. 'It is also a way of having the audience bear witness to the show as a show, and not as an illusion'.[*] And the feeling the spectator has is indeed one of sharing a moment of creation more than its result. That is why the impromptu as a form is both the 'touchstone of the wit'[†], the quintessence of the work of the STAN, and the mark of a peculiar style: 'All that I do, I do it naturally and without practicing'.[‡]

The presence onstage of the actor and of his character simultaneously points to another stylistic aspect of the collective and consequently to another famous impromptu, Molière's 'play of and by actors'.[§] *The Impromptu de Versailles* develops a double structure. The first one is that of the show and its theme, the tale of the actors' rehearsal. The second is about the conditions of the show itself, the rehearsal and the *real* presence of the actors on stage.[¶] In the *Impromptu XL* the first aspect would be the different extracts being performed whereas the second one would be endorsed by the whole structure, the relative lack of any notion of offstage and the ambiguous presence of the actors. Far from adopting a classical *mise en abyme* structure and despite the setting-up of episodes that are more or less dramatic inside a framework that does not avoid commentary (especially when Frank Vercruyssen names the extracts performed), the show offers a maximum exhibition of theatricality, detached from any

---

* Franck Vercruyssen, 'Anvers et contre tout', art. cit.
† Abstract from *Les Egotistes*. Text adapted from Molière, part of *Poquelin*. The character is played by Damiaan de Schrijver: 'Il faut que je vous dise un impromptu: la pierre de touche de l'esprit'.
‡ Ibid., 'Tout ce que je fais, c'est naturellement et sans étude'.
§ 'Une pièce de comédiens'. The expression is in *L'Impromptu de Versailles*, in *Œuvres Complètes, tome 1*, textes établis, présentés et annotés par Georges Couton, Paris, Gallimard, Bibliothèque de la Pléiade, 1971, p.678.
¶ These two aspects of the impromptu as a theatrical form are underlined in the analysis Georges Forestier gives of the *Impromptu de Versailles* in his definition of the impromptu as a theatrical form. (In *Dictionnaire de théâtre*, op. cit., p.452)

kind of illusionism. Having 'lost faith in scenic illusion' and in 'the embodiment of the character by the actor',* performers here hardly ever embody the characters they have to play. For them, 'the actor doesn't come on stage, he simply is who he is. He is just himself, with his qualities and his faults'. The aim is 'to show a bare way of playing, to expose the mechanisms of identification, to break away from formal aesthetics, to discuss with spectators the questions raised by a text.† Thus the spectators can choose 'to see or not to see characters or actors, or both'.‡ In any case, and even if the text is very well known, or the play already seen, the spectator cannot know in advance what will happen.

Former plays that became part of the show take this question into consideration. For example, *My Dinner with André* plays with the boundaries between actors and characters: Wallace Shawn writes a scenario staging himself as well as André. They both played their own role in the film by Louis Malle. And Damiaan de Schrijver and Matthias de Koning play here with this ambiguity.§ *Du Serment de l'écrivain, du roi et de Diderot*,¶ based on *Le Paradoxe du comédien* by Diderot, questions theatrical illusion, the relationship between the actor and his own character, or the need to act in a 'real-world' way. This questioning is noticeable in the way the STAN play: they refuse to hide behind a character and prefer to deliver a text rather than become avatars of characters nobody believes in,** and they do so by adopting a very blurred presence on stage.

---

*   In *Le Monde*, 'La bande des 4 du Tg STAN', 14 September 2005
†   In 'Le jeu mis à nu', art. cit.
‡   Ibid.
§   Here is what Wallace Shawn writes in the preface to the scenario: 'I'd have to distort us both slightly – our conflicts would have to be sharpened – we'd have to become – well – *characters*.' (Wallace Shawn, Preface to *My Dinner with André*, Grove Press, New York, 1994, [1981] p.14)
¶   *Du Serment de l'écrivain, du roi et de Diderot*, created in Dutch, on 14 June 2001, Westergasfabriek, Amsterdam. In French on 12 November 2003, Théâtre Garonne, Toulouse. Adapted from *Le Paradoxe sur le comédien* by Denis Diderot. Tg STAN, De KOE and Maatschappij Discordia production.
** See Anne Pellois, 'Les intermittences du je(u), à propos du Tg STAN', in *Autofictions scéniques ou l'auto-figuration au théâtre: L'auteur de soi à soi?*, op. cit.; '*En Quête* du Tg STAN: Spectateur en monologues pour acteur polyphonique', op. cit.

The Master of Time

What is more, the presence of a particular man has aroused a lot of questions, that of Frank Vercruyssen as the master of time. Every spectator can quite clearly identify the actor as the master of ceremonies, he who controls time in the show. At the beginning of the *Impromptu XL* he puts on stage a clock to indicate the starting hour (noon) and shows the clock again to indicate the end of the show, at midnight on the dot. It is he who announces what has just been performed and who speeds up or slows down the pace of the show. In this cheerful mess, something has to structure the whole show and it is time that does this. And yet, if this role is explained by Vercruyssen in a very pragmatic manner ('because I like doing this'), the perception of this role and the discussions raised about this role are worthy of some analysis. The mastering of time by one of the members of the collective sets him up as the leader, even though the collective firmly claims its radical opposition to any kind of leadership. The mastering of time is therefore perceived as the control of the whole show.* But this presence of time, embodied by Vercruyssen, far from showing the actor's leadership and control of the show, leads to the perception of real time, real duration, our time; the time that we all share.

The Temporality of Theatre: a Struggle against Oblivion

The great originality of the STAN lies for me in the desire to give the audience food for thought about the question of temporality in theatre. The experiments with duration, continuity and reiteration *all* converge to question the need for a common time, be it simply of the present or of the past. As a form of 'art of the here and now', theatre is a 'unique moment when some people, actors, speak to other people, spectators, and a place where we can take the time to ask questions and to think together',† thinking about present times, by evoking the news or significant current events, but also thinking about the moment of theatre, this shared moment where everyone lives in the present, leaving only traces of memories.

---

* This absence of a leader in the collective is a question that is often raised, as if all the critics or journalists doubted that creation could ever be possible within the context of a direct artistic democracy.

† 'Le jeu mis à nu', art. cit.

Theatre and News

Among the multiplicity of materials used in the *Impromptu XL* is real material, documents, that take a form that is more or less raw.

Some of the dramatic texts have a political resonance, even if they are not directly political. We can take for example this extract of *Sauve qui peut, pas mal comme titre*, based on the *Dramuscules* by Thomas Bernhard.[*] In this extract Damiaan de Schrijvers and Jolente de Keersmaeker, play neighbours who comment on the death of a certain Mister Geissrathner, a man who had been hit by a car driven by a Turkish man a few days ago. The dialogue quickly turns into a demonstration of ordinary racism. Indeed, even though Mister Geissrathner, an honourable Austrian citizen, was clearly responsible for the car accident, it is the presence of the Turkish man himself, in this car, in this place on earth and on Austrian land which is sufficient to prove him guilty, according to simple and simply absurd reasoning. If the Turkish man had not emigrated, he would not have been at this very particular place in this car and would not have hit Mister Geissrathner. At the end of the scene, the two actors get to an extremely uncomfortable moment when they repeat, one after the other, the sentence 'They ought to be gassed'.

The show contains statements in which assessments of ideological values are made in a very direct way. Jef Lambrecht's statement appears to be the least transformed material in the show. After Eric Morel's sax solo, the journalist comes in and sits on a bar stool on stage and starts his speech by apologising: 'Sorry to bother you with my problems', he begins, before giving a disenchanted description of his job as a journalist: 'I have met the powerful and I have met the victims. It was beautiful, and it was disgusting'. The picture of the world depicted by the journalist is far from brilliant: a dumbed-down audience 'that only exists below the belt' and varied assertions converging to describe a European logic of fear, withdrawal and hate. The delivery is quiet, even a bit weary, and Lambrecht announces his desire to quit his job as a journalist, after having noticed the scandalous relationship between media and power and serial obstructions to the practice of ethical journalism. Lambrecht's statement ends with the need for everyone to wake up in these times when the media are directionless: 'It's time to see how you are manipulated', and with an invitation: 'I'd like to politely invite you, dear victims, to the waltz of sweet insurrection'.

---

[*] This text is from this specific short play by Thomas Bernhard, *Le Mois de Marie*, in *Dramuscules*, Paris, l'Arche, 1991.

At the end of this speech, all the STAN's actors appear on the stage, with plastic bags in their hands. The spectators see them from behind. They begin to engage in a curious dance, the Tank Man Tango Dance. It is only when the model for this choreography, that is to say pictures of the man alone in front of the tanks on Tiananmen Square, are projected onto a screen in front of them, that the spectators are able to recall, if they hadn't made the connection earlier, the Chinese events of 1989. The fact that actors are seen from behind puts the audience on the victims' side, faced with oppression, here depicted by the tank. The choreography is not new, having been on the net for some time now, but its use sets up a striking image of oppression only slightly magnified by art. In any case, this sequence tells of the need for memory, and draws a parallel between the real and the media crushing of the student rebellion in Beijing. The Tiananmen events function as a symbol of the decadence of the mass media.

Thus, whether through the theatrical text or through a direct and sincere statement, the show questions the collective (in the civic sense) and its responsibilities, calling for, if not action, at least a kind of informed awareness.

Permanence

The real political gesture lies also in the temporality of the show and in the generosity of the process. Of course, the show was made to celebrate an anniversary, but in a very particular form, that is to say in the celebration of some time spent together *by* some time spent together. There is no nostalgia in this celebration, the celebration is of shared happy times. There is nothing to regret in the acknowledgement of past time. The passing of time is celebrated in an 'Eluardian' way, like a succession of pure instants of a perpetual present, not dramatic at all, but 'as happiness'.*

Moreover, these twelve hours of show might be a form of resistance, by imposing another quality of time, in a world of zapping and virtual sociability. If the artists demonstrate a high degree of generosity towards the spectators through the size and density of what is represented then Frank Vercruyssen underlines the huge generosity of the audience, able to stay for twelve hours, and on top of this, able and willing to travel through

---

*   Frank Vercruyssen's expression, made during an interview in Lyon on 2 December 2010.

a multiplicity of emotions. But more than duration it is continuity that creates the specificity of this time spent together. Even if the spectators can leave the theatre, *something* is always playing, it never stops, they never stop playing. It does not mean theatre does not need the presence of spectators to exist. On the contrary, as seen earlier in the text: it means that theatre is always playing somewhere, that there is something like a permanence of theatre. The length of the show is then a kind of manifesto for a permanent theatre, one that stands as perpetual witness and recorder of the world that surrounds us.* This kind of theatre vision of theatre is, as Vercruyssen says 'a love declaration against the virtual world, advertisement and the neo-liberal world. It is against Dubaï. In that sense, it is militant. In fact, it is completely natural, but nowadays, it is militant, while it was natural in the sixteenth and seventeenth centuries'.† The reference to earlier periods of theatre leads us to the last part of our memories of this show, concerning precisely the process of memory in theatre.

The Memory of Theatre

Impromptu XL questions the relations between theatre, its history and its memory. Because theatre asserts a 'crossroad between memory and the ephemeral', theatrical time is more of a mythological type than of a historical

---

* As such, the XL experiment could be compared to the 'Théâtre Permanent' by Gwénaël Morin, experiment that started in Lyon in 2008 at the Théâtre de l'Elysée with *Le Foyer-Le Chœur*, and carried on at the Laboratoires d'Aubervilliers in 2009 in its definitive form of 'Théâtre Permanent'. The idea is basically to create a form of theatre that is permanent, that is to say which never stops. For more information on the Gwénaël Morin Theatre, see the interviews by Barbara Métais-Chastanier and Anne Pellois: Gwénaël Morin, 'Un point d'engagement', *Agôn* [En ligne], Entretiens & Portraits, updated on: 19/10/2010, URL: http://agon.ens-lyon.fr/index.php?id=866. And Gwénaël Morin, 'C'est tous les jours qu'il faut faire la revolution', *Agôn* [En ligne], Les tiers lieux, Enquête : Engouffrés dans la brèche, no. 3: Utopies de la scène, scènes de l'utopie, Dossiers, updated on : 10/01/2011, URL : http://agon.ens-lyon.fr/index.php?id=1444.

† 'C'est une déclaration d'amour contre le virtuel, contre la publicité, contre le monde néolibéral. C'est contre Dubaï. Dans ce sens, c'est militant. En fait, c'est complètement normal, mais dans notre ère, c'est militant. Alors qu'au 16e, 17e, c'est complètement normal'. Franck Vercruyssen's interview extract.

type.* It is always a 'fictive memory',† without being 'pure imagination'. This 'fantasmatic past has got the very real weight of a collective inheritance',‡ even if all the memories are personal. The peculiar experience the STAN proposes to us in this show, above the exceptional length and the principle of non-interruption, is something like the dissection of the process of the spectator's memory in theatre.

Whilst pictures, recordings, writing, testimonies and notes are always useful for the memory of a spectator, the ways of remembering *Impromptu XL* make the real greatness of the show. The work pays infinite tribute to the always-living show, the one that persists in the actors' and spectators' memory and not the one, mummified, set in books, videos and audio recordings. In this way, memories of theatre remain living memories without calcifying into history.§

Two types of theatrical memories are summoned by the STAN, one that has something to do with the origins of theatre, with a former theatre that is purer than ours; one that does not exist anymore. The other relates to the sheer scale of company's work. Taken together, these impact on the spectator's memory processes at the same time as they address the specificity of memory in theatre.

The fact that spectators do not have to be sitting down for twelve hours¶ brings us back to the period from the seventeenth to the nineteenth century of long theatre evenings, a long time before the spectator was obliged to sit

---

* Georges Banu, 'La Mémoire, une mythologie de l'intérieur', in *Art du Théâtre*, no. 2–3, 1985, pp.85–6

† The term in French is 'Mémoire fictive'. Martial Poirson, 'Mémoire vive: archiver, conserver, inventorier, actualiser', in *Revue d'histoire du théâtre*, January–March 2008.

‡ Anne-Françoise Benhamou, 'Le Déjeuner sur l'herbe du spectateur contemporain', in *L'Art du théâtre* no. 9, 1988, p.85

§ 'As soon as there is a trace, a distance, mediation, we are not in the real memory, but in history' ('Dès qu'il y a trace, distance, médiation, on n'est plus dans la mémoire vraie, mais dans l'histoire'). These are the words of the historian Pierre Nora, quoted by Denis Plassard in 'La scène peut-elle être un lieu de mémoire?', in *Mémoires en éveil, archives en création*, (collective), Paris, L'Entretemps, 2006.

¶ Except for very precise moments, intimate ones, when the doors are closed.

quietly in the stalls during the whole show.* The audience's freedom to move around gives theatre something of its social element back, where the show emphasises the links between the artists themselves, but also within the audience, between the spectators. There is no 'consumer' relationship between actors and spectators, no preset scheme, where the spectator has to sit, and the actor has to 'frolic around'.† The very principle of the anniversary brings theatre back to the time when it was a real celebration and not just a reiterated representation, the time when theatre was an event and not just cultural entertainment. And because the STAN's particular method of playing is open to accidents, no show can be the same and the show is always its own unique and unrepeatable moment. Far from contradicting this, the rerun of extracts from former shows, put together in a 'best of' way, shows that Tg STAN take into account the peculiar nature of memory in theatre.

The first process of recollection is the one used during the show, which sends us back to one or to various shows that may not necessarily be represented as such during the show. This is the case with the video/speech/music superimposition set up during the Jef Lambrecht/Tank Man Tango Dance episode, a section that is immediately reminiscent of *En Quête*,‡ a show about the Gulf War and Western-centrism.

But the more common process is the concentration of dramatic means, as if the STAN were proposing, from an extract, the quintessence of the former show. Of course, for someone who has already seen the entire show, the first words directly lead one back to the show. But the thing is that the remembrance starts before the recital of the text, with the introduction of accessories or actors. That is why, when Damiaan de Schrijvers and Jolente de Keersmaeker arrive on stage each with long thin planks in their hands,

---

* Which happened roughly at the end of the nineteenth century, when the audience was plunged into darkness.

† 'You are here, you are seated, and I'm supposed to frolic around' ('vous êtes ici, vous occupez un siège, et je suis censé gambader'). (Frank Vercruyssen in *En Quête/Questioning*)

‡ *En Quête*, created in 2004. Original show made with a montage of texts by Frank Vercruyssen and Jolente de Keersmaerker, with extracts from novels by Kureishi, Carver, Murakami, texts by Eric Bogosian, an American actor who is famous for his stand up comedy, but also texts by Camus or Handke. All these extracts are interspersed with questions from the *Journal* by Max Fricht, and introduced by a text called introduction. This show is a long monologue by Frank Vercruyssen.

and when they lay them in a cross on the floor and climb on these planks at the very edge of the stage, we see immediately the set made of bits and pieces, planks, ropes and veils in *Sauve qui peut, pas mal comme titre* and we remember the moment of the death of Mister Gassheitner. Also, when the ceiling-light descends for the final scene from *Poquelin*, when a particular atmosphere is created with light, when the sofa and armchairs are brought on, the spectator knows immediately which part of the show will be played.[*] This concept also works for all the emblematic accessories like the little rubber sticks the STAN use for the fight scenes in *Poquelin*.

But the most interesting example might be the re-run of *My Dinner with André*. This show was based on the real duration of a dinner between two theatre men, Wallace Shawn and André Gregory. A kitchen was set upstage and the protagonists ate for four hours, to the great displeasure of the spectator who has not eaten before the show. During the re-run, the STAN sets the table up very quickly, Peter van den Eede and Damiaan de Schrijvers sit down for dinner. But instead of the sumptuous dinner offered during the original show, Frank Vercruyssen, as waiter, offers them a pitiful dinner, served hastily and mainly made of junk food (mostly crisps). With this single extract of about twenty minutes,[†] the device adopted enables the spectator to remember the theme of the show – a conversation about theatre – the length of it – the length of a dinner – and the meta-theatrical characteristic of this show – two actors chatting about their art. What remains of this show in one's memory, what enables the process of memory to be set off, is a temporality, a space and an attitude to a text whose details we do not need to remember, but whose general meaning remains.

The example of *My Dinner* is for me something like a focal point of this show, a kind of summary of the way the STAN invest theatre, in duration, in the reflexive process inherent in their particular way of acting and relating to the text, in the friendly space that has been created. The aim of the STAN is to make spectators 'think of what they have *lived* when they saw the show'[‡] in terms of sensations of time, space, emotion, thought… and in terms of sharing.

---

[*] Although the ceiling light is here from the beginning of the show, but at a higher level than during this scene.

[†] The chosen part of the show is the conversation on Grotowski explaining his experiments in a forest with a group of women.

[‡] 'Nous voulions faire en sorte que vous puissiez penser à ce que vous avez vécu quand vous avez vu le spectacle'. (Frank Vercruyssen, during the interview)

Conclusion

With its device, the Tg STAN's show pays a tribute to live performance. The memory summoned is both the memory of the creative process and the memory of the spectator, set into motion by the minimally evoked re-run of moments of shows, like a quintessence of former work.

The 'defence and illustration' of the live show is not without consequences. First of all, the specificity of the STAN's 'unstable' way of playing and the live re-run of the show prevents it from being reproduced in an identical form, showing the specificity of theatre with regards to other art forms, as well as the impossibility of its reproduction.[*] The live reiteration of extracts, far from bringing the spectator into the spectator's present,[†] maintains the play seen a few years ago in a state of memory. We were all here to 'celebrate our story together: ours and the audience's',[‡] said Vercruyssen. The show never falls into nostalgia of times past. The passing of time and the time shared together is a joyful one, joyfully celebrated together.[§]

Index of Shows Referred to, in Chronological Order

My Dinner with André, Tg STAN, de KOE production
    In Dutch on 17 September 1998, in Het Toneelhuis in Antwerp
    In French on 11 October 2005, in Théâtre Garonne in Toulouse
In Real Time, Tg STAN, AKA Moon and Rosas production
    In English at the Théâtre de la Monnaie in Brussels, on 18 May 2000
Tout est calme, Tg STAN production
    In Dutch on 12 May 1999, at Minard Schouwburg/Vooruit, in Ghent
    In French on 9 October 2001, at the Théâtre des Bernardines, in Marseille

---

[*] See Walter Benjamin, 'L'œuvre d'art à l'époque de sa reproductibilité technique', in *Œuvres III*, Paris, Folio Essais, 2000. 'Nothing, indeed, is opposed more radically to the work of art completely invaded by technical reproduction, …than theatre'. 'Rien, en effet, ne s'oppose plus radicalement à l'œuvre d'art entièrement envahie par la reproduction technique, …que le théâtre'. (291–2)

[†] 'By allowing reproduction to offer itself to the receptor in the situation that he is, the reproduction actualise the reproduced objet'/'En permettant à la reproduction de s'offrir au récepteur dans la situation où il se trouve, elle actualise l'objet reproduit'. (Id., p.276)

[‡] Frank Vercruyssen, during the interview.

[§] I would like to thank Nichola Barnes and Frédéric Hermann for their help and corrections for the translation of this chapter.

Du Serment de l'écrivain, du roi et de Diderot, Tg STAN, De KOE and Maatschappij Discordia production
  In Dutch on 14 June 2001, Westergasfabriek, Amsterdam
  In French on 12 November 2003, Théâtre Garonne, Toulouse
Poquelin, Tg STAN production
  In Dutch on 21May 2003, in Kaaitheater / KunstenFESTIVALdesArts, Brussels
  In French on 1 October 2004, at the Théâtre Garonne, Toulouse
En Quête, Frank Vercruyssen
  In Dutch (*Vraagzucht*) on 17 January 2003, the Monty, Antwerp
  In English (*Questionism*) on 23 Mars 2004, B.I.T., Bergen
  In French on 10 June 2004, Théâtre de la Bastille, Paris
Sauve qui peut, pas mal comme titre, Tg STAN production, with the participation of Matthias de Kooning
  In Dutch on 16 February 2005, at the Kaaitheater in Brussels
  In French on 17 October 2007 at the Théâtre de la Bastille
Impromptu, Tg STAN production
  In French 10 November 2005, at the Théâtre de la Bastille
Impromptu XL, Tg STAN production, and many others...
  In Belgium:
  24-hour version: Premiere: Kaaitheater in Brussels, on 16 and 17 October 2009, from 8 p.m. to 8 p.m. the next day; then at the Monty, Antwerp, on 30 and 31 October, also from 8 p.m. to 8 p.m. the next day
  In France:
  4-hour version at the Théâtre Garonne in Toulouse, on 21 November, from 7 p.m. to 11 p.m.; 12-hour version at the Théâtre de la Bastille in Paris, on 19 December 2009, from noon to midnight

Works Cited

Dictionnaire du Théâtre, Michel Corvin (dir.), Paris: Bordas, 1995
Banu, Georges, 'La Mémoire, une mythologie de l'intérieur', in *Art du Théâtre*, no. 2–3, 1985, pp.85–6
Benhamou, Anne-Françoise,
'Organiser le secret: Patrice Chéreau, le texte et l'acteur', in *Brûler les planches, crever l'écran, la présence de l'acteur*, Gérard-Denis Farcy et René Prédal (dir.), Editions l'Entretemps, coll. 'Les Voies de l'acteur', Saint-Jean de Védas, 2001, pp.69–78
'Le Déjeuner sur l'herbe du spectateur contemporain', in *L'Art du théâtre* no. 9, 1988

Benjamin, Walter, 'L'œuvre d'art à l'époque de sa reproductibilité technique', in *Œuvres III*, Paris, Folio Essais, 2000

Pellois, Anne,

'Les intermittences du je(u), à propos du Tg STAN', in *Autofictions scéniques ou l'auto-figuration au théâtre: L'auteur de soi à soi?*, joint publication soon to be published at the Presses Universitaires de Dijon

'En Quête du Tg STAN: Spectateur en monologues pour acteur polyphonique', in *Le Monologue contre le drame?*, joint publication soon to be published at the Presses Universitaires de Rennes

'L'acteur déjà là', contribution to a two-day workshop about 'l'entrée en scène' organised by the ENS de Lyon and the University of Lyon II, 29 and 30 May 2009

Plassard, Denis, 'La scène peut-elle être un lieu de mémoire?', in *Mémoires en éveil, archives en création,* (collective), Paris, L'Entretemps, 2006

Poirson, Martial, 'Mémoire vive: archiver, conserver, inventorier, actualiser', in *Revue d'histoire du théâtre*, January–March 2008.

Plays and Scenarios Quoted:

Bernhard, Thomas, *Le Mois de Marie*, in *Dramuscules*, Paris, l'Arche, 1991

Molière, *L'Impromptu de Versailles*, in *Œuvres Complètes, tome 1*, textes établis, présentés et annotés par Georges Couton, Paris, Gallimard, Bibliothèque de la Pléiade, 1971

Shawn, Wallace, *My Dinner with André*, Grove Press, New York, 1994, [1981]

Interviews:

Interview with Frank Vercruyssen by Anne Pellois in Lyon, on 2 December 2010

'Drôle de drame', broadcast live in 9 December 2009, from the Théâtre de la Bastille, from 8 p.m. to midnight, France Culture

'Anvers et contre tout', interview by Catherine Firmin-Didot in *Télérama*, 9 November 2005

'Le Jeu mis à nu', interview of Jolente de Keersmaeker and Frank Vercruyssen by Gwénola David, in *Mouvement*, October 2001, www.stan.be

'La bande des 4 du Tg STAN', *Le Monde*, 14 September 2005

Métais-Chastanier Barbara, Pellois Anne: Gwénaël Morin, 'Un point d'engagement', *Agôn* [En ligne], Entretiens & Portraits, uploaded: 19/10/2010, URL: http://agon.ens-lyon.fr/index.php?id=866. And Gwénaël Morin, 'C'est tous les jours qu'il faut faire la revolution', *Agôn* [En ligne], Les tiers lieux, Enquête: Engouffrés dans la brèche, no. 3: Utopies de la scène, scènes de l'utopie, Dossiers, uploaded: 10/01/2011, URL: http://agon.ens-lyon.fr/index.php?id=1444

CHAPTER FIFTEEN

The Oberammergau Passionsspiele

DAVID MASON

It's certainly a big show. The auditorium, re-designed and renovated specially before the 2000 production, holds more than 4,500 people and there were no empty seats on the day I saw the Oberammergau Passion play in August 2010. One performance takes six hours and involves 120 distinct characters and many more indistinct characters in the various crowds that come and go in the play's plot and fill up the theatre's broad stage. More than 2,000 people are cast in the play. Many of the roles are double-cast to allow Oberammergauers off-nights while the play goes on. The crowded stage is inflated by a director's nightmare of ten-year-old children, sheep, goats, donkeys, horses, and a couple of camels. At least 35 backstage jobs, credited to multiple people, are listed in the programme, including stitchers, sculptors, welders and master electricians. The costume crew, by itself, consists of at least 27 people.

This is to say nothing of the thousands of people in Oberammergau and elsewhere who are not directly involved in the Passionsspiele production, but whose lives are inextricably entwined with it. Hundreds of guesthouses in this small, southern Bavarian town, operate to provide overnight accommodations to the deluge of patrons who attend the Passionsspiele over the course of its 102 performances. Restaurants and outlets for woodcarvings that cluster around the great Passion play Theatre are packed during the play's three-hour intermission. Public services and infrastructure stretch tight around visitors, who, on any given performance day, outnumber Oberammergau residents two-to-one.

The show is so big that its reach extends far beyond Oberammergau. Hotels in Munich, which is close enough to house audiences, fill up during Passionsspiele summers. Travel agencies – not only in Europe,

255

but worldwide – begin selling tour packages to eager audiences years before opening night. Airlines, train systems, buses, automobile rental companies, law enforcement agencies, shopping centres, media outlets – even universities – anticipate the Oberammergau Passion play. They make plans for it, years in advance. They must. More than half a million people attended the play during the summer of 2000.

Part of what accounts for the widespread interest that sustains the play's grandeur is, simply, its infrequency. The show only goes on during one summer of every decade, going back nearly four centuries. In 1633, according to the legend, the residents of Oberammergau collectively entered into a vow to perform the play every ten years should they escape the plague, which, at that time, was decimating villages in southern Germany.[1] Following the community's pledge, so the story is told, deaths from the plague ceased and the first production followed in 1634. Since then, with remarkably few lapses and with a few extra performances to make up for the gaps, the residents of Oberammergau have staged the play every tenth year.[2] The production's infrequency nourishes interest and its regularity sustains its appeal as a rare event that a person can, nevertheless, hope for, plan for and save for.

Another feature that sustains widespread interest in the play, interest that only seems to grow during the show's decade-long intervals, is its religious content. The relationship some audiences have with the religious content of the play makes repeat customers of many Passion play patrons. The Passionsspiele, like other Passion plays, dramatises the New Testament accounts of the last days of Jesus's life. Beginning with his triumphal entry into Jerusalem, the play includes Jesus's conflict with local authorities (Jewish and Roman), his Passover meal with his disciples, his arrest and the climactic moment of his crucifixion. The play concludes suddenly with a brief suggestion of Jesus's resurrection. The *raison d'être* of the production, then, is the central myth of the world's two billion Christians. The tradition of Passion plays, extending across history and across geography, shows that Christians do not tire of stagings of the Jesus story. Like going to church, attending Passion plays can be a regular, repeated exercise of faith, so that Catholic, Protestant, and Other Christians look to Oberammergau for a representation – and, sometimes, re-presentations – of the story that reiterates their very faith. The Passionsspiele reaches out to a vast and ever-renewed audience, for which the play's subject matter always matters.

There are other big shows. Other big Passion plays. The Eureka Springs New Great Passion play in the United States plays for half the year, every year, with hundreds of actors and its own menagerie of exotic animals. The play's staging of Jesus's ascension into heaven is spectacular. More than 100,000 people paid to see the Eureka Springs play in 2009. Down from a peak of nearly 300,000 in 1993, but still enough to double Oberammergau's attendance over the course of ten years. But the Eureka Springs production has no historical mooring. Born in 1968, this Passion play in a Mid-Western United States forest has only its own, forty-year-old, Evangelical Christian tradition for a pedigree. It's a dynamic performance but one that has an ineluctably American aura to it, as though re-packaged and reissued to evoke the fond memory of the original. Vestiges of the great cycle plays emerge from time to time in England, but these come and go. Even the regular staging, from 1951, of the York plays as part of the Festival of Britain, have been a tradition of discontinuity, as they've moved from venue to venue and from the hand of one director to another.[3] There are other Passion plays to see around Europe. None of them are The Event, in the same way.

Oberammergau's own dramatic history augments its play's appeal, so that even within its worldwide cohort of Jesus plays, many of them very big, the Passionsspiele still has cachet. Unlike its new-world and old-world cousins, the Bavarian play offers audiences the rare experience of a dramatic spectacle whose tradition of performance is continuous across four centuries, and that kind of longevity imbues Oberammergau with a peculiar quality. Audiences go to southern Bavaria every ten years, not only to see the Passion play, but to see the Passion play that survives from medieval days, the Passion play that was performed to avert the plague, the Passion play that has marked every decade since Galileo's trial.

It's likely, actually, that the play is even older. James Shapiro has shown how the story of the vow that instigated the Oberammergau tradition stands on shaky legs.[4] But the suggestion that the town had already been performing the play for some time makes it all the more interesting as an historical artefact. The plague did run through southern Germany in 1633. Some people in Oberammergau did die of the plague. And, in 1634, the town did perform the first of what is now regarded as a nearly four-century tradition. The texts, both Catholic and Protestant, that seem to have been combined with a third, lost play to provide the material of the 1634 production, date from a century earlier.[5] Whatever the legends, Oberammergau does give us a remarkable piece of living history.

Nevertheless, while the performance tradition in the Bavarian village is unbroken from the seventeenth century, what is performed there today is not the same thing. The tradition includes variations and developments on the theme of a Passion play; and, perhaps, that's for the better, as the contemporary production plays not so much as the (hopeless) attempt to preserve a centuries-old form but as an art that derives its current life from learning as it goes along.

Each staging of the Passionsspiele introduces revisions but there are three major versions of the Oberammergau play. What we know of the first production of 1634 comes in the oldest surviving script from 1662. This version of the script provided the material for the performance until Ferdinand Rosner, a local monk, produced a new text in 1750, which was radically different in content and style. For the 1811 production, Rosner's play was abandoned in favour of a script prepared by Othmar Weis, another monk. It is Weis's text, through the revision of Joseph Alois Daisenberger in the later 1800s, that productions up to the present follow.

The 1662 script appears to be the legitimate scion of medieval Passion plays, both in the Catholic and Protestant traditions. Shapiro describes the play as 'a characteristically medieval affair.'[6] The play brought Satan and other devils on stage to inflate the rambunctious theatricality of the story. Satan, for instance, interrupts the prologue to read a letter that 'encourages the audience to ignore the Prologue, desecrate the play with laughter, and join him in Hell.'[7] The play then does almost all it can to explode the Jesus story with grotesque spectacles that must have been both horrific and thrilling in performance, such as the host of devils who devour Judas's intestines on stage.

The huge medieval stagings of the Bible, sometimes called 'cycle plays' were similar exercises in theatricality and they took visceral delight in the combination of the sacred and the profane. The *Second Shepherds' Pageant* from the cycle of Bible plays staged in Yorkshire, England, is ostensibly about the shepherds who were afforded the sacred privilege of seeing Jesus's nativity. But the bulk of the episode concerns one shepherd's theft of a sheep and his subsequent attempts to pass the sheep off as his own baby, asleep in a crib. From underneath the crib's coverlet, the sheep's bleating undermines the thief's deception. The medieval Bible plays also took particular delight in the theatrical possibilities afforded by demons. The fifteenth-century

Castle of Perseverance was not, technically, a Bible play but it gives us some frightening hints as to how far the medieval stages were willing to go to wring the spectacular out of devils on stage. The *Castle*'s ground plan, a drawing that indicates how the play was to be staged, advises the medieval designers, 'He that shall play Belial, look that he have gunpowder burning in pipes, in his hands, and in his ears, and in his arse, when he goeth to battle.'[8] To some extent, the onstage animals of the contemporary production at Oberammergau reiterate this medieval interest in spectacular theatricality.

Ferdinand Rosner's late-eighteenth-century *Passio Nova* is sometimes called the 'Baroque version'. Much more formally poetic and also twice the length of the previous script, Rosner's play emphasised the otherworldly elements of the Jesus story through more overt allegory, the explicit ascription of blame to Satan and his company of devils, and a formal arrangement of tableau scenes as typological commentaries on the Jesus story.[9] Shapiro notes that eleven thousand people attended Rosner's version in 1750 and 1760, which indicates its appeal to audiences.[10] Nevertheless, the township eventually traded Rosner's for Weis's version on account of Rosner's not being quite Biblical enough.[11] Even so, the appeal of the *Passio Nova* persisted over two centuries. In the 1970s, a serious movement to re-adopt the Rosner script – at least in part as a less anti-Semitic version of the Oberammergau tradition – raised funds for a 'trial production' of Rosner's play in 1977. The town rejected Rosner by referendum (as they had previously, in 1970).

War drastically truncated performances in 1800. In 1810, Oberammergau found itself again under a ban on religious theatre. A special petition convinced Maximilian Joseph to allow the Passionsspiele to go on, not as religious theatre but as 'folk festival'.[12] Othmar Weis provided a new script for performance in 1811, free of the poetic and allegorical encumbrances of the Rosner script. A young Rochus Dedler wrote new music, partially for 1811, and then a complete score for 1820.[13] Weis's own student, Joseph Daisenberger, did some rewrites of Weis's script in the mid-1800s to produce the script that went largely unchanged into the 1980s. The Weis–Daisenberger play purported to follow the Gospels much more closely. One consequence of this effort was the ascription of blame for Jesus's death to the Jews of Jerusalem, as opposed to Lucifer and his disembodied devils. An 1890 German–English version of the play features several long scenes in which Pilate excuses himself, telling his wife Claudia, for instance, that he plans to do everything he can to save Jesus.[14] Pilate's role ends when the

Jerusalem citizenry shouts the Gospel of Matthew's infamous 'blood oath', not only once, but twice.[15] Perhaps more down-to-earth than Rosner's, the Weis–Daisenberger script returned this most problematic element of the Passion play tradition to Oberammergau's stage.

The Christian theatre of the Middle Ages that directly informs the contemporary Passionsspiele was rife with rather un-Christian excesses maligning and slandering broad groups of people. One of the primary tensions in the Passion play tradition was the consequence of performances for European Jews. In the thirteenth century, the Fourth Lateran Council forbade Jews to leave their homes during Holy Week – perhaps for the sake of their own safety at a time of year when Passion stories that vilified Jews were read and played in public. In the sixteenth century, officials in Rome shut down an annual Passion play to prevent the obligatory sacking of the ghetto that annually followed.

Oberammergau's Passionsspiele tradition is undeniably and inextricably linked to this history of anti-Semitism. The regular re-staging of the play in Oberammergau in all its big-ness is, for many, a regular reiteration of European bigotry. In response to criticism, in the past half-century Oberammergau has undertaken successive revisions of the script and global transformations of the production's design. James Shapiro's book, cited earlier, provides comprehensive documentation of the Passionsspiele's history, of the dialogue between critics of the production and the play's officials, and of the way that Oberammergau's play has moved to overcome this aspect of its character.

Shapiro suggests how Oberammergau may yet show us how radical and how conservative the Passion play tradition can be. Writing of what he saw at rehearsals for the 2000 production, Shapiro describes a 'veteran actor' who objected to what he perceived as discontinuity in the logic of the script when Jesus and his disciples deny that they seek to undermine the Law of Moses. As Shapiro relates the incident:

> Christian Stückl (the director) patiently explained to the older actor that there was no mistake in the text. Peter and the other disciples, even Jesus himself, were all Jews. The play, then, was not about a conflict between Christians and Jews.... I'm sure this actor left still somewhat confused, and I am equally sure that he went home thinking about it. And so did I, and so did a lot of other people in that room. And when members of the cast went to eat and drink after the rehearsal, they were still talking about it. There

would be seven months of rehearsals to come and five months of performing the play for the message of a Jewish Jesus and his followers to sink in. Instances like these offer the most compelling argument I know against banning or boycotting Passion plays. All censorship does is hide the problem.[16]

For Shapiro, only the continuing performance of Passion plays can over-write the ignorance and injustice inherent in the tradition. I would add to Shapiro's assertion the claim that the same traditional authority that reinforces the 'veteran actor's' confusion about Jesus's identity and mission also lends to the Oberammergau Passion play the confidence that the assertions it makes about Jesus will not be dismissed or denied. More than other, extant examples of the tradition, more than the flighty York productions in Britain, more than the saccharine spectacle at Eureka Springs in the United States, the persistence, the regularity of Oberammergau's Passionsspiele, its resistance to change (even while it *does* change), give the decennial Oberammergau ritual its power to say the most radical things.

The most recent revision has chased after the Passionsspiele's anti-Semitic elements. Rather than abandon the Weis–Daisenberger play, the township has opted to try to make it work, as a twenty-first century, global-village play. Otto Huber, whose efforts to address the play's more distasteful elements took him far from Bavaria to discuss the play with Jewish leaders in the 1990s, and Christian Stückl, director of the Munich Volkstheater, have been cooperating on a text that the published 2010 script describes as 'extensively edited and expanded'.[17]

Among the significant changes that Huber and Stückl make to the traditional script, Pilate comes onstage early in act three to threaten Caiaphas with the Roman-style destruction of Jerusalem if he fails to maintain order. 'If there is conflict in the land' says Pilate, 'I will come with the army's might and plunge you, your land, and your people into ruin and perdition.'[18] Stückl and Huber's Caiaphas then – more of St. John than of St. Matthew – motivates the Jewish leadership in Jerusalem not to murder the Christ, but to sacrifice Jesus to save Jerusalem from Roman wrath. And Matthew's 'blood oath' does not appear in Stückl and Huber's text at all. More than half a million people saw this version of the story in 2010. Only the efforts of such established traditions as Oberammergau's play can transform a story as baggage-laden in Western tradition as that of Jesus.

Whatever the intent of the production, what audiences see in Oberammergau differs from audience member to audience member and the differences are as wide as the play is big. An instructive contrast is found between the descriptions that Isabel and Richard Burton give us of their experiences. Both widely travelled (Richard is famous as one of the first Europeans to see Mecca), both highly literate (Isabel published several titles, including *The Revival of Christianity in Syria*), they went to Oberammergau together and saw the same Passionsspiele performance in 1880. Although impressed by aspects of the production, Richard wrote, 'the piercing of the side is badly done. It looks like a surgical operation, opening a tumor, and as if Longinus were feeling with his spear for a hidden bladder or bag of mauve-colored fluid.' Isabel, on the other hand, reported that the production 'must surely be a vision of Calvary.'[19] Something appeared to Isabel that did not appear to Richard, though they saw the same performance. Presumably, the actors that Richard saw were the same actors Isabel saw, performing the same actions with the same implements on the same stage. The experiences of these two audience members, presumably seated next to each other at the same performance, however, were wholly different. To Isabel, something living, something tangible, something more real than the material of the performance itself manifested on Oberammergau's stage.

The promise of seeing something in the material of Oberammergau has been one of the things that has always drawn visitors. Nineteenth-century visitors to the town could 'stay in the homes of the actors, which for many visitors meant the thrill of being in close contact with Jesus, Mary, or Peter.'[20] One such traveller, Anna Maria Howitt, visited Oberammergau in 1850, and stayed in the home of Tobias Flunger who, at the time, was playing Jesus in the Passionsspiele. After the day's performance, Howitt records that she 'was overwhelmed with questions regarding Flunger, questions which his most intimate friends could not have answered satisfactorily.'[21] Howitt suggests that her companions were particularly taken by the actor's portrayal of Christ. But travel writer Michael Counsell suggests something else has moved Oberammergau visitors from Howitt's time until the present day, when he writes that some patrons regard the Passionsspiele as 'a way of meeting the real Jesus face to face.'[22]

Travellers, *pilgrims*, have not only been after a glimpse of Jesus or Mary in Oberammergau. The place itself has become a manifestation of another world, the 'old world', according to one visitor.[23] Besides expressing the essence of a romanticised, pre-Christian Palestine, the land of Oberammergau manifests a romanticised Europe. In 1890, British traveller Ethel B.H. Tweedie wrote of her visit, 'Sitting among those simple surroundings, it seemed almost impossible to realise that one was living in the nineteenth century. Living in an age of machinery, steam, electricity and invention, an age when it is all hurry and bustle, it is strange to be suddenly transported back, as it were, to the Middle Ages.'[24]

Part of what accounts for the zeal for proximity to the play's leading actors is merely a delight in celebrity. Part of what accounts for the fantasies about Oberammergau's rustic and pseudo-historical charm is a simply romantic longing for a (lost) golden age. Oberammergau never was Jerusalem and Tobias Flunger never was Jesus. But for some patrons, some kind of Jerusalem and some kind of Jesus do materialise in the course of the play. Part of what must account for the glamour that seems to have rubbed off on Anna Maria Howitt, part of what must account for the 'old world' that people found in Oberammergau's hills and valleys, comes from the complimentary capacities of theatre and ritual to facilitate devotional vision.

In such responses, Oberammergau's Passion play shows us rather starkly that theatrical performances do not impose experiences on audiences. While it may seem self-evident that *Oklahoma!* can't make an audience swoon over waving American wheat, we still may not appreciate just how much an audience member contributes to his or her own theatrical experience, sometimes even in spite of what the actors and the production itself do. We know something of how actors prepare for performances and we know something of what actors do during performances, and we know a lot about design and direction and space and literature and what they contribute to a theatrical production. The varying experiences of Oberammergau's Passionsspiele, from Richard Burton's blasé account of a botched spear thrust and Isabel Burton's 'vision of Calvary' to the face-to-face experience of Jesus himself, remind us that we don't know much about what the *audience* does during a performance.

The fortunate coincidence in Oberammergau that can open our understanding of what audiences contribute to their theatrical experiences is the convergence of theatre and religion. The religious environment in which this show exists shows us that some kinds of theatrical experiences come from the audience's very active involvement. In fact, what audience members bring to a play often contributes to the play's effect as much or even more than that which directors, designers and performers create.

One peculiarity of the Passionsspiele stands out in this regard. At the outset, and 10 more times during the course of the performance, this very big, very dynamic, very dramatic production comes to a stop. Surviving from Rosner's 18 tableaus are 13 *lebende bilder*, or 'living images', which stand still in the midst of the inexorable action of the Jesus story. Built of very flat panels and the round bodies of living actors, these scenes don't *do* anything, they only *are*. For some time, several minutes in some cases, the actors in these scenes do not move and do not speak. The only activity during the *lebende bilder* comes from the orchestra, which supplies music for the singing of a chorus and its soloists, who do not themselves appear in the living scenes, but remove themselves to the far sides of the stage.

Following the obligatory prologue to Act III, for instance, declaimed from centre stage by a player identified in the programme only as 'Prologue', the chorus, lined up shoulder to shoulder across the broad stage, parts in the middle and retreats to either side to reveal, centre stage, an image titled 'The Ten Commandments and the dance around the golden calf'. Within the chorus's subsequent description of the scene, several actors recreate the well-known event from Exodus in still-life poses: Moses, on the hill, with the tablets of the law in the arms of angels; wayward Israelites below, in the attitude of idolatry. The colours are saturated and bright and the palette is simple. The arrangement of the scene, the postures in which the human participants are cast, the style of the characters' dress and the tenor of the landscape evoke the style of early renaissance painters such as Fra Angelico, but especially of the Flemish artists such as Rogier van der Weyden and Jan Provoost.[25] In fact, a lesser-known Biblical episode appearing in *tableaux vivants* at the beginning of Act Four includes a slaughtered sheep that seems taken directly from Jan van Eyk's Ghent Altarpiece.

On a contemporary stage that inherits Aristotle's insistence on the elimination of anything unnecessary, these frozen moments are so inactive in an otherwise active medium, so odd, so *useless* they arrest attention and make some demands. The experience an audience member has of the Passionsspiele very much depends on how he or she responds to these demands because these scenes, above the others, invite the audience to join the players on the stage: the *lebende bilder* interface with the active play going on in the spectator's mind to facilitate the spectator's own role-playing in the stage's story. And the spectator's own role-playing, ultimately, constitutes the quality and tone of the spectator's experience.

To some degree, these *tableaux vivants* survive only as curious vestiges of the religious theatre of the medieval period. In the span of the thirteenth and sixteenth centuries, the incorporation of such frozen Biblical scenes into the mechanised processions of Europe's Corpus Christi festivities were commonplace. Flatbed carts, some quite large, winding parade-style through many medieval towns during this celebration of the Eucharist, drew townspeople arranged in still scenes of Adam and Eve, Abraham and Isaac, John baptising in the Jordan and so forth past onlookers toward the church or to some common marketplace for on-going display.[26] Tracing its heritage to the seventeenth century, a time when many of these cycle dramas were still extant, it may be that the on-going peculiarity of the Oberammergau Passionsspiele's tableaus is the living preservation of this medieval practice. If for only the purpose of a kind of archival preservation, the *lebende bilder* would be valuable.

However, Oberammergau's living images are the key element that facilitates the heightened experience of the play as the non-representational – or 'unmediated' – manifestation of divinity. Devotee patrons of such religious theatre as Oberammergau's bring with them to the theatre identities that partake of the metaphysical reality they long to see through the stage, identities for which that metaphysical reality is real, indeed.

The culture that engendered the Passion plays from which Oberammergau's Passionsspiele derives appreciated how representation could also be manifestation. In the late middle ages, iconography of all sorts, including the iconography-in-motion of the Passion plays, did more than represent what had been: it revealed something with immediate and on-going, substantial reality.

Theatre in late medieval Europe inherited a well-developed theology of role-play, which drove the development of the religious theatre from which Oberammergau's Passionsspiele derives. In the eleventh century, new conceptions of the incarnation and of its proxy, the Eucharist, as manifestations of God, gave new value to mechanisms of physical representation. In the next few centuries, new devotional practices that sought to exploit the vivifying power of representation came into vogue and role-playing, as spiritual exercise, came into popularity among men and women of widely divergent cultures, backgrounds, and social status. Not coincidentally, the tradition of staging the Bible – the so-called cycle plays – rises in the thirteenth century and persists in great popularity until the religious violence that comes on the heels of the Reformation leads to widespread banning of religious theatre of all sorts in the 1500s.

Theologians of the eleventh century placed new emphasis on Jesus's humanity. Historiographer Michal Kobialka asserts that this new emphasis redirected the attention of Christian devotees to the physical realities of

Jesus's life: 'Studies by Bernard of Clairvaux, Abelard, Bruno of Segni, Odo of Cambrai, and Peter Lombard in the twelfth century... show a new concern for a better understanding of Christ's humanity and a need to discuss the details of his life as a man.'[27] The new interest in the physical life of Jesus had a significant impact on religious practices, which, in the following century, informed representational art.

The significance of the eleventh-century Christological shift is evident in Berengar of Tours' argument against the doctrine of transubstantiation established in the ninth century. Rather than a physical transformation of the host, Berengar argued that consecration facilitated a transformation of the experience of devotees. Kobialka summarises Berengar's argument as conceding that a change in the host takes place at consecration, but that the change 'did not take place in the physical space of a ritual site. It took place in the mind of the faithful, rather than in the realm of the senses.'[28] Berengar did not argue that God was not present in the host, only that the material of the host, the physical stuff of the Eucharist, need not change to make that presence possible. Although they were inimical to each other, the 'material bread and wine could coexist with... the spiritual body and blood of Christ.'[29] The stuff, averred Berengar, that was just stuff, managed nevertheless to be a conduit of divinity for devotees.

Berengar's scholasticism presaged a new interest in physical stuff as a mechanism by which devotees might experience divinity. In the twelfth century, Bernard of Clairvaux and others advocated meditations on Jesus's physical condition as a way of gaining direct experience of God. Subsequently, in addition to the Eucharist itself (as a physical conduit for the divine as Berengar had characterised it), other physical means came to be the physical stuff of God's manifestation for the devoted, especially representational imagery. The literary and visual arts, from this point, adopt subject matter and style intended to facilitate better the contemplation of the physical Jesus, of his humanity, so as to effect a physical and metaphysical experience. Kobialka characterises the trend in devotional art as a move away from 'symbolic or dogmatised representation' towards the depiction of a human drama in 'a realistic way', with images of Jesus 'contorted with pain... with blood dripping from his wounds.'[30]

But the new realism was not only concerned with realising the human suffering of the crucified Jesus. The passion for imaginatively entering into the human experience of Jesus moved artists and devotees to celebrate even the most mundane aspects of the man. In the thirteenth century, the

Meditationes Vitae Christi, probably written by a follower of St. Bonaventure, became widely popular as a rubric for attaining to a transcendent sort of spiritual experience by visualising the incarnate Jesus – and not only his suffering and death but such ignoble mortal necessities as nursing and swaddling. The *Meditationes* advises readers to visualise Jesus's infancy, to imagine meditatively Mary nursing her baby and caring for him, and enjoins readers: *Ita et tu adjuva eam, si potes; in his delectare, jucundare, ac sedulo meditari memento, et quantum potes famuleris Dominae et puero Jesu, et intuearis faciem ejus saepe, in quam desiderant angeli prospicere.* ('Even so, assist her, if you can; being mindful to take delight, to rejoice, and to contemplate these things earnestly, and serve her and the child Jesus as much as you can, and always keep your mind on his face, on which the angels ever long to look').[31]

The *Meditationes* thus advocates a meditative style of role play as legitimate devotional activity. The faithful can imagine themselves not only as witnesses at the nativity but as helpers. The 'simple' devotional imagining that the *Meditationes* advocates becomes complex and elaborate in subsequent texts, encouraging the kind of re-imagining of the mundane elements of the individual's real-world environment as pieces of the Jesus story. James Shapiro notes the fifteenth-century *Zardino de Oration* as an example of a text that encourages readers to conflate imaginatively their real-world lives with the world of the Gospels:

> You must shape in your mind some people, people well known to you, to represent for you the people involved in the Passion – the person of Jesus himself, of the Virgin, Saint Peter, Saint John the Evangelist, Saint Mary Magdalene, Anne, Caiaphas, Pilate, Judas and the others, every one of them you will fashion in your mind.[32]

After the twelfth century, the increasingly popular Franciscan spirituality looks for increasingly theatrical ways of seeing and finds ways of conflating the everyday with the reality of the Gospels.

The practices of the *Meditationes* and the *Zardino de Oration* catch on not only as a mental or conceptual exercise but as a physical practice. The festival commemoration of Palm Sunday that developed in many parts of Germany included a real donkey bearing a figure of Jesus in procession into the church. Shapiro implies that this practice was not yet the realisation of dramatic practice, since a wooden figure representing Jesus was used and 'human impersonators were not allowed'.[33] But the point of the activity did not need a moving, breathing actor. The activity meant to position the onlookers as the mythic inhabitants of Jerusalem – to help *them* play their audience roles in the story.

In the fourteenth century, the pilgrim Margery Kemp travelled briefly with a group of Italian women who kept a baby Jesus doll in their luggage. In the evenings, they would remove the doll and dress it, hold it and talk to it as though it were the baby Jesus.[34] Among many others who took up the practice, the fourteenth-century German nun Margaret Ebner kept a baby Jesus doll with which she not only played the role of nursemaid, but which, according to her report, kept her awake at night by kicking in its cradle, speaking to her and nursing at her breast.[35]

In this case and in many others of the same period, devotional role-playing brings about an experience that is more vivid, more visceral, more real. The playing of the role vivifies the world of the role. By acting out the part of Jesus's nursemaid, Ebner came to experience the doll *as* Jesus's nursemaid. Ebner's acting anticipates Jesus's response as an infant, so it's only natural when that response comes in the form of a doll that cries and complains. It is not enough to say that Ebner is simply imagining the doll's response. Ebner's adoption of a role shapes her psychological and cognitive experience.[36] In the twelfth century, Saint Francis instituted the *crèche*, the practice of setting up artificial nativity scenes as devotional visual aids. Thomas of Celano's and St. Bonaventure's biographies of the saint record that the first such nativity scene at Greccio sent Francis into a spiritual swoon, under the influence of which both he and others saw and interacted with the baby Jesus, who appeared in the empty manger.[37] In this case, it was enough for Francis to play the role of the spectator. Entering physically into the part of the shepherd or Joseph or an angel or some other onlooker at the event of Jesus's birth shifted Francis's perception of the scene so that he experienced the scene *as* a true onlooker.

Not only do manuscript illumination, painting, stained glass, mosaics and three-dimensional media such as sculpture become in the twelfth century important tools that people of all stations and educations use to facilitate their own role-playing to the effect of realising Jesus, an important Christological shift begins to characterise the incarnation itself as a representational device. By arguing for a dual nature of Jesus that placed emphasis on his humanity, St Anselm's eleventh–century treatise *Cur Deus Homo* (*Why God* [*became*] *Man*) promoted an incarnation with distinctly theatrical overtones. The human Jesus, necessary for the satisfaction of divine justice, reveals God. For art, this 'manifestational' Jesus rescued the use of images from the stigma of idolatry and 'gave sacred authority to image making.'[38] The great cycle plays that arise around Europe beginning in the twelfth century seem to appreciate the sacred value of images and give audiences living, breathing images of Jesus on which to fix their devotional eyes.

In these circumstances, where the eyes of the meditative faithful are present, the actor not only represents Jesus but provides the physical material whereby the divine Jesus may be manifest. Anselm's notion that God 'is not at all contained by anything else' but, nevertheless, 'can be said to be in every place and time because it is absent from none' provided the groundwork for a doctrine that characterised individuals – including audiences and actors – as essential manifestations of divinity that needed only eyes to see it.[39] For scholar Sarah Beckwith, the several individual scenes that together comprise the Passion in the York cycle offered its fifteenth-century audiences a 'real presence' that exceeded 'the parameters of representational space'.[40] In the late medieval period, like the manuscript illuminations and stained glass and statuary that brought Jesus in fact into the experience of devotees, the actor who looked like Jesus could be Jesus.

Given the pervasive extent, by the fourteenth century, to which images and objects were used in Europe by monks and nuns and laity to realise the presence of Jesus and to experience interaction with him, the dramas in which Jesus moved and spoke surely brought real presence to theatre patrons. The vernacular religious drama of medieval Europe did, therefore, perform 'essential ritual functions', as Gail McMurray Gibson and Clifford Flanigan have suggested.[41] Catherine Dunn agrees. The 'vernacular drama' of medieval Europe, she writes, was 'a paraliturgical form of spirituality.'[42] In their liturgical function, rather than likenesses of historical figures, the actors in these popular performances 'were iconic aids to worship.'[43] In addition to *representing* the body of Jesus, in the sense of typical, Aristotelian mimesis, the actor in the cycle dramas also manifested the divine reality of God's presence to audience members who were engaged in looking at the plays as witnesses of God's presence.

The Jesus story of late medieval and early renaissance art was always on-going, always available to the devotee who would see it. Paintings of religious scenes from this period commonly combine anachronistic imagery. A typical example is Rogier van der Weyden's *Adoration of the Magi*, in which a crucifix is fixed to a beam in the stable of Jesus's nativity. Hans

Memling's 1490 painting *The Virgin and Child Between St. James and St. Dominic* shows what the title claims: the infant Jesus on Mary's lap between a fully grown character from Jesus's adult life and another man from the thirteenth century (holding a crucifix). Memling's great 1480 *Advent and Triumph of Christ* tries to combine all the episodes of the Jesus story, of course, into one sprawling panel; but more interesting is the painting's combination of first-century and fifteenth-century people, costumes, and architecture. The painting even includes two ships of distinctly European design. These anachronisms speak not of an ignorance of history but of an appreciation of history's irrelevance to the always on-going Jesus narrative. The European Passion plays, too, are fraught with anachronisms that serve not only, or not merely, a humorous purpose.[44] Art of the period intended to yield to the open eyes of the faithful spectator the story of Christian salvation that was not a historical event but an immediately accessible one. The late medieval eye saw the manifestation of that story in painting, sculpture and on stages not as a representation but as an expression of it.

The Reformation and then the Enlightenment may have been a double-whammy blow to the kind of seeing that Anselm's Christology engendered in Christian Europe. Protestant modes of worship marginalised the use of images, and recurring violence between Catholics and Protestants convinced many renaissance administrations to discourage religious theatre or ban it altogether. The Age of Reason made a fantasy of all but ocular types of seeing. And in its current, postmodern condition, much of the Christian world has forgotten that it once saw things differently. But as Isabel Burton indicates, the inclination to see differently is not dead, even in the world now dominated by her husband's eyes. Indeed, even in the twenty-first century, much of the non-Christian world still encounters God through pictures, statues and stage actors, and these extant practices may suggest how Isabel Burton's description of Oberammergau's Passionsspiele as 'a vision of Calvary' could be more than mere metaphor. They might even remind us how to see in a way we once did.

In fact, in spite of the Reformation, the Enlightenment and the fearful scepticism of the twentieth century, theatre-goers know very well the religious kind of seeing in which representation ends. The kind of seeing that commonly happens during performances commonly sees things that aren't materially there, even if twenty-first century theatre-goers can't articulate how that seeing happens.

The Oberammergau Passionsspiele

One need not look very long at examples of theatre before one finds an instance in which a performance stops *representing* and starts *being*. At the climax of one performance of Arizona State University's production of *Oleanna* in the late 1990s, an older gentleman in the audience shouted at an actor on stage, 'Hit her again!' I recall audiences cheering at the end of screenings of *Star Wars* in the late 1970s, as though thrilled that the emperor's Death Star had finally, *really* been destroyed. For Bert States, theatre most engages us when representation stops. Referring to Launce's dog in *The Two Gentlemen of Verona*, the animal that we audiences know stands between our world and the world of the play, States writes, 'we find ourselves cheering its performance precisely because it isn't one.'[45] We often appreciate theatre most, not for the way it re-presents life, but for the way it reveals life.

The so-called 'paradox of fiction', a term theatre borrows from literary theory, denotes the phenomenon in which art reveals real presence. An audience member's gasp at Lear's entrance in Act Five, dishevelled, distraught and bearing the corpse of his dear daughter, is not an expression of the audience member's 'suspension of disbelief', the willingness simply to pretend that things are happening: it is the confirmation that the audience member's body has seen something. The tears an audience member sheds over Cordelia and Lear do not ask *what if that happened?* but state *look what happened!*

Such theatrical experience resembles the kind of religious experience in which the presumably make-believe strikes the individual as quite real. Dramatic instances such as Margaret Ebner's Jesus doll, when it insists on sleeping in her bed, or Saint Francis's vision of the child Jesus through the *crèche*, may be variously read as striking examples of the paradox of fiction or as instances of psychosis. But everyday religious experiences, the *feeling* of God's presence in a cathedral, the *sense* an impressive vista can give of the oneness of existence, the intimation we get of the human family from the singing of a song, exemplify the ways in which we all know something immaterial in a visceral way.

Religion and theatre converge here, in the manifestation of 'real presence'. Both facilitate the materialisation of something that was not there before and which becomes, in the material of the performance, *really* there. The surge of reverence a parishioner feels in the mass, the rush of delight that animates the devotee at the *kirtan* and the dread that hangs over us at *Trojan Women*, are not delusions or wishful thinking, but corporeal and real experience. Theatre and religion resemble each other for so often making *look!* things rather than *what if?* things.

The Passionsspiele's *lebende bilder* invite devotees to assume the roles of onlookers within the always-on-going reality of the story indicated by the tableaus. Devotees who bring these roles with them to the Oberammergau theatre, roles for whom the Jesus story has an immediate and continuous reality, may interface with the *bilder* through their own playing of those roles to see in the play's unnatural – even uncanny – living images the truth that is usually obscured by the exigencies of day-to-day living.

And the artistic stylisation of the *lebende bilder* matters. Audience members do not need reminders that what happens on the Oberammergau stage is a play, but the strangeness of the tableaus draws audience members' conscious attention to the fabrication of the stage. The aesthetic distance that arises from this juxtaposition of art and observer is essential to the development in the audience of the state of mind that perceives the ineffable in the corporeal. The audience's subsequent, necessary, consideration of the stage art, as art, and the stage's high artistry, as artistry, conspire to incorporate the stage and audience into that mystical realm where aesthetic qualia have substance.

'Realism' (inasmuch as it is possible at all on a stage) can only disrupt the process by which the Passionsspiele vivifies the individual visions of the Bible and its various episodes that devotee audience members bring with them. The strange artistry of the *lebende bilder* brings the audience's own devotional vision into focus and makes it tangible in the combined space of the stage and the mind. If I might speak for her, Isabel Burton did not see 'a vision of Calvary' but *her* vision of Calvary, enlivened in the highly artificial apparatus of Oberammergau's Passion play.

In addition to the tableaus, the iconic moments of the Jesus story that the play does put into motion, such as the so-called last supper, the scourging and, of course, the crucifixion itself, take a mind-numbing amount of time to play out. When Oberammergau's Jesus washes his disciples' feet, he washes *all* their feet. For the uninitiated, there are twelve disciples, each with two feet. It takes Jesus an awfully long time to go through the motions of washing each foot of each of the twelve. A scene like this might just as well be a *lebendes bild*, for all the good that playing it out in fully realised motion does it. And this kind of pace-killing, redundant business makes most modern directors polish their editorial knives.

The Passionsspiele, on the other hand, by design or good instinct instilled in it by staging its *lebende bilder*, knows how to accommodate the devotional sensibilities of its audience. Indeed, devotee audiences know the iconic scenes, such as the foot-washing episode, so well and are so invested in them as expressions of the spiritual truth of the story as a whole, that such scenes are already accomplished and alive in their minds.[46] The patience that the Passionsspiele exercises estranges these scenes from the stage. Rather than looking for *abbreviated* expression, the devotees, for whom these episodes indicate most distinctly the always on-going reality of the Jesus story, look for a prolonged moment in which to look on as witnesses. The tableaus have the greatest potential to realise the story in the eye of piety through which devotees look and to incorporate the devotees themselves in the roles of witnesses of the spiritual narrative for which the play on stage is a mere proxy.

The experience that an audience has of a play proceeds primarily from what the audience brings to the theatre and from the roles that the audience is willing to play. An audience that won't watch *Lear* through the eyes of an exhausted Celtic army, or of a father whose children die for his folly, or even as a devotee of the Bard, will have a much different experience from those who will. The experiences of the Passionsspiele (whatever they may be) proceed from the roles the Oberammergau theatre's audiences take up. This play – this historic, controversial and very big play – best succeeds where it imposes itself on audiences least and where it offers instead a stage on which its audiences can impose themselves.

Endnotes

1   During off-seasons, Oberammergau residents also perform a play based on the circumstances of the Passionsspiele's origins.
2   The community marks the beginning of each production season with a ceremony commemorating the legendary vow. See chapter three of Shapiro, J. (2000) *Oberammergau: The Troubling Story of the World's Most Famous Passion Play* (New York: Pantheon)
3   The kind of unhappiness Sarah Beckwith notes over the staging of the York plays inside the Theatre Royal in 1992, rather than outside in the ruins of St. Mary's Abbey, is the kind of thing that inhibits the development of a long-standing tradition. See Beckwith, S. (2001) *Signifying God: Social Relation and Symbolic Act in the York Corpus Christi Plays* (Chicago: University of Chicago Press) p.9

4   Shapiro, op. cit., pp.103–9
5   Ibid., p.59
6   Ibid., p.59
7   Ibid., p.60
8   Reproductions of this stage plan abound. For one, see Wickham, G. (1987) *The Medieval Theatre* (Cambridge: Cambridge University Press) p.118.
9   Among other allegorical figures that appear in Rosner's play to deliver homiletic speeches to the audience are Death, Sin, and Avarice. Lane, E., and Brenson, I. (trans.) (1984) *Oberammergau: A Passion Play* (London: Dedalus) p.28
10 Shapiro, op. cit., p.61
11 While still Cardinal Ratzinger, Pope Benedict XVI himself opposed Rosner's play 'on the grounds that it was no longer possible to bring the Devil and Hell to life'. (Ibid., p.66) But the story is more complicated than this. Bans on Passion plays, as a genre, were widespread in Europe after the sixteenth century and a specific ban in 1770 by Maximilian Joseph put Oberammergau's century-and-a-half tradition in jeopardy. Fellow monk, Magnus Knipfelberger, offered government officials a refined version of Rosner's play for the 1780 production, which promised to be much less grotesque and to play the story more strictly as the Gospels told it. It may be that Oberammergau finally abandoned Rosner's version of the play in order to sustain the tradition of playing at all.
12 Lane and Brenson, op. cit., p.29
13 The story goes that Dedler's score was lost to a fire in 1817 and he rewrote it from memory for the 1820 production.
14 Stead, W.T. (ed.) *The Passion Play as Played To-day at Oberammergau* (New York: Charles E. Merrill & Co., n.d.) p.87
15 Ibid., p.101
16 Shapiro, op. cit., p.220
17 Weis, O., Daisenberger, J.A., Stückl, C. & Huber, O. (2010) *Oberammergau Passion Play 2010*, Shafer, I. (trans.) (Oberammergau: Gemeinde) p.4
18 Ibid., p.36
19 Shapiro, op. cit., p.132
20 Ibid., p.119–20
21 Ibid., p.117
22 Ibid., p.90
23 Ibid., p.114
24 Ibid., p.116
25 German critic Werner Spies compares the designs of the *lebende bilder* in the 2010 production to the work of early renaissance Italians, including Fra Angelico and Mantegna. Spies also points out the influence on Hageneier's

design of contemporary artists, such as photographer Cindy Sherman. See Spies, W. 'Zeige deine Wunde', *Frankfurter Allgemeine Sonntagszeitung*, 29 August 2010

26 Some historians speculate that these still-photo scenes on 'pageant wagons' developed into the grand and raucous 'cycle play' spectacles. Such evolutionary models of the development of theatre in medieval Europe are suspect.

27 Kobialka, M. (1988) 'Historic Time, Mythical Time, and Mimetic Time: The Impact of the Humanistic Philosophy of Saint Anselm on Early Medieval Drama', *Medieval Perspectives* 3.1: 172–90, p.179

28 Kobialka, M. (2003) *This Is My Body: Representational Practices in the Early Middle Ages* (Ann Arbor: University of Michigan Press) p.111

29 Ibid.

30 Kobialka, 'Historic Time, Mythical Time, and Mimetic Time', p.178

31 See Bonaventure, S. (1868) *Opera Omnia* (Paris: Ludovicus Vives) – part of the this text, including Book 7, is available online at http://www.ultramontes.pl/bonaventura.htm

32 Quoted in Shapiro, p.49

33 Ibid., p.53

34 Kemp. M. (2000) *The Book of Margery Kemp*, Staley, L. (ed) (New York: W. W. Norton & Company) p.57

35 Ebner, M. (1993) *The Revelations of Margaret Ebner*, Hindsley, L.P. (trans.) (Mahwah: Paulist Press) pp.132, 134

36 The study of the cognitive effects of theatrical playing and spectating is in its infancy. For a fuller discussion of the Role-Play Theory of Religious Experience, as formulated by psychologist Hjalmar Sundén, see the collected papers from the Symposium on Hjalmar Sundén's role-theory of religion in *Journal for the Scientific Study of Religion* 26 (1987).

37 Cunningham, L.S. (2004) *Francis of Assisi: Performing the Gospel Life* (Grand Rapids: William B. Eerdmans) p.75

38 Gibson, G.M. (1989) *The Theater of Devotion: East Anglian Drama and Society in the Late Middle Ages* (Chicago: University of Chicago Press) p.13

39 Quoted from Anselm's *Monologion*, in Kobialka, *This Is My Body*, p.113

40 Beckwith, S. (2001) *Signifying God: Social Relation and Symbolic Act in the York Corpus Christi Plays* (Chicago: University of Chicago Press) p.66

41 Gibson, p.41

42 Dunn, C. (1973) 'Popular Devotion in the Vernacular Drama of Medieval England', *Medievalia at Humanistica* 4: 55–68, p.57

43 Happé, P. (1994) 'A Guide to Criticism of Medieval English Theatre', in Beadle, R. (ed.) *The Cambridge Companion to Medieval English Theatre* (Cambridge: Cambridge University Press) pp. 312–43, 324. Happé, here,

is summarising the historical perspective of Richard Axton. See Axton, R. (1974) *European Drama of the Early Middle Ages* (London: Hutchinson)

44 Though some of them, certainly, were intended to be funny. Humour and reverence coexisted quite comfortably on the medieval stage.

45 States, B.O. (1985) *Great Reckonings in Little Rooms: On the Phenomenology of Theater* (Berkeley: University of California Press) p.34

46 Consider, as illustration, theatre scholar Glenn Loney's admission concerning the Passionsspiele that 'it is always difficult to separate the performance from a lifetime of thinking about this pivotal event in history and its significance'. See Loney, G. (1991) 'Oberammergau, 1634–1990: The Play and the Passions', *New Theatre Quarterly* 7.27: 203–16, 212

Contributors' Biographies

Colin Chambers   is Professor of Drama at Kingston University. A former journalist, drama critic and Literary Manager of the Royal Shakespeare Company (1981–1997), he co-wrote *Kenneth's First Play* and *Tynan* with Richard Nelson (RSC, 1997 & 2004 respectively). Books include *The Story of Unity Theatre* (1989); the award-winning *Peggy: the Life of Margaret Ramsay, Play Agent* (1997); *The Continuum Companion to Twentieth Century Theatre* (editor, 2002); *Inside the Royal Shakespeare Company* (2004); *Here We Stand: Politics, Performers and Performance – Paul Robeson, Isadora Duncan and Charlie Chaplin* (2006); and *Black and Asian Theatre in Britain: A History* (Routledge, 2011).

Constantin Chiriac   studied at the Theatre and Cinematography University, Bucharest. After graduating he began a successful career as a stage and film actor, with 45 theatre characters and 17 film roles to date, as well as 23 one-man shows, presented in 56 countries. He is the recipient of numerous awards and prizes for acting and cultural management, including one of the highest distinctions of the Romanian Theatre Union (UNITER). Chiriac was awarded a Master's Degree in Cultural Management from Hull University (1999) and a PhD in Theatre Arts from Lucian Blaga University, Sibiu, Romania. He is General Manager of the National Theatre Radu Stanca Sibiu, manager of Sibiu International Theatre Festival and Sibiu Open Market for Performances and professor at the Lucian Blaga University. Vice-president of the Sibiu – European Capital of Culture 2007 Association, he is a member of the European Capital of Culture selection and monitoring panel.

Anthony J. Faulder-Mawson   studied at Salisbury and at West Surrey College of Art and holds a Multimedia Design & Production and Web Design diploma from Cimdata, Akademie für Digitale Medien, Berlin. In 1993 he developed a light texturing method for use in high-temperature theatre lamps; this led to the development of 'light painting'. He subsequently developed systems for the construction of painting and cross-disciplinary forms, creating multi-layered, multi-dimensional Textured Installation Environments. His main focus lies in inter- and cross-disciplinary work with Ursula Mawson-Raffalt. As Co-founder, Artistic Director and Producer of the artist association known under the graphic logo) + (= a0 *International Platform for Innovation in the Arts* he is actively involved in theoretical writing and is responsible for multimedia production, web design, and design and layout of all) + (= **a0** projects.

Kathy Foley is a Professor of Theatre at the University of California, Santa Cruz. She is author of the Southeast Asia section of the *Cambridge Guide to World Theatre*, current editor of the *Asian Theatre Journal* and her articles have appeared in *TDR, Modern Drama, Asian Theatre Journal, Puppetry International* and other publications. She trained in mask and puppetry in Indonesia and was among the first non-Indonesians invited to perform in the prestigious all Indonesia National Wayang Festival. Her research has been supported by Fulbright, East-West Center, the Asian Cultural Council and other grants. Her exhibits have appeared at the National Geographic Society and other venues. She is also a Punch and Judy professor.

John Freeman joined the Performance Studies team at Curtin University, Perth, Western Australia from Brunel University London, where he was Reader in Theatre. The founder editor of *Performance Practice*, Freeman is author of *Tracing the Footprints: Documenting the Process of Performance* (2003), *New Performance/New Writing* (2007) and *Blood, Sweat & Theory: Research through Practice in Performance* (2010). His extensive writings on solo performance, identity construction, theatre pedagogy and approaches to artistic research have been published in edited collections and numerous international journals. Freeman has presented and staged work at major festivals, conferences and festivals worldwide, alongside residencies at universities, theatres and academies in New York, Helsinki, Sarajevo, Malta, Bavaria and Belgrade .

David Jortner teaches theatre history, theory and dramatic literature at Baylor University. He received his PhD in Theatre and Performance Studies from the University of Pittsburgh in 2003. He is the co-editor of *Modern Japanese Theatre and Performance* and has essays in several texts, including *Inexorable Modernity: Japan's Grappling with Modernity in the Arts* and *Revenge Drama in European Renaissance and Japanese Theatre*. He has published articles on Japanese theatre and film in *Asian Theatre Journal, Postscript, Text and Presentation* and *Tirai Pangung*. As a director he has staged works such as *The Odyssey, Lysistrata, Picasso at the Lapin Agile, The Caucasian Chalk Circle, Angel City* and *Fefu and Her Friends*.

Jean-Marc Larrue is co-director of the Research Center on Intermediality (CRI) at Université de Montréal, president of the International University Theatre Association (AITU-IUTA) and professor of theatre history and theory at the College of Valleyfield. His research mainly focuses on theatre, modernism and media. He is the author or co-author of several works: *Yiddish Theatre in Montreal* (Lansman-Jeu), *Les Nuits de la "Main"* (VLB – with André-G. Bourassa), *Le Monument inattendu* (HMH-Hurtubise), *Le Théâtre à Montréal à la fin du XIXe siècle* (Fides), *Théâtre au Québec – repères et perspectives* (VLB – with André-G. Bourassa and Gilbert David). He is the editor and co-editor of books and journals on theatre. More recently, *Lives and Deaths of Collective Creation* with Jane Baldwin and Christiane Page (Vox Theatri), « Mettre en scène » (*Intermédialités*, 2008) and « Le son au théâtre » *Théâtre/Public*, 2010). He is the recipient of grants from the Social Sciences and Humanities Research Council of Canada (SSHRC) and the Fonds québécois de recherche sur la société et la culture (FQRSC).

Edward Lewis holds degrees from the Open, Lancaster and Cambridge universities and has undertaken Forum Theatre training with Augusto Boal. Inspired by the production of *Nicholas Nickleby* about which he writes in this book, he has written and directed for the stage a number of adaptations including Margaret Atwood's *The Handmaid's Tale*, Aldous Huxley's *Brave New World* and Dickens' *Our Mutual Friend*. His most recent commissioned work is an adaptation of Emile Zola's *Nana*, performed in Russian in Minsk, Belarus, under his direction. This project is a continuation of work which, for the last twenty years, has been created in contexts as varied as war zones, prisons, professional theatres and sites for political intervention. Dividing his time between Britain, Eire and continental Europe, Lewis combines university teaching and applied drama practice with theatre work as director, writer and actor.

David Mason is Associate Professor of Theatre at Rhodes College. A former Fulbright Fellow in India, Mason has written articles on India's *râs lîlâ* theatre, classical Sanskrit aesthetics, and Shakespeare in India for such journals as *Theatre Research International*, *New Literary History*, and the *Journal of Dramatic Theory and Criticism*; his concerns with the intersection of religious and theatrical practices in Vrindavan, India are explored in his 2009 book, *Theatre and Religion on Krishna's Stage*.

Ursula Mawson-Raffalt holds a BA in Performing Arts, Choreography and Dance from the Academy of the Arts, Arnhem and a Certificate in Arts Management from the Akademie für Kultur und Bildung, Berlin. She has, since 1989, written, conceived, composed, choreographed, directed and performed multi-layered Installation Matrices for Choreographic Theatrical Environments, work which carries her unique signature, the **focus-point technique) uM_R**, a compositional method and training system for body and voice which is a key element in defining her approach to movement and stage language. Since 1993 her main focus is on cross- and interdisciplinary work with Anthony J. Faulder-Mawson. As the Co-founder, Artistic Director and Producer of) + (= a0 she is also actively involved in theoretical writing and the strategic and promotional planning and coordination of the production process for all their projects.

Guilherme Mendonça trained at the Institut Franco-Portugais and the Guildhall School of Music and Drama, before completing a Master's degree at Kings College and RADA. He is a published poet, essayist and playwright and, in 2003, integrated the international residency for playwrights at the Royal Court Theatre. Mendonça has worked with many companies, including Barraca, o Teatro da Cornucópia and Workhorse Productions, editing, translating, casting and directing; more recently he was casting director and acting coach on films in Portugal and Africa. He has recently completed PhD research into conceptual connections between acting theory and literary theory, exploring the extent to which given circumstances and objectives can be incorporated in a dramaturgical theory.

Allan Owens is Professor of Drama Education at the University of Chester and is a UK National Teaching Fellow. Practice and research interests centre round the intercultural and interdisciplinary applications of process drama in a wide range of contexts including education, theatre, health, justice and organisational settings. His extensive international work includes long-term collaborative projects across Europe, the Middle East and East Asia. The author of numerous articles, chapters and books, most relevant to this publication Owens is co-author with Naomi Green and Yuri Kobayashi of the first book on applied drama originated in Japan, *'Applied Drama: Communication through pre-texts'* (2010); co-editor of the *2007 IDEA Dialogues: Hong Kong* (2009); and editorial-board member of *DaTEAsia*, the first journal for drama and theatre education in Asia (2010).

Anne Pellois is Senior Lecturer in Theatre Studies in the Arts Department of the Ecole Normale Supérieure (ENS) in Lyon. She holds a PhD in Literature and Theatre Studies: *Symbolist Utopias: theatrical fictions around Man an City*, directed by Professor Bernadette Bost, and has published widely on symbolist theatre. This work continues with a reflexion on the relations between theatre and utopia, from the end of the nineteenth century to the present; and the history and techniques of actors from the nineteenth century to the present. Pellois is currently working on the practice of theatre as a way of learning French and developing her methodological constructions into a series of research papers.

Peter Snow is Professor and Director of the Centre for Theatre and Performance at Monash University and a professional theatre artist. He has made many performance research productions in Europe, Asia and Australia, including, with Tess de Quincey, *Guilt Frame* (Sydney Theatre Company 2008) and, with Frank Van de Ven, *Thought/Action Suites* (Copenhagen, Amsterdam, Brussels, Gent, Leeds 2002–5). His research interests, on which he has written widely, are in contemporary performance, philosophy of performance, and performance making. He spent the winter semester of 2010–11 as DAAD Guest Professor in Australian Studies at the Free University, Berlin.

Kevin J. Wetmore, Jr. is an Associate Professor of Theatre at Loyola Marymount University. In addition to being an actor and director, he is the author of *The Athenian Sun in an African Sky*, *Black Dionysus: Greek Tragedy and African American Theatre* and *The Empire Triumphant*, among others, and the editor or co-editor of another six books, including *Portrayal of Americans on the World Stage*, *Suzan-Lori Parks: A Casebook* and *Modern Japanese Theatre and Drama*.

Index

A Floresta d'Água 145
Active Music Listening (AML) 146, 150, 157
  see also Audição Musical Activa
Actividades de Enriquecimento Cultural 150
Adams, John 10, 163–166, 168, 170–174, 176–178
Admiral's Men, The 168
Adoration of the Magi 269
Advent and Triumph of Christ 270
Aesthetic Distance 272
Age of Reason, The 270
Aguilera, Christina 128
Aka Moon 235, 237, 240, 252
Akademi Seni Tari Indonesia (Indonesian Academy of Dance, ASTI) 191
Aldwych Theatre 17, 24, 35, 39, 44, 50, 51
Alfreds, Mike 43
Alleyn, Edward 168
Amagatsu, Ushio 113
Anachronism 19, 28, 31, 185, 269, 270
Anagnorisis 163
And the Light Shines in Darkness 216
Anderson, Laurie 9
Angelico, Fra 264
Angels in America: Part 1: Millennium Approaches 102
Angelus Novus 165
Anti-Semitism 259–261
Antony and Cleopatra 30
Apartheid/Post-Apartheid 88–91, 93, 98, 100–101
Appia, Adolphe 29
Apreotesei, Doru 202
Arden from Faversham 217
Arden, John 39
Aristotle 109, 122, 123, 264
Artaud, Antonin 54, 182, 195, 197, 198
As You Like It 217
Associazione Lirica e Concertistica Italiana 157
Atomic Energy Committee 172
Audição Musical Activa 158

see also Active Music Listening
Audience 61
Augustijnen Koen 235
Aussie Aussie Aussie Oi Oi Oi (Democratic Torture) 119
Australia 13, 15, 105, 107, 110, 111, 112, 113, 116, 117, 118, 119, 120, 121, 122, 123, 124
Australian Bicentennial/ Bicentenary 118, 120
Ayckbourn, Alan 4, 47, 52

Baal 216
Bacchae, The 216
Bach, Joahnn Sebastian 151
Bahkouche, Simon 235
Bailey, Brett 8, 88, 90, 104
Bakker, Kuno 235
Balanța Hall 212, 217
Balcony, The 27
Bamboo to Bronze 181, 191, 193, 198
Banu, Georges 210, 218, 249, 253
Barber, Felix 49
Barbican Theatre 13
Baris Gede 185
Barker, Howard 31, 240
Barnett, Laura 10, 15
Barthes, Roland 7
Baudrillard, Jean 230
Bausch, Pina 220
Bazzo, Lucie 63
Beck, Julian 54
Beckett, Samuel 4, 27, 236
Beckwith, Sarah 269, 273, 275
Bellefeuille, Robert 57–58, 62
Belo, Jane 181, 188, 195–196, 198–199
Benedict, Ruth 195
Benhamou, Anne-Françoise 242, 249, 253
Benjamin, Walter 165, 196, 227, 228, 252, 254
Bennett, Susan 6, 15, 233
Berata, I Dewa Putu 12, 181, 191–193, 198
Berengar of Tours 266
Berliner Ensemble 24
Bernard of Clairvaux 266
Bernhard, Thomas 237, 240,

241, 246, 254
Bernstein, Jeremy 173
Bernstein, Leonard 196
Bestel, Mélanie 235
Bettens, Stijn 235
Beuys, Joseph 225
Bevington, David 170
Bhagavad Gita 166, 177
Billington, Michael 50
Birmingham Repertory Theatre 19, 20
Blau, Herbert 113, 123
Bleak House 43
Bloos, Coca 205, 206
Blue Monster, The 217
Bockenheimer Depot 213
Bogosian, Eric 250
Bomb, The 173
Bond, Edward 31
Bonnema, Anneke 221
Booth, James 22
Born, Max 172
Boulez, Pierre 151
Bousset, Sigrid 233
Bower, Sharon 48
Bowie, David 230, 231
Brando, Marlon 2
Brassard, Marie 57, 62
Bratton, Jackie 29, 33
Brecht, Bertolt 2, 4, 7, 14, 27, 45, 54, 113, 220, 221, 224, 233, 241, 242
Brenton, Howard 2, 39
Brine, Daniel 7, 15
Britten, Benjamin 196, 217
Broods, Natali 235, 242
Brook, Peter 8, 10, 11, 12, 13, 15, 18, 19, 20, 21, 22, 23, 24, 25, 26, 27, 28, 29, 30, 31, 32, 33, 41, 52, 100, 213
Brothers Karamazov, The 217
Bruno, Giordano 169
Büchner, Georg 240
Bulandra Theatre 216
Bunuel, Luis 6
Burning Daylight 113
Burton, Isabel 262, 263, 270, 272
Burton, Richard 262, 263

Cabral, Pedro Álvares 145

INDEX

Caganisso 149
Cage, John 7
Caird, John 40, 49, 52
Caltech 172
Camerlain, Lorraine 59, 62
Camillo, Giulio 226, 231
Camus, Albert 250
Carbone 14 theatre company 61
Carl Malcomess High School 89
Carlson, Marvin 227, 228, 233
Carriere, Jean 12
Carver, Raymond 250
Casault, Jean 57, 62
Casey, Edward 109, 123
Cassidy, David 173
Cassol, Fabrizio 235
Castle of Perseverance 259
Castor and Pollux 216
Caux, Patrick 57, 60
Caux, Robert 63
Ceaușescu, Nicolae 203, 205, 217
Centre for New Dance Development 71
Centro Cultural de Belém 155
Ceremony 91, 96, 273
  see also Sydney 2000 Olympics Opening Ceremony
Cerita, I Nyoman 12, 181, 191, 192, 197, 198
Cerita, Pak 187, 193
Chaillet, Ned 50
Chamberworks 80
Chants Andalou 230
Chaplin, Charles 128
Chaudhuri, Una 174, 178
Chelba, Constantin 217
Cherry Orchard, The 216
Church, Tony 23
Churchill, Caryl 4
Churchill Play, The 39
Cincinnati Playhouse in the Park 173
Circulations 57
City Council of Sibiu 203
Ciulli, Roberto 216
Cloudstreet 122, 124
Coast, John 194, 195, 196, 197, 198
Cognitive Experience 268
Collège International de Philosophie 77
Collier, Patience 22
Colonialism/Neo-Colonialism/

Post-Colonialism 88, 196, 231
Comedy of Errors, The 24, 28
Conant, Jennet 173
Concertos para Bebés 155
Concertos para Bebés e Famílias 155
Cooley, Eileen 184
Copeau, Jacques 29
Coplan, David 99, 100, 101, 104
Côté, Lorraine 57, 62, 66
Counsell, Michael 262
Couture, Jean-François 63
Craig, Edward Gordon 29
Cricot 2 Theatre 226
Crimp, Martin 240
Crosby, Bing 196
Cross-Gendering 188
Cubism 22, 23, 32
Culinary Theatre 224
Cultural Materialism 31
Curious Productions 12
Cushman, Robert 50
Cymbeline 28

Dahl, Hans Petter 221, 230
Daisenberger, Joseph Alois 258, 259, 260, 261, 274
Danaides, The 204, 206, 216, 217
Daneliuc, Mircea 217
Dante (Durante degli Alighieri) 75, 110
Darlington, W. A. 29, 33
Darwin, Charles 164
David, Gwénola 242, 254
Davidson, John 170, 178
Davis, Judith 235
Davis, Tracy 175, 176, 178
Day, Doris 87, 97
De Clerck, Paul 235, 237, 240
De Keersmaeker, Anne Teresa 232, 237, 239
De Keersmaeker, Jolente 235, 236, 240, 242, 246, 250, 254
De Koe 237, 239, 244, 252, 253
De Koning, Matthias 235, 237, 239, 244
De Muynck, Viviane 220, 222, 232
De Roo, Sara 235, 236, 239, 240, 242
De Schrijver, Damiaan 235, 236, 237, 242, 243, 244, 246, 250, 251
De Wet, Reza 87

Dead Class, The 226
Dead Dreams of Monochrome Men 12
Death in Venice 196
Death of Klinghoffer, The 164
Dedler, Rochus 259, 274
Dee, John 169
Deleuze, Gilles 111, 123
Dench, Judi 2, 30
Dennis, Armand 196
Dewa Ayu Eka Putri 188
D'Huys, An 235
Dias da Música 155
Dickens, Charles 11, 35, 36, 40, 42, 43, 46, 47, 49, 52
Diderot, Denis 240, 244, 253
Digges, Thomas 168
Dinescu, Mircea 208, 217
Dinică, Gheorghe 204, 205
Direcção Geral das Artes 154
Disneyland, Paris 217
Divine Comedy, The 75
Djakapurra Munyarryun 110
Doctor Faustus (character) 10, 164, 167, 168, 169, 170, 171
  see also Dr Faustus Lights the Lights
Doctor Faustus (Christopher Marlowe) 10, 168, 169
Doctor Faustus (Thomas Mann) 170
Doctorow, E. L. 163
Doinaș, Ștefan Augustin 202, 209
Dole, Bob 208
Dom Juan 237
Don Juan 217
Donellan, Declan 102
Donka: A Letter to Chekhov 12
Donne, John 163, 165, 166, 171
Downey, Misha 220
Downs, Jane 45, 52
Dr Faustus Lights the Lights 12
Dragons' Trilogy, The 4, 9, 53–67
Drake, Sir Francis 169
Dubé, Gilles 63
Dumas, Claire 235
Dumitrescu, Andu 202
Dunn, Catherine 269, 275
DV8 12

Each One Tell One 103
East Asia, influence of 13
Ebner, Margaret 268, 271, 275

Edgar, David 35, 37, 40, 42, 46, 47, 48, 49, 52
Edinburgh International Festival 10, 207, 211, 213, 214
Egnos, Bertha 99
Elegy from Marienbad, The 208
Elizabeth I 169
Elton, Ben 14
Embrechts, Tine 235, 242
Enlightenment, The 214, 270
EPED 147, 148
Esrig, David 205, 216
Etchells, Tim 7
Eucharist, the 265, 266
Eugene Onegin 216
Eureka Springs New Great Passion play 257
Expresso Bongo 20
Eynaudi, Alix 235
Eyre, Richard 31, 33

Fabre, Jan 220, 232
Fauré, Julien 222, 223
Faust 10, 13, 201–215
see also Doctor Faustus
Feinstein, Elaine 31
Fellini, Federico 208, 220
Fenton, James 50
Ferguson, Elian 201, 218
Festival du théâtre des Amériques (FTA) 54
Festival of Britain, The 257
Figgis, Mike 5
Fink, Richard Paul 163
Finley, Gerald 163
Firmin-Didot, Catherine 241, 254
Fitful Muse, The 226
Fitzgerald, Ella 128
Flanigan, Clifford 269
Fleming, Tom 17
Flunger, Tobias 262, 263
Flying Dutchman, The 217
Foco Musical 12, 145–161
Focus Point Technique 72, 79–83, 85
Fonoteca Municipal 147
Forced Entertainment 9
Forestier, Georges 241, 243
Frankenstein, Dr 164
Frankfurt Goethe Festival 213
Fréchette, Richard 58, 62
Freeman, Cathy 1, 116, 117, 122
Fricht, Max 250
Fuchs, Elinor 221, 233

Fugard, Athol 88, 89, 100, 226

Galileo, Galilei 164, 166, 257
Galland, Stéphane 235
Gamelan Çudamani 181, 198
Gamelan Sekar Jaya 184, 192, 193
Gardner, Lyn 9, 15, 218
Gaskill, William 29
Gellert, Roger 29, 33
Gender Dynamics 185
Genet, Jean 27
Germain, Jean-Claude 54
Gheorghe, Ilie 202, 207
Gibson, Gail McMurray 269, 275
Gielgud, John 20
Gignac, Marie 57, 62
Gil, Jose 77, 78
Gilbert, Helen 107, 114, 124
Gilbert, William 169
Glass Menagerie, The 226
Gob, Benoît 221, 225
God 46, 48, 67, 140, 163, 171, 201, 265, 266, 268, 269, 270, 271
Goddard, Jim 42, 52
Godinho, José Carlos 150
Goebbels, Heiner 1
Goethe Institute 208
Goethe, Wolfgang Amadeus 208
Gold Fever 216
Good 39
Goodbody, Buzz 30
Goona-Goona 196
Gorky, Maxim 216
Gould, Glenn 237
Grand Cirque Ordinaire 54
Granville Barker, Harley 23, 26, 29
Graver, David 100, 101, 103, 104
Gregory, André 237, 251
Grootboom, Mpumelelo 87
Grotowski, Jerzi 11, 251
Groves, Leslie 172, 176, 177
Gruarin, Alano 235
Guardian, The 33, 50, 67, 218
Guinness Book of Records 207
Gurdjieff, George Ivanovitch 6
Gusti Ayu Raku Rasmin 192
Gusti Ayu Suryani 187

Haas, Conrad 203

Hall, Peter 21, 23, 24, 31
Halprin, Anna 55
Halprin, Lawrence 55
Hamlet 19, 20, 30, 94, 216
Handke, Peter 250
Hard Times 40
Hardy, Thomas 14
Hare, David 2, 29, 31, 33
Harriot, Thomas 169
Harrison, Cathryn 45
Harrison, Jane 122
Harrison, Katherine 'Kitty' 172
Hatzigeorgiou, Michel 235
Haussmann, Leander 216
Hawkins, Andrew 48
Haynes, Rosalynn 167, 168, 170
Hébert, Chantal 60
Herken, Gregg 173
Hideki, Noda 102
Hiroshima 58, 172
Hirst, Damien 229
Hitler, Adolf 37
Holman, James 224
Holy Sonnet XIV 163, 165, 171
Hope, Bob 196
Hopes of the Living Dead 103
Hopkins, Anthony 2
House in Bali 196, 199
Houston, Whitney 128
Howitt, Anna Maria 262, 263
Huber, Otto 261, 274
Hughes, Ted 9
Hytner, Nicholas 9

I Dewa Putu Berata 12, 181, 191
I Gede Manik 188
I Ketut Kantor 192
I Ketut Wirtawan 192
I Made Arnawa 191, 192
I Made Bandem 191
I Made Lebah 195, 196, 199
I Nyoman Cerita 12, 181, 191, 192
I Nyoman Kakul 192
I was Looking at the Ceiling and then I Saw the Sky 164
I Wayan Gandera 188, 196
Il Campiello 216, 217
Ilbijerri Theatre Company 122
Illusion, The 102
Împăratul Romanilor 211
Impromptu XL 11, 235–252
iMumbo Jumbo 103
Incarnation 28, 242, 265, 268

Index

Indigenous Australian Performance 109–110, 123
Ineffability 272
Institut Seni Indonesia (ISI) 191
International Centre for Theatre Research 30
International WOW Company 173
Ionesco, Petrika 216, 217
Iordache, Stefan 204, 205, 206
Ipi Zombi? 4, 8, 12, 87–104
Isabella's Room 12, 219–233
Island of the Mighty, The 39
Italian Straw Hat, The 216

Jackson 5 (music group) 128
Jacobs, Sally 30
Jail Diary of Albie Sachs, The 40
Jane Eyre 43
Jesus 256, 257, 258, 259, 260, 261, 262, 263, 264, 265, 266, 267, 268, 269, 270, 271, 272, 273
Johnson, Haynes 174, 175, 176, 178
Jones, Bill T. 12
Jordens, Filip 235, 237, 240
Joseph, Maximilian 259, 274
Jowitt, Debra 184, 199
Judas 258, 267
Judson Church 71

Kabuki 211, 212
Kane, Sarah 4
Kantor, Tadeusz 4, 12, 226, 233
Kanzaburo Nakamura-Za 211, 212
Kaye, Lila 45
Keaton, Buster 128
Keidan, Lois 7, 15
Kemp, Margery 268, 275
Kempner, Teddy 37
Keneally, Thomas 120, 121, 124
Ki energy 125, 130, 131, 132, 135, 138, 140, 141, 143
King John 19, 20, 31
King Lear 8, 10, 11, 15, 17–33, 87, 271, 273
Kingsley, Ben 30, 50
Kinoshita, Liz 235
Kirby, Ernest T. 3, 15
Kjartansdottir, Vedis 235
Kobialka, Michel 226, 233, 265, 266, 275

Kojin, Nishido 138
Komisjaresvky, Theodore 29
Kott, Jan 27, 33
Kreitzer, Carson 173
Kroll, Jack 29, 33
Kruger, Loren 90, 91, 99, 103, 104
Kureishi, Hanif 250
Kushner, Tony 102

La Rochefoucault, François 240
Lady from the Sea, The 20
Laing, R. D. 27
Lakier, Gail 99
Lamb, Charles 26
Lambrecht, Jef 235, 237, 240, 246, 250
Lamour, Dorothy 196
Landscape 226
Large, Duncan 233
Laughton, Charles 21
Lauterbach, Konstanze 216
Lauwers, Felix 222, 223, 228, 231
Lauwers, Jan 219, 220, 222–226, 228–232
L'Avantage du doute 237, 239
Lavoie, Louis-Marie 63
Le Rail 61
Le Roy, Frederick 233
Le Titanic 61
lebende bilder 264, 265, 272, 273, 274
Lecat, Jean Guy 213
LeCompte, Elizabeth 220, 225
Leggatt, Alexander 29, 32, 33
Legrand, Nadir 235
Lepage, Robert 4, 9, 53, 55, 57–60, 63, 64, 65, 67
Les Miserables 50
Lessard, Jacques 55, 56, 57
Levin, Bernard 50
Life and Adventures of Nicholas Nickleby, The 11, 35–52
Lifton, Robert Jay 174, 175, 178
Little Dorrit 40
Live Art 15
Living Theatre 54
Lo, Jacqueline 107
Lombard, Peter 266
Lone Anzac 118
Look back in Anger 228
Lord of the Flies 25
L'Orfeo 74–77
Love Song of J. Robert Oppenheimer 173
Love's Labour's Lost 19, 20, 21
Lowland Hall 213, 214, 215, 218
L.S.D. 12, 225, 226
Lucia di Lammermoor 216
Lucian Blaga University of Sibiu 203, 277
Lucifer/Satan 206, 258, 259
Lulu 216
Lyotard, Jean-Francois 220, 233

Maatschappij Discordia 237, 239, 244, 253
Macbeth 2, 29, 30, 216, 217
Machado, Manuel 230
Magic 66, 72, 85, 90, 95, 102, 103, 116, 167–169, 184, 195, 196, 210
Maheu, Gilles 61
Malle, Louis 237, 244
Man and Superman 20
Mandela, Nelson 89
Manhattan Project, the 172
Manţoc, Lia 202, 207
Maponya, Maishe 89
Marat/Sade, The 41
Marier, Yves-Éric 58, 62
Marin, MIhaela 207, 217
Marlowe, Christopher 10, 167, 168, 169, 177, 178, 179
Marowitz, Charles 21, 22, 23, 26, 27, 32
Marrugeku 113, 124
Marsalis on Music 155
Martin, Hugh 127, 128, 144
Mary Barnes 40
Master and Margarita, The 216
Maxwell, Richard 225, 226
May, Thomas 164, 166, 170, 178, 179
McAlindon, Tom 1, 15
McCowen, Alec 18
McKay, Fulton 50
McKellen, Ian 2, 30
McMillan, Priscilla 173, 179
McNamara, Robert 176
McPhee, Colin 189, 194, 195, 196, 199
Mda, Zakes 100
Measure for Measure 19, 21, 28
Mecaru: Appeasing the Playful Earth Spirits 185
Meditationes Vitae Christi 267
Meet Me in St. Louis 128

285

Memling, Hans 270
Memory Theatre 226
Mendes, Marco 151
Mephistopheles 168, 169, 202, 204, 205, 209, 210, 214, 215
Meron, Dovrat Ana 105
Michaud, Marie 57, 62
Micu, Dan 217
Mills, Jonathan 211, 213, 214
Mimesis 269
Ministry of Culture, Cults and National Heritage of Romania 203
Mitoma, Judy 184, 192, 193, 196, 199, 200
Mnouchkine, Ariane 100
Modernism 222, 279
Mofokeng, Jerry 100, 101, 104
Molière 237, 240, 241, 242, 243, 254
Moment I Saw You I Knew I Could Love You, The 12
Montaigne, Michel De 226, 233
Monteverdi 73, 74, 75, 76, 77, 78
Morandi, Giorgio 220, 226
Morel, Erik 235, 240, 246
Morimura, Rumiko 126, 127, 128, 129, 130, 131, 132, 134, 135, 137, 138, 139, 140, 141, 142, 143, 144
Morin, Gwénaël 248, 254
Morley, Christopher 29
Moscow Art Theatre 24
Moses 17, 264
Mother Courage and her Children 2, 14, 222
Mozart, Amadeus 20, 81, 151, 152, 161, 164
Mozart effect, The 152
Mugur, Vlad 216
Mullins, Mike 118, 119
Multiple Viewpoints 31
Murakami, Haruki 250
Murdoch, Rupert 38
Murnau, Friedrich Wilhelm 195
Murray, Brian 18
Music Academy of Bucharest 217
Musicology 148, 149, 150

Nagasaki 172
Napier, John 49
National English Literary Museum 87
National Theatre, London 9, 15, 20, 102
National Theatre of Craiova 216
National Theatre Radu Stanca 201, 202, 203, 206, 212, 215
Nederland Subtheatre 12
Needcompany 11, 219, 232
Nelson, H. G. 117
New Historicism 31
New Realism 266
New Wave 27
New York City Players 225
Ni Ketut Alit Arini 192
Ni Wayan Febri Lestari 187
Nicholas Nickleby 11, 35–52
Nicolae Grigorescu Fine Arts Institute 216
Nietzsche, Friedrich 228, 229, 233
Nihon Kogakuin Digital Open Space 13
Nixon in China 164
Nora, Pierre 249
Noren, Lars 240
Northwest Arts Drama Company 87
Nosferatu, a Symphony of Horror 195
Not with my Gun 87
Nouryeh, Andrea 176, 179
Nunn, Trevor 2, 30, 39, 40, 45, 47, 49, 50, 52

O Achamento do Brasil 12, 145–161
O Conquistador 145
Oberammergau Passionsspiele 5, 11, 255–276
O'Connor, Garry 29, 33
Odalan Bali 4, 12, 181–200
Odo of Cambrai 266
Oh, What A Lovely War! 24
Ohashi, Yosuke 126–144
Oklahoma! 263
Old Vic Theatre 42
Oleanna 271
Oliver, Stephen 47, 48, 49
Olivier, Laurence 20, 21, 25
Olympic Games *see* Sydney 2000 Olympics Opening Ceremony
On the Transmigration of Souls 164
Opera 19, 23, 48, 78, 113, 118, 120, 145, 147, 154, 157, 161, 163–166, 170–174, 176–178, 196, 199
Oppenheimer, J. Robert 10, 163–179
Oresteia, The 216, 217
Orquesta Filarmónica de Gran Canaria (OFGC) 157, 158
Orquesta Didáctica da Foco Musical 12, 145–161
Orquesta Metropolitana de Lisboa 159
Osborne, John 228
Other Place, The 30, 39
Our Country's Good 120, 124
Ouspensky, P. D. 6, 15
Owen, Eric 176

Page, Stephen 109, 112, 121, 124
Palacios, Alma 235
Palazzo Ducale 75
Palm Sunday 267
Pantagruel's Sister-in-Law 217
Paradox of Fiction 217
Paris Colonial Exposition, 1930 182, 194, 195
Parish, Paul 183, 184, 199
Parr, Mike 119, 120
Passio Nova 259
Pavarotti, Luciano 197
Pavlovic, Diane 63
Pearson, Keith Ansell 233
Peck, Bob 44, 47
Pedagogy 146, 148, 151, 155
Pedro, Risoleta Pinto 145
Perelli-Contos, Irène 60
Pernes, Miguel 145, 146, 149, 150, 151, 152, 153, 158
Persecution and Assassination of Jean-Paul Marat... see Marat/Sade, The
Peter and the Wolf 155
Petherbridge, Edward 43, 45
Phèdre 9
Phelan, Peggy 113, 124
Phoenix Theatre 19, 20
Physicists, The 24
Picasso, Pablo 22
Pilgrim 13, 125–144
Pingbody 9
Pinter, Harold 4, 226, 240, 241
Pintilie, Lucian 217
Piţa, Dan 216
Plassard, Denis 249, 254

INDEX

Poel, William 29
Pogrebin, Robin 225, 233
Poirson, Martial 249, 254
Polygraph 57
Popii, Ofelia 202, 207, 214, 215
Porello, Federica 235, 237
Post-Dramatic 31
Postmodernism 222, 229, 230, 231, 233
Power and the Glory, The 20
Pravda 2
Prévert, Jacques 240
Princeton Institute for Advanced Study 172
Prokofiev, Sergei 155
Provoost, Jan 264
Psychological Experience 268
Punchdrunk 10
Puppets/Puppetry 136, 186, 189, 204
Purcărete, Silviu 10, 201–218
Purgatorio 75

Quebec Conservatory of Dramatic Art 55
Quick, Andrew 226, 233
Quinta da Amizade 145

Raaijmakers, Boy 235
Racine, Jean 9
Răduḅă, Daniel 202, 207
Rameau's Nephew 205
Rawls, Lou 128
Recruiting Officer, The 120
Red de Organizadores de Conciertos Educativos (ROCE) 157
Reed, Larry 192, 199
Rees, Roger 43, 45, 47, 49, 51, 52
Reformation, The 270
Rich, Alan 165, 170, 179
Richard, Emily 50, 52
Richard III 217
Rigg, Diana 17
Riggs, David 169, 179
Rijnders, Gerardjan 237
Ring Round the Moon 20
Ritual 3, 15, 17, 88, 91, 92, 95, 96, 99, 101, 114, 115, 182, 183, 186, 220, 261, 263, 266, 269
Road to Bali, The 196
Roberto Devereux 216
Roberts, Jason 224, 233

Robinson, Dave 220, 221. 233
Rock 'n' Roll Suicide 230
Rodgers, Richard 196
Rodrigues, Tiago 235, 242
Role-Play 264, 265, 268, 275
Romeo and Juliet 19, 20, 26, 47
Ronfard, Jean-Pierre 61
Roosevelt, Andre 196
Rosas 237, 239, 252
Rosenberg, Pamela 164, 170
Rosner, Ferdinand 258, 259, 260, 264, 274
Rotimi, Ola 103
Royal Court Theatre 30, 120, 124
Royal Shakespeare Company 11, 13, 17, 20, 21, 23, 24, 25, 26, 27, 28, 30, 31, 32, 35, 38, 39, 40, 41, 50, 51, 52, 216
Rozik, Eli 3, 15
Rubin, Leon 40, 42, 46, 50, 52
Rudakoff, Judith 100, 104

Sacks, Oliver 156
St. Anselm 268, 269, 270, 275
St. Bonaventure 267, 268
Saint-Denis, Michel 21
St. Francis 268, 271, 275
Salgueiro, Jorge 145, 146
Sampermans, Erwin 235
Sarafina 101
Satyagraha 216
Savarese, Nicola 182, 196, 200
Savran, David 226, 233
Scapino, the Trickster 217
Scenography 207
Schechner, Richard 3, 15, 100, 229
Scofield, Paul 17, 18, 20, 23, 24, 25, 28, 29, 31, 33
Seagull, The 217
Second Shepherds' Pageant 258
Seghers, Maarten 222, 230
Sekhabi, Aubrey 87
Sellars, Peter 9, 10, 163, 164, 165, 166, 168, 171, 172, 173, 174, 176, 177, 178, 179
Semiotics 1
Şerban, Andrei 216
Shakespeare Birthplace Trust 41
Shakespeare Our Contemporary 27, 33
Shakespeare, William 4, 11, 13, 15, 17–33, 39, 47, 240

Shaking the Blues Away 97
Shamanism 3, 93
Shankar, Ravi 197
Shapiro, James 257, 258, 259, 260, 261, 267, 273, 274, 275
Shared Experience 43
Shawn, Wallace 237, 244, 251, 254
Shepherd-Barr, Kristin 166, 167, 179
Shichiji, Eisi 138
Simerom Halls 203, 204, 212
Simon, Barney 100
Sinatra, Frank 128
Şirli, Vasile 202, 207, 217
Sisterly Feelings 47, 52
Sitsho thina, sifela emathongweni 92
Sizwe Bansi is Dead 88
Slam Poetry 240
Slaven, Roy 117
Snow in Midsummer 94
Social Drama 112, 115, 120, 122
Sofer, Andrew 169, 170, 179
Song for Budhanton 222, 231
Sorrows of Young Werther, The 216
South Bank Show 46
South Pacific 196
Spencer, Charles 7, 15, 218
Spies, Walter 182, 194–198, 200
Spirituality 96, 127, 138, 143, 191, 197, 267, 269
Stalpaert, Christel 219, 233
Stan, Nicu 217
Standard Bank National Arts Festival 87, 96, 102
Stanislavski, Konstantin 113, 225, 227, 242
Star Wars 271
States, Bert 271, 276
Stein, Peter 204
Stelarc 9
Stolen 112, 122, 124
Stone Wedding, The 216
Strangelove, Dr 164
Stratford, Ontario 20
Stratford-upon-Avon (theatre/place) 17, 19, 20, 24, 25, 30, 31, 39, 42
Strauss, Botho 240
Stravinsky, Igor Fyodorovich 151

287

Stückl, Christian 260, 261, 274
Sturm, Nico 235
Stürmer, Helmut 202, 206, 215, 216
Styx 10, 69–86
Susilo, Emiko 181, 184, 187, 191, 193, 197, 200
Susilo, Hardja 193
Sydney 107, 108, 109, 111, 115, 116, 117, 118, 119, 120, 121, 216
Sydney 2000 Olympics Opening Ceremony 4, 12–13, 105–124

Tableaux Vivants 264
Tabu 195
Tabuchi, Eisei 126, 127, 128, 131, 134, 135, 139, 140, 142, 143
Taichi-Kikaku 13, 125–144
Takeaway Theatre Company 87
Tănase Scatiu 216
Tate, Nahum 26
Taylor, C. P. 39
Teatro Sunil 12
Tectonic Plates 57
Tempest, The 19, 21, 216, 217
Temporality 238, 245, 247, 251
ten Cate, Ritsaert 5, 15, 233
Terry, Keith 192
Tg STAN 11, 235–254
Thackeray, William 26
Thatcher, Margaret 37, 38, 46
Théâtre des Nations 24
Théâtre du Même Nom (TMN) 54
Théâtre Euh 54
Theatre of Cruelty 30
Theatre of the Absurd 27
Théâtre Repère 9, 53–67
Theatre Workshop 24
Theatrum Anatomicum 12
Theweleit, Klaus 75
Third World Bunfight (TWB) 87–104
Thomas of Celano 268
Thorpe, Charles 173
Three Sisters, The 216
Threlfall, David 43, 45, 49, 52
Thyestes 94
Tiny Alice 125
Titus Andronicus 19, 21, 26, 216
Today is My Birthday 12

Tokyo Metropolitan Theatre 125
Tolstoy, Leo 26
Transcendence 76, 167, 267
Trilogie des Dragons 4, 9, 53–67
Troilus and Cressida 20, 216, 217
Trojan Women, The 216, 271
Truskowski, Jakub 235
Turner, Victor 3, 15, 115, 124
Tweedie, Ethel B. H. 262
Two Gentlemen of Verona, The 271
Tynan, Kenneth 37

Ubu Rex with Scenes from Macbeth 216
Ulrich, Allen 183, 200
Umewaka Noh Stage 130
United States' House of Representatives 174–175
Universidade Nova 149
University of California, Berkeley 172
University of California Davis 181
University of Göttingen 172
University of Hawaii 191, 193
University of Lisbon 77

Van Boxelaer, Wim 223
Van den Eede, Peter 235, 237, 239, 251
Van der Weyden, Rogier 264, 269
Van Eyk, Jan 264
Van Gennep, Arnold 115, 124
Vandekeybus, Wim 232
Venice Preserv'd 20
Vercruyssen, Frank 235, 236, 238, 240, 242, 243, 245, 247, 248, 250, 251, 252, 253, 254
Verdi, Guiseppe 161, 164
Verhaegen, Peter 235
Verney, Cathy 235
Village Voice 184, 199
Vinci 57
Virgin and Child Between St. James and St. Dominic, The 270
Visual Arts University, Cluj 207
Vitale, Wayne 183, 184, 200
Volkstheater, Munich 261
von Goethe, Johann Wolfgang 201, 202, 203, 204, 207, 209, 214, 215, 217

von Goethe, Wolfgang Amadeus 208
von Plessen, Viktor 196
Vusa Dance Company 87

Walker, Matt 102
Wars of the Roses, The 26, 30
We Will Rock You 14
Webb, Alan 18
Weigel, Helene 2
Weis, Othmar 258, 259, 260, 261, 274
Welles, Orson 20
Wertenbaker, Timberlake 120, 121, 124
Wesemann, Arnd 219
West End, The 19, 20, 39
Wilde, Oscar 4, 240
Williams, Raymond 221, 233
Williams, Tennessee 2, 4, 226
Williams, William Carlos 28
Wilson, Robert 12, 220
Wilson, Ronald 122, 124
Winter's Tale, The 19, 216, 217
Witchcraft Act (1562) 217
Witness, Acts of 2, 9, 29, 62, 72, 86, 94, 115, 121, 177, 178, 212, 243, 248, 267, 269, 273
Witts, Noel 226, 233
Wolf, Matt 3, 15
Wonders Are Many 166, 179
Woods, Donald 100
Woodvine, John 45, 48, 51, 52
Wooster Group 4, 12, 225, 226, 233
World War II 11, 118, 172, 176, 195, 196
Worth, Irene 22

Yates, Frances A. 73, 226, 233
Yelena 87
York Mystery Cycle 257, 258, 261, 269
Yoshida, Asahi 126, 133, 134, 136, 137, 138, 139, 140, 141, 142, 143

Zardino de Oration 267
Ziggy Stardust 230
Zinder, David 6, 15
Ziporyn, Evan 196
Zombi 90
Zombies 87, 90, 91, 94, 95, 96, 97
see also *Ipi Zombi?*

www.ingramcontent.com/pod-product-compliance
Lightning Source LLC
Chambersburg PA
CBHW021054080526
44587CB00010B/248